Willful Monstrosity

ALSO BY NATALIE WILSON

Seduced by Twilight: *The Allure and
Contradictory Messages of the Popular Saga*
(McFarland, 2011)

Willful Monstrosity

*Gender and Race
in 21st Century Horror*

NATALIE WILSON

McFarland & Company, Inc., Publishers
Jefferson, North Carolina

ISBN (print) 978-1-4766-7344-8
ISBN (ebook) 978-1-4766-3726-6

LIBRARY OF CONGRESS AND BRITISH LIBRARY
CATALOGUING DATA ARE AVAILABLE

Library of Congress Control Number 2019054112

Front cover image © 2020 Igor Link/Shutterstock

Printed in the United States of America

*McFarland & Company, Inc., Publishers
Box 611, Jefferson, North Carolina 28640
www.mcfarlandpub.com*

To my mom and dad,
thank you for that Betamax player
(and for letting me watch *Jaws* on repeat).
And to Graham,
for seeing me through the scariest of times.

"In demonstrating, we assume the form of monster, becoming an obstacle, a physical fleshy thing."
—Sara Ahmed

Table of Contents

Acknowledgments

First and foremost, I must acknowledge Sara Ahmed's phenomenal scholarly contributions to the world which have indelibly impacted my thinking. Her influence on this book will be obvious. Her theory provided the "willful" foundation upon which my reading (and book title) rests upon. I hope that if she is to come across my work, she finds my reading to be a respectful one undertaken in the spirit of admiration and deference. I feel as if a copyright symbol should be affixed to the world "willful" in my title—she, to me, has patented this concept in a remarkable way that I can hope I have done justice to.

Writing this book required immersion in many shadowy places, sinister hide-outs, and laboratories of monstrous creation. I am very grateful to the folks who made my time in such dark places and spaces possible.

To the friends and family who willingly watched monster shows along with me, who discussed the merits (or lack thereof) of the latest monster fiction, and who accompanied me to the cinema despite my predilection to scream, thank you from the bottom of my monster-loving heart. Thank you also to the many horror aficionados and critics whose guidebooks, podcasts, websites, and blogs helped me navigate my way through the very dense terrain of horror and its monsters.

Thanks also to those who provided feedback on early drafts—Simon Bacon, Shelley Rees, Tom Connelly, Graham Clift, Melissa Ames, Rebekah Bachnick, and Jennifer Meneray among them. McFarland and Layla Milholen, thank you for being so pleasant to work with, and so very patient.

Thank you to the Popular Culture Association and American Cultural Association for providing conferences both national and regional that engage at length with horror and monster studies. Thanks also to the National Women's Studies Association for supporting feminist scholars, myself included, and for featuring Sara Ahmed as a keynote speaker a few years back. Hearing her speak about willful subjects profoundly impacted the trajectory of this book.

Appreciation also to Cal State San Marco, and the departments in which I teach, Women's, Gender, and Sexuality Studies and Literature and Writing. The teaching and learning opportunities these academic homes provide are invaluable. Much, much gratitude also belongs to my wonderful students, past and present. Their enthusiasm is infectious. Their dedication and determination inspiring. Their fresh-eyed, savvy, slick commentary a joy. Their responses to and analysis of various pop culture monstrosities greatly enhances my own.

I am indebted primarily, however, to my family. Thanks goes to my mom and dad for instilling within me a love of learning. And for not believing the many friends who warned them a degree in literature would surely result in life-long penury for their daughter! Thanks are owed to my children, Naomi and Shane, who not only indulged my endless requests to watch ANOTHER monster movie, but also regularly supplied me with homemade, generously buttered popcorn.

Last but not least, huge thanks are due to Graham. His willingness to binge-watch movies and television shows is but one of the many things cementing us together. That, and he didn't let me give up on this book, even when the finish line seemed to be receding further and further from view. For this, I shall be eternally grateful—remaining so even beyond the grave.

And now for the very last—thanks go to my granddaughter Lena, whose monster laugh lights up my world. May she grow up to be exceedingly willful.

Preface

Shall I begin with how I became a monster lover or how I became a feminist? Or, should I address how, as a feminist, I am viewed as a monster?

As the fear of feminism is still so great it might drive readers away, perhaps I should keep my identity secret. A Hyde safely wrapped in a Dr. Jekyll. But I fear it's too late for that. I have let my monster out of the closet. To distract you from this revelation, allow me to shift to how this terrible progeny was born.

* * *

She crept from her lair in the middle of the night while still a baby beast, barely eight years old. Her devious little claw turned the television on, twisting the volume dial to nearly mute. She, like Carol Ann, was sucked in. Glued to the pulsing light, she found herself transfixed by a demonic girl and her putrescent green skin. She knew she should not be watching. This made her nighttime secret all the tastier. As Aristotle would have it, she was born bad.

Years passed. Her mass consumption of monster movies grew right along with her, accelerating thanks to a wonderful new addition to her home: a Betamax player.

Convincing her mother to rent all manner of horror, she soon found herself watching and re-watching *Jaws*. She recognized the villain of the film from the moment he scratched his nails across a blackboard. She then eagerly awaited the braggart's demise with each repeated viewing. She took worrisome pleasure in seeing him bit in half.

This she, this monster, is me...

* * *

Thinking back to falling in love with a disreputable genre and a much maligned movement, aka feminism, I am unable to separate my fascination with monsters and my burgeoning feminism. Yet, something rendered

1

me willful, an attribute Sara Ahmed (of feminist killjoy fame), deems necessary to resist our misogynistic, racist, queer-phobic world.[1]

Looking back on my fascination with Captain Quint's demise in *Jaws*, I now read willfulness in my repeated viewing.

Quint is a macho braggadocio, toxic masculinity in captain form, his ship a metonym for a patriarchal power. As Jane Caputi astutely argues, *Jaws* is a "ritual retelling of an essential patriarchal myth—male vanquishment of the female symbolized as sea monster," the purpose of which is to "instill dread and loathing for the female." While the great white is referenced as "he" many times over, the monster, in her estimation, "actually represents the primordial female and her most dreaded aspects"—a reading substantiated when Quint, upon first eyeing the shark, croons "Come here, darling" (1993, 23–5).

In Quint's first appearance on screen he boasts "I'll catch this bird for you," characterizing the shark as a "bird," a common epithet used to refer to women. Quint later describes the sea-dwelling creatures as having "lifeless eyes ... like a doll's eyes," something that evokes not only a formative female toy (one invented to further "proper" mothering instincts), but also the tired tradition of referencing women as "dolls." When Quint is later bitten in half by the toothy broad, the blood gurgling from his mouth registers as the silencing of his male voice, one that promised to destroy, "the head, the tail, the whole damn thing." Instead, he is taken in by a man-eating piece of tail, bitten in half above penis-point by the classic vagina dentata in monster shark form.

Of course, my pre-pubescent self didn't give much thought as to why I was fascinated by this scene, but now I recognize my child-self found in such scenes something I was hard pressed to find elsewhere—scenes which framed females and femininity as *not only* monstrous, but also *powerful*, as able to kill the patriarchal beast.

Over the years, despite encountering many who assuredly told me horror was bad, silly, dangerous, a waste of time, and not for females, I persisted in my pursuit of all things monstrous and gory. Though some folks still assert "good feminists" should not like horror, I heartily disagree. Consuming monstrous tales en masse in researching this book, I am more convinced than ever that horror not only *matters,* but that it is of deep feminist import.

Consuming horror, the narrative has gone, is to revel in male power and female victimhood, to find pleasure in female death, to perpetuate ideas of the feminine as monstrous, dangerous, inferior, and ultimately other. To be sure, many examples of the genre eroticize violence, solidify the woman-as-evil-monster equation, and sideline women (both in front of and behind the camera). Yet the genre also regularly features women who endeavor to break free of patriarchy's stranglehold, to destroy white supremacist sentiment, to claim sexual agency.

The first two decades of the 21st century, as many have pointed out, brims with phenomenal horror texts. Many place not only female characters—but also many feminist ones—front and center. Behind the camera, directors such as Jennifer Kent, Ana Lily Amirpour, Karyn Kusama, Julie Ducourno, and Anna Biller add to a long line of female horror filmmakers—many of them feminist. At the same time, horror is tackling issues of racial import. This is not a new phenomenon, of course, but the critical acclaim and widespread consumption of such horror is heartening to those who are more than ready to see white supremacist ideology die for good. Attesting to this race-aware-renaissance in horror are filmmakers such as Jordan Peele, authors such as Helen Oyeyemi and Nnedi Okarfor, and characters such as Michonne, Sasha, and Glenn of *The Walking Dead*, of Chris and Rod in *Us,* and many protagonists of color, as in popular TV series and films like *The Passage, The Girl with All the Gifts, American Horror Story*, and the CW's reboot of *Charmed.* Indeed, with horror currently positioned as the Amazon prime of genres, it's an opportune time for "woke" monster lovers.

Concentrating on an array of novels, movies, and TV series, my aim in what follows is to document a prominent feature of the current horror landscape—one I am deeming "willful monstrosity." Informed by the theoretical work of Sara Ahmed, I seek to valorize willful monsters and the texts in which they appear. Monstrosity of this ilk—true to the etymology of the term—warns us we must not be complacent in the face of villainy—especially when that villainy is being emboldened by misogynists, white nationalists, trigger-happy police, anti-abortion extremists, and orange-hued tyrants.

That horror is doing political work is by no means new, what is new, I contend, is the embrace of the progressive politics horror is currently proffering. Sure, regressive texts still hoist their tired sexism, racism, and homophobia into narrative, but such texts are not the ones being heaped with praise, winning awards, changing minds. They are, with any luck, a dying breed. I will consider a few such regressive texts in the coming chapters, but the bulk of the discussion will focus on justice-minded horror and its many willful monsters.

The chapters revolve around particular monstrous figures and the texts in which they appear—Chapter 1 on the zombie, Chapter 2 the vampire, Chapter 3 the witch, Chapter 4 the female monster. The films, television series, and fiction examined—some 75 texts in all—are mostly from the United States, though a smattering hail from Canada, Britain, New Zealand, Australia, Sweden, and Korea. The close readings of individual texts, most of which run from 1,000 to 3,000 words, are intended to allow readers to dip in an out of the monograph, reading about those texts they are most interested in, some of which are already deemed "classics" and others of which are not yet well-known. While the narratives featured are united in their championing of willfulness, some stray from traditional notions of the monstrous and/or horrific. Much like the monster, which refuses to abide by any easy classification, the tales transform classic conceptions of the zombie, vampire, witch, and female monster.

Overall, the work reflects my abiding interest in monsters, something also in evidence in my previous book, *Seduced by Twilight*. My intellectual curiosity about monsters—of how they speak to the inequities of our world—as well as how they might be deployed to change our ways of thinking—is informed by rich body of scholarly work on horror and its monsters. Formative texts by the likes of Barbara Creed, Robin Wood, Linda Williamson, Carol Clover, Isabel Cristina Pinedo, Barry Keith Grant, and Jack Halberstam, as well as more recent studies by scholars such as Robin Means Coleman, Sylvia Federici, Erin Harrington, David McNally, Stacey Abbott, Simon Bacon, Sarah Juliet Lauro, Roger Luckhurst, Melissa Ames, Kyle William Bishop, W. Scott Poole, Dawn Keetley and Bernice Murphy have indelibly enhanced my thinking. Also of note is the rich and varied work being carried out in horror magazines, blogs, and podcasts. Listening to episodes from *Faculty of Horror*, reading essays at *Horror Homeroom*, and eating up critical takes provided at *Graveyard Shift Sisters* provides delicious sustenance for the monster hungry among us. As these necessarily partial lists convey, critical engagements with horror and its monsters are undergoing a renaissance of their own.

My hope is that what follows contributes to this fascinating, ever-mutating, monstrous conversation.

Introduction:
Monster Matters

I was fairly deep into my research when I came across Sara Ahmed's foundational usage of the Brothers Grimm tale "The Willful Child." Quoted in full in her 2014 book *Willful Subjects*, the tale reads as follows:

Once upon a time there was a child who was willful, and would not do as her mother wished. For this reason God had no pleasure in her, and let her become ill, and no doctor could do her any good, and in a short time she lay on her death-bed. When she had been lowered into her grave, and the earth was spread over her, all at once her arm came out again, and stretched upwards, and when they had put it in and spread fresh earth over it, it was all to no purpose, for the arm always came out again. Then the mother herself was obliged to go to the grave, and strike the arm with a rod, and when she had done that, it was drawn in, and then at last the child had rest beneath the ground [Grimm Brothers, 125].

Refuting the "moral" of the above tale, that children should do as their told, Ahmed's book charts a story of willful bodies that raise fists in the air, march with angry feet, and create blockages made of flesh. Characterizing such bodies as assemblages of "disobedient parts"—as made up of "hands which are not handy" and "parts that will not budge"—Ahmed's conception of willfulness prioritizes the corporeal, doing so in a way that also foregrounds the monstrous (194).

In the Grimm tale, the willful child's arm *demonstrates* refusal. Embodying the *demonstrative* aspects of *monstrosity,* her recalcitrant arm indicates the social order and the authoritative power on which it rests are not to be trusted. As a result, the girl is deemed a monster and beaten into submission, much like bodies across history beaten down for resisting the social systems they are expected to serve.

Though the tale closes with the assurance the girl's arm is at last "drawn in," a willful reader might interpret her rest beneath the ground as *only* a rest, a time to gather strength until she, zombie-like, rises again. A willful reader might further interpret her as *choosing* to remain under-

5

ground—a place where she might befriend what Ahmed deems "the many willful girls that haunt literature" (3). Perhaps the girl, in "drawing in" her arm, is *drawing* a new mode of existence, one penned with the blood of her rod-beaten arm, an arm transformed into revolutionary fist. Ahmed, refusing the call to be a reader of "good will," reads the resistant arm in this vein (pun intended)—as a willful part that "keeps coming up, acquiring a life of its own, even after the death of the body of which it is a part" (1). The girl's arm, in such a reading, is a willful part which refuses to be buried beneath cultural expectations to "be a good girl"—a passive girl, a voiceless, dead thing. The arm is a "disobedient part" threatening the body politic. Such parts, as Ahmed puts it, "become a problem" (3). Yet willful parts and bodies, as Ahmed makes plain, can be advantageous to those seeking to resist the general will and its oppressive formations—indeed, sometimes willfulness is an urgent necessity, one required to change conceptions of which lives and bodies matter.[2] In this regard, willfulness holds out promise. The same is true of monstrosity. Ahmed specifically suggests as much in *Willful Subjects* when she likens "the promise of monstrosity" to the "promise of willfulness" (161).

In what follows, I explore such promise via what I am deeming "willful monstrosity," an approach informed by Ahmed's valorization of willfulness, the ever-expanding body of monster studies, and progressive reads of the horror genre. Just as texts focusing on monstrosity revolve around disruptive figures, so too does analysis of horror and its monsters disrupt traditional notions of what counts as scholarship. For example, the recent anthology *Monsters in the Classroom,* in its valorization of studying monster-laden texts, explicitly extends the monster's reach into the pedagogical realm. Monstrosity, framed thus, is not only able to tear down the master's logocentric house, but just might storm the ivory tower. Of course, not all monsters are willfully disruptive "subjects of the left" any more than all monster theory is transgressive (Ahmed 249).

To the contrary, monsterizing the Other was—and continues to be— one of the primary ways to maintain power and shore up existing hierarchies. One such enduring hierarchy, that of East/West, lies at the heart of colonialism and conquest. While denigrating the Other has spanned history, the Western world, as Partha Mitter puts it, "forged a monopoly on this" (339). Importantly, this monopoly is linked to the emergence of race as a concept, something evident when, around about the first century, the Latin term for "people" (gens/gentes) came to mean "races of people," thus laying the groundwork for the concept of "monstrous races" (Friedeman xxx). Early catalogs of race not only attributed certain proclivities to the Muslim, Jewish, and Mongolian, but also to backward-footed, one-legged and hirsute people, thus equating human races/types with imagined monsters. "In a set of continuous historical variations," in which the "furthest away was represented as the most monstrous," certain bodies were deemed "eminently disposable" and certain places deemed in need of being "civilized" (Braidotti, 1996, 142–3, 136). Such designations continue to define "who is due moral consideration and who is not," in the words of Margrit Shildrick (2002, 5). From the geographical determinism of the ancient world through to the eugenics movement of the twentieth century, monsterizing the Other laid the groundwork—and still continues to justify—colonization, imperialism, notions of racial superiority, and the casting of certain bodies as expendable. Like the maps of old that depicted dragons, sea serpents, and other monstrous figures in as-yet unchartered areas, such representations position monsters in the margins—as marginal.

Whereas far-away places were imagined as being inhabited by a whole range of fantastical creatures, "discovered" lands repeatedly instigated cautionary tales that characterized racialized Others as monstrous. As Persephone Braham chronicles, claims indigenous populations of the so-called New World were cannibals "became a convenient justification for conquest, enslavement, and other abuses" (22). W. Scott Poole similarly explores how monsterization was informed by "ideological efforts to marginalize the weak and normalize the powerful, to suppress struggles for class, racial, and sexual liberation, to transform the 'American way of Life' into a weapon of empire." Arguing "monsters register our national traumas," his work reads American history *as* horror—a suitable endeavor given how monstrous constructions served to bolster America's "founding fathers"—genocide and slavery (23).

Just as race has long served as a basis to identify others as monstrous, so too has gender—from Plato's discussion of female beasts to Odysseus encounter with Scylla and her multiple heads (or in other iterations, a lower body made up of snarling, canine mouths), ancient descriptions of the womb as a hungry animal, women said to birth "parasitic offspring," to the many variations of the vagina dentata (Miller, 320). Repeatedly associated with excessive, dangerous consumption (particularly of the cannibalistic variety) as well as perverse sexuality (particularly of the emasculating or castrating variety), such associations buttress the "necessity" of patriarchal rule. This consistent discourse is cogently documented in Braham's "The Monstrous Caribbean" and Sarah Alison Miller's "Monstrous Sexuality: Variations on the *Vagina Dentata*," both of which appear in *The Ashgate Research Companion to Monsters and the Monstrous*.

Braham, naming the monsterization of women as "a prerequisite to conquest and colonization," details Christopher Columbus' and Amerigo Vespucci's reports of cannibal warrior women and the resulting allegory of the New World as a monstrous female (17). From the devouring sea-hydra and Charbydis, each said to consume passing ships, to land-dwelling libidinous women reported to have a taste for male genitalia, female monsters were characterized as a particular threat. As evidenced in many historical accounts, females are repeatedly positioned as paradigmatic monster. A tale from India, for example, warns of a woman with three teeth in her vagina. The leader of her village desires to marry her, so dispatches servants to rape the woman (apparently believing this will remove her teeth). After one of these men has his penis bitten in three, the others rip out her vaginal teeth. The village leader then marries her, an act reported to bring her consolation and happiness.[3] This is but one example of the many tales of the vagina dentata.

As the above examples indicate, women and people of color are repeatedly depicted as "regressive agents capable of dragging down white civilization by feeding off the precious resources, both economic and bodily, accrued by right-living men" (Shildrick, 2002, 30). Such racialized and gendered representations also pervade literary and cinematic texts. From the hairy-palmed Eastern dwelling Count Dracula to the vampiric creatures of Robert Matheson's *I Am Legend,* from the devil-worshipping witch to the terrifying "She-who-must-be-obeyed" from H. Rider Haggard's 1886 novel *She,* narratives across history deem the non-white and the non-male as monstrous. While depictions such as these uphold what bell hooks refers to as white supremacist capitalist patriarchy, other representations critique hegemonic power, courting sympathy for those deemed Other. Mary Shelley's novel—and the empathy for the monster and disdain for the monster creator it exhibits—is definitive in this regard. Her "hideous progeny" eventually mutating to directly address racism in the U.S., something extensively documented in Elizabeth Young's *Black Frankenstein.* While such reclamation is generally enacted via a male Frankenstein creature—thus speaking especially to racialized masculinity—notable examples deploy a female creature to infuse monstrous femininity with radical potential. Young cites Nnedi Okorafor's *The Book of Phoenix* and *Who Fears Death* in this regard. In another recent example, the Showtime series *Penny Dreadful* features a female Frankenstein figure intent on destroying the patriarchy—one which foregrounds a working-class creature.

Other quintessential monsters speak to race, gender, and class as well. Grendel and Caliban each speak to gender (Grendel is avenging the murder of his mother, Caliban's mother was condemned for practicing sorcery) and race (Caliban is commonly read as colonized and—in some retellings—as a black slave). In terms of class, the monster often comes from "the underclass"—a factor symbolized via their linkage to underground lairs, charnel houses, cellars, and caves. They are the slum dwellers, the enslaved, the proletariat masses threatening the bourgeoisie. Yet, as with sympathetic gendered and racialized monsters, they often serve to condemn class hierarchy.

Contemporary descendants of such sympathetic monster types include the sentient zombie (Romero's Bub serves as an early example), the heroic vampire (as witnessed in contemporary television series such as *True Blood* and *Vampire Diaries*), the subversive witch (common in contemporary fairy tales from feminist authors such as Angela Slatter and Margot Lanagan), and the radical female monster (a fan favorite in this camp is Dawn, from the film *Teeth*, who wields her vagina dentata to take down sexual predators).

Just as monster narratives regularly redeem creatures that have historically been construed as diabolical, horrific, and/or irredeemably other, so too does a substantial body of theory celebrate the "promises of monsters" (a promise addressed, in various ways, by Margrit Shildrick, Sara Ahmed, Jeffrey Jerome Cohen, Rosi Braidotti, Donna Haraway, and Simon Bacon, to name but a few). Cohen and Shildrick, perhaps the best-known theorists in this regard, valorize monstrous constructions as able to destabilize delimiting constructions of self and other. Monsters, according to Shildrick, codify "who is due moral consideration and who is not" (2002, 5). Interpreting attempts to project monstrosity onto the Other as inextricably linked to repudiations of the self, Shildrick examines the "fragility of the distinctions by which the human subject is fixed and maintained," one that speaks to "the failure of the monster to occupy only the space of the other" (2001, 163). As her work suggests, interrogations of the monster are inevitably bound up with attempts to define the human. In order for there to be "normal humans," abnormal monsters are needed as counterpart. Cohen's work also champions the disruptive potential of the monstrous in his influential "Monster Culture (Seven Theses)." Offering "a method for reading cultures from the monsters they engender," his seven postulates emphasize the monster as a transgressive figure that disrupts binary logic, refutes being disciplined or destroyed, and exists in an and/or realm. "The monster of abjection resides in that marginal geography of the Exterior, beyond the limits of the Thinkable," he writes. Putting forth claims such as "The Monster Dwells at the Gates of Difference," "The Monster Polices the Borders of the Possible," and "The Monster Stands at the Threshold," he is interested in the ways monsters break/transcend that which culture tries to fix in place. Various other theorists make similar claims about the transgressive aspects of the monster, as with Noell Caroll's concept of "category jamming," Jack Halberstam's exploration of skin as a "wall" holding in and exposing the monstrosity, and Robin Wood's framing of the monster as putting the very concept of normality into question. More recently, Elizabeth Young's *Black Frankenstein*, Robin Means Coleman's *Horror Noire*, Kinitra Brooks' *Searching for Sycorax*, and Elizabeth Aiossa's *The Subversive Zombie* deploy redemptive readings of key monstrous figures and texts. Especially pertinent to this study is Ahmed's conception of the willful subject as one that comes up against (and attempts to breach) the (sometimes literal and sometimes figurative) walls erected by dominant culture. Relating the willful subject to the monstrous one, she champions the "wall-busting" capabilities of those that destabilize meaning, threaten to erode hierarchies, and call into question the general will.

Many of these theorists focus on corporeal specificities as foundational to monsterization. Just as naming others monstrous bolsters societal notions of us/them and civilized/savage, designating certain corporeal manifestations monstrous serves to maintain the normality and fixedness of certain selves. In the same way that all bodies are materialized through discourse, constructions of monstrosity rely on naming certain bodily forms deviant, deformed, and/or freakish. Infamously furthered via Aristotle's claim the birth of females was the most common deformity, the naming of certain bodies as deviant informs the western imagination, serving as "a paradigmatic element in the oppression not only of women, but a range of other others" (Shildrick, 2002, 1). As such, as convincingly argued by Shildrick, (re)embracing corporeal otherness has the potential to foment an ethics of embodiment in which we are not haunted by bodily specificities but "in communion with, the differences between, and internal to, us all" (2001, 171) Ahmed also identifies rethinking the body as key to rethinking otherness, doing so through the metaphor of the willfully monstrous subject. Making explicit connections between the willful subject, the monster, and the political dissident, her work provides a philosophical lens on otherness grounded in the politics of the corporeal. "Together bodies can become monstrous," Ahmed writes, calling for the creation of a "willful army." Emphasizing "the fleshiness of arms" that would make up this willful army—as well as hands clenched into protesting fists—Ahmed valorizes the dissenting, demonstrating body. Characterizing willfulness as "a politics that aims for no," she repeatedly draws upon corporeal analogies in her work, for resisting "a social body that treats others as supporting limbs." In animating the double meaning of "arm"—one being the upper limb and the other being weapon—she characterizes the willful army as a collective of dissenting parts—"arms as fleshy limbs" that act as "willful agents" rather than "tools of war" (161–194).

Mining the slippage between *monstrare, monstrum, monster,* and *demonstrate*, her theories speak not only to monstrous bodies, but to the destabilizing possibilities of language. "To demonstrate is to be involved in the creation of ominous signs," she writes. Such signs, she suggests, are made flesh when bodies demonstrate together and "assume the form of monster, becoming an obstacle, a physical fleshy thing." Positing that "willfulness can be an electric current, passing through each of us, switching us on. Willfulness can be a spark. We can be lit up by it," her assertions speak to the *charge* to "become woke" that animates the current cultural moment. In becoming lit up—or, to use the contemporary parlance—in becoming woke, monsters negate the charge of the general will much as Frankenstein's creature rejected the charge of his creator, much as the girl from "The Willful Child" refuses the charge to be obedient (163–8). Though the price for such willfulness is often rejection (as with the creature) or annihilation (as with the girl), many monster types nevertheless choose resistance. Others, of course, do not. Sometimes they aim for inclusion. To be granted as much, the monster must shape themselves into "proper" form; they must be willing to prop up existing systems and/or do the bidding of the powerful. In the case of capitalism, for example, willing monsters need adopt what Wood names the basic tenet of capitalism, "that people have the right to live off other people" (84).

In *Monsters of the Market: Zombies, Vampires, and Global Capitalism*, David McNally offers a fascinating analysis of "willing capitalist monsters." Critical of economic exploitation and the class hierarchy it engenders, or what he calls "capitalist monstrosity," his study explores how "monsters of the market" feed off "the blood and flesh" of those they dominate. Warning against a one-dimensional read of the monster, his work questions what he characterizes as an overly "giddy embrace of monstrosity." Reminding readers that "not all monsters are created equal," McNally's thesis—that monsters are just as capable of shoring up inequitable systems of power as they are at destabilizing them—is crucial to keep in mind when attempting to map the political terrain of horror. If one follows what McNally claims is postmodernism's "universal injunction to be on the side of monsters," the political potential of monstrosity is lost. One becomes a willing reader rather than a willful one. While McNally oversimplifies postmodernism's take on monstrosity in my view, the point he seems to be getting at—that we must not simply "embrace the monster" without taking a good look at it first—is a valid one. As he puts it, "It is one thing ... to be on the side of monstrous others ... in the face of political persecution and repression. But it is quite another thing where multinational corporations, racist gangs or an imperial war-machine are the monsters in question" (2–11).

In some senses, the difference between oppressive and subversive monsters is similar to Ahmed's concepts regarding being willing versus being willful. When one is a willing subject, they go along with the general will. In doing so, they bolster existing systems of power. When one is a willful subject, they resist the very same systems. Examples from Jordan Peele's films are illustrative here. In *Get Out*, Rose Armitage is a willing subject. She abides by the expectations of her privileged family, and by extension, the white supremacist mindset they represent. What she and her family do is monstrous, but not subversively so. In contrast, the tethered bodies that hold hands across great swathes of land at the close of *Us* (Peele's second feature-film) willfully resist their designation as sub-human. Many other 21st century monster narratives feature similarly willful subjects that refuse to "stay in their place"—whether that place be physical (an underground prison, for example) or conceptual (a racialized norm, for instance). Such subjects *will not* abide by cultural norms and expectations. This "willing not" is the crux of the willful monstrosity I seek to valorize—a monstrosity that resists assimilation, exploitation, and annihilation. This type of monstrosity is particularly prevalent in contemporary horror narratives—something that aligns to Robin Wood's contention that horror is especially relevant during times of "cultural crisis and disintegration"—times, in other words, like our own (76).

In spite of—or perhaps because of—several years of marked global unrest and political divisiveness, the horror genre has served up hopeful tales of apocalypses averted and communities united against villainy. We have seen life-affirming visions of zombie children saving the planet (as in *The Girl with All the Gifts*), vampires eager to prevent humanity's demise (as in *The Passage*), and witchy women dedicated to thwarting reproductive injustice (*Red Clocks, Penny Dreadful*). Monstrous outcasts have taken down mad scientists (*Stranger Things, The OA*), military corruption (*The Shape of Water, The Passage*), and devilish patriarchs (*The Chilling Adventures of Sabrina, Get Out*). As these examples convey, some of the most successful horror narratives of our times not only let the monster live, they also applaud the paradigm-busting and wall-breaching capabilities of cultural outsiders. With its feminist Middle-Eastern vampires, its deaf female heroes, its queer renegades, its autistic geniuses, its children-of-color world-saviors, and its gnashers of patriarchy, the 21st century horror landscape has thus far been chock-full of progressive, counter-cultural, monster-celebrating tales. Indeed, there are so many narratives of this ilk, it would be impossible to mention them all, let alone cover them in detail within the space of one book. So as to limit the scope into manageable size, I will foreground four specific monstrous types in the chapters that follow—zombies, vampires, witches, and monstrous women. Examining some seventy-five texts, the discussion will be comprised in the main of close textual analysis. Informed prominently by feminism, critical race theory, and cultural studies, the analysis seeks to illuminate the political work being carried out by the many willful monsters populating the contemporary horror canon.

Chapter 1 addresses the zombie and zombie texts. Beginning with an overview of the four key zombie types dominating the 21st century narrative landscape—the Haitian/voodoo zombie, the post–Romero zombie, the sympathetic zombie, and the viral zombie, the chapter then turns to a discussion of early zombie films and their engagement with race and gender—*White Zombie, I Walked with a Zombie,* and *Voodoo Man.* Arguing that a handful of recent films rectify the conservative messaging of these examples, I take a close look at three post-millennial films informed by the voodoo zombie tradition, *Fido, Get Out,* and *Us.* In the second section of the chapter, the powerhouse series *The Walking Dead,* the heavily Romero-esque *As the World Dies* saga, and the independent film *Avenged* are examined in relation to the continuum of sexual violence. Child heroes, zombie and human alike, are taken up in the third section via analysis of *The Girl with All the Gifts, The Boy on the Bridge, Train to Busan,* and *The Reapers Are the Angels.* The closing section turns to narratives I hope will die out soon given their reanimation of regressive notions (*Deadgirl* and *World War Z* among them). Overall, the chapter maintains that if we don't overcome outmoded ways of being—whether based in a capitalist profit motif, a misogynist rape culture world, or a white supremacist mindset—we are as good as dead.

Texts featuring willful vampires are the focus of Chapter 2. While *Twilight* arguably turned vampire politics to the conservative right, narratives from the late 1990s on have consistently deployed vampires in the service of leftist critique.[4] Concentrating on tales of this ilk, the chapter aims to elucidate the continuing progressive potentialities of the vampire figure. In the first section I consider Jewelle Gomez's foundational feminist vampire Gilda. I then turn to Gilda's kindred descendent, the activist vampire girl from *A Girl Walks Home Alone at Night.* The second and third sections of the chapter focus on what I am deeming "post-traumatic vampire disorder" and "ethical vampirism." Section two centers on two coming of age narratives. In the first, the British novel *White Is for Witching,* Miranda Silver struggles with her vampiric female ancestors in a tale heavily imbued with feminist, post-colonial, and Gothic elements. In the second, *The Transfiguration,* a 2017 independent film, a young teenager copes with personal trauma by "becoming vampire."[5] Vampire families and their attempts to lead ethical blood-drinking lives is taken up in section three via examination of Matt Haig's *The Radleys,* Neil Jordan's *Byzantium,* and Susan Hubbard's YA trilogy, *The Ethical Vampire Series.* In the final section of the chapter, viral vampires and dystopian landscapes are given center-stage. Primarily concerning itself with Justin Cronin's series *The Passage* and its television adaptation, the section also analyzes *Daybreakers* and the 2007 adaptation of *I Am Legend.*

Chapter 3 sets out to prove the witch is undergoing a renaissance of her own. Though witches are admittedly less common than their zombie and vampire brethren, the new millennium offers a plethora of magical females, many of which are interested in using their powers to foment a more just world. The first section of the chapter addresses three novels set in the witch-hunt era, Jeanette Winterson's *The Daylight Gate,* Maryse Conde's *I, Tituba, Black Witch of Salem,* and Colleen Passard's *Diary of a Witch.* Closing with an assessment of Leni Zumas' *Red Clocks,* which is set in the near-future U.S., the section as a whole concerns itself with the historical demonization of the willful and witchy. In section two, I examine the witches of *Penny Dreadful, American Horror Story: Coven, Sisterhood of Night, All Cheerleaders Die, The Chilling Adventures of Sabrina,* and the 2018 *Charmed* reboot in relation to their willful damnation of patriarchal formations. In the third section, contemporary fantasy and fairy tale witches are the focus. Novels by Margot Lanagan, *Tender Morsels* and *The Brides of Rollrock Island,* as well as a novella by Angela Slatter, *Of Sorrows and Such,* are read as offering feminist intervention related especially to family and marriage. The closing section assesses the witches featured in *Hex, The Autopsy of Jane Doe, The Witch, The Woods,* and *The Love Witch,* maintaining that the kidnapping of babies, killing of innocents, and hexing of the living results from the oppressive contexts in which these witches reside rather than in any natural wickedness.

Chapter 4 scrutinizes the myriad females coded as monstrous in texts of the new millennium. Concentrating on narratives animated by modern Medusa figures, New Woman types, female Frankenstein creatures, ghostly brides, monstrous mothers, femme fatales, and rape-avengers, the aim of the final chapter is to illuminate how negative conceptions of the monstrous feminine can be reconfigured in ways that intersect with feminist aims. As such, this last chapter differs from the first three in that it is not organized around a specific monster, but instead around the enduring characterization of females as abject, evil creatures patriarchy must vanquish and/or tame. The first two sections concentrate on Gothic texts, some of which accord to traditional conceptions of this mode and others of which combine elements of the Suburban Gothic with the house horror sub-genre and the monstrous mother trope. In addition to examining monstrous permutations of the New Woman in *Penny Dreadful* and *Crimson Peak,* the opening section addresses *I Am the Pretty Thing That Lives in the House,* a ghost story, house-horror, and feminist mediation on female authorship/agency all in one. The second section looks at two very different films united in their focus on the mother/child relationship, *The*

Babadook and *Housebound.* Whereas one is a meditation on grief and the other a comedic take on familial dysfunction, both frame patriarchy as a systemic monster that fails to support its citizenry, especially its women and children. In the third section, *Stranger Things, The OA, The Shape of Water,* and *A Quiet Place* are read as modern iterations of the Creature Feature. In each, powerful indictments of the reigning social order are proffered, ones which condemn corrupt government establishments, military officials, and/or exploitive scientific research. Crucially, all four narrative place willful females front and center. To close out the chapter, four movies helmed by post-millennial Medusa figures are analyzed—the vagina dentata wielding Dawn from *Teeth,* the succubus from *Jennifer's Body,* the murderess from *All the Boys Love Mandy Lane,* and the final girl figures Rocky and Needy (from *Don't Breathe* and *Jennifer's Body*). Addressing contemporary film, fiction, and television as brimming with willful female subjects, the chapter foregrounds the monstrous woman as an exemplary figure in the post-millennial horror landscape.

Combined, the four chapters aim to reveal the exceedingly promising potential of post-millennial horror and its many willful monsters. Instead of furthering the message found in the (grim) Grimm Brothers story quoted at the outset of this introduction—that the monster must be annihilated—the tales analyzed in the chapters to follow champion willful monsters in all their rebellious, messy, rage-fueled, killjoy glory. I hope you, dear readers, will find such monsters not only intriguing, but inspiring.

1

Staying Woke
in an Undead World

Political Undercurrents
in Zombie Narratives

"Well, there's no problem. If you have a gun, shoot them
in the head.
That's a sure way to kill 'em. If you don't, get yourself a
club or a torch.
Beat 'em or burn 'em. They go up pretty easy."
—Sheriff McClelland, *Night of the Living Dead*

In contrast to real world trends such as racial profiling, anti-immigrant sentiment, refusal to take in refugees, and a shoring up of us/them binarisms, many post-millennial zombie texts call for tolerance, disapprove of indiscriminate killing (of humans *and* zombies), and suggest communalism is the way forward. At the same time, characters that wed themselves to outmoded ways of being—whether based in a capitalist profit motif, a misogynist worldview, or a colonial mindset—are oft condemned. Pertinent to this study in particular, many recent zombie narratives decry prejudicial aspects of society, indicating that if we don't overcome these, we are as good as dead. The dead-end zombies portend is no longer a definitive end in many tales. Instead, zombie arrival provides opportunities for a radically changed world, something this chapter will explore in relation to three primary types of zombie: (1) the enslaved zombie figure emerging out of Haiti (and associated with voodoo), (2) the classic zombie (most often linked to Romero's zombie canon), and (3) the viral, fast-moving, rabidly infectious zombie (as featured in films like *28 Days Later*). The first section will address three early zombie movies, *White Zombie, I Walked with a Zombie*, and *Voodoo Zombie*, as well as three contemporary films that draw upon Haitian conceptions of the zombie, *Fido*,

Get Out and *Us*. In the second section, the zombie figure is considered in relation to interpersonal violence and rape culture. The championing of child heroes, both zombie and human, will be taken up in the third section. To close the chapter, the fourth section turns to a consideration of recent zombie narratives which are more regressive in their messaging.

Zombies Here, There and Everywhere

Infectiously popular, zombies shuffle through comic books, graphic novels, and video games at a seemingly unstoppable pace. Since 2010, they have pervaded the living rooms of millions of homes via the rabidly popular *The Walking Dead* (*TWD*). Far from the only zombie-based series, *TWD* is joined by its spin-off series, *Fear the Walking Dead*, along with several other stand-alone shows. Hundreds of zombie films have also been produced since 2000, many of them making indelible marks on the genre (*28 Days Later, Fido, Shaun of the Dead, Zombieland,* and *World War Z*, for example). This zombie-obsessed century has infected the literary world as well, as with *Warm Bodies, Zone One, The Rising, My Life as a White Trash Zombie, The Forest of Hands and Teeth,* and many others too numerous to name. From apocalyptic tales featuring zombie hordes threatening to decimate humanity to narratives featuring sympathetic, humane zombies, tales of this undead monster—whether in film, television, or fiction—continue to call upon the zombie, very often doing so to proffer subversive imaginings. This subversive bent of zombie tales is by no means new. Coming to particular prominence in Romero's films, "zombie politics" can be linked to a number of factors. First, zombie lore is profoundly informed by the lasting legacies of imperialism, colonialism, and enslavement. Second, the lack of consciousness and will that marks the figure allows for interrogations of agency, domination, and power. Third, the liminal, boundary-disrupting nature of the zombie—a figure that is most often presented in multiple/multiplying form—lends itself to narratives that eschew closure and fixity. All three primary categories of this monster, the Haitian, voodoo inflected zombie (or zombi), the flesh-eating undead zombie (or the "post–Romero" zombie), and the fast-moving, viral zombie, populate millennial tales in vast number. Before turning to readings of several millennial zombie texts, an exploration of these zombie types is in order.

The voodoo-inflected zombie has its origins in Haiti and the African Diaspora.[1] This zombie, is, as Roger Luckhurst puts it, "branded by the murderous history of slavery and colonial dispossession," and shaped by "the systematic violence, appropriated labour, rebellion and revolution" the slave trade fostered (15). The figure entered the U.S. cultural lexicon largely as a result of William Seabrook's 1929 book *The Magic Island*. Seabrook's work describes the zombie as "a soulless human corpse ... taken from the grave and endowed by sorcery with the mechanical semblance of life—it is a dead body which is made to walk and act as if it were alive" (93). Written during the era of the U.S. occupation of Haiti, Seabrook's account furthered the colonialist mindset of the racialized other as less-than-human. Rather than bringing about the apocalypse, this zombie promises tractable labor and tends to be utilized so as to justify enslavement/control. Zombie-ism of this ilk is often reversible with the removal or nullification of the "spell" causing the zombified state (though, of note, generally only white zombies are returned to their human, non-zombie selves). Given the zombie "shuffled out of the margins of empire," it's no surprise the figure brought with it the racist, classist, and sexist hierarchies upon which empire depended (Luckhurst 7). Such sentiments are readily apparent in early movies featuring the figure, something that will be considered in more detail below.

Another primary type of zombie, the slow-moving, infectious one, sometimes called the "classic" or "traditional" zombie, emerged most famously in Romero's 1968 film *Night of the Living Dead*. Instead of an enslaved figure turned zombie via voodoo forces, this iteration of the zombie has more nebulous causes. In *Night*, for example, no definitive reason for the zombie outbreak is given, though it is suggested their emergence was caused by radioactive fallout. What is definitive is the fact Romero's *Night* brought the zombie as a figure rife with political possibility to cinema screens across the U.S. Incorporating issues that continue to inform the zombie canon, *Night*, in Romero's words, insisted "the monster, the evil, is not something lurking in the distance, but something actually inside all of us" (Williams, 2011, 78). While *Night* ends on a bleak note with the lone black male survivor shot by a group of white vigilantes, Romero's later *Land of the Dead* finds both humans and zombies poised to survive under improved conditions. Unlike the Haitian zombie, which exists as a soulless automaton with no agency, the classic version of the zombie generally has at least some capacity to learn, emote, and form relations to others. We see such zombies in Romero's Bub and Big Daddy and, more recently, in the self-reflective zombies of Hugh Howey's *I, Zombie* and the BBC television series *In the Flesh*.

The third prominent type of zombie is the viral zombie. Compared to the Haitian zombie and the Romero zombie, this zombie is faster, more infectious, and harder to kill. Turning zombie in this type of narrative is quick—often a matter of seconds—as opposed to the slower deterioration into a brain-hungry Romero-esque zombie or the hypnosis-like transformation witnessed in texts drawing upon the voodoo zombie. As the turn to viral zombie happens at a rapid pace, infestation happens quickly and, in turn, whole societies and/or swathes of the globe are extinguished in a matter of days. As such, the tales in which viral zombies appear are often informed by anxieties associated with corrupt state power, fear of disease/contagion, and the dehumanizing effects of living in a hyper-technological, war-ridden world.[2]

Significantly, regardless of the types of zombie deployed, many recent narratives deploy the zombie figure to champion the type of willfulness Sara Ahmed construes as necessary to bring about a more just world. In various texts, such willful resistance is witnessed in characters—some human and some zombie—that are dedicated to changing society as it stands, or what Ahmed calls the *general will*. Echoing her explorations of the general will as one which fosters inequity so as to keep existing power systems in place, many post-millennial zombie tales take on the deleterious effects of systematic inequity. Such narratives often intimate there is nothing inherently monstrous or evil about humans per se, but rather that the competitive, top-down systems within which they are encouraged to view certain others *as other* leads to prejudice and violence. By framing the zombie as ultimate other and then exploring how those humans who challenge this otherizing—whether by not gleefully killing zombies, by attempting to co-exist with zombies, or simply by not intentionally experimenting on, abusing, or needlessly harming zombies—narratives of this type intimate that only through refusing to frame existence around us/them binaries can we become more humane. Yet, as scholar Gerry Canavan reminds us, "the powers that be tend to fear such leveling." Noting that in many tales "the evocation of the zombie conjures not solidarity but racial panic," Canavan points out that when zombies emerge "we build fortifications, we hoard supplies, we 'circle the wagons' and point our guns outward." "The really radical move," Canavan counters, "would be to refuse the demarcation between life and anti-life altogether." Construing this demarcation as one that keeps racism and other forms of injustice intact, his work reminds readers that:

> despite the protestations of biopolitical state racism, despite the endless blaring declarations of national emergencies and states of exception, we don't live inside the zombie narrative; we live in the real world, the zombie-less world, where the only zombies to be found are the ones we ourselves have made out of the excluded, the forgotten, the cast-out, and the walled-off [450].

This "self-decentering and self-depriviliging" is, according to Canavan, "the necessary precondition for a final end to our collective zombie nightmare, the nightmare called history itself" (433–50).

Sarah Juliet Lauro and Karen Embry, like Canavan, name dialectical conceptions of life/death and subject/object as stumbling blocks on the road to more radical, liberatory politics. Asserting the zombie "reveals much about the crisis of human embodiments, the way power works, and the history of man's subjugation and oppression of its 'Others,'" their manifesto positions zombies as able to bring about the destruction of dominant ideologies. Drawing inspiration from Donna Haraway and Judith Butler, they frame the zombie as the "most apt metaphor" for the current historical milieu. As a "figure as indebted to narratives of historical power and oppression," they contend the zombie "reveals much about the way we code inferior subjects as unworthy of life" (87–92). Similarly, in her introduction to *Zombie Theory*, "Wander and Wonder in Zombieland," Lauro names the zombie as a "valuable figure for meditating on our culture's enduring demons" (180). She, like other recent zombie scholars, links the proliferation of this monster to defining components of our era: "the global economic downturn; the advent of new, anesthetizing pocket technology; the increased sense of terrorist threats in the wake of 9/11; the perpetuation of a state of constant warfare; the looming sense of ecological disaster; a shift in demographics toward an overall aging population" (187). To these, I would add increasing awareness of the ubiquity of sexual violence, an expansion of white supremacist sentiment, a growing global repugnance towards immigrants and refugees, and the reigniting of fears related to nuclear energy/weaponry. Such trends notably inform zombie scholarship of late, a field of study that "goes beyond commentary on zombie fictions to read our real world as a landscape peopled with the undead" (Lauro 256).

To be sure, the post-human, apocalyptic sentiment some zombie scholars insist is the sine qua non of the genre speaks to the reactionary ways of thinking characterizing large swathes of our 21st century milieu. If we take racism as an example, we can think about, as Canavan argues, the "racial myth of inimical Otherness the zombie narrative replicates" as "not just some deceased artifact of the 'bad past'" but a myth that is "alive and well" (446). Citing Hurricane Katrina specifically, Canavan considers the survival mode events of this ilk instigate, arguing this mode often instigates attempts to contain or destroy those deemed other. Akin to police brutality enacted against innocent black bodies in the contemporary United States, such an exceedingly violent survival mode positions white (human) bodies against non-white (zombie) bodies. The heavily criticized practice of separating immigrant children from their families that dominated U.S. news in the summer of 2018 is an example of this type of reactionary survival mode—one that shores up exclusionary, nationalist notions. This case, one in which children were separated from their families only to be kept in fenced cages, is not so different to zombie containment. In fact, in many zombie texts we witness the use of walls/cages/chains to imprison zombies or keep them out of human zones. Likewise, the infectious zombie horde is not all that far removed from the way refugees and migrants are characterized as undesirables via mainstream rhetoric. These examples are accompanied by the undead's emergence in our vernacular, as in "zombie economics" and "zombie computer."[3] Though the deployment of zombie figures and metaphors continues to mutate, earlier conceptions of the figure still circulate, as evidenced in the groundbreaking, multi-award winning *Get Out* and the earlier cult-classic *Fido*, each of which further themes inaugurated in some of Hollywood's earliest zombie films.

Section 1: Lurching Engagements with Gender, Race and Class

As noted above, the zombie which emerged from Haiti (and, more generally, the African Diaspora) speaks to the history of slavery and imperialism. Especially pertinent to the present study is what this iteration of the figure reveals about gender formations upheld and perpetuated via these systems, particularly in relation to white womanhood. As noted by Sherronda Brown, many films featuring this zombie type "place white women and the obsessive need to protect them from Black men at the center." Referencing "the distinct history of white womanhood and the ways in which it has traditionally operated in horror," Brown argues films such as *White Zombie* (1932), *I Walked with a Zombie* (1943), *The Skeleton Key* (2005), and *Bag of Bones* (2011) rely on "fears of phantasmagorical Blackness." That they do so by constructing the white woman as in need of protection is key, but so too is the way they construct females as property. In effect, white women are denied agency in much the same way as black (zombified) slaves. Herein, in addition to justifying colonialism due to its purported civilizing aims, early zombie films present patriarchy as a necessary, natural order through which women can be kept in their "proper" place. In turn, the horror of early zombie films is more about becoming enslaved to the will of another rather than about being turned zombie (or eaten by one). For the privileged male elite of the early twentieth century, whose status was changing due to the erosion of empire and growing unrest regarding industrial capitalism and the like, such fear of losing power and agency was projected onto women and people of color—something we see in the early zombie movies *White Zombie, I Walked with a Zombie,* and *Voodoo Man.* To be sure, the construction of men of color and women as other exists across early horror films, yet the zombie genre enacts this characterization in a way uniquely indebted to colonial occupation and enslavement. Notably, both black men and white women are controlled via zombification. However, it is only the white women that are presented as in need of saving from this zombified fate—black men, in contrast, are depicted as permanent zombies. As Chera Kee argues, early films mark Haiti as "a nation of eternal slaves" and solidify notions of people of color "as less than human." In so doing, Kee contends, the narratives enact a "fantasy of empire" wherein "certain bodies could be made to work endless hours, supplying the rest of the world's needs" (14–23). The three post-millennial movies considered in the latter half of the following section revolve around such fantasies, *Fido, Get Out,* and *Us*—the first of which features white males who fear becoming zombies and the latter of which interrogates the continuing project of normalizing the zombification of people of color.

Black Magic as Imperiling White Womanhood: *White Zombie, I Walked with a Zombie* and *Voodoo Man*

The 1932 film *White Zombie* draws on Stoker's *Dracula,* a text rife with imperialistic conceptions of gender, race and class. Relocating the narrative from a European context to the Caribbean, the movie features white male patriarchs, black zombie slaves, and a white woman turned zombie. Said woman, Madeline, is rendered a zombie so that the wealthy Beaumont, a plantation owner, can force her to marry him in lieu of her current fiancé, Neil. Functioning as the passive corpse bride the patriarchal imaginary is so fond of, Madeline is depicted as sexually threatened by the voodoo master Legendre, something Tony Williams reads in relation to her treatment as sexualized property (18). Meanwhile, Haitian zombie slaves toil endlessly in a sugar cane mill, toppling to their deaths to be ground by millstones without remark. The narrative never questions whether or not black Haitians "deserve" to be zombified; instead, it circulates around the horror of a besmirched white woman in what Robin Coleman names "a fantasy of post-slavery docility" in which slaves labor "forever and without complaint" (51). The white supremacist attitudes that underscore the film are made particularly apparent in Madeline's fiancé Neil's response when he learns she may have been kidnapped by the native population: "Surely, you don't mean she's alive? In the hands of natives? God, no! She's better dead than that!" In truth, the horror of the film, as Coleman rightly points out, is framed as "the threat made against a White woman" (52).

In the narrative, black Haitians are controlled via a "black magic" practicing "middle-man" (Legendre) while the white female love interest is zombified.⁴ Colonialism and enslavement are thus displaced (and never explicitly mentioned) via representing voodoo as the zombifying force that imperils white women. Voodoo is most strongly associated with Legendre in the film, a Dracula-like figure (fittingly played by Bela Lugosi). In contrast, Beaumont and Neil (the white males of the film, the first French and the latter American) conquer the "dark threat" endangering white womanhood. Representing "the archetypal white female victim ... in danger from Indians, monsters, flying saucers, foreign invaders," Madeline becomes the battleground not only between good and bad men, but between colonizers and colonized—she is, as Williams contends, akin to Haiti itself. Whereas Haiti is possessed land, she is "the possessed partner within the capitalist marriage institution" (20). Further, by replacing historical realities with a voodoo villain, the film is able to frame its white male characters positively. "Saving" Haiti from voodoo by destroying Legendre, these white male heroes awaken Madeline to her true self and "true" American husband, Neil.

This depiction of marriage as a property right combined with the unquestioned colonized "zombie state" of people of color is also apparent in *I Walked with a Zombie*, a 1943 movie inspired in part by *Jane Eyre*. Similar to Bronte's novel, *I Walked with a Zombie* gives us two wifely characters—the compliant Betsy, and the "insane" Jessica, the film's Bertha Mason. Betsy is a nurse hired to take care of Jessica, the zombified wife of Mr. Paul Holland, a plantation owner in the West Indies. Implying Jessica married Paul for his money and had plans to run away with his half-brother Wesley, the story arc relies on voodoo to "solve" the problem of "gold-digging" wives. Jessica's mother-in-law, who orchestrated the voodoo ceremony that rendered Jessica a compliant zombie so as to "enact punishment upon her transgressive daughter-in-law," is the film's Legendre character—the one who "turns" a woman for the sake of a powerful white male (her son Paul). Significantly, Jessica's zombification transforms her into "a big doll" that is "bereft of will-power" and "unable to speak or even to act by herself" (Bishop, *Zombie Gothic* 91). Noting "she will obey simple commands," the plantation's doctor, Maxwell, describes Jessica as a perfect wifely figure, one who does as she is told without pesky thoughts or ambitions of her own. Meanwhile, Betsy takes it upon herself to save Jessica. Markedly, Betsy does so as she hopes it will make Paul—whom she has fallen in love with—happy.

As in *White Zombie*, enslavement of blacks in *I Walked with a Zombie* is overshadowed by attempts to save a white woman, though this time a woman is saving another woman—albeit in order to gain male approval/love. Convinced Jessica can be awakened from her zombified state, Betsy leads Jessica through sugar cane fields towards the island's voodoo encampment. During their travels, the two encounter Carrefour, the iconic black zombie figure with wide, unseeing eyes. As with the enslaved zombies of the sugar mill in *White Zombie*, Carrefour is a silenced character not given any narrative arc, let alone any dialogue. Hence, though *White Zombie* and *I Walked with a Zombie* each nod towards the horrors of being a zombie, they replace the horror of slavery with the specter of white female zombies. Further, the ending of each film releases the white females from their zombie-status. Whereas Madeline is returned to her human self in *White Zombie*, in *I Walked with a Zombie*, Jessica is released through death. To "free" her, Wesley kills Jessica as he can't bear to see her with "no mind, no sense—no love, no hate, no feeling." After stabbing her, he carries her body out to sea, drowning himself in the process. In this scene of murder/suicide, the black zombie Carrefour walks slowly towards Wesley and Jessica. It is not clear if he is following them in order to try and save them from drowning, or if he too yearns for release through death. As he nears the ocean's edge, Carrefour puts up his arms, mirroring Wesley's arm positioning as he carries the dead Jessica out to sea, a move which suggests Carrefour wanted to carry (or even love) Jessica—or, perhaps, that he desires to also be carried out to sea and/or freed from his zombie existence.[5] Alas, Carrefour remains a zombie and, as with the ending of *White Zombie*, sympathy is directed only towards the white female, not the black male.

The 1944 film *Voodoo Man*, instead of silenced black zombies, erases black characters entirely. Transplanting zombie-ism to the United States, the movie puts the racial dynamics of the Haitian zombie under erasure. While white women are constructed as love interests whose purity is threatened by "black magic" in *White Zombie* and *I Walked with a Zombie*, in *Voodoo Man*, young white women are constructed as bodies ripe for zombification. Building on the long-standing historical construction of the female body as devoid of agency, the film plays upon the supposed ease with which women can be "zombified" as well as on the enduring obsession with the female (as) corpse. In the narrative, several women have been kidnapped by Dr. Marlowe (played by Bela Lugosi). Marlowe is experimenting with voodoo in hopes he can find a way to revive his wife Evelyn from the coma she has been languishing in for years. Using his hypnotic stare to zombify the women he kidnaps, Marlowe cages them in his basement. Deploying closed circuit cameras to watch his captives,

Marlowe is a mad-scientist figure using his phallic eye in hopes of "penetrating" the life/death divide. Though Marlowe does not directly sexually assault the women, tropes that will emerge in later zombie films featuring rape are here in latent form—women in a basement space (as in *Deadgirl*), the desirability of female corpses (as in *Contracted*), and the zombified woman as object/property (as with Tammy in *Fido*). Further, the fact Marlowe is seen clutching items of clothing from his female victims while commenting upon their beauty visually codes him as a would-be rapist. Like Dracula (also played by Lugosi), Marlowe sucks the life force from women, but he does so in order to turn them zombie, not vampire.

In films such as these, white females emerge as desirable objects which men vie over, experiment on, and rob of agency. Meanwhile, the enslavement and zombification of black males serves as a mere backdrop or, as in the case of *Voodoo Man*, is put entirely under erasure. Though George Romero's 1968 *Night of the Living Dead* shifted the zombie landscape to one of flesh-eating zombie hordes—the representation featured in the majority of texts that came after—three millennial films of note deploy the Haitian-style zombie that characterize the movies discussed above: *Fido, Get Out,* and *Us.* In *Fido*, colonialism is linked to corporate capitalist militarism. In place of the sugar plantation owning Beaumont, we have the CEO of Zomcon, John Bottoms. Technology supplants the "black magic" middle man Legendre with a "zombie domestication collar" invented by Zomcon to end the zombie wars—or, in other words, to enslave all zombies. Said collar both animalizes and humanizes the zombies wearing it, pointing to zombie primitivism on the one hand and announcing the zombie as a human worker under a militarized leash on the other. In this updated version of tyrannical power, women are forced into submission and serve their husbands/masters so as to be guaranteed the suburban good life. As if *The Stepford Wives* had been imbued with the racial consciousness of Audre Lorde or bell hooks yet emptied out of all people of color, the film acts as a screed against oppression of zombified workers and wives—all of them white. Though it fails to incorporate people of color into its narrative, *Fido* does resurrect one of the key elements of Haitian notions of the figure, that of "the economic exploitation of the underclass" (Murphy 117).

While *Fido* is a sort of *I Walked with a George W. Bush Era Zombie*, *Get Out* is more of a *Post-Racial Voodoo Man*. Rather than the nefarious Dr. Marlowe featured in *Voodoo Man* who attempts to supplant his dead wife with the living brains of abducted young women, *Get Out* gives us not one but two mad scientists—Missy and Dean Armitage. As with *Voodoo Man*, an emphasis on eyes and cameras loom—so much so one wishes Bela Lugosi were still around so that he could have played the insanely creepy blind art dealer who hungers for the eyes of the young black photographer, Chris Washington. In contradistinction to *Fido*, *Get Out* does not bracket out race—instead, white supremacy and scientific racism become primary foci.

Peele's second film, *Us*, also has elements of the Haitian zombie lore. Akin to *Get Out*, the zombie making capability of the *bokor* (or "witch doctor") is positioned in the contemporary U.S. Whereas *Get Out* concentrates more on the micro impacts of white supremacy, focusing on the Armitage family to do so, *Us* offers a macroscopic take on enslavement wherein the U.S.—a "Big Brother Bokor"—attempts to create a compliant populace that can be controlled like zombified puppets. When this agenda fails, the zombie-like doubles are "tethered" underground and forgotten. Just as the willful protagonist of *Get Out* resists being zombified by Rose and her family, so too do "The Tethered" of *Us* resist their underground incarceration. They are the willful monsters of the tale—a dissident army clothed in red, the color of revolution.

Notably, all three films echo strains of the iconic *The Stepford Wives*, itself a tale reliant on the transformation of suburban women into roboticized zombies—and, like that text, they are destined to become classics.[6]

Fido: Zombie Father Knows Best

In *Fido*, the colonial enslavement which gave rise to the zombie as a figure is repackaged into the oppression of the newly risen dead, something made possible via a "breakthrough domestication collar" which renders zombies compliant workers and nullifies their hunger for human flesh. Disseminated via the Halliburton-esque corporation Zomcon, these collars turn zombies into productive capitalist workers while also creating high-end, high-status jobs for the white men who control the working-zombie-class. Going by the motto "a better life through containment," the Zomcon corporation acts as a zombified form of "homeland security," building ever taller fences to keep out the wild, un-collared zombies. In the film-within-the-film that opens the narrative, we, like the school-children of this zombie infiltrated society, watch a propaganda video detailing the history of the zombie wars and subsequent emergence of Zomcon. Only scant details about these wars are provided, but what is made clear is that white male humans won—a victory that assures their dominance over zombies and women. Michele Braun aptly encapsulates the film's revisionist history as follows: "Instead of the civil rights movement and second-wave feminism of the 1950s and '60s, America spent the 1950s fighting the Zombie Wars and now survives as a post-zombie white middle-class utopia in which questions of racial and gender equality appear not to have been asked" (162). Of course, this world is only a utopia for (white) human males. In contrast, zombies serve as unpaid manual labor while women are kept in the limited role of "happy housewife."

A sort of *Pleasantville* with zombies, *Fido* is set in Willard, a small-town with a 1950s feel replete with cookie cutter houses, big shiny cars, men in dapper suits, and women with perfectly coiffed hair. Offering an important cinematic critique of hegemonic gender roles and nuclear family formations, the film is centered in the main around Helen and Timmy Robinson, mother and son, and their changing views of Fido (played by Billy Connolly), the zombie Helen (Carrie-Anne Moss) purchases near the outset of the movie. Initially treating Fido with disdain, Timmy eventually realizes Fido is more-human than his robotic, conservative father Bill Robinson—a man who so fears becoming a zombie that he is obsessed with purchasing proper "head funerals" to prevent reanimation. Here, Bill's fear of "becoming-zombie" equates to the white male fear of losing power to men of color, a fear prevalent not only in the 1950s era evoked via the film but also of the post–9/11 milieu in which *Fido* was released. Notably, the anxiety Bill harbors seems less about dying or becoming a monster than it is about the prospect of becoming a member of the oppressed zombie class.

Helen seems at first to agree with the construction of an exploitable zombie class. However, she will eventually come to realize her wifely status renders her similarly exploited. This awakening is spurred by Fido's entry into the Robinson household and Helen's growing sense of dismay regarding Bill's ineptitude as father and partner. Symbolically, Helen wakes up to her own status as a quasi-zombie figure—one "domesticated" not by a collar, but by her circumscribed status of wife. Meanwhile, the narrative's white male patriarchs, John Bottoms and Bill Robinson, exemplify not only "the inhumanity that Zomcon's commodification of the zombie has created," but also the inequity of a marriage/kinship system that dehumanizes women and children alike (Braun 171). The macro Zomcon plutocracy that runs Willard with a militaristic, corporate fist and constructs zombies as exploitable slave labor is repeated in the micro patriarchal marriages wherein the males exploit and mistreat their wives, much as the colonially occupied Haiti is echoed in Beaumont's attempt to "colonize" Madeline into a slavish wife in *White Zombie*. While the Haitian setting of the 1932 film allowed for a move away from the breadlines of depression era America and into the palatial Beaumont estate, the nostalgic setting of *Fido* captures, as Murphy puts it "what 1950s upper-class suburbia might have looked like had slave labor still been available" ("Imitations" 117).

Though the former movie promoted exotic, fright-filled escapism, the latter satirically suggests modern-day America has not shed its 1950s era racism and sexism, simultaneously mocking nostalgia for a pre-feminist age—or, to put it in zombie parlance, for a time when men were men and women were zombies.

By equating the control of zombies to that of women and children, the film suggests such unequal power dynamics are part and parcel of the wider inequity fostered by patriarchal capitalism. At the same time, women and children are presented as well-positioned to bring about a change to the status quo. As Murphy notes, "Timmy's questioning of the status of the zombie sets the stage for a potential liberation of the zombie from its status as slave" (172). In the film, such liberation triumphs when a zombie outbreak results in Bill's death and John's zombification. Herein, the primary patriarchal baddies of the movie are rendered null and void, leaving Helen, Fido, and Timmy to enjoy a summer barbeque— wherein, significantly, Fido is positioned as the new and improved father of the Robinson family. Instead of the conservative narrative at the heart of *White Zombie*—one which does not question women's status as marriageable object or the exploitation of zombified workers—*Fido* deploys the zombie to condemn both class and gender based oppression. While it fails to proffer a direct engagement with race, it nevertheless provides a politicized zombie narrative for the post-millennial age.

Zombies in "Post-Racial" America: Jordan Peele's *Get Out* and *Us*

Jordan Peele's phenomenally successful films—2017's *Get Out* and 2019's *Us*—wowed audiences, impressed critics, and garnered numerous awards. Contributing to the body of horror films that overtly deal with race, the films, each set in modern day America, are steeped in U.S. history and mythos. On the surface of both narrative are black characters who have "made it"—successful college graduates, happy couples, upstanding families. Behind this surface-level American good-life specters of enslavement, genocide, and white supremacy loom. As will be revealed, the "good life" the characters lead—with its summer homes, garden parties, and days at the beach—depends upon a great underbelly of oppression and exploitation. To explore this dark underbelly, Peele references a number of horror films with similar sociopolitical messages, films which engage with sinister aspects of life in the U.S. He also draws on zombie lore—something that has as of yet received minimal attention in existing analysis.[7] His work proves there is life in the zombie yet, offering a corrective to how, "zombies have always been constructed/(mis)understood through the white imagination" (Sherronda Brown).

As an African American director and writer, Peele addresses the "white imagination" and the continuing racism in the contemporary U.S., doing so by taking zombie lore—and the Voodoo practices that inform the figure—back to its Haitian roots. The Haitian zombie, as noted in the chapter introduction, encapsulates the traumas of enslavement and the dehumanization wrought by colonialism. The horror at the heart of this zombie figure is not of the zombie itself, but of *being zombified*. Both *Get Out* and *Us* address this horror. In *Us*, The Tethered are akin to a mass zombie underclass while in *Get Out* those implanted with white brains as a consequence of the "Coagula procedure" *embody* the enduring impacts of colonialism, enslavement, and systemic racism. Whereas *Us* engages with an oppression of the masses, *Get Out* focuses on the racist enterprise of a privileged white family who colonize black bodies by implanting them with white brains and forcing them to exist only as silenced "passengers" as, in effect, soulless zombies.

In keeping with this more macroscopic focus, *Get Out* highlights the constant micro-aggressions experienced by its main character, Chris Washington (Daniel Kaluuya). It also depicts white supremacy as an immortal ideology, one that even "good white liberals" are far from immune to. Gesturing towards common "post-racial" pronouncements such as "I don't see race," the narrative portrays white Americans as blind—often willfully so—to the continuing impact of racism and white supremacy. Emphasizing this post-racial blindness via a marked emphasis on sight, eyes, and cameras, the film offers a snapshot of current race relations as they pertain to Chris, a young black man dating Rose Armitage, a wealthy white woman. As in the early twentieth century film *Voodoo Man*, surveillance is used as a tool of oppression, but, in this iteration, it is black male bodies put under a predatory gaze rather than white female ones. Chris, the imperiled protagonist, is able to escape this gaze (and the aggression it portends) by using his camera and phone as tools of resistance (something that brings to mind recent use of smart phones to record incidences of police brutality).

The pre-credit segment of *Get Out* establishes this focus on vision and technology. A black man is talking on a cell phone as he walks through what he deems a "creepy confusing-ass suburb." When a car pulls up, he tries to mitigate his deepening fear, telling himself "Not today, not me." The driver of the car emerges, knocks him out, and forces him into the trunk. It is not clear if he is dead nor are any details of his attacker provided (notably, the night-time setting impedes the audience's vision as well). In a sense, the monstrous attacker is (white) suburbia itself—a place not safe for black bodies (as evidenced via real-world incidents such as the murder of Trayvon Martin and countless other black citizens). As Cayla McNally observes, this opening segment launches "the film's dual focus on the objectification of black bodies and the white supremacist vision that structures our world." After this harrowing opening, the film switches gears to focus on Chris, an urban dwelling photographer, and his relationship with Rose. Chris has agreed to go with Rose to her parents' house, yet is clearly apprehensive about the pending visit. While he is well aware his success as a photographer may mean nothing to Rose's parents, she shrugs off his concerns. "I don't want to get chased off the lawn with a shotgun" Chris explains. She insists her parents are not racist and convinces Chris he is being paranoid. His friend Rod, on the other hand, later warns him via telephone not to go, insisting "Don't go to the white girl's parents' house!" As the narrative continues, Rod's concerns prove all too justified, something ominously foreshadowed when Rose hits and kills a deer on the drive out to her parents' upstate mansion. After a difficult to watch scene in which a white law officer demands to see Chris' I.D. even though Rose was driving, the two continue on to the Armitage estate.

After their arrival, as Rose relates details of hitting the deer, her father Dean interjects: "I do not like the deer. I'm sick of it. They're taking over. They're like rats, destroying the ecosystem. I see a dead deer on the side of the highway, I think to myself 'That's a start.'" The deer clearly stand-in here for the people of color oft construed as "taking over" in white supremacist rhetoric. The Armitage family, in turn, are the hunters, something confirmed in a later scene when Chris spies a deer head mounted to their basement wall (or as when Rose wears hunting jodhpurs near the close of the film, eventually chasing Chris with a shotgun—the very fear he voiced at the film's outset). Via conflating Chris with deer, *Get Out* invokes the long historical tradition of viewing blacks as animalistic. The plantation-like Armitage estate, complete with modern-day slave auctions, furthers such historical realities, as do characters representative of the house slave (Georgina), the field slave (Walter), and the Uncle Tom (Andre). Meanwhile, Dean and Missy Armitage, Rose's parents, serve as white master figures whose "performative white guilt" is suspect from the get go (James).

As a neurosurgeon and psychiatrist respectively, Dean and Missy act as modern day eugenicists. They use their scientific acumen to take control of Chris' mind (via hypnosis) with the goal of ultimately colonizing his body (via neurosurgery). That this will occur in the Armitage basement is hinted at when Dean warns Chris it is infested with "black mold" as they tour the house. This so-called black-mold, as we will eventually learn, is not a fungus, but an operating theater in which black bodies become the

A promotional poster for *Get Out* depicting Chris (Daniel Kaluuya) as a teacup, evoking Missy's tool of hypnosis and presenting Chris as the "bodily mold" for the Armitages' zombifying enterprise (Universal Pictures, 2017, directed by Jordan Peele).

"mold" in which to pour white brains and identities. Dubbed the Coagula Procedure, this modern-day zombification of black bodies is the true enterprise of the Armitage family—a venture that relies on auctioning off black bodies to cultural elites so that they can take over their chosen bodily hosts via brain transplantation.

As Kendra James parses it, *Get Out* offers "a literal and visual representation of building a better life in America on the backs of the subjugated." In a continuation of the construction of blacks as mere bodies (devoid of mental acumen), the whites featured in the film view blacks as having superior physical and athletic ability which they can "build upon." Such beliefs are first brought to the fore when Dean tells Chris his father was a runner that lost against Jessie Owens during Olympic finals. The suggestion that blackness equates to athletic superiority is furthered when Rose's brother Jeremy tells Chris he would make a great athlete and has the potential to be "a beast," something that evokes the construction of black men as "black bucks." Of course, this construction was not used to celebrate black athleticism, but to "justify" using blacks as "beasts of burden" during slavery as well as to ignite fears of their "beastly sexuality" and the dangers it purportedly posed to white women.[8] Chris is further dehumanized at the Armitages' party that follows. Treating him as a body on display, guests make multiple comments about his assumed strength and virility. One woman squeezes his arm as she asks Rose if sex with a black man really is better. This scrutiny of Chris in these scenes variously alludes to slaves at auction, the systemic exploitation of black athletes, and the fetishizing of the muscular/sexy black body. The film also engages with the divide-and-conquer strategy white supremacy depends upon. We see this in a number of strange encounters between Chris and the other black characters associated with the Armitage family—Walter, Georgina, and Andre.

Walter is the first fellow black person Chris sees. When he and Rose first drive up to the house, Walter is stock-still, as if a statue, and dressed in work clothes, exuding the lifeless aura of the typical Haitian zombie. When Chris goes outside later that night to have a cigarette, Walter runs directly towards him at full speed, as if an attacking animal (though we don't know it yet, Walter has been "taken over" by Roman Armitage, Rose's Olympic-running grandfather). In a conversation between the two men the next day, Chris indicates Walter is being exploited. "They working you good out here, huh?" he asks. Walter, redolent of the "happy slave," replies "Nothing I don't want to be doing." Georgina, the "house slave" of the narrative, will further insinuate nothing is amiss at the Armitage estate. After Chris confides in her that "if there's too many white people I get nervous," Georgina, donning a white voice and affect, avers "That's not my experience. Not at all. The Armitages are so good to us. They treat us like family." Dean made a similar claim earlier in the film, telling Chris that Georgina and Walter are "like family." Indeed, they *are* family—the black bodies known as Walter and Georgina house the identities of Rose's grandparents—something made possible by the Coagula Procedure.

In order to provide bodies for the transplantation at the center of the film's plot, Rose trolls dating sights to find black candidates and then lures them to her parents' estate. Her brother, as insinuated in the opening segment, likely also provides black bodies. While Rose uses feminine wiles, Jeremy uses physical violence. These stereotypically gendered tactics echo that of their parents—the hypnotic power of Missy and the surgical power of Dean. Yet, in a gender reversal, Missy acts as the newfangled voodoo master—a role traditionally cast as male. On the evening of Chris's arrival, we observe her in this capacity as she puts Chris into a hypnotic state by rhythmically tapping a spoon against a teacup (an action which evokes the slave era practice of summoning house slaves in similar manner). As Missy takes control of his mind, Chris experiences himself falling into "the sunken place"—a dark void where he can no longer control his body or his thoughts (much like a zombie). He hears Missy talking from a television-like portal far above him. An encapsulation of black experience in a white supremacist world, the sunken place strips Chris of agency. Later, he will sit wide-eyed and helpless in the sunken place, watching a screen showing his mother's death as tears stream down his face. Forced to view the images Missy directs him to, his vision is controlled by a white gaze, something that parallels how the Coagula Procedure forces black victims to view the world through the (white) brains transplanted into their bodies. Though hypnotized against his will and eventually captured in the Armitages' basement, Chris is able to prevent such a fate thanks to his strong powers of observation—his willful black vision, if you well—something associated with his camera and smart phone. At the party, when Chris takes a photo of Andre the flash from his camera awakens Andre from his zombified state. He grabs Chris frantically and urgently repeats "Get out!" He is then whisked away only to be re-hypnotized. This brief scene, from which the film takes its title, calls to mind the joke "Why are there no Black people in horror movies? Because when an ominous voice says 'GET OUT!', we do!" This joke, as Coleman notes, traditionally served as an "offhanded justification to help explain the virtual absence of Blacks in horror movies made before the 1970s" (xi). In Peele's film, "Get out!" instead warns of the danger Chris faces due to the white supremacist mission of the Armitage family.

Convinced he should "get out" as Andre advised, he gathers his things from Rose's room. While doing so, he makes an ominous discovery: a stack of pictures of Rose posing with numerous black men (including Walter) and one black woman (Georgina). These photos hint at the role Rose plays in abducting blacks for the Coagula Procedure. In the movie within the movie that provides background to this contemporary enslavement enterprise, Rose's grandfather explains blacks are chosen due to their "physical advantage." Echoing claims used to "justify" colonialism, enslavement, and eugenics, this modern enterprise finds Dean and Missy Armitage functioning as 21st century witch doctors and slavers. Like the black bodies in Haitian lore robbed of will so as to make enslavement possible, those abducted for the Coagula Enterprise have their agency stolen from them. Rather than having their souls removed so as to become eternal slaves (as in Haitian lore), the modern-day victims are hypnotized and then locked in the Armitage basement until it is time for their "transmutation." As it is later described to Chris by Jim Hudson, the winning bidder for his body, this "transmutation" will turn Chris into a "passenger." As Jim explains, "You won't be gone, not completely. A sliver of you will still be in there ... your existence will be as a passenger, an audience." Thus, the black subjects that undergo "transmutation" are forced to watch their own bodies—now controlled by the white brains transplanted into them—carry on existing. Like the Haitian zombie, which served as a "nightmarish figuration of a slavery that would continue even after death," these "passengers" are stripped of agency (Canavan 447).

Rose, responsible for ensnaring and then ferrying soon-to-be passengers to the Armitage estate, plays a crucial role in this modern-day zombification enterprise. Overturning the "innocent as a rose" notion of young white femininity, Rose acts as beast. Clothed as colonial white hunter figure in the closing scenes, she hunts for black victims on online dating sites as she sips a glass of cold milk. With a confident, icy demeanor that suggests she is sure Chris's transmutation is a foregone conclusion, she is a chilling embodiment of a white woman happily upholding a white supremacist system. Yet, her over-determined whiteness prevented her from seeing that Chris—observant, determined, and "woke"—was not a good target. As her ears are plugged with headphones as she hunts for future victims from her bedroom lair, Chris is plugging his ears with cotton pulled from the chair he is strapped to in the basement so as to drown out the sounds keeping him hypnotized. Using a symbol indelibly related to slavery, Chris figuratively tears down the master's house and then proceeds to use one of the master's trophies—a mounted deer head—to attack his captors.[9] Not willing to be rendered into a mere bodily housing for a white master to occupy, Chris dismantles the Coagula apparatus one Armitage at a time— first Dean, then Jeremy, then Missy, and, finally, Rose. Before the credits roll, however, Peele has another twist for his viewers: Rose, who has been shot, mistakenly assumes the sirens and flashing lights of the approaching car mean the police have arrived. Shouting "Help me," she puts her hands in the air and readies herself to be rescued by (white) law enforcement. Instead, Rod emerges from a TSA vehicle and bellows at Chris "I told you not to go in the house!" This comedic twist allows our black protagonist to survive (and his best friend to act as savior).

Meditating on how we might "get out" of the collective nightmare that is white supremacy, Peele's *Get Out* provides a corrective to the sentiment proffered in early twentieth century zombie films that "pure" white women were threatened by dark forces attempting to zombify them. Instead, it is a white woman (and her family) that threaten and enslave black bodies—a representation far more in keeping with reality. In its positioning Chris and Rod as heroic rebels at the film's close, *Get Out* offers an on-screen echo of the uprising in Haiti that led to the fist nation to be ruled by the formerly enslaved. Peele's second film, *Us,* more directly engages with this history, drawing on zombie iconography and lore to do so. Most notable in this regard are The Tethered, the supposedly soulless automatons surviving in an underground world. The apparent result of a failed government experiment, this population, with their halting, robotic movements and blank stares, share several similarities with the post–Romero zombie— they act in horde-like fashion, they lack agency, they kill humans. They are also very much, as the title suggests, like "us"—something Peele spoke of in ways redolent of Romero at the SXSW film festival in 2019:

> … when I decided to write this movie, I was stricken with the fact that we are in a time where we fear the other, whether it is the mysterious invader that we think is going to come and kill us, take our jobs, or the faction that we don't live near that voted a different way than us. We're all about pointing the finger. And I wanted to suggest that maybe the monster we really need to look at has our face, maybe the evil is us.

The Tethered, though remarkably like "us" humans, are forced to live beneath ground in the "Abandoned subway lines, road networks and deserted mines"—presumably those referenced in the on-screen quote that precedes the film.

As the prologue of *Us* begins, a lone white rabbit fills the screen. The camera zooms out to reveal a vast wall of caged rabbits. After providing brief glimpses of the sparse underground world that seems part abandoned train station, part subterranean science facility, the camera cuts to a television airing a commercial for Hands Across America, a 1980s fundraiser aimed at alleviating poverty. The faint reflection of a young girl's face provides the first glimpse of one of the film's central characters. In the scene that follows, the girl is with her parents at a beach-side amusement park.

When her dad wins the carnival game he is playing, he lets her pick the prize. She chooses a Thriller t-shirt (another key zombie reference).[10] Her mom grouses about how Michael Jackson's video terrified her, declaring the t-shirt will give her nightmares. Annoyed with her husband's drinking and lackadaisical parenting, the mother heads off to the bathroom, asking him pointedly "Can you watch your daughter, please?" The girl soon wanders away from her distracted parents and descends a staircase leading down to the beach. Once there, she enters the "Shaman Vision Quest Forest," a funhouse attraction. As she makes her way through the attraction's American wilderness themed walkways, a stereotypical "noble warrior" voice narrates. An animatronic owl pops out from the wall, startling her.[11] The lights go out. She whistles a tune to keep herself calm as she walks towards the exit. She is stopped short when she encounters something terrifying—the back of another girl's head that looks exactly like her. This doppelganger turns to face her. Her eyes widen in terror before the camera cuts to the present day.

Adelaide Wilson, presumably the girl from the prologue, now an adult, sleeps blissfully in the passenger seat of a moving car. Her husband Gabe is driving the family to their summer vacation home, establishing the Wilsons as privileged economically. Once they arrive at the house, Zora, their daughter, complains the Wi-Fi doesn't work. Jason, their son, asks to get a dog. The family eat a take-out meal and chat amiably with one another. Alas, their upper-middle class lifestyle is soon to be punctured, something hinted at when Jason gets locked in a hall closet. Adelaide's behavior is especially ominous—she furtively looks out the windows as if scanning for intruders and searches through the house as if hunting down a ghost. That something menacing is afoot is further substantiated when Gabe tries to convince Adelaide to go to the beach. "It's crowded there," she asserts. "There's weirdos at the beach," she continues, insisting "I am not going. We're not going." She eventually gives in, however, and the Wilson family heads to the beach.

Adelaide has a flashback to her childhood as they are driving. She is a girl again, riding in the back of her parents' car on the way home from the beach boardwalk following the funhouse incident. She has an odd, blank look about her. The mother is distraught and assumes the fact her daughter isn't talking means something horrible happened to her when she wandered down to the beach on her own. Adelaide is then pulled back to the current moment as the family nears the beach. Once there, they locate their friends Josh and Kitty. Not long after, Adelaide notices Jason has gone missing. She panics and scans the beach for him. After locating him, they return home and Adelaide tells Gabe about her childhood experience at the boardwalk:

I wandered off.... I ended up in that hall of mirrors. There was another girl in there. She looked like me. Exactly like me.... She wasn't a reflection. She was real.... I ran as fast as I could. My whole life ... I've thought that she's a devil coming for me.... Since we've been here ... I feel like ... she's getting closer.

Gabe, always the joker, offers some ill-timed witticisms. The power goes out. Jason enters their bedroom, announcing "There's a family in our driveway." They go to look. A family of four, clad in prison-like jumpsuits, stand as if statues, holding hands at the edge of the driveway. Adelaide immediately calls 911. Gabe, nonplussed, insists "It's just a family standing outside. It's probably the neighbors."[12] Annoyed his vacation has been interrupted, he goes outside. "Can I help you?" he inquires in a friendly tone. Troubled by their lack of response, he becomes agitated, shouting "I need y'all to get off my property." Here, Adelaide's and Gabe's actions speak to their privilege—on the one hand, Adelaide has no qualms about calling 911 (something many people of color are reluctant to do given a less than stellar history of how emergency services and law enforcement deal with marginalized folks)—on the other, Gabe's lack of worry smacks of an easy life while his "get off my property" commandment is predicated on the sentiment he *owns* the land. The family, unaffected by Gabe's command, don't "get off"—instead they invade the home.

Once inside, they round up the four Wilsons and assemble them in the living room. "It's us," Jason announces, pointing out what has yet gone unsaid—the invaders are doppelgangers—a duplicate family of four. Their matriarch, known as Red, proceeds to tell a story:

Once upon a time, there was a girl. And the girl had a shadow. The two were connected. Tethered together. When the girl ate, her food was given to her warm and tasty. But when the shadow was hungry, she had to eat rabbit, raw and bloody. On Christmas, the girl received wonderful toys. Soft and cushy. But the shadow's toys were so sharp and cold. They'd slice through her fingers when she tried to play with them.

As Red continues, it becomes increasingly clear she is the shadow of the tale. Describing how she was forced to marry and have two children, her experiences echo that of African women enslaved in the U.S. who were denied marital choices, regularly raped, and made to bear children they were then separated from. Unmoved by her tragic tale, Gabe asks in exasperation, "What do you want?" Failing to realize the threat the doppelgangers pose, he sees the world through a material lens. "You could have my wallet. You could have the car.... You could have the boat," he offers. His follow-up inquiry—"What are you people?"—further emphasizes his privileged worldview—one in which the family of others are referenced via the racially loaded "you people." In return, Red responds, "We're Americans"—a proclamation that is as shocking to the Wilson family as it is to the audience. How can this freakish family of four, with their wide staring eyes, guttural grunts, and peculiar demeanors, be American? They must be mistaken—surely they are aliens, counterfeits, monstrous cyborgs—or perhaps zombies. They have dead-looking eyes and fixed facial expressions. They move as if not human. None but Red speak. Abraham, Gabe's double, embodies the murderous aspects of the American zombie and communicates in grunts and growls. Zora's counterpart wears a vacant expression. Pluto, Jason's counterpart, seems part canine and is said to worship fire. They proceed to pursue their human doubles with murderous intent. The narrative then turns to the Wilsons' white friends, Josh and Kitty. They too have their home invaded by doppelgangers, ones who successfully murder the entire family. The Wilsons eventually travel to their friends' house, hoping to find shelter or aid. When they discover Josh, Kitty, and their twin daughters dead, Adelaide again tries to contact 911. Gabe, incredulous that 911 puts them on hold, continues to put faith in authority and rule of law, suggesting they stay inside until help arrives. Adelaide, in contrast, suggests they flee to Mexico, insisting the doubles will not give up in their lethal pursuit.

After learning from a local newscast that masses of the red-suited others have emerged from underneath the beach boardwalk, the Wilson family take Josh's SUV in hopes of escaping the town. As they drive, they encounter Pluto, Jason's double, standing in front of a burning vehicle near the boardwalk. Their way blocked, they get out of the vehicle. Red sneaks up from behind and grabs Jason. Red runs off with him towards the funhouse. Adelaide pursues her. The Tethered stand holding hands in the distance, creating a long human chain reaching out into the ocean. Gabe and Zora spy another human chain circling the boardwalk and hide away in an ambulance. Adelaide soon finds her way to the underground labyrinth that runs beneath the beachside funhouse. She finds Red in a classroom space, drawing chains of paper-doll like figures on a chalkboard. Red shares details about her existence and identity leading to the film's big reveal: Adelaide, who has functioned as the heroic mother of the narrative thus far, is not in fact the grown up little girl whose trip to the boardwalk went awry near the film's start—she is instead The Tethered double—the one encountered in the funhouse mirror. She abducted her human counterpart from the funhouse years ago and imprisoned her underground. As subsequent flashbacks reveal, The Tethered doppelganger (who will continue to be referred to as Adelaide) chained Red (the girl from the film's start) underground. She stole Red's Thriller t-shirt, walked away with a sinister smile, and proceeded to steal her aboveground identity. This revelation puts Red's violent pursuit of Adelaide and her family in a much different light—she is not simply a murderous double, but a wronged woman

Red (Lupita Nyong'o) cuts a chain of red paper dolls as she stands in front of a chalkboard, upon which is drawn a long chain of stick figures. The chains represent "The Tethered," who are both victims and villains, in *Us* (Universal Pictures, 2019, directed by Jordan Peele).

trying to take back the life Adelaide stole from her. Importantly, she is not only pursuing a personal vendetta—she also aims to free to her tethered counterparts.

In accordance with the political undercurrents that shape the voodoo religion, Peele positions Red as part voodoo priest, part zombie, part revolutionary. Instead of sticking dolls with pins, she draws as well as cuts out long chains of paper dolls, effectively conjuring the red-clad masses to rise up in solidarity.

She is at once part of The Tethered masses, a virtual zombie, but at the same time a powerful bokor—one who commands her family to join her in overthrowing their Wilson "masters." As she later explains it to Adelaide.

> The Tethered saw that I was different. That I would deliver them from this misery. I found my faith. And I began to prepare. It took years to plan. Everything had to be perfect. I didn't just need to kill you. I needed to make a statement that the whole world would see. It's our time now. Our time up there.

In other words, Red finds her (voodoo) faith and prepares The Tethered for a revolution. While some critics have argued Red's actions and those of her brethren are irredeemably violent, if we read them in light of the historical injustices the film revolves around, their actions are politically motivated. If viewed through the lens of Haitian history and voodoo belief, their violent uprising is akin to a slave rebellion—or, in more monstrous terms—a zombie takeover. As Red describes it, humans "figured out how to make a copy of the body but not the soul. The soul remains one shared by two." They created these doubles, she claims, "so they could use them to control the ones above. Like puppets." Said humans thus enacted something similar to zombification. Their acts tie to lore of voodoo priests, or Bokors, able to split human victims into two distinct parts—one being the spirit zombie (or soul) and the other being the zombie cadaver (or revived corpse). The Bokor then keeps the spirit zombie trapped, enabling complete control of the body. As Red explains it, the creation of The Tethered enacted just such a split. That they ultimately revolt against their subjection can be further linked to the slave uprising in Haiti—one that led to the formation of the first independent republic in the Western Hemisphere. Cited as a key turning point in the eradication of the U.S. slave regime by many, this large-scale rebellion was grounded in the beliefs of the largely African-born slaves of Haiti. Associating slavery to an eternal bodily imprisonment which disallowed ever transitioning to the afterlife, the Haitian revolution emerged out of the horrors of slavery and was animated by voodoo faith. The resistance enacted by The Tethered in Peele's film is in some senses a similar uprising.

The Tethered can also be read as the colonized peoples of what is now America—those derogatorily deemed "*red* Indians." Like indigenous peoples, they are construed as savage and inferior. They are forced to migrate underground and left to barely survive for generations. Put in this light, Adelaide's theft of Red's identity is a response to her own oppression.

Yet, rather than trying to free her brethren once aboveground, Adelaide takes an individualist route, stealing Red's identity to do so. As Tasha Robinson puts it, "She knows full well that her comfortable, happy life came at someone else's expense, and that she chose to hold someone else down so she could be free." Red, in contrast, leads the tethered to rise en masse.

The virtual proletariat breaking the chains the bourgeoisie have bound them in, The Tethered admittedly commit heinous acts of violence, leaving the streets of Santa Cruz strewn with dead bodies in what looks much like a zombie killing spree. Yet, Adelaide comes off as even more villainous as the narrative concludes. She brutally kills Red in a scene that finds her snarling and growling with wide-eyed ferocity—and which culminates in Adelaide chomping her jaws in zombie-like fashion. She then returns to her aboveground life, joining her family as they drive away from the body-strewn streets in a shiny SUV. In the distance, clouds of smoke billow above a wall of bodies holding hands across the landscape. The swarms of helicopters hovering above them indicate they are under attack, much as protestors gathered in peaceful assembly have been across the generations. This foregrounding of bodies holding hands as far as the eye can see at the film's close powerfully tethers present U.S. inequities to past injustices. If such injustices are to be overcome, the film suggests, the Us/Them divide must be eradicated.

Responding to what Richard Brody aptly describes as "a moment of growing recognition that the deeds of the past still rage with silent and devastating force in the present time," *Get Out* and *Us* each portray the "American Dream" as nightmare. Drawing on voodoo mythos to enact the horrifying critiques proffered in *Get Out* and *Us*, Peele's films prove Haitian zombie mythos has life in it yet. Indeed, as argued by Max Gordon, his "filmic ideas are so powerful that they are transforming the language we use to talk about race."

Section 2: Eradicating Rape Culture Zombie-Style

Contrary to the long silences and inaction surrounding sexual violence in the real world, especially regarding legal ramifications that punish rapists, many recent zombie texts expose and condemn rape culture.[13] Though the term "rape culture" arose in the 1970s out of second wave feminism, the phrase became part of mainstream rhetoric rather recently.[14] An umbrella concept that encompasses the entire spectrum of sexualized violence carried out between individuals as well as that condoned by institutions (the military, for example), rape culture references the many ways sexual violence is normalized. At the heart of such normalization is hierarchical power, or what Brownmiller named "the ideology of rape"—one that makes sexual violence seem a *natural*—or at least a to-be-expected—part of culture (2).[15] Though zombie texts have received much scholarly attention in recent years, only recently has a focus on rape culture in/and zombie texts begun to emerge.[16] In what follows, I expand this conversation, arguing that many zombie texts reveal how societies defined by top-down power systems (including patriarchy, militarism, capitalism, white supremacy, and so on) foster a rape culture world.

As feminist analysis reveals, one of the foundational impetuses normalizing such a world is the construction of females and people of color as property. Angela Davis' influential article "Joan Little: The Dialectics of Rape" convincingly establishes as much. For our purposes here, the ways in which this construction plays itself out within zombie texts is apparent via the attempts of those in power to maintain control over women *and* zombies, as well as in relation to the treatment of women, people of color, and zombies *as property*. When these marginalized others are not willing to be treated as such, they are deemed monstrous, as when Michonne is the "angry black female" who tortures the Governor for raping her in *The Walking Dead* comic series or as with undead female figures such as Deadgirl (from the film of the same title) or Sam (from *Contracted*) who are framed as infectious monsters as a result of being unwilling to act as sexual objects. In contrast to these more reactionary representations, many zombie texts directly include narrative arcs dealing with sexual violence, often condemning those who take pleasure in sexually violating others—whether they be zombie or human. Such is the case with characters from the televised version of *TWD* such as Negan as well as Major West from *28 Days Later*, the sexual traffickers of the *Kellie's Diary* series, the sexually abusive father from *AfterTime*, and in scenes of domestic abuse, sexual assault, and gang rape in *As the World Dies*. In examples such as these, perpetrators are framed as posing more of a threat than zombies. The three post-millennial narratives featured in the following section represent a necessarily small sample of zombie texts engaging with rape culture—the first is (thus far) the most popular post-apocalyptic zombie tale of the 21st century (*TWD*), the second is a book series building upon (and inspired by) Romero's zombie canon (*As the World Dies*), and the third offers a unique permutation of the rape-revenge genre (*Avenged*).

The Walking Dead: Rape Survival Rules in a Post-Zombie World

TWD provides scholars with a plethora of entry points to consider its import. Notable for its focus on human survival in the years that follow a zombie outbreak, the series introduces a large cast of characters as they forge new lives in a decimated world. The series' representation of various communities—the Prison, Terminus, Alexandria, Hilltop—champions more communal, egalitarian models while condemning dictatorial leaders, especially those that promote torture and brutality. Though Rick at one points insists "This is not a democracy," a claim that surely informed fan references to the "Ricktatorship," he is, in the main, a more democratic leader than other males in the saga—and becomes more so in later seasons. Meanwhile, the most positively portrayed communities are women-led, as with Hilltop and Alexandria, the former helmed by Maggie and the latter by Michonne following Rick's departure in season nine. These human enclaves suggest egalitarianism presents the best hope for surviving the threat zombies portend. Significantly, each adopts permutations of a democratic voting system, something non-existent until late in the story arc. Importantly, these battles for suffrage are waged by women within the narrative, a factor that links to historical calls for equitable voting as well as to contemporary issues pertaining to voter suppression. In season nine, Michonne is instrumental in bringing about a more democratic Alexandria, one based on voting rather than the so-called "Ricktatorship." Herein, a woman of color brings about more equity, doing so within a show that had a rather shaky start in terms of its engagements with race.

In the first season, for instance, Glenn and T-Dog were the token men of color while Jacqui, an early woman of color, was killed at the season's close. T-Dog, whom Elexus Jionde reads as embodying the "magical negro" trope, died in the fourth episode of season three. Yet, as the show progressed, *TWD* included more characters of color with more screen time and more complex narrative arcs, doing so in ways that moved beyond the stereotypical. Glenn lived through six seasons, dying in the opening episode of season seven. As Helen K. Ho discusses in her article "Becoming Glenn: Asian American Masculinity," his narrative moved well beyond the "model minority" trope and featured him not only as a heroic male lead, but one who was involved romantically with a white woman, Maggie, one of *TWD*'s lead female protagonists. In addition to primary heroes such as Glenn and Michonne, the series includes several other characters of color, Sasha, Morgan, Tyreese, Rosita, Gabriel, Ezekial, and Siddiq among them. At the same time, authoritarian white males such as The Governor and

Negan are cast as the most monstrous creatures of all within the walker world. Whereas many other characters change in ways that aid in their own and others survival, these white male tyrants of the series undergo "barbaric transformations" that lead to multiple deaths (Bishop, *How Zombies* 79). Other white male baddies, such as Shane (Rick's former best friend), Ed (Carol's abusive husband), Merle (Darryl's racist brother), Gregory (the cowardly and traitorous leader of Hilltop), Gareth (leader of the cannibalistic Hunters) and Joe (head of the Claimers gang) are similarly barbaric. Notably, several of these baddies enact sexual violence at multiple points throughout the series. In what follows, I will address episodes featuring domestic violence, sexual assault, sexual coercion, attempted rape, and rape in order to argue that *TWD* frames perpetrators of domestic and sexual violence as *more rotten* than the ever-present walkers. In contrast to the common tendency to present sexual violence as titillating on the one hand and as an aberrant act carried out by "bad apples" on the other, the show sheds light on the contexts within which this type of sexualization and normalization of violence thrives. As in the comics, where Michonne, after being repeatedly raped and abused by the Governor, seeks vengeance, in the TV series, various characters avenge those who abuse/rape them. In the process, the show provides a number of "rules" for eradicating rape culture within post-zombie U.S.A. Via several narrative arcs that explore the continuum of interpersonal violence, the show positions such violence as resulting from the white heteronormative patriarchy that is still very much in evidence in the walker world.

In season one, the "Tell it to the Frogs" episode introduces key themes related to domestic abuse in particular. This early episode additionally frames norms of masculinity as leading to escalating cycles of violence—something nodded to in an early conversation in which one of the leading males (Shane) instructs a young boy (Carl) how to be "a real man." Later, several females talk and laugh while doing laundry by the river. As they do so, Carol, a battered wife, keeps looking back nervously over her shoulder at her husband Ed. Hearing their laughter, Ed instructs the women, "You ought to focus on your work, this ain't no comedy club." He then orders Carol, "Let's go … come on now, you heard me." When another woman intervenes, Ed warns, "Don't think I won't knock you on your ass." It is here made clear that Ed is more than willing to threaten and attack any woman, not just his wife. Frustrated by the fact Carol seems more interested in her friends than his commands, Ed thunders, "You gonna come on now, or you gonna regret it later?"

Shane, who along with Rick is one of the early male leaders of the series, is watching these interactions from the sidelines. When Ed hits Carol across the face, Shane intervenes. He violently pulls Ed back, throws him to the ground, beats him mercilessly, and then threatens, "Put your hands on your wife, your little girl, anyone else in this camp one more time.... I will not stop next time ... you hear me? ... I will beat you to death." Carol, her mouth bloodied, runs to Ed's side, bawling, "Oh god, Ed, I'm sorry." Although some argue this scene "fails to serve an educative function" as it "positions rescue by another man as the solution," I would counter that the "educative function" is the framing of male control/violence as damaging not only to women, but to the entire community (Green and Meyer 69). Moreover, such scenes are utilized to condemn normative gendered expectations—including that women should "make nice" and men should jump to aid damsels in distress. Though Shane "saves" Carol in the moment, he does so via blows—an intervention that will not produce lasting effects. When Ed is later taken out by a walker, the implication is that the type of violence Shane represents must be eradicated, not merely interrupted by a lone "heroic" act. Thus, while Shane tells Carl to "be a man" early on, Shane's definition of masculinity is more rotten than curative, something that becomes even more apparent in the final episode of the first season, "TS-19."

Set at the Centers for Disease Control, "TS-19" fittingly portrays sexual violence as a disease that is decidedly *not* under control. It does so through further focus on the hyper-masculine Shane. Chafing at the fact he has been "un-manned" as the primary leader of the group due to Rick's return, and frustrated that said return led Lori, Rick's wife, to end their sexual relations, he violently channels his frustrations at her. As she peruses a bookshelf in the CDC game-room, Shane leers at her from the doorway, whiskey bottle in hand. Stomping into the room, he commands, "I'm going to tell you a few things, and you're gonna listen." In addition to harassing her verbally, he attacks her physically. Insisting that she loves him (because who wouldn't love a fist-wielding, whiskey chugging muscle man?), Shane traps Lori against a pinball machine—a nice visual evocation that he's "got balls"—ones that are better than Rick's—and that she *must* love him, godammit! Apparently not wowed by his testicular bravado, Lori responds not with desire but fear. As she tries to push him away, he puts his hands around her neck. "Get your hands off me, don't you dare," Lori warns. The camera then cuts to Shane's hand, forcing its way between Lori's legs. Lori pushes him away, this time leaving nail marks that stripe his neck with blood. Shane retreats, punching the doorframe on his way out. The camera then cuts back to Lori, crying and gripping her head in fear.

By episode's close, Shane's escalating abusive behavior is set against Carol's burgeoning self-confidence—something we might link to the fact her husband Ed is no longer in the picture. In closing scenes, the group discover the CDC is due to explode in less than 30 minutes. With reinforced glass barring their exit, the group frantically tries to figure out a means to escape. As they do so, Carol rummages through her bag quietly. Shyly telling Rick she thinks she has something that will help, she is mocked by Shane: "I don't think a nail file is gonna do it." Yet, what Carol has is a grenade, one which will ultimately make it possible for the group to escape the CDC. Here, Shane's gendered presumption that a woman could never save the day is put in its place—*filed* away, perhaps. As the series progresses, Carol's trajectory reflects the continuum of abuse and the difficulties victims face in extracting themselves from such situations. For example, in "Indifference" Carol reveals she reset her dislocated shoulder rather than go to the ER and court more attacks from Ed, something that depicts the pre-zombie world as *more dangerous* for victims of domestic violence. In effect, the zombie apocalypse provides Carol the opportunity to escape Ed's abuse as well as to use her survivor's knowledge to help herself and others, as when she finds the women's shelter for her and Daryl to take shelter. Later in the series, she morphs into a domestic-abuse-avenger when she intervenes to take out the abusive town doctor at Alexandria. Before that point, various other narrative arcs address sexualized violence and the rape culture continuum, one that apparently lives on in the zombie-populated world.

For instance, in "When the Dead Come Knocking," from season three, Maggie is violated in ways reminiscent of the sexualized torture of Abu Ghraib prisoners in the real world. Here, the series allies post–9/11 xenophobia to the rise of inhumane atrocities and nods towards the military mindset as one that frames women and racialized others as less than human. Scholars such as Melissa Ames and Kyle William Bishop read the show in this light. Bishop sees the "traumatized heroes" of the show "as an indictment of the arguably aggressive stance U.S. politics and foreign policy have taken since 9/11," while Ames emphasizes how the series reflects anxieties shifting gender norms produce (12). The aggressive stance Bishop references is embodied in the show via uber-aggressive white male leaders: Shane, The Governor, and Negan. The Governor's monstrosity is focused on extensively in season three, and especially so in "When the Dead Come Knocking." In the episode, Maggie and Glenn, a couple from Rick's community, are being held prisoner by The Governor, who hopes to force them to reveal Rick's whereabouts. While Glenn is tortured and beaten in one room, The Governor sexually assaults Maggie in another. Removing his belt as they are locked alone together, it is unclear whether he is preparing to beat Maggie or rape her. Positioning himself behind her, he caresses her hair before shoving her head to the table. "Do whatever you're going to do, then go to hell," Maggie cries. The camera cuts away, leaving Maggie still prone on the table. Later in the episode, The Governor brings Maggie, topless and clearly traumatized, before her partner Glenn—the suggestion being that he raped her. Before letting Maggie go, The Governor hugs her in a sadistic embrace. Importantly, the narrative does not simply move on from this assault. Rather, subsequent episodes highlight Maggie's trauma and the resulting impacts on her relationship with Glenn.

As the series continues, rape threats are directed at a number of other characters. In "A," from season four, Rick rips out the jugular vein of the man orchestrating sexual threats against Carl, Michonne, and Daryl. In season five, "Slabtown" features a similar jugular-ripping scene when a recently-turned female zombie attacks her rapist. In the episode, the sexual enslavement and rape of women is equated to zombification (much like *Fido* equated being a housewife to being a zombie). Set at Grady Memorial Hospital, this "slab town" has as its foundation a slew of rotting bodies. Symbolic of the general rot of human decency that one would hope *not* to find in a hospital, the episode circulates around Beth, Maggie's younger sister, and her encounters with a violent, exploitive police officer (Dawn Lerner), a predatory rapist (Officer Gorman), and a self-serving doctor (Edwards). As the episode opens, Beth wakes up in hospital and stares at the clock, a visual evocation of the time she has spent separated from her community—one instigated, significantly, by the same group of violent men that threatened to rape Carl. Soon after, as Beth wanders the halls of Grady Memorial, she encounters Officer Lerner. Decked out in full uniform, Lerner ominously warns her, "You owe us." As the episode continues, it becomes clear Lerner provides her cadre of officers with sexual slaves, whom she calls "wards," with the indication Beth's "debts" will be paid through "ward service."

Beth soon witnesses one such ward being commandeered by officers down a hall and forced into a surgical room. Officer Gorman (a prime villain of this narrative arc) looks on, calling the woman, whose name is Joan, a "smart-ass whore." Though Joan has been bitten on her arm by a zombie, she resists amputation. "I am not going back to them!" she shouts (the "them" she refers to surely being the officers raping her in her role as ward). In the scene, various characters hold Joan down as Edwards cuts off her arm in a scene evocative of a gang rape. Later, to prevent becoming a ward herself, Beth goes to Gorman's office to search for keys that would allow her to escape from the hospital. Once inside, she finds Joan dead on the floor. The insinuation is Joan killed herself to escape her sex-slave existence. As Beth proceeds to search the office, Gorman walks in. He pushes Beth against the desk and starts to put his arm up her shirt, noting it will be a "win win situation." Beth, noticing Joan is turning zombie, smashes

Gorman over the head with the lollipop jar from his desk, knocking him to the ground. Joan, now turned walker, pounces on him, ripping out his jugular. Here, Gorman's actions come back to bite him (quite literally) when Joan reanimates. The scene, reminiscent of the jugular-biting enacted by Rick in the "A" episode, positions Gorman as similar to Carl's would-be-rapist. And, just as sympathy was directed at Carl (and Rick) during that parallel scene, so too are sympathies directed at Joan in "Slabtown." In both cases, the monstrous act of ripping out another's jugular vein is rendered *less monstrous* than rape/attempted rape.

As the series continues, the Alexandria safe-zone will further *TWD's* engagement with rape culture. By this point in the series, Carol has fully transformed from battered wife and grieving mother into avenging warrior. Once at Alexandria, she strategically dons the guise of a Susie-home-maker, baking cookies, wearing comfy cardigans, and offering an ever-smiling face.[17] Underneath this facade, Carol remains vigilant and always-on-watch. Secretively amassing weapons from Alexandria's armory, she is the first to recognize, with her knowledgeable survivor's gaze, one of Alexandria's hidden horrors: Pete Anderson, the community doctor. After an interaction with Sam, Pete's young son, Carol deducts his father is a batterer and informs Rick. Rick then approaches Deanna, Alexandria's leader, telling her "He's beating his wife, we have to stop him." Deanna, in disbelief, explains "Pete's a surgeon. He has saved lives." Herein, the show depicts the tendency to question the veracity of these types of revelations, especially when directed at otherwise respected white males. Ultimately, Rick takes it upon himself to rid the community of this violent male. Coming one season after "A," when, as noted above, Rick ripped out another man's jugular to prevent Carl's rape, Rick here again seeks to rid his world of those who perpetrate sexual and domestic violence. Though some read such violence as indicating Rick is losing his moral compass, it seems more apt to castigate those (such as Diana) who deny this type of cruelty exists.

Through narrative arcs like these which highlight the cyclical, interconnected nature of domestic abuse, sexual assault, rape, and sexual slavery, *TWD* suggests such violence is as pervasive and dangerous—if not more so—than the walkers. As Melissa Leon puts it in her *Daily Beast* post from 2014, "the real source of terror within the world of *The Walking Dead* is not walkers, it's rape." Negan, the tyrannical leader introduced in season six, furthers this type of terror. He rapes his amassed "harem of wives" and offers other men the "privilege" of doing the same. Referencing what he deems "happy hour at the pussy bar" and regularly bragging about the size of his penis, Negan is arguably the show's most extreme example of toxic masculinity. He subscribes to the view of women as men's property and promotes rape with glee, all while claiming to be anti-rape. Ruling not with an iron fist but with a bat wrapped in barbwire, Negan at one point brags to Rick, "I just slid my dick down your throat, and you thanked me for it." He further proclaims the best way to have power over another man is "by fucking his vagina." Herein, Negan is positioned not only as violating women, but also as one who tries to emasculate men with his (phallic) bat.

Though Jessica Valenti argues the lack of on-screen rape and sexual violence makes *TWD* more feminist-friendly than other current fare, I would counter the way show *deals* with domestic violence and rape culture is key. Instead of sensationalizing abuse, eroticizing it, or showing it as an individual tragedy, the series presents violence itself as an infection, as a key "patient zero." The suggestion is thus that while you might be able to out-live the walking dead, you are less likely to survive rape culture unscathed. This portrayal aligns the series with several other zombie narratives that imply interpersonal violence and sexual assault pose a threat similar to that of zombies—one that refuses to die, that rises, again and again, in all sorts of contexts, polluting those it "bites." In such tales, the terror of living in a zombified world *as a human* is equated to the terror of being construed as a *rape-able object* in the real world, something taken up specifically in the next series up for consideration.

The Rise of Female Solidarity: *As the World Dies*

As the World Dies, by Rhiannon Frater, pays homage to the Romero canon, something the author notes as a key intention ("This Author Doesn't Bite").[18] Made up of three novels, *The First Days, Fighting to Survive,* and *Siege*, this trilogy is what one imagines Romero's zombie films might read like if transferred into novel form. Not only is the series helmed by strong female leads (a Romero trademark), it also contends racism, homophobia, and sexual violence pose as much danger—if not more—as zombies. Set in Texas, the series has two female protagonists at its narrative center, Jenni and Katie. The first book opens as Jenni is being pursued by her husband Lloyd, now a zombie. Locked inside her home, Jenni watches Lloyd through the thick glass of their front door as she thinks about the hidden money and packed suitcases she "squirreled away" in hopes she and her children could one day escape Lloyd's abuse (14). Meanwhile, Lloyd consumes their infant son, his destruction of the family here literalized. Inverting the far more common representation of woman as child killer, this scene takes something all too common, a father/husband who beats his family, and renders him terrifyingly aberrant. Each book of the saga will open similarly, documenting Jenni's traumatic memories of Lloyd and his abuse, thus effectively likening the ongoing trauma survivors face to the now ever-present zombie threat. Though Jenni suffers from recurring nightmares in which Lloyd's ghost comes back to torment her, she takes to eradicating zombies with gusto, an endeavor that the series implies is far easier than surviving an abusive marriage.

In book two, *Fighting to Survive,* Jenni's best friend's Katie is attacked in a public restroom by fellow survivor Shane. A bi-sexual woman, her near rape serves as a textual exploration of the ways compulsory heteronormativity perpetuates sexual assault. Shane, a homophobe seeking to "cure" Katie of her same-sex desires, functions as gatekeeper of the general will, one the saga as a whole indicates is problematically heteronormative. In the scene in which he attempts to rape Katie, Shane implores "It's a damn shame that a fine piece of ass like you is a carpet muncher" as his friend guards the bathroom door (a nod to "cock-block" culture and the call for men to "support" their friends' sexual pursuits, violent or otherwise) (197). Katie punches Shane as he tries to rip off her clothes, but he pushes himself between her legs, hissing "I will show you what it's like to be with a man" (198). Depicted as "more than willing to turn the lesbo straight," Shane hews to heteronormative notions that bisexuality isn't real, that queer women only need a "real man," and that forced sexual interaction is the "cure" (205). Later, as the community of survivors discuss Katie's assault, some imply Katie's sexuality is to blame, causing one survivor to intervene: "Gay or straight, it don't make no difference.... Shane was trying to rape her" (205). This exchange echoes the cultural tendency to blame victims for the assault they experience rather than to focus on the perpetrators, something that often leads to victims blaming themselves, as it does in the novel. As Katie listens to her fellow survivor's conversation, still crying and shivering from the ordeal, the "voice inside her head" is "full of self-recrimination" (206). Jenni comforts her, saying "It's okay Katie. Every time Lloyd beat me, he told me it was my fault. I kinda believed him even though I knew it was a lie" (206). Noting such support "forced the accusing voice in her mind to fall silent," Katie thinks back to her former work as an attorney defending victims of sexual assault (206). Though she spent years assuring victims "being raped was not their fault," Katie finds it difficult to heed this dictum when she is assaulted (206).

The final book of the trilogy delves even deeper into the corrosive nature of rape culture and heteronormativity, denouncing religious fundamentalism as well as male characters who feel women owe them sex. This, along with the series allying how Katie feels as a survivor of sexual assault to how it feels to be bisexual in a heteronormative world, encourages consideration as to why, as Katie puts it, "a good portion of the world hated you simply because you looked at your own sex and saw no issue with loving them" (223). Via plot points like this, Frater's saga extends the gendered critiques evident in the work of her cited inspiration, George Romero. Importantly, the first book of the series also includes a key scene which finds Nerit, a fearless female sniper, aiding a zombie woman in avenging her rapists. In her recounting of this incident, Nerit details seeing "the girl's face. It was ... wild ... dead ... hungry.... Her thighs were raw and covered in blood. Her breasts bruised and cut. To me, it looked like they raped her until she was dead. But she was alive again" (326). Sharing "I knew then what to do," Nerit relates:

> I shot off her bonds.... I watched her get up. I watched her get her revenge on the one who had been kicking her. The other men panicked, and some shot at her.... I shot the weapons out of their hands and let her have them. All of them. And when they rose, I put them down, one by one. And at the end, I gave that poor girl her peace [327].

Here, Nerit facilitates another female's revenge, suggesting a solidarity between human women and zombie women forged within the cruel reality of a rape-culture-world. Another narrative, *Avenged*, extends this rape revenge focus within the post-millennial zombie canon.

Rape-Revenge Goes Zombie: *Avenged*

Written and directed by Michael S. Ojeda, *Avenged* is a zombie rape revenge film with a racial retribution twist. The movie opens as Zoe, a deaf white woman, is about to embark on a cross-country road trip to visit her fiancé, Dane, a black man. After entering New Mexico, texting Dane while driving causes Zoe to nearly hit an indigenous man running down the middle of the highway as he attempts to evade a truckload of white supremacists. When this truck pulls up to her car, Zoe runs. One of the men shoots her in the leg. The camera then cuts to her immobilized on her back, bound to a gurney with barbed wire. As her neo-Nazi abductors are going through her belongings, they find a picture of Dane. Scoffing that she must be "color-blind," they proceed to gang-rape Zoe, "reclaiming" what they see as rightfully "theirs" (a white woman), and killing her in the process. Characterized by an in-your-face style heavy on the gore, *Avenged* feels part Western, part action, and part horror. Dealing with intersections of gender, race, class, and (dis)ability, the film finds Zoe morphing from sweet fiancée into a savage warrior replete with face-paint and a warrior cry, something made possible by the fact Zoe is aided into an undead state by Grey Wolf, a local indigenous healer.

Variously wielding a tomahawk, a bow and arrow, and a hunting

A promotional poster for *Avenged* showing Zoe (Amanda Adrienne Smith), a young deaf woman who morphs into a zombie avenger after being gang-raped by a group of white supremacists (Uncork'd Entertainment, 2013, directed by Michael S. Ojeda).

knife, Zoe's rape revenge arc is put in conversation with white supremacy and toxic masculinity. Linking the decay of self-identity brought on by sexual assault to the rotten history of conquest and genocide, *Avenged* highlights racism and sexism as mutually supportive systems via its deployment of a white supremacist gang, most of whom hail from the same depraved family. In one telling moment, the leader of the gang pounds his chest as he wields a container of skulls, those of the indigenous people he and his family hunt and kill. In addition to segments such as this, the film is riddled with racist and sexist language. For example, the white supremacist group call their indigenous targets "injun," brag about having "kicked some major Apache ass," promise to "put a can of whoop-ass on this nigger," and note they are "not gonna hesitate ... sodomizing that sweet virgin ass." Coupling pervasive micro-aggressions with extreme acts of violence, *Avenged* proffers a story which speaks to the wide swath of actions and beliefs that bolster imperialist white supremacist patriarchy.

The undead-zombie-warrior Zoe resists the racism and sexism plaguing her world, doing so specifically through a rape-revenge narrative in which she dispatches her perpetrators one by one. As she does so, her decaying body sustains more and more wounds. Eventually infested with maggots, Zoe's body evokes the rottenness at society's core, a rot that she alone cannot quell. With only the top half of her body remaining by film's end, Zoe succumbs to death. As she does so, the moon, a symbol of the divine feminine, casts a luminous glow over the night sky. Aligned with a celestial body in the closing shot, one wonders if she might become divinely able to avenge rape and racist acts from beyond her grave.

Attending to the as yet undead system of rape culture, the three narratives discussed above suggest that life with zombies (or as a zombie) is less horrific than the sexism, homophobia, and racism that undergirds a system that deems other bodies as rife for sexual, heteronormative, and/or imperial conquest. Whereas *TWD*, As *the World Dies*, and *Avenged* castigate rape culture, doing so through willfully monstrous characters, the texts examined in the forthcoming section position child protagonists, some human and some zombie, as able to rectify various forms of societal rot.

Section 3: The Hopeful Apocalypse and the Zombie Child

From survivors of domestic abuse saving entire communities (as with Carol of *TWD*) to adolescents that save humanity (as with Melanie from *The Girl with All the Gifts*), many heroes in recent zombie tales veer from the white, male, heterosexual norm. No longer do such heroes merely escape the zombie-infected mall alive (as did Fran in *Dawn of the Dead*), they now solve crimes (Liv Moore in *iZombie*), and bring down sexual traffickers (Kellie in *Kellie's Diary*). Many of these heroes are hybrid, liminal figures who queer identity in monstrously productive ways.[19] In Alden Bell's *Exit Kingdom*, for example, Vestal Amata is an admixture of divine savior, sexual dissident, circus freak, and trickster. A millennial vestal virgin, she holds the potential to keep the fire of humanity alive via her zombie-resistant body. In another iteration of the queer-hybrid-hero, Amy from the BBC series *In the Flesh* functions as a rebellious zombie who rejects the "masquerade of living-normativity" (Abbott, *Undead* 172). Refusing to wear the make-up required to appear human, Amy queers zombie femininity, something that allies to the series' depiction of the hetero-monogamous imperative as itself monstrous. Other queer zombie heroes take on white supremacy (as in *Avenged*), take down serial killers (as in the short story "The Third Dead Body")—and give rapists a taste of their own medicine via zombified permutations of the vagina dentata (as in the delightfully gruesome story "Blossom").

The child hero is particularly prominent in the millennial zombie canon, a subject I take up in the following section. In addition to the heroes featured in the four texts analyzed below (*The Reapers Are the Angels, The Girl with All the Gifts, The Boy on the Bridge*, and *Train to Busan*), many other children play integral roles in post-zombie worlds (Carl in *TWD*), zombie-apocalypse narratives (Hannah in *28 Days Later*), eco-zombie tales (Thoomi in *Cargo*), YA series (Mary in *Forest of Hands and Teeth*), and animated movies (Norman in *Paranorman*). Child characters are of course integral to the horror genre, something explored by Vivian Sobchack in "Bringing It All Back Home." Linking the "privileged figure of the child" to the "crisis experienced by American bourgeois patriarchy since the late 1960s," Sobchack documents representations of children as terrorized victims on the one hand and terrorizing forces on the other (144). Admitting such children invoke the possibility of "a radically transformed future," Sobchack documents that most characters deliver "something other than radical" even while they speak to "the terror and rage of *patriarchy in decline*" (149, emphasis in original). In her estimation, child characters within the horror genre often conserve the status quo. Colette Bailman makes a similar argument in "The Enemy Within: The Child as Terrorist in the Contemporary American Horror Film." She writes "The traditional function of the child within bourgeois mythology is the perpetuation of the past into the future, the propagation of the same rather than the embodiment of difference, and a promise of the continuation of the dominant ideological order" (137). Diverging from the traditional, regressive functions of children in horror Sobchack and Bailman document, the four young heroes discussed below instead willfully refute dominant norms and systems. In so doing, they provide a palliative bandaid—if not a cure—to the tyranny of the norm.

Hunting Miracles in a Meatskin World: *The Reapers Are the Angels*

Alden Bell's *The Reapers Are the Angels* is set in a zombie infected United States in the not-too-distant future. Societal infrastructures are gone and violent groups of surviving humans roam the now barren U.S. landscape. Other survivors hole up in homes or abandoned buildings. The story concentrates on Temple, a girl who has never known a world without zombies. As the novel opens, she is living in an abandoned lighthouse in relative safety from the zombies (otherwise known as "meatskins") that populate her world. However, once the zombies discover her make-shift safe house, Temple takes to the road. Confident, independent, and fearless, Temple regularly shares philosophical musings in her journey of survival. "Them meatskins are just animals is all," she reflects early on, noting that "Evil's a thing of the mind. We humans got the full measure of it ourselves" (79). Here, her words suggest humans are evil by *mindful* choice, whereas zombies are merely following their *animal* instincts. Sentiments like this are notably prevalent in the zombie canon, often framing humans as more monstrous than the undead. Furthering this trend, Temple repeatedly insists humans have a great propensity for evil, so much so that she worries about her own ability to remain good, as when she observes "Stayin alive ain't the hard part. The problem is stayin' right" (175). Willfully subverting the norms of her society, Temple manages more than staying right—she helps various others in her trek across the U.S., trying to set society right as she does so.

As she traverses the zombie-filled landscape, Temple keeps butting up against the types of figurative walls Ahmed warns of in *Willful Subjects*. In the novel, such walls come in the form of people and places that work to keep the inequitable ways of the world intact. One wall-abiding human of the text is Moses, a man hunting Temple to avenge his brother Abraham (whom Temple killed when he attempted to rape her). Temple, as her name hints, seeks sanctuary in the meatskin-ridden world, an aim made more difficult as she is being hunted not only by Moses, but also must navigate various other groups of violent men. When Temple meets one such group, they "circle around her," forming a figurative wall, asking "You runnin away from a boyfriend? Lookin for someone to take care of you?" (24). Further proof that her post-apocalyptic world is *not* post-patriarchal is made evident when Ruby, a woman who steps in to help Temple assimilate into a co-ed survivors' encampment, warns her to avoid "unmarried men" as "they can get a little rough" (28). Later, as Temple watches these men on patrol, she notes they "wind their way down the street like a tactical serpent," likening them to "one body with many parts" (29). During a game of poker with this group of "serpents," Temple meets Abraham, who tells her about "this girl that one of the other men nearly choked to death because she teased him and got him into one of the storage rooms and wouldn't let him have any" (32). Temple, noticing "when he says it, his tongue slithers across his lips," describes Abraham's gaze as "wanting to bite on her" (32). The continuing use of serpent imagery is key here, suggesting that Abraham is not a lone rapist, but part of a "tactical serpent."

Abraham ultimately breaks into Temple's room and "pulls out his flaccid genitals," ordering her "Put it in your mouth.... Make it big" (36). By way of reply, Temple punches him in the crotch. He then grabs her knife and tries to strike her. In return, she breaks his arm. Hoping to quiet his screams, she stuffs a bra in his mouth. The imagery is evocative here—a female undergarment silences a would-be rapist. Though Temple tries to allow Abraham to breathe, he suffocates. Temple realizes his death means she will have to take to the road again, to run from the cadre of men who have "curious notions of brotherhood" (40). Ruby affirms Temple will be retaliated against for her willfulness, relating, "I don't like the look in their eyes.... I've seen it before" (41).

The remainder of the novel charts Temple's journey as Abraham's brother Moses pursues her. In her travels, she encounters a wealthy family holed up in their mansion as well as a clan whose poverty does not afford a protective domicile. Through such details, the novel documents socio-economic inequity all while celebrating the willful resistance of an orphan girl whose guiding principle is "We're all of us beholden to the beauty of the world, even the bad ones of us" (9). Part Orphan Annie, part Scout Finch (of *To Kill a Mockingbird*), Temple holds true to her matter-of fact convictions throughout. In a typical example of such convictions, she imparts at novel's end "the world is wondrous even when your stomach is empty and there is dried blood in your hair" (25). Temple also lives up to her name, providing service and sanctuary to various others less equipped to survive post-meatskin life (as with a young mentally impaired boy). Even Moses, with his eye-for-an-eye vengeance, comes to admire Temple as "a warrior princess of the wastes" and "hunter of miracles" (184, 226). This Temple is certainly a joy to behold and is thankfully not the only refreshingly rebellious child hero of the zombie canon.

Hungry for More: *The Girl with All the Gifts* and *The Boy on the Bridge*

The Girl with All the Gifts (Gifts) introduces us to the "weird kid" Melanie, an intelligent zombie child. *The Boy on the Bridge (Bridge)* centers on Stephen, a 15-year-old autistic boy. Linking the overriding will of patriarchy and its reliance on militarism, exploitation, and environmental ruin to the near destruction of the planet, each narrative champions outsiders as key to survival. *Bridge*, though published after *Gifts*, functions as a prequel. Both novels are set in post-apocalyptic Britain after zombies, known as hungries, have decimated the human population. Remaining humans have migrated to survivor outposts or joined the "junkers"—scavengers who have built "ruthlessly patriarchal" packs that steal from and attack other humans; representing the apex of toxic masculinity, the junkers "reduce women to pack animals," treating them as "breeding stock" to ensure their own survival (216). Through these and other details, *Gifts* and *Bridge* each condemn the ethos of "might makes right."

The narrative of *Boy* takes place some twenty years prior to *Girl*. Stephen, the boy of the title, is on a mission aboard the Rosalind Franklin, a mobile research lab inhabited by a group of soldiers and scientists tasked with studying "Cordyceps," the fungus that caused the zombie outbreak. Having invented "e-blocker" as a child—the cream that prevents the hungries from detecting humans—Stephen is a scientific whiz-kid who has a difficult time navigating emotions and human interaction. Dubbed "robot," he is treated disdainfully by most of those aboard the Rosalind. Dr. Khan is the exception. Soon after meeting the orphaned Stephen, Khan tells him that, as refugees, they should stick together. Eventually orchestrating Stephen's inclusion on the Rosalind, she serves as both mentor and quasi-mother to Stephen. Becoming pregnant during the mission, Khan does not tell anyone, fearing the revelation will ruin her career. Her supervisor confirms this to be the case upon discovering the news and gives her an ultimatum: have an abortion or kiss goodbye to being a scientist. Balking at his directive, Khan responds, "Your authority ends at my skin" (Loc. 666). Sentiments such as this one—of bodily agency—are a recurring motif in *Boy*.

In positioning this unplanned pregnancy within a narrative detailing the birth of a new society founded by feral zombie children, Carey's post-apocalyptic vision not only supports reproductive choice but also recasts the "dead end" zombies portend as a new beginning—one that will be populated by sentient zombies and (one hopes) more equity-minded humans. Pleasantly, the novel avoids the "reproductive futurism" that hinges on the replication of a (hetero)normative societal model (Edelman

2004). Indeed, Carey's twin *Boy* and *Girl* novels queer the future via child protagonists that insist on the humanity of zombies, the value of protecting the natural world, and the need to transform the weed-like invasiveness of militaristic capitalism. The future in this fictional world is not for the nuclear family, nor for the nation, not even for individual gain. It is, in some senses, not even for human reproduction—something shown to be unpredictable, dangerous, and counter to planetary survival. This "'Proper' control over wombs, and anxiety that they will somehow be captured, polluted, or compromised, is a kind of Ur-myth for the apocalyptic genre" according to Canavan (444). In Carey's work, the policing function of this myth is called into question. Womb-control, *Boy* contends, is solely up to the body containing the womb, while planet-protection (the womb of existence) is framed as already tragically compromised by a capitalistic, militarized state apparatus.

In this deadening world, Stephen and Melanie represent the gift of monstrosity which is, to link it to Carey's title, the bridge upon which to enter into a new mode of living. Key to successful cohabitation of the planet, these narratives impart, is a refusal to frame some lives as monstrous and therefore unworthy. In Carey's depiction, the world itself is a monstrous fungal-zone able to absorb humanity if necessary. The virus in need of curing is not the presumed zombie plague, but rather the disregard for life in all its (queer) variation. This is made clear near the ending of *Boy* when Stephen refuses to reveal the cure for Cordyceps, which lies within the bodies of the feral zombie children. As Stephen explains to Khan,

> the main ingredient of the cure would be the children, and I can't do that to them. Can you imagine, Khan? Half a million people in Beacon. Half a million doses of vaccine, just to start with. If I bring this home, if I tell them.... We'll scour the whole country, from one end to the other. Probably we'll have to send some raiding parties across the Channel, too. And then when that isn't enough—not nearly enough—we'll start a breeding program. Capture female hungries alive and impregnate them.... The children are human in every way that counts. Growing up in the wild, with no adult role models except the hungries, figuring it out for themselves. It's a miracle they have come so far so fast. That they have formed a family instead of beating each other's skulls in and eating the best parts ... they're nobody's monsters. What would be monstrous would be pulping their brains and spines to make medicine [Loc. 4048–5].

Khan concurs with Stephen's sentiments. Infected herself, she is horrified by the prospect of "massive battery farms" that would render zombie females "insentient brood mares." Recognizing the baby she carries will likely be born with the virus, Khan begs Stephen to protect her zombie-child after her death. In turn, Stephen comes to ultimately see himself and his fellow humans as "the plague, the pathogen that could destroy them." As a result, he warns the leader of the feral children, a young girl, telling her "Men with weapons will come after you—many, many more than are here now. They'll take you and turn you into medicine. Kill you all, just so they can have a few more years of life themselves. They won't even feel sorry about it." Believing that the children represent "the potential to be something else," to move beyond "humanity 1.0," Stephen gives himself over to the virus near the close of the narrative, doing so by holding his hand out for Khan's newborn baby to bite. Described as letting go of his humanity "with much more relief than fear" as it was "an awkward burden to carry at the best of times," Stephen thus makes the willful choice to become zombie. In line with the aforementioned argument made by Canavan, that the truly revolutionary move would be to stop creating an us/them binary, Stephen refuses to align himself with "us" against "them" (Loc. 4084–4853).

Carey offers a similar message in *Girl*. Set two decades after *Boy*, the novel opens at an army base where "weird kids"—sentient, second generation zombie children—are being kept as prisoners at a repurposed military base. Miss Justineau, a research psychologist, serves as their teacher and develops a soft spot for Melanie, the most intelligent of the so-called weird kids. Meanwhile, Dr. Caldwell, the lead scientist at the base, dissects the brains of select child subjects in hopes of finding a cure. Her pursuits are stalled, however, after a breach of the base by the hungries. Though her plan to cut open Melanie's skull is interrupted by this breach, Caldwell and Melanie fortuitously end up escaping the base in an armored vehicle along with Miss Justineau, Sergeant Parks, and a smattering of soldiers. While Justineau views Melanie as a child rather than as experimental fodder, her views are not shared by the others. Instead, they see her a posing a severe threat and proceed to treat her as a dangerous captive, locking her hands behind her back and placing a muzzle over her mouth. Shaved bald, "painted like a savage," and muzzled at the outset of their journey, Melanie's treatment evokes colonialism and slavery, each of which relied upon treating others as dangers to destroy, force into bondage, or "educate" into submission/assimilation (120).

Despite the way she is treated by the group, Melanie does all she can to avoid hurting them, becoming their protector in the process. Associated with the Pandora myth threaded throughout the novel, Melanie offers the gift of hope.[20] Rather than blaming a female for transforming the world into a place of suffering, or furthering the misogynistic bent of tales about first females (Pandora and Eve among them), the novel positions Melanie as able to provide the inhabitants of earth the gift of another chance.

Like the book, the film adaptation foregrounds the healing power

Melanie (Sennia Nanua) is *The Girl with All the Gifts*, the girl-zombie savior deemed a threat and muzzled at the behest of Dr. Caldwell (Glenn Close) (Saban Films, 2016, directed by Colm McCarthy).

of cross-generational, cross-racial, human/zombie relations. While each keeps Justineau as the teacher figure and Melanie as the kind-hearted child-zombie, the movie swaps the racial identities of Melanie and Justineau. In the novel Melanie has "skin white as snow" and Justineau's skin is described as "dark brown" (24). In the film, the young black actress Sennia Nanua plays Melanie and the white actress Gemma Atherton plays Justineau. Though with different inflections, both the novel and the film suggest that the mother-daughter and monster-human bond formed by Melanie and Justineau transcends limited conceptions of race. While the book has an ultra-white blue-eyed and blonde-haired zombie child looking up to, learning from, and loving a woman of color, the movie, by presenting Melanie as black, tells a more radical story. As Kevin Wayne Williams argues, this change gives the tale "more of a civil-rights metaphor" wherein "Melanie isn't growing up so much as forcing the powers-that-be to recognize her value, that she has things to contribute if she is allowed to contribute them on her own terms, that taken out of the shackles and the mask, she is a person." The casting of a black actress in the role of Melanie also puts the narrative more in line with the Haitian zombie tradition, especially via suggestions of how militarism, scientific racism, and imprisonment perpetuate enslavement.

Sherronda Brown, in her reading of the film, similarly notes that presenting Melanie as black "adds more gravity" to the tale's conclusion—one in which a young black zombie informs an older white male (Sergeant Parks) that the world is "not over … it's just not yours anymore." Arguing that "To create a story in which this hierarchy (of white supremacy) becomes dismantled through the intentional actions of a Black child enhances the theme of decolonization that is already present in the zombie narrative," Brown interprets the film adaptation as speaking to what she terms "apocalyptic whiteness," or white fears of no longer being in power. Fittingly, Williams and Brown each read the narrative via a Trump era lens. Whereas Brown argues the film echoes real world moves to strengthen borders and keep people of color "contained and subjugated," Williams notes his admiration for Melanie's closing speech about bettering the world, imparting the sentiment "I can't imagine a more anti–Trump, anti–Sessions, anti-everything-2016-came-to-be moment."

The close of *Boy* extends this type of sentiment into the future in an epilogue that jumps twenty years forward in time which finds Melanie helming a group to a remote mountain in northern Scotland as they search for human "legends." When they encounter human survivors, Melanie imparts, "we thought you were all gone and we're so happy that we were wrong." (Loc. 5009). Her sentiment notably counters the closing suggestion of Matheson's novel in which Neville's last line, "I am legend," indicates the world would be a better place without humans. In contrast, Melanie and her group seek to prevent humanity from dying out only to become the stuff of legend. This closing segment of *Boy* was interpreted as an anti-climactic let-down by some—and, in particular—a less revolutionary vision than that proffered in *Girl*. For example, in "Queer Revolution, Zombie Uprisings, and the Problem with M. R. Carey's *The Boy on the Bridge*," Christine Prevas contends *Boy* lacks the ethical gravitas of *Girl* with its examination of "the morality of scientific experimentation, the rights of the hungry children as not-human but not-quite-monster, the questionable prioritization of human life over a kind of life that is not yet understood." Yet, I would counter that *Boy* also engages with which types of "life" matter.[21] Framing the most sympathetic characters, Khan and Stephen, as outcasts and refugees whose lives are deemed less worthy by others aboard the Rosalind Franklin, *Boy* continues to trouble any easy divide between human/monster. Doing so via narratives arcs that include an unplanned pregnancy and a refusal to let female hungries be turned into brood mares, *Boy* puts (re)productive justice, individual agency, and human/planetary survival in conversation with one another. And, as with *Girl*, it is children that save the world and indicate there is hope for a better future. The same is true of the zombie-apocalypse film I turn to next, one that features a willful young girl as hero.

The Light at the End of the Tunnel: *Train to Busan*

Train to Busan (*Train*), a huge box-office hit in Korea, generated major buzz at Cannes in 2016. It captivated American audiences as well—so much so, in fact, that a bidding war for English-language remake rights ensued not long after the film's U.S. release. Though a remake of the film is arguably unnecessary given the excellence of the original, if an English language version results in more seeing *Train*, and, even more importantly, in a predominantly Asian cast—something exceedingly rare in U.S. cinema—then perhaps a new iteration is justifiable, especially if it succeeds in doling out social commentary apace with its uber-fast zombies.

Described by critic David Ehrlich as "a high-speed collision between *Snowpiercer* and *World War Z*," *Train* features a workaholic divorced dad, Seok-woo, and his kind-hearted daughter, Su-an. So focused on work that he misses his daughter's school performance singing Aloha 'Oe (a song Su-an will again sing at film's close), Seok-woo arrives home late on the eve of Su-an's birthday near the start of the movie only to give his daughter something she already has—a Nintendo Wii. The fact her other Wii sits still in its box not only indicates Seok-woo's lack of knowledge about his daughter, but also nods to her lack of interest in techno-gadgetry, something that sets her apart from the gaming systems and smart-phone obsessed milieu from which she hails. Though Su-an lives in a culture saturated with technology, she herself is more interested in human connection. This is emphasized when she insists all she wants for her birthday is to visit her mother, a request her father reluctantly agrees to. A man who is mainly concerned with his career, Seok-woo is not inclined to travel with his daughter on the journey to Busan given it will take precious time away from his work as a hedge fund manager, a job that links his character to the economic downturn instigated in part by hedge fund moguls. Like the culprits made infamous in the early 2000s, Seok-woo has few qualms about carrying out ethically questionable actions as long as they have profit potential. Yet, he will ultimately transform thanks to witnessing the selflessness and bravery of his daughter. A man who instructs Su-an soon after the zombie outbreak, "At a time like this, only watch out for yourself," by film's end, he has adopted Su-an's communal ethos, an ethos the film champions. At the other end of the spectrum, *Train* condemns those only out for themselves, pointing a finger at capitalist greed. Significantly, this greed is tied to ruination of the ecosystem, too heavy a reliance on technology, and the possible annihilation of humanity. Environmental devastation and the accompanying destruction of animal life is emphasized in *Train's* opening scene wherein we discover polluted waters have turned fish toxic. Soon after this revelation, a man hits a deer after trying to answer his cell phone while driving, one of the film's many nods to the dangers of technology. Before switching to the main narrative featuring Seok-woo and Su-an, we witness the dead deer mutate into a crazy-eyed zombie, a moment that foreshadows the zombie apocalypse to come while also linking planetary ruin to capitalist greed.

Once Seok-woo and Su-an are on the train to Busan, we are introduced to several other key characters—two elderly sisters, a veteran with PTSD, a working class couple expecting their first child, a baseball team, a teen schoolgirl, and a ruthless businessman. The fleshing out of these characters furthers the film's main conceit: communalism is key to survival. In the case of the elderly sisters, one is cast as selfish, while the other is generous, offering to share her food with her greedy sister. Regarding the homeless veteran, he is indicated as the possible cause of the zombie outbreak on the train, something introduced when the greedy businessman, Eui-sung, complains to a conductor that an unseemly character has boarded the train without purchasing a ticket. Yet, such class bias proves faulty. It is not the veteran he (and we) suspect who spreads the virus, but a woman who boarded the train just before it left the station. In a further castigation of class prejudice, Eui-sung, as he later looks at the veteran with disgust, warns Su-an that if she doesn't study and apply herself, she will end up like the veteran once an adult, poor and alone. Su-an doesn't hesitate to refute his prejudice, telling Eui-sung her mother taught her opinions like this are cruel and misguided. The train setting of the film furthers this focus on social status and socio-economic hierarchy. While Eui-sung espouses a hierarchical view of class status and believes he should rightly be at the front of the train (literally and metaphorically), various other characters work to erase dividing lines based on class, age, status, and so on. As film critic Dorothy Woodend emphasizes in her review, the train setting serves to highlight "segmented containers of the population." Eui-sung revels in such segregation, as when he tries to keep the passengers from further back in the train from entering the first class section. Framing Eui-sung as cannibalizing capitalist and associating his nearsighted greed with the zombie outbreak, *Train*, as Woodend interprets it, emphasizes how "Good old global capitalism keeps devouring everything in its path."

The film also castigates the apathetic, willing-blindness of many living within global capitalism, using both the first class passengers and the zombies to do so. Whereas the zombies of the film have poor vision and are easily confused by sounds (especially of the smart-phone variety), those positioned in the "good segments" of the train fail to see how their privilege comes at the expense—and very lives—of others. Like those portions of the population hailed in Trump's bombastic speeches and tweets that seem blind to deep-seated inequities, the zombies in *Busan* are easily duped and distracted. This is emphasized in an early scene where Seok-woo slides a phone across the train floor after realizing sound distracts the zombies. Drawn by the beeps of technological gadgets—which we might link to Trump's distracting tweets and sound bites—the zombies encapsulate the techno-crazed blindness the film condemns. Moving as an unthinking horde towards the front of the train, they are cast both as sheepish masses and selfish individualist monsters vying for the "human food" the train holds. Significantly, Eui-sung, the greedy capitalist, is turned zombie after an extended segment in which he exits the infected train, causes several others to be turned zombie, and is ultimately turned himself after trying to prevent the three remaining survivors— Su-an, Seok-Woo, and Seong-kyeong (the pregnant woman)—from joining him on another train car he has commandeered in hopes of driving out of harm's way. Seok-Woo is bitten in the scuffle that follows as zombies attack the train car. By scene's end, only Su-an and Seong-kyeong remain alive.

In the film's final scene, Su-an and Seong-kyeong head towards Busan. As they walk through a darkened tunnel, the soldiers positioned at tunnel's end are instructed to shoot them. However, when the soldiers hear Su-an singing, they realize those approaching are human and hold their fire. Here, the tunnel acts as a figurative birth canal, one that "rebirths" hope for the two female survivors (one a child and one a pregnant woman). Moreover, the pregnant Seong-kyeong serves as a visual encapsulation of communal resources, her swollen belly functioning as a bodily reminder of the necessity of human interdependence. Su-an is the primary hero of the narrative though, one whose concern for the well-being of strangers is heralded as inspiring others to be similarly compassionate. As kind to the homeless veteran with PTSD as she is forgiving of her workaholic father, Su-an's empathetic worldview is akin to that of Temple, Stephen, and Melanie, the other child heroes discussed above. As in Bell and Carey's work, a willful child is the savior figure of *Train*, one who similarly impacts the adults of her world, rendering them more benevolent. The film is, as one reviewer puts it, "what *World War Z* should have been—a nightmarish vision of the end of the world, and a provocation to ask ourselves what it is that really makes us human in the first place" (Tallerico). Regarding this, the use of the song "Aloha 'Oe" at the outset and close of the film is significant. A melancholy farewell song, in its first use, it foreshadows the farewell to humanity the zombie outbreak instigates; at the close, it both acts as Su-an's farewell to her father, but also as a farewell to the world as it was. Perhaps, as in *Girl with All the Gifts*, Su-an and her fellow survivors will forge a new and improved world for the generations to follow, one where humans can "meet again" rather than continue in their attempts to survive—and profit—on their own. In contrast to the optimistic outlook of *Train*, one which hangs its hope on female characters, the narratives taken up in the fourth and final section are infected with misogyny—a viral scourge in much need of eradication.

Section 4: Undead Conservativism: "Legitimate" Zombie Rape and "Necessary" War

While many millennial era texts draw on the zombie figure to address misogyny, racism, and the dog-eat-dog world of capitalism, others mock environmental sentiment and poke fun at "bleeding heart liberals." Still others draw on the abject female body to justify rape, casting toxic males as heroes, hen-pecked husbands as victims, and sexist men as affable lads. In contrast, women are framed as inconsequential or infectious in texts of this ilk. Akin to early cinematic zombie forays which circulated around treating women and/or people of color as property (as in *White Zombie* and *I Walked with a Zombie*), narratives that accord to the more regressive strains of the zombie canon normalize sexism, xenophobia, and the power-over mentality that informs patriarchy (and militarism). The tales considered in this final section proffer such sentiment, proving that post-millennial tales featuring zombies, are, in some cases, not nearly as "woke" as one would hope.

Enlightened Sexism Goes Zombie: *Doghouse*

Doghouse, a 2009 British film directed by Jake West, centers on a group of male friends unable to keep their flats clean let alone their female partners happy. The movie pokes fun at these males via a mode Susan Douglas characterizes as a guys-are-so-dumb-wink, one integral to her concept of enlightened sexism, or the notion that we are so *beyond sexism*, so "enlightened," that we can now make fun of it. That the film

A zombie-bride (Victoria Hopkins) from *Doghouse* (Vertigo Films, 2009, directed by Jake Wes).

enacts its enlightened sexism via equating women with zombies is of particular interest. Suggesting modern males suffer "social gender anxiety" brought about by female nagging, the film's protagonist, Neil, is a macho man-child who boasts "women love me." Near the outset of the narrative he informs his soon-to-be-divorced friend Vince, "today is the day you're going to rediscover your inner bloke." To discover this "inner bloke," Neil and Vince, along with a few other friends, set off to the village of Moodley, where they plan to, as one of them puts it, "go caveman." Yet, Moodley is hardly a good place to celebrate manhood, something intimated via visual reference to mummified penises, one of the "treasures" sold at the local occult store. Moodley is also not "manhood friendly" thanks to the *moody* zombie females that populate the village. Though admittedly light-hearted zombie fare, *Doghouse* relies on "casual sexism" as the basis for its comedic moments. In the tradition of *The Man Show*, an American comedy celebrating loutish male behavior, misogyny is treated as funny and harmless. "Now is not the time to stop objectifying women," one character jokes as he ogles a "hot zombie." With female zombies presented as castrating bitches, rotten brides, and angry housewives, the film offers a tired vision wherein "real men" are put upon by annoying girlfriends (in London) and imperiled by bitchy, angry zombies (in Moodley).

When we learn, near the close of the film, that these female zombies were created to use as weapons so as to "fight wars without armies," the depiction of women as mere bodies for men's use (whether for sex or as

A promotional poster for *Doghouse* presents a zombie woman (Annie Vanders) with a cake she has decorated with the severed fingers of one of her male victims (Vertigo Films, 2009, directed by Jake Wes).

bodily fodder for the war machine), is taken to a logical, though misogynist, conclusion. The creation of the female zombies, otherwise known as "Project Cathouse," results in an "army of pissed man-hating feminist cannibals." Here, the naming of the zombies as feminist echoes real world terms like "feminazi" and "man-eater" while also casting feminism as a "brainless" movement which turns its followers into mindless hordes. That the zombie virus is spread via laundry detergent further suggests that (gasp!) feminism could bring an end to men having their laundry done by obedient women. At film's end, the threat this female zombie horde poses is eradicated and the lads return to London, back to the "doghouses" their nagging female partners put them in. Thus, while the zombie-feminazis of Moodley have been overcome, females remain a scourge to the heterosexual men of London. Perhaps if there were to be a *Doghouse 2*, males might do laundry and come in contact with infected laundry detergent, leading to a man-spreading horde of undead lads. The experience of losing their living manhood could lead them to become socially justice minded zombies, ones who adopt the personal is political mindset and take to the streets to join Slutwalk marches and the like. I am not holding my breath for this imagined *Doghouse* sequel, but it's nice to dream.

Making America Gun-Loving Again: The Works of Max Brooks

The notion furthered in *Doghouse*, that men need to find their "inner bloke" and forget about annoying "zombirds," is similarly evident in the works of Max Brooks. His greatest hit so far, *World War Z* (*WWZ*), though aptly described as including a "global mosaic of voices," is tellingly male-centric: out of over forty narrative voices, only five are women (Collins and Bond 188). One, Mary Jo Miller, though a mayor, does not tell us anything about being a leader. Instead, her narrative focuses on her children, her weight concerns, and her internet shopping habits. Meanwhile, Maria, a Russian soldier, is late to her military drills due to being immersed in teen magazines whereas Jessica, another of the few female characters, is presented as ill-equipped to cope with the zombie-infected world. Sharon, another female of the text, mindlessly mimics the monstrous moan of the zombies. The last of the five female narrators—Colonel Christina—as Molly Todd puts it, "simply becomes a mouthpiece for the male-orientated world of the military, albeit one with breasts." While the film adaptation adds in more central (and less stereotypical) female characters, it still frames white western heterosexual masculinity—and the power it wields—as preventing human annihilation (casting the ever popular Brad Pitt in the lead role to do so).

WWZ is not only male-centric, however, but also xenophobic and jingoistic. It frames the U.S. as instrumental to humanity's survival while presenting militarism as what allows the war against zombies to be won. As such, Brooks, who describes himself as a "fanatical patriot," pens a narrative in which "human victory is never in doubt" thanks to the U.S. and its military dominance (Collins and Bond 192, 188). This "hopeful apocalypse," as Margo Collins and Elson Bond deem it, leads to, in their estimation "the discovery of a common, even improved, humanity" (188). Yet, how hopeful is a vision that depends on perpetual war, sidelines women, and frames "undesirables" of the world as akin to a zombie threat? Further, in indicating that zombies do not deserve any compassion—that they should be destroyed by any means necessary—the novel holds out a staunchly anti-zombie stance, one that echoes the us/them binary wherein "us" are superior and "them" are disposable enemies. What Brooks seems especially keen to protect—or reanimate—are "good old fashioned" traditional values—ones in which the military is respected, male dominance is a given, and borders are rigidly policed.[22] At the same time, the history of imperialism is put under erasure in *WWZ* while facile nods to the global village try (but fail) to indicate all of the world's inhabitants are equally deserving. Any consideration of how America's reliance on a dominator model has harmed the planet and its peoples is absent—par for the course, I suppose, for a "fanatical patriot."

Brooks' later story "Steve and Fred" contains similar side-lining of women and pro–USA sentiment. Constructed as a story within a story, the framing narrative features Fred, a janitor hiding out in a bathroom stall after zombies have inundated the hotel where he works. To take his mind off impending death, Fred reads his favorite section of a zombie novel over and over—one which centers on Steve, a heroic former marine turned zombie killer. This story within a story constitutes the pages Fred reads and re-reads as he is trapped in the bathroom stall. In it, Steve, a former marine, rides on a motorcycle through a zombie-infested zone. Dominated by his misogynist, anti-environmentalist, and pro-militaristic thoughts, this portion of the story characterizes Steve as overjoyed by the zombie apocalypse as it provides him with a new and exciting "enemy" to eradicate. As he rides through the area on a large motorcycle, he triumphantly shouts "OOOOH-RAHHH!" noting how his zombie-killing reminds him of being "back in the cockpit, shrieking over the Iraqi dessert, showering fire and death in a star spangled storm" (205). After his motorbike smashes into a Prius during this murderous rampage, he celebrates leaving the driver "armless, faceless" and scoffs, "Too bad the 'save the Earth' car couldn't do the same for its owner" (205). His weapon-fueled path of destruction then leads him to a run-in with Doc Schlozman, a Nobel Prize recipient turned zombie whom Steve greets with a "Hey, Doc.... Still tryin' to save Mother Earth from her spoiled children?" Steve then happily destroys "The brain that had once been hailed as 'Evolution's Crowning Achievement'" (207). This derision for environmentalism is typical in Brooks' work, as it is in *WWZ*, a sort of wet-dream ode to global militarism (193). As for this particular story, in a few short pages, the "hero" manages to champion the war with Iraq, wax poetic about the power of weapons, and deride "wimpy intellectuals" who *think* instead of *do* (he also notably derides women via misogynistic references to his ex-wife as well as to female scientists).

Importantly, the format of "Steve and Fred" gives readers two narratives to choose from—that of Steve *or* Fred. Brooks clearly suggests Steve's hyper-militaristic, macho story is the better choice. In so doing, Brooks not only offers an OOOOH-RAHHH celebration of killing, he also proffers a tale in which, Fred, the janitor, is presented as the working-class loser while Steve, the marine-ninja warrior, is the type of hero that will save us not only from zombies, but also from bitchy ex-wives, annoyingly talkative women, and Prius-driving ninnies. Though the story, like *Doghouse*, seems to be aiming for humor, the narrative message supports Steve's hyper-masculinity, showing his violent credo not only necessary, but joy-inducing. Enacting "enlightened sexism" writ large, the tale provides an approving wink to the laddish Steve, encouraging readers to laugh at misogyny while celebrating the "fun" of killing.

Deadgirl: The Rapist Gaze of Patriarchy

Lacking the light tone that characterizes *Doghouse* and "Steve and Fred," the 2008 film *Deadgirl* circulates around a pair of high school friends, JT and Rickie, who find a naked undead young woman (the eponymous girl) in an abandoned asylum. JT wants to keep this "Deadgirl" as a "personal sex object" but Rickie is loath to do so. Importantly, Rickie's objections are not about raping her (or at least he never says as much). Rather, he believes he and JT could get a reward for finding her. JT focuses instead on the "sex slave" opportunities her body poses. This sexualization and objectification of the female body is in evidence from the opening scene. In it, Rickie ogles Joann, a girl he kissed in fourth grade, as she walks across their high school quad. The scene aligns viewers with Rickie's line of sight as the camera tracks Joann's body. When JT approaches Rickie, he first teases him about cutting gym class: "You're missing the fuckin' gay Coach Hankens. And fuckin' faggot gym showers and fuckin' queer jock motherfuckers." Realizing Rickie is busy watching Joann, he remarks, "You should have fucked her when you were nine, when you had the chance, boy!" Not only does this exchange conflate homophobia, male entitlement, and sexism, it also hints the elementary school kiss between Rickie and Joann was not consensual.

When JT and Rickie discover Deadgirl tied to a gurney in a remote room of a defunct mental asylum sometime later, JT's objectification of females is further cemented. Staring at her, JT gushes "She's like someone in a magazine.... I could spend all day looking at that body." Yet, he does far more than look, soon touching her breast and encouraging Rickie to do the same. "We could keep her," he enthuses. Rickie is averse to this suggestion, however, and leaves. The next day, JT insists he has to show Rickie something back at the asylum. Once there, he conveys that Deadgirl seems unable to die. Relating his interactions with her (which were clearly acts of rape, though he—nor the script—never use the term), JT explains

> She woke up. She started to struggle ... tried to bite like a wild fucking dog.... I hit her.... I hit her again and it felt good.... Then I hit her harder.... And harder and harder ... after a while, she stopped moving. I stuck my thumbs real deep into her neck until she quit moving. A few minutes later, she starts kicking again. I killed her three times now.

While JT construes the fact she can't be killed as "awesome," Rickie responds, "We could destroy her. Ain't you suppose to get her kind in the brain pan or something?" Here, Rickie interprets her as a zombie and thus deserving of annihilation, but JT avers, "Sure, she is some kind of monster or something, but she's our monster." He then continues in his pursuit to convince Rickie Deadgirl would make a great sex toy, enthusing, "What you think? ... hot pussy? Straight out of porn! Anytime we want it, boy." Rickie responds, "I'm not fucking touching her, man," citing the fact he doesn't want to deal with "trouble I don't need." Importantly, Rickie does not condemn JT's rapist pursuits. Here, as elsewhere, he is only interested in how finding her body might benefit him on the one hand and/or could get them in trouble with the law on the other.

As the movie proceeds, JT encourages other high-schoolers, Wheeler, Johnny, and Dwyer, to "get some" via Deadgirl. When Rickie discovers as much, JT again tries to entice him to join in, saying, "We can call her Joann if you want." Questioning him, "But you know that ain't a real human being ... right?," Rickie's refusal is couched in the fact Deadgirl is not a "real human" rather than in a repugnance for rape, let alone any ire regarding JT's suggestion they name Deadgirl after his crush Joann. This incident also brings up a central question regularly posed in the zombie canon: Are zombies equivalent to things, to non-life—and, if they are, does that make it acceptable to kill, exploit, torture, and/or rape them? Screenwriter Trent Haaga, who claims Deadgirl's inhumanity makes the film inoffensive, answers this central question with a resounding yes. Referencing Deadgirl as akin to "just a blob of space protoplasm with a bunch of fuck holes in it," Haaga fails to address the "blob" is female—a former human girl— something the film's title directly names her as. Further, as argued by Steve Jones in "Deadgirl and the Sexual Politics of Zombie Rape," Haaga's film implies *only* females are useful "fuck holes." This is made evident when JT realizes "one bite from her and I can make another," recruiting Wheeler to help him abduct a female to do so. However, Dwyer has already been bitten and thus there already is "another." As Jones points out, "If Haaga's comparison with a blob were accurate, Dwyer should have been chained up and abused, since he also has 'fuck holes'" (527). Yet, even though the males have capitalized on any opening/orifice in Deadgirl's body, including her bullet wounds, Dwyer's orifices are clearly off limits. The film thus "revolves around male sexual violation of the female body exclusively"—a violation that is cast as a way for these teens to assert they are "real men" (Jones 527).

Though Haaga insists the agenda of the film is to critique toxic masculinity, the film portrays the male teens rather sympathetically. Rickie, for example, pines away for Joann, is seemingly neglected by his mother, and is treated to appalling "man up" speeches by his alcoholic quasi-stepfather, Clint.[23] As for JT, the lead antagonist, he comes from an impoverished family and only has his grandmother to love him. "Folks like us are just cannon fodder for the rest of the world," he laments at one point. Arguing that the abandoned asylum where they find Deadgirl allows folks like him to be "in control" and "call the shots," and that doing so "Feels good," JT clearly wants to live up to ideal codes of masculinity—ones which he has correctly associated with inflicting violence on others. Telling Rickie at one point, "You don't have to be the nice guy down here [in the asylum]," JT associates agency and power with not being nice. Alas, an underprivileged teen such as himself is only able to enact power "outside" the confines of normative society—in the asylum.

Haaga defends his film in DVD commentary by contrasting it to torture porn, saying "you have a zombie girl that these guys fuck, and it's not like you're taking a blowtorch to her nipples or pliers to her vagina." "You're not getting off on torture," he continues, "you're using her as a sex object." Or, in other words, torture is bad, but "normal rape" is A-ok. Claiming "I always saw the original *Deadgirl* as a condemnation of misogyny as opposed to being misogynous—the boys were the monsters, not the 'monster' of the title," Haaga indicates his film is not misogynist because it portrays males badly. Yet, the narrative itself fails to condemn male characters as "toxic" for raping, instead implying the female body (and its refusal to be open to male penetration) is what turns men monstrous. Describing the film as asking viewers to decide whether they are JT or Rickie or an admixture of the two, Haaga implies audiences should decide what type of rapist they would like to be—the "bad rapist" like JT or the reluctant "nice rapist" like Rickie (who has turned Joann into another "dead fuck toy" by film's end). In so doing, Haaga calls on viewers to pity "nice guys" in much the same way news stories involving sexual assault call on people to see (white) male perpetrators of sexual violence as "good boys" and star athletes, as with Brock Turner, for example. Such males, hegemonic narratives insist, are to be pitied for what allegations of sexual misconduct do to their lives and careers. Their female victims and accusers, on the other hand, are dehumanized in much the same way as is Deadgirl—rendered silent, made to endure threats (or acts) of violence, and cast as "asking for it."

Contracted: Zombie-ism as Sexually Transmitted Disease

Contracted, like *Deadgirl*, relies on the motif of a zombified/undead female. The movie opens with an image of a female corpse, a biohazard tag on her toe, lying on a gurney. Rhythmic squeaking sounds soon reveal a male morgue worker (BJ) is raping her corpse. After cleaning up his workspace and suggestively fingering various glass beakers, we see BJ get in his car. The next scene introduces us to Sam, the female protagonist of the film, as she is arriving at a house party. Later, BJ arrives at the same party and sneaks a roofie into Sam's drink. Soon after this, the camera cuts to the two of them in his car. Sam groans in pain and flails her hands against the car window desperately, indicating she is being attacked. She contracts a virus from this assault, one that initiates her slow transformation into a zombie. Thus, after being drugged and assaulted by a man in the habit of raping female corpses at the morgue where he works, Sam is turned into a corpse herself—albeit not a fully dead one.

Problematically, *Contracted* marketing posters referenced this rape as a "one night stand," suggesting Sam made a bad choice in sexual partners. The language on one promotional poster was particularly telling: "If *Jaws* was the film that made people never want to go into the water again, *Contracted* is the one that will make them think twice before having sex." Not only is rape referred to as "having sex," but Sam is equated to the voracious great white shark, itself a symbol of the monstrous female body and her devouring vagina.[24] Further, the film itself, rather than framing BJ as a sexual predator, depicts Sam as an infectious monster. Given that Sam's most horrific symptoms manifest via her female genitalia (which bleed copiously and eventually produce maggots), the horror in *Contracted* is presented *as* the female body, *not* rape and the damage it causes. Sam's body is the host for what the film suggests is a zombifying STD. Meanwhile BJ, the lead rapist that causes Sam's zombiedom, is never encountered after the opening scenes. Though no specific reason is given regarding how BJ became a carrier of the zombie virus, one can assume raping dead bodies as a morgue worker might have something to do with it. Yet, BJ does not manifest symptoms. In other words, he gets away with raping while the victim is punished. These factors, along with the movie's construction of Sam's female body as the site of horror, propagates a profoundly anti-woman narrative, one that is thankfully countered in more recent films like *It Follows* where the amorphous entity stalks and infects males and females alike, and, moreover, where the acts of the entity are framed as sexual assault, *not* one night stands.

The sequel to *Contracted*, *Contracted: Phase II*, admittedly is less "rapey" than the first. It focuses on Riley, a male Sam had sex with in the first movie soon after she was infected. *Phase II* opens with a replay of the scene that ended the first film: Sam attacking and killing her mother. It then cuts to Sam's body in the morgue, being creepily caressed by a man with a tattoo on his finger that reads ABADDON. The suggestion here indicates Sam was raped not only by BJ, but by this man as well. According to screen headings, it has been four days since the virus was initially given to Sam. The sequel will take us through day six. During day four, Riley visits a doctor to be tested for STDs. As Riley is waiting for the nurse to come in, he runs his fingers over the scratch marks Sam left on his shoulder and discovers a protruding object. Grabbing a nearby medical tool, he removes what turns out to be a fingernail, presumably Sam's, and has flashbacks to their sex

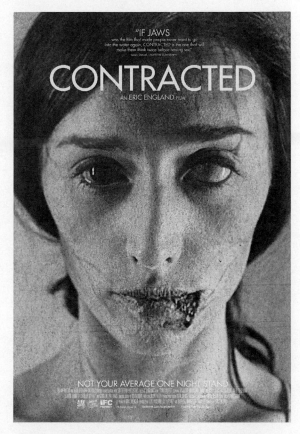

A poster from *Contracted* with Sam (Najarra Townsend) with ad-copy that makes light of her having been raped and drugged at a party: "Not Your Average One Night Stand," and distorts the nature of that scene: "If *Jaws* was the film that made people never want to go into the water again, *Contracted* is the one that will make them think twice before having sex" (IFC Films, 2013, directed by Eric England).

scene, including the maggots that fell out of her vagina. Body gore of this ilk continues throughout the film, but this time around the infection is an "equal opportunity" STD that also infects male bodies. Though we never learn why BJ, the original rapist, is immune to the disease he spreads, we do find out his full name—Brent Jaffe—and that he is wanted for sexually assaulting four other women. This alone makes for an improvement on the first film, which never names BJ as a rapist. However, the fact that Riley degenerates slowly, as opposed to Sam's quick turn to zombie, implies that females are more prone to zombification—more "naturally zombie" if you will. Further, while Sam only sleeps with/kills others after she is infected, Riley pro-actively forges a crusade to rid his body of the infection, even vowing to find BJ to put an end to the spread of the zombie STD.

Though the sequel never reveals the meaning of the ABADDON tattoo, which we see on another man near the film's end, it evokes the word "abandon." Perhaps the suggestion is those who wear the tattoo are abandoning civility, any hope for humanity, and will do whatever it takes to spread the STD pathogen. Whether or not rape is their primary weapon in this pursuit is never disclosed, however. If it were, there would be more opportunity for politicized critique and a better chance of rectifying the misogynist narrative the first film put forth. Instead, we are left with a male hero (Riley) and numerous dead females, including Riley's grandmother and pregnant sister. At least this time around bodily rot is not only associated with the female form and the rapist is finally named as such.

The narratives discussed above, written/directed by Brooks, West, Haaga, and England, exude rather regressive messaging. In them, women are characterized as cock-blockers and/or cock-destroying bitches (especially so in *Doghouse*), liberals as pansies (as with the environmentalist characters in Brooks' works), mothers as useless and/or bitchy (as with Samantha's mother in *Contracted*, killed by her daughter in the closing scene) and cisgender hetero white males as heroes (or, in the case of *Deadgirl*, *tragically* rejected by females). While four of the six texts focus on sexual violence, a common element in post-millennial zombie texts generally, they notably do so in ways that minimize violence. Suggesting rape, STDs, and deaths occur as a result of the monstrous female body and its abilities to entice "nice guys" to carry out not-so-nice acts, the narratives sympathetically frame their various perpetrators, casting them as harmless lads (*Doghouse*), horny teens (*Deadgirl*), or heroic best friends (*Contracted II*). Thankfully, the above examples of less-than-woke zombie tales are countered by a slew of narratives deploying the zombie to decry such attitudes, as documented in the first three sections of this chapter.

* * *

Various elements in post-millennial zombie narratives work to further realize the revolutionary potential of this monstrous figure. As Elizabeth Aiossa argues, "These radical monsters and the apocalypse they incite can ... rattle if not fully dismantle problematic Western heteronormative traditions, ideals, and dichotomies to their very core" (Loc. 147). In the article "Zombies in Revolt," Dunja Opatic similarly references the "counter-hegemonic liberatory potential of the rising masses," linking zombie contagion to the spread of revolutionary consciousness (1). Lamenting that zombie texts often close with a return to the status quo, Opatic notes there is "hope for further counter-hegemonic development of the zombie trope" (15). Written in 2014, the piece actually precedes some of the most hopeful and subversive tales discussed above, including *The Girl with All the Gifts*, *Train to Busan*, and the ninth season of *The Walking Dead*, arguably its most hopeful yet. Along with other works discussed in this chapter that take on capitalism, militarism, racism, and sexism so as to resist the status quo, zombie tales of this type offer revolutionary dead ends which "open up a possibility for creating the world anew" (Opatic 9). As comparably argued in Shaviro's "The Cinematic Body," zombies are not only "monstrous symptoms of a violent manipulative, exploitive society" but "potential remedies for its ills" (87). Such potential is witnessed in the narratives considered in the first three sections above as well as in numerous other examples space does not allow for inclusion—*Shaun of the Dead*, *In the Flesh*, *Otto*, *Wasting Away*, *I Was a White Trash Zombie*, *Juan of the Dead*, *AfterTime*, and *iZombie* (to name but a few). This post-millennial canon of zombie texts continues its rapid (rabid?) expansion as we lurch towards the close of the second decade of the 21st century. Here is hoping the undead and their human counterparts will continue to infect our narratives in promising, politically expedient ways—perhaps even imparting how we can outlive the deadening effects of the current "Trump-ocalypse."

2

Draining the Imperialist White-Supremacist Capitalist Patriarchy

The Post-Millennial Vampire

"I am on the side of the vampires, or at least some of them"
—Donna Haraway

Many vampires gracing our screens and pages in the last several decades seem intent on driving a definitive stake through the decrepit heart of patriarchy and its attendant formations. As with the post-millennial zombie canon, recent narratives featuring vampires reimagine the iconic monster and the worlds it inhabits, presenting us not with a dreadful end, but with hope for a *revamped* world. A number of these vampires are intent on bringing about a more socially just world—one in which human life is not rendered less than oil (as in *A Girl Walks Home Alone at Night* and *Daybreakers*), sexual predators are condemned (as in *The Radleys*, *Let the Right One In*, and *Byzantium*), and inter-dependence is championed (as in *The Gilda Stories*, *The Passage*, and *The Ethical Vampire Series*). While *Twilight* arguably turned vampire politics to the conservative right (as I argued in *Seduced by Twilight*), texts from the late 1990s on, and especially those from the first decades of the 21st century, have consistently featured vampires as a conduit through which to offer leftist critique.[1] As Simon Bacon—whose work significantly informs my own—argues in *Becoming Vampire*, "the vampire inherently manifests a resistance to all forms of normative (patriarchal, heteronormative) categorization, queering all attempts to contain its innate, excessive un-name ability, and enacting forms of becoming" (14). As the following chapter aims to prove, such resistance is particularly evident in vampire narratives from the first two decades of the 21st century.

With the over-riding goal of elucidating recent vampire texts as politically expedient in what follows, I will focus in the main on texts featuring willful vampires who challenge imperialist white-supremacist capitalist patriarchy (to use bell hooks' phrasing). The first section considers "vampire activists" seeking to eradicate violence against women and people of color. In addressing racism and misogyny, vampires of this type shed light on slavery and colonialism as historical legacies that continue to perpetuate inequity. The second section draws on the field of trauma studies to contemplate what I am calling "post traumatic vampire disorder." Considering psychosocial damage resulting in particular from imperialism, war, socio-economic inequity, and 9/11, the section explores vampire figures as apt conduits through which to critically engage with trauma. The third section takes as its focus moral components of being a vampire via an examination of several characters who struggle to forge ethical relationships with other vampires, with humans, and with their respective environments. The final section turns to the viral vampire in apocalyptic landscapes.

The Willful Vampire as Mightier than the Phallocentric Script

Vampires tend to go in one of two primary directions in post-millennial texts: they become more *humane*—more deserving of empathy, more vulnerable, and more enmeshed in the political realities of the world—or they become more akin to the horde-like zombies we see in *28 Days Later* and *Train to Busan*—gruesome, ruthless creatures who threaten apocalyptic doom.

The more sympathetic iterations of the figure often draw on the traditional lone vampire figure—one who lives on the fringes of society and whose difference necessitates hiding their true selves and/or attempting to pass as human. Though the sadistic vampire Count Dracula spawned many evil vampire descendants (as in the iconic novel *I Am Legend* and the more recent vampire saga *The Strain*), sympathetic vampire figures have multiplied as well. This vampire type has been with us since the monster entered the literary scene early in the eighteenth century but became increasingly common in the latter portions of the twentieth century, coming to global prominence in Anne Rice's *Interview with a Vampire* and multiplying ever since. As Patrick Day documents, the last third of the twentieth century witnessed well over a thousand narratives featuring this vampire type, one he argues solidified the vampire's shift from reviled monster to tortured outsider. Milly Williamson similarly reads the modern vampire as "a misfit with a good image" whose "painful awareness of outsiderdom" informs a desire "to *matter* in the light of day and not just in the shadows" (186, 2). This misfit but affable vampire is in evidence not only in the texts this chapter analyzes, but in myriad others: *The Vampire Diaries, True Blood, What We Do in the Shadows, Being Human, Preacher, The Hamiltons, The Coldest Girl in Coldtown, Certain Dark Things, The Moth Diaries*. Indeed, the "good vampire" is so prominent in the post-millennial era that the figure is the subject of a series of monographs plus academic anthologies. At the same time, in accordance with what Stacey Abbot argues is an increasing cross-over between the zombie and the vampire, viral, mindless, and infectious vampires populate numerous contemporary narratives such as *Blade, Underworld, Ultraviolet, The Strain, Stakeland.*

Given contemporary concerns regarding pandemics, refugee crises, natural disasters, nuclear threats—all fears often addressed in modern zombie texts—it is not surprising this other side of the "undead coin" has turned to the viral vampire as an expedient metaphor (Abbott, *Undead*, 4). In both of these dominant vampire types, traditional or viral, the figure continues to be a useful vehicle through which to explore societal inequity, particularly as it relates to imbalances of power based in gender, sexuality, racial, socio-economic difference, and bodily difference.

As a monster argued to exude "ubiquitous political symbolism," it is noteworthy how often "vampire politics" has a leftist bent—especially in texts from the late twentieth century on (George and Hughes 3). Whereas *Dracula* is informed by pro-patriarchal, xenophobic sentiment, many recent narratives feature social-justice-minded vampires keen to dismantle hierarchies of domination. In several instances, vampires (and humans) are placed within matrixes of privilege and oppression to trouble normative formations. Donna Haraway argues the vampire figure is especially conducive to such positioning in her work. Writing of vampires as "vectors of category transformation in a racialized, historical, national unconscious" which feed off "the normalized human," Haraway contends the infecting nature of the figure troubles "whatever poses as pure" (214). In so doing, she encourages a liberatory read of vampires, calling upon us to question "Who are my kin in this odd world of promising monsters…. Who are my familiars, my siblings, and what kind of livable world are we trying to build?" (52). Noting that she is "on the side of the vampires, or at least some of them," her work, like the vampire narratives this chapter takes as its focus, questions hegemonic power formations (265). Simon Bacon, akin to Haraway, examines the way vampiric identities are able to exceed "the restrictions of the normative," arguing their "strategic constructions of gender" allow for "a trajectory away from patriarchal control" (99). Deeming "problematics of difference" as revealing "the complications of social otherness," Bacon construes the vampire as a distillation of things/

people being other than they seem (143). This, he posits, fuels the violence surrounding the vampire on whom we project our fears of the Other. Citing how the vampire functions as "racial, sexual, or ethnic Other," Bacon's reading of vampires as "the eruption of difference within the beating heart of normality" characterizes vampiric difference as "a magical thing" that offers an "irrepressible expression of excess that cannot be contained" (146). "Vampiric becomings," as he terms them, resist dominant ideologies in transformative ways. Drawing on the work of Deleuze and Guattari, Bacon names the vampire a radically destabilizing figure.

In order to claim agency and "become" in the sense of the aforementioned theorists, vampires must forge new self-identities and life scripts. Death herein becomes rebirth. Such "productive deaths" can be usefully linked to the contemporary concept of "becoming woke." In more theoretical realms, awakening of this type is often tied to writing the self, as in, for example, Deleuze and Guattari's notion of writing and becoming (304). Vampire texts reflect such linkages between writing and becoming in their consistent foregrounding of characters as writers, diarists, and storytellers[2] In some cases, these writers *are* sympathetic vampires, in others, they *empathize with* vampires. By extension, consumers of such tales are often encouraged to be *on the side of vampires* (to use Haraway's phrasing).

If we think of this in relation to vampiric becoming and movement, as Bacon does, being on the side of vampires allows for identification with monstrous difference, with a liberatory "un-belonging" that is "beyond borders" (44). That many contemporary tales explore un-belonging through vampire figures who either take up the pen (as in *Byzantium* and *The Transfiguration*) or adopt activist agendas (as in *A Girl Walks Home Alone at Night* and *The Passage*) confirms what scholars like Bacon and Haraway contend—that being on the side of the vampire is being on the side of writing identity (and the world) anew.

Many post-millennial vampire texts champion this type of re-writing, doing so especially through "woke" vampire figures. In some cases, humans opt to live "vampire lives" by literally or metaphorically becoming vampire. By allowing their monsters to thrive in some cases and by suggesting productive ways humans can "become vampire" in others, contemporary narratives call for an embrace of the (vampiric) Other. To be sure, the vampire is not always an uplifting figure, and rarely so in texts focusing on the viral vampire. Yet, in some of the most provocative cases, the "depressed vampire" and/or the "apocalyptic vampire" exist within stories offering imaginative responses to personal trauma, which suggest how to navigate an inequitable world, and/or insist fighting for humanity's survival—even against all odds—is a worthwhile goal. Informed by *willful* characters who *choose* to become vampire, remain human, or transform into an admixture of the two (whether literally or metaphorically), the tales circulate repeatedly around individuals determined to forge (undead) lives that matter. In contradistinction to Stoker's ur-text, in which *Dracula* forced his vampiric will onto others, in several post-millennial accounts, humans and vampires alike have agency whether they will—or will not— become vampire. In a number of cases, the narratives encourage us to "invite the vampire in" so as to "become different" in the way Bacon's theorizations valorize. Like my own contention that engagements/embodiments of (and with) monstrosity do not bring about definitive dead ends but instead make space for the new to emerge, I interpret the vampire as championing, as Bacon puts it, "beginnings rather than endings" (1). This life-affirming aspect of the vampire allies to the willfulness this text takes as crucial to the formulation of progressive imaginings. To begin examining such willful vampires, I will first discuss "vampire activists," beginning with the queer, feminist vampire Gilda, from the fictional works of Jewelle Gomez.

Section 1:
The Rise of the Vampire Activist

Politics saturates the vampire story as much as it does the theoretical responses to it. Colonialism, nationhood, (im)migration, racial identity, economic systems all come under narrative purview within vampire texts. Though often read in relation to sexuality, the vampire does far more than kiss you with those red lips. Yes, *Dracula* drips with themes of sexual seduction, penetration, and "staking," yet it also, as theorists like Ken Gelder, Stephen Arata, and Franco Moretti argue, is in conversation with imperialism, capitalism, and race relations. Most often read as maintaining the status quo via staking its animating monster, *Dracula's* conservativism is countered by many a progressive vampire tale in the twentieth century, something that only becomes more pronounced in the twenty-first. While conservative tales of the figure have not gone away (hello, *Twilight*), a number of texts inject not only a progressive viewpoint, but incorporate vampires who are themselves activists, or, in more contemporary parlance "social justice warriors." Arguably inaugurated most extensively in Jewelle Gomez's 1991 novel *The Gilda Stories,* vampire activists are also in evidence in narratives such as *The Ethical Vampire Series* and *Byzantium* (each considered later in this chapter). In the section that follows, I first examine Gomez's queer, feminist vampire extraordinaire, Gilda, and then move into a discussion of the titular girl from *A Girl Walks Home Alone at Night*, an apt, millennial descendant to Gilda.

A Feminist Vampire Manifesto: *The Gilda Stories*

Championed for its use of the vampire as a vehicle through which to interrogate racism, sexism, and homophobia, *The Gilda Stories* intentionally invokes *Dracula*. Gomez shares as much in her afterword to the novel, naming Stoker's text as a "compelling mythology" that she, as a lesbian, feminist, and activist, "needed to excavate and reshape" (256). Gomez undoubtedly reshapes, penning a narrative that features gender fluid characters across a range of time periods. In its two century trajectory, the novel addresses slavery, workers' rights, monogamy, sex work, and the capitalist-fueled ruination of the planet. Gilda, a queer, black female vampire, is an undeniably heroic figure, but also one Gomez importantly describes as experiencing typical "issues imposed on girls by western society—surviving abuse, discovering her self-worth, shedding the social construct of girls as victims" (257). Herein, Gomez frames her vampire creation as an "every woman" whose experiences speak broadly to female oppression.

Gilda's story traverses two hundred years of U.S. history, offering a meditation on how wounds of the past (and specifically those rendered against the bodies of women and people of color) bleed into the present. The book opens in Louisiana circa 1850 as Gilda, at this point only referred to as "The Girl," is raped by a bounty hunter. Described as "stiff for conquest" and as "swelling with power at the thought of invading her," the bounty hunter serves metonymically for the sexual violence white males perpetuated against female slaves (11). Equating the rape of the female body to the rape of entire peoples/lands, the novel here constructs sexual violence as part of the continuum of imperialist, patriarchal formations. In order to be effective against these massive forces, Gilda's narrative will insist females and other oppressed peoples must rise up. Such rising is made possible when "The Girl" consents to being turned vampire by the three-hundred-year-old Gilda, whose name she will eventually adopt. During the two-centuries long journey that follows, Gilda takes part in various forms of political activism related to abolition, the Jim Crow era, and the civil rights movement. Her journey culminates in 2050 in the post-apocalyptic "Land of Enchantment" wherein society is bifurcated into haves and have-nots. The "haves" of the future go "Off-World" to escape the now-toxic environment while hunters remain on the seemingly doomed planet to seek out vampires like Gilda as the "full transfusion of their blood gave eternal life to the hungry rich" (235). Evoking the bounty hunter the young Gilda was nearly raped by at the outset of the novel, these hunters bring the narrative full circle. In so doing, they suggest a continuity from slavery to the ruination of the planet, a ruination that is linked to the attack and exploitation of female bodies and bodies of color. In addition to this condemnation of bodily exploitation, the novel calls for economic equity, addresses the need for literacy and social justice education, and condemns us/them thinking. Regarding the last point, Sabine Meyer notes, "one of the most striking aspects of *The Gilda Stories* is the fact that it actively foregrounds reductive categorization and social normativity as very 'real' horrors that spread across time and cultures insidiously" (3). Much the same is true of two other vampire stories by Gomez, each discussed below.

Fight the (White) Power: "Joe Louis Was a Heck of a Fighter" and "Caramelle 1864"

In the first narrative she wrote about Gilda, "Joe Louis Was a Heck of a Fighter," Gomez sets the stage for the larger vampire-infused critique realized in *The Gilda Stories*. In the tale, racism faced by black athletes serves as a backdrop to a violent street encounter Gilda has with a young black man while walking home one evening. Hidden in the shadows of a tree, Gilda describes this man as "leering out from behind an empty grin," something that causes her to wonder "what drove men ... to need to leap out at women from the darkness." As the man verbally harasses Gilda, "his voice scraped and scratched at her" causing her to reflect, "This one reeked of his enjoyment of power over someone else he considered weaker, unworthy. An assault in the dark was the substitution for truly taking power." In other words, as his race and class exclude him from systems of power, the man opts to enact his male privilege, using it against someone "weaker," a woman (266–7).

When the man seizes her arm, Gilda envisions her fingers around his neck "snapping the connection to the spine." However, recalling a memory from thirty years prior, Gilda sublimates her rage. Recalling the time a boxer attacked a man for saying "boxing was just a 'coon show,'" Gilda is prompted to spare her sexual aggressor, instead knocking him unconscious with a punch to the jaw. After doing so, Gilda slices his neck open and holds him "in the grip of her hands and her mind" as she rummages through his brain looking for a place "where there was no anger or hatred." Significantly, she only finds "places seared white with disappointment turned into rage." The use of "white" is key here. In its evocation of white supremacy, something the story links not only to male supremacy but also to violence enacted *between* people of color rather than *against* systems of power (267–8).

Within the body of the narrative itself, the violence endured *by* people of color is connected to the history of staging violence *between* people of color through the titular reference to the real-world boxer, Joe Louis, the reigning heavyweight champion from 1937 to 1949. One of the first black athletes to achieve national fame, Louis was a regular target of racist sentiment. By incorporating him into her story, one which takes place in the 1980s, Gomez nods to enduring, seemingly trans-historical racism, something Gilda consistently works to dismantle. By resisting the urge to lash out at her black male attacker after being reminded of a racist comment directed at Louis in an earlier era, Gilda chooses not only compassion over aggression, but also racial solidarity over vengeance. This type of compassionate willfulness is, the story implies, made possible by an awareness of the matrix of power/privilege, one Gilda (as a woman) and her attacker (as a black male) are similarly disempowered by.

In the later story, "Caramelle 1864," inspired by and dedicated to Sheridan LeFanu's *Carmilla*, Gomez continues her literary revisions of the vampire, this time penning a story set near the close of the Civil War. The story is narrated by a young girl whose father runs his farm as a depot for runaway slaves. Like LeFanu's 1872 novella, the tale features a mysterious mother and daughter who enter the narrative by way of a horse-drawn carriage. The pair are heading north to escape their master, a vampire who turned them. As the character Caramelle relates, "One night he tried to mess with me and I guess he forgot … about changing us … and mama got mad and killed him." In other words, the unnamed man turned Caramelle and her mother with the aim of having (immortal) sexual slaves yet did not have the foresight to see that by making them vampires, he was also giving them the strength to revolt. After killing him, mother and daughter take to the road, ending up at the depot for runaway slaves. Asked for details of how she and her mother survived on the road by the narrator, Caramelle imparts, "We met a woman on the road, Gilda." Describing Gilda as the strongest women she ever met, Caramelle ends the story with the insistence "You'll want to hear about her." Published in 2011, the story contributes to Gomez's willful vampire canon. Much like the narrator, we as readers want to hear more about such vampires—and thanks to the new breed of millennial vampire to be examined in more detail below, we can. Just as Gomez transforms the lead vampire of LeFanu's story from "a hideous black woman, with a sort of coloured turban on her head," into a woke vampire of color, so too does *A Girl Walks Home Alone at Night* transform the typical male-helmed vampire narrative into one featuring a female vampire, one who willfully challenges the patriarchal, imperialist, exploitive world in which she resides (Le Fanu 25).

Vampire Vengeance: *A Girl Walks Home Alone at Night*

The 2014 independent film *A Girl Walks Home Alone at Night* (*GWHAN*), written and directed by Ana Lily Amirpour, tells the story of "Bad City," a fictional Iranian oil town. Blending elements of the western and the road movie, the film circulates around a teen vampire, the "girl" of the title.[3] Targeting male predators within Bad City, the girl functions as an apt avenging vampire descendent not only to Gilda but also to Nadja from the film of the same name and Kathy from *The Addiction*. As Stacey Abbott and Simon Bacon each document, female vampires have a history of infiltrating city streets in the (male-associated) night-time. This tradition is extended in Amirpour's film, one wherein the girl vampire protagonist partakes in a blood-thirsty version of "take back the night," traversing the streets in the dark as she watches for incidents requiring toothy intervention.[4] That she has no proper name—only referred to with the generic "girl"—suggests her experience as a female in a city full of abusive men is far from unique, while the title of the film references the dangers females face when alone in public at night. Though this title cues viewers to expect the girl to be victim, she is in fact an attacker, one that targets bad men. Alas, individual bad men are not all that make the city bad. Rather, as the opening shot indicates, Bad City is marred by a crumbling infrastructure resulting from an imperialist oil economy. Abandoned buildings dot the barren landscape as dark plumes from the looming oil finery pollute eerie, empty streets. This dreary setting is heightened by the washed out black and white format, one which speaks to the hopelessness of Bad City's inhabitants. The sense of hopelessness and stasis of the locale is embodied in the first character we meet in the film's opening moments, Arash. A James Dean type, he exudes ennui as he smokes a cigarette on the outskirts of the city, not far from a ravine filled with dead bodies (ones which could be casualties of war or victims of the girl vampire, it's never made clear).

In the next scene, set in the dilapidated apartment Arash shares with his drug-addicted father Hossein, we watch Hossein shoot heroin between his toes. In the background, a TV commentator directs criticism towards a female audience, warning they had better be good to their bread-winning husbands, as, if they are not, their spouses will replace them with younger versions. This background snippet highlights a double-standard—one where men have the privilege to be "bad" while women are expected to be "good" *or else*. This focus on gender inequity the film proffers is furthered by the introduction of Atti, a sex worker victimized and abused by her pimp (Saeed) as well as by Hossein, both of whom are metaphorical blood-suckers.

Much like the white bounty hunter that attempts to rape the young Gilda in Gomez's novel, Saeed is a sexual predator. Part of a depraved chain of consumption, he sells drugs, pimps women, and steals jewelry, cars, and other valuables. When the girl vampire arrives at his home in a key scene, heaps of watches and cash are piled in his living room, accentuating Saeed as a greedy capitalist (something further hinted at via the paintings of large cats that adorn his walls and the animal print décor of his opulent [if gaudy] living room). Saeed, assuming the girl has come for pleasure, first dances provocatively in front of her and then offers her drugs. She walks away indifferently. He approaches her again and strokes her mouth. Her fangs pop out.

He releases an excited "ahhhh," apparently interpreting her fangs as a sign she is turned on, and forces his finger into her mouth. Instead of leading to the blow job his fingering suggests, the girl bites off his finger, symbolically castrating him. He falls to the ground. The girl shoves his finger back into his mouth, forcing him to "swallow" what he previously doled out on others (as when he forced Atti give him oral sex in a previous scene). The girl consumes him, something she will soon do to Hossein as well. Though her dispatching of "bad men" is read by most as vengeance, her murderous tactics are not entirely championed within the arc of the film. On the one hand, the girl is a ruthless killer, one who attacks and consumes a homeless man without any obvious cause, and who perhaps is also responsible for filling the ravine on the outskirts of town with dead bodies.[5] On the other hand, she takes out the primary villains of the film, Saeed and Hossein, and provides

The moment from *A Girl Walks Home Alone at Night* when Saeed (Dominic Rains) puts his finger in the girl vampire's mouth (Sheila Vand), causing her fangs to pop out (Ice Films, 2014, directed by Ana Lily Amirpour).

Atti with resources to escape Bad City. Herein, the movie functions as a contemporary permutation of the rape revenge genre. Though Amirpour insists she didn't set out to make a feminist film, *GWHAN* undoubtedly engages with the politics of gender. Whether or not Amirpour set out to provide this type of critique is moot, as any good post-structural theorist would agree. More important is the text itself (and the production of meaning rendered by those who consume it).

Naming *GWHAN* "Perhaps the most important horror film since Danny Boyle's *28 Days Later*," W. Scott Poole construes the film as feminist, writing, "it explains post-revolutionary Iran both in terms of its complex relationship to modernity and the struggle of women caught in the rip-tides of Shi'a traditionalism and an indigenous middle eastern feminism that wants to mutilate patriarchal systems, old and new" (6). On the other side of the spectrum, Megan Goodwin insists the film is far from the feminist battle-cry it has been hailed as. Contending such interpretations serve as evidence of the way western feminists and American audiences "are eager to elide women's violent agency with feminism," Goodwin is critical of what she interprets as the film's "attempts to map western feminism onto nonwestern agents." In this, she is certainly onto something, especially as Amirpour's movie arguably appropriates images of the veiled Muslim woman without interrogating the multivalent meanings of donning a chador.[6] Yet, at the same time, the movie counters, as Goodwin puts it, "facile stereotypes of Muslim women."

In addition to its gender politics, the film is informed by an anti-imperialist ethos of the narrative is also worthy of note. With oil derricks munching into the surrounding city and a gigantic refinery spewing toxic plumes into the atmosphere, the "badness" of Bad City and its environs nods to a decimated Iran, one that is positioned as resulting from the oil industry and the imperialist, militaristic capitalism that fuels it. Rob Latham's argument that vampire texts "illuminate specifically the historical phases of capitalism in which they are produced" is pertinent here (128). The film, produced in an era increasingly concerned about the end of oil, as well as one in which swathes of the world are being sucked dry to feed the vampiric thirst for this resource, addresses the realities of global capitalism—a "badness" that seeps through the ruined spaces imperialism has wrought, infecting them with nihilism, vice, and decay.

If the deadening rot of capitalism and its colonization of places and peoples is to be overcome, the film hints, the resulting badness must be annihilated or left behind. While the girl initially opts for annihilation, she ultimately leaves Bad City with Arash. Though he too plies drugs to get by and pockets earrings to bestow upon the girl, he has not a whiff of the male sexual and monetary entitlement of Saeed nor any of the addicted, manipulative demeanor of his deadbeat dad, Hossein. This brings me to the young boy who begs Arash for money at the outset of the film. Will he be another "bad man" or will he grow up to be more akin to Arash, the caretaker of street cats and lover of renegade vampire girls? If the girl has any say in it, the boy will grow into a "good man." Warning him that "Til the end of your life I'll watch you," so he had better "be a good boy," the girl's threats to take out his eyes may be terrifying, but they are also arguably necessary to ensure he too does not grow into an abuser of women and exploiter of others. As for the girl, she too might be growing towards a less violent existence given she leaves Bad City with Arash (and his cat) in the closing scene. Perhaps like her fictional antecedent, Gilda, she will journey the landscape so as to drain post-colonialism, misogyny, white supremacy, and global capitalism of their predatory hold.

Section 2:
Post-Traumatic Vampire Disorder

Reading the vampire figure as suffering from (and sometimes causing) an undead permutation of post-traumatic stress disorder (PTSD) provides a useful lens through which to consider the individual and collective trauma the vampire both causes and experiences. As Milly Williamson argues, "to embrace the vampire is also to embrace pain; a painful awareness of outsiderdom, a recognition of inhabiting an unwelcome self, a life at least partly lived at the edges" (2). I read such pain in the following section through the lens of what I am terming "post traumatic vampire disorder." In so doing, I invoke *PTVD* as a form of *PTSD* not to make light of trauma, but rather to highlight the ways in which vampire texts engage with both personal and collective trauma. In so doing, texts deploying the traumatized vampire perform a sort of "literary healing," one which intimately engages with physical and psychological trauma so as to render it more manageable (even if only at the level of fiction). As I hope to illuminate, the texts explored below are of note due to the effective linkages they provide not only to PTSD/PTVD but to the field of trauma studies generally. Akin to recent developments within trauma studies as a discipline, the vampire narrative generally eschews "the traditional event-based model of trauma" in which "trauma results from a single, extraordinary, catastrophic event" (Craps 31). Looking at the vampire within this type of framework is apt given they are figures of ongoing—even immortal—trauma. While the turn to vampire is a key catastrophic event, this primary event is re-enacted as the vampire feeds on/wounds others and/or experiences the pain of not feeding. Further, given writing is cast as an effectively therapeutic way to process trauma, the vampire's writerly bent can be linked to attempts to ameliorate PTSD symptoms. As Bacon points out in his discussion of the figure's association to authorship and narrative, many vampires "explicitly use the act of writing in some way to construct a new identity or as a way to incorporate their trauma into the ongoing trajectory of their existence" (115). Though in some cases this writing cures or at least alleviates "PTVD," in other cases, the traumatic turn to vampire cannot be overcome (as in two of the texts discussed below).

Including a post-colonial approach to vampire trauma is also instructive. Asserting traditional trauma studies suffers from a problematic centering of the Western world, Sonya Andermahr documents the need "to bear witness to traumatic histories in such a way as to attend to the suffering of the other"—especially the non–Western, racialized other (500). As the vampire figure is associated extensively with the foreign in many guises—geographical location, appearance, belief, traditions, world view—and given the racialization of the figure in iconic narratives—as gypsy (*Carmilla*), Eastern (*Dracula*), Jewish (*Nosferatu*)—post-colonialism's emphasis on race, nation, and global (dis)placement is an apt methodology to employ when considering vampire trauma.[7] The following discussion will address three texts that depict such trauma in ways that link individual wounding to collective histories related to imperialism, socio-economic inequity, and the post–9/11 milieu.

Vampirism as Post-Colonial Trauma: *White Is for Witching*

Helen Oyeyemi's *White Is for Witching* explores the harrowing life of Miranda Silver. Miranda lives in "The Silver House," a bed and breakfast named after her matrilineal line, one whose ghosts traumatize Miranda as well as the surrounding Dover community. Part Gothic mystery, part vampire-coming-of-age-tale, part post-colonial polemic, the novel opens soon after Miranda is released from a long stint in mental hospital. Told from four different viewpoints, that of Miranda, her twin brother Eliot, her girlfriend Ore, and the Silver House itself, all unreliable, the plot trajectory is non-linear at the level of form, its pages repeatedly "pierced" via singular words set in white space that disjointedly shift the narrative between differing viewpoints, time periods, and literary modes (Gothic, fairy tale, folklore, etc.). The Silver House is the "foundation" of the intertwining tales the novel charts. The house has been passed down from generation to generation in Miranda's family, seemingly taking on more and more sinister life in the process. Figuratively "consuming" its inhabitants and sometimes its guests, this haunting bed and breakfast is melded with European vampire mythos, the vampiric Soucouyant of Caribbean lore, and myriad references to *Snow White* (a tale whose fateful bites and cannibalistic themes are aptly vampiric).

The vampire is associated with mental and physical disorders in the novel, particularly those related to aberrant consumption. Miranda has pica, an eating disorder that involves consuming non-nutritional items. Miranda also has inherited a vampiric hunger from her maternal line. Repressing her hunger for flesh and blood, Miranda instead eats chalk and chews on plastic. With the chalk, she figuratively consumes bits of the white cliffs of her Dover locale and their evocation of the imperial conquest and xenophobia which shape English nationhood generally. Also an instrument of writing, Miranda's chalky diet constitutes a seeming attempt to "write over" her history and pulverize her identity so as to render them erasable/invisible, much like chalk marks on white skin. Alas, it proves difficult for Miranda to escape the indelible marks wrought by colonialism on the one hand and the ancestral "purity" of her white British family on the other. Meanwhile, her chewing on plastic and bending it into new shapes with her sharp teeth can be viewed as an attempt to form a more malleable, modern identity, one that can slice through the racist beliefs her (now dead) great-grandmother Anna tries to force onto her.

Miranda's aberrant consumptive practices have led her to the point of near starvation as the tale begins. Represented as skeletal and repeatedly associated with bone, she is described as "[i]mmaculately carved" like an "ivory wand" (219). Like ivory, she is a product of empire, one who is meant to "trade" in the racism and xenophobia "carved" by her maternal legacy. Other descriptions indicate a vampiric identity—she has pale skin, blood-red lips, jagged teeth, and an "odd smell" (3). She sleeps wrapped in sheets, her form evoking that of a corpse. She finds sunlight hard to bear and has a morphing appearance (her hair appears long at some points and short at others, while photographs of her suggest she is sometimes a different person altogether). Though often "giddy with hunger," Miranda refrains from eating almost entirely, instead shuffling food around on her plate and counting bites in her head (197). Telling herself "I am good, I am" like a mantra, Miranda tries to ward off her vampirism as well as her pica, both passed down to her from her great-grandmother (227).

Her grandmother, or "Grand Anna," used to eat "leaves by the handful," chomp on acorn husks to feel them "splinter down her throat," and chipped her teeth eating pebbles (26). An ancestral double to Miranda, she experienced a "really big crack-up," making her and Miranda the madwomen of the Silver House. In Anna's case, her mental disorders were brought on by the World War II bombings of Dover coupled with her husband being killed on active duty, a death Anna blames on "Blackies.... Germans, killers, dirty killers" (137). Framing the ravages of war as caused solely by other nations/peoples, Anna comes to see her beloved country as "twisted" by these traumatic events. In response, she carries out "some witching" and conjures up the "goodlady," a ghostly doppelganger that thereafter haunts the Silver House. Together, the goodlady and the monstrous bed and breakfast infect Miranda, eventually leading her to declare "We are the goodlady ... the house and I" (202). This collective identity of "goodlady" is later linked to an inhabitant of the house from long ago, likely another ancestor, who would "slash at her flesh" as if trying "to get at food that is buried" and then "drink off her blood ... bite and suck at the bobbled stubs of her meat" (22). This not-so-good-lady is one of the many monstrous women surrounding Miranda, all of whom coalesce around a traumatizing white femininity, one associated with Dover's white cliff's, white Englishness, and the white clothing, hair, and skin of Grand Anna. In fact, Anna is the "white witch" the title invokes, one who believes "White is for witching, a colour to be worn so that all other colours can enter you, so that you may use them" (136). Significantly, Anna sees other colors as something to "use," much like British imperialism treated people of color (and their lands) as exploitable. An individual symptom of colonialism, she wants to consume the labor of non-white bodies on the one hand (as does the bed and breakfast via its employ of Kurdish and Nigerian workers), on the other, she *consumes* non-white inhabitants to cleanse Britain of its "impurities" by murdering several members of Dover's immigrant population.

Such predatory whiteness infuses one of the novel's most memorable scenes: a ghastly meal attended by Miranda and her dead mother, grandmother, and great-grandmother in which it seems the (white) Miranda has fed on the blood of a (dark-skinned) immigrant—that of her friend Jalil. In the interlude, the desiccated bodies of Miranda's ancestors are clothed in corsets as they sit before a table that looks as if made of "very clean bone." An array of food is laid out in front of them but their mouths are padlocked shut, preventing consumption. Standing nearby, Miranda is said to be hungry "for what was not there," something linked to the fact she "grew new teeth inside her." When Miranda notices "holes bored into the wall" and realizes the brown fingers poking from them are not attached to a body, these new teeth seem the likely culprit—something further substantiated when Miranda realizes she is covered in blood as a result of seemingly having killed Jalil. As with other nightmarish scenes in the text, it is never made clear if this horrific meal is part of a dream, an hallucination of a disordered mind, or an actual event. Similarly, the reasons behind Miranda's consistent refusal to eat food are not given a definitive cause. Is she a vampire, an anorexic, and/or mentally ill? (147–150).

Miranda later successfully resists her desire to consume her girlfriend Ore. As they are lying together, she compares Ore's heart to an oyster in a serving dish and "her head spun with the desire to taste" (220). "Ore would hardly have felt it," she muses, noting she was stopped from "tasting" via the ticking of her wristwatch. Described as "the sound of a tongue slapped disapprovingly against the roof of a mouth," this watch belonged to Miranda's mother, Lily. Apparently castigated from beyond the grave by Lily for contemplating attacking Ore, Miranda stops herself from doing so, instead biting into her own wrist. "Manage your consumption.... Behave yourself.... Ore is not food," she chides herself (221). Yet, when she informs the house and its vampiric ghosts "I'm in love," they are disgusted and take to attacking Ore. "We saw who she meant," they respond to Miranda's declaration of love, "[t]he squashed nose, the pillow lips, fist-sized breasts, the reek of fluids from the seam between her legs. The skin. The skin" (223). Lamenting "These are the things that happen when you're not looking, when you're not keeping careful watch ... a taint creeps in," the house and its ghosts expect Miranda to carry on the "rule Britannia" code and champion Englishness/whiteness (222). Unwilling to reject/consume Ore (who is a dark-skinned daughter of an immigrant), Miranda comes to realize she "could not be herself plus all her mothers"—she cannot, in other words, promote their racist decrees and calls to destroy the (immigrant) other (269). Eventually swallowing watch batteries that were given to her by Ore, Miranda symbolically destroys the time from which these racist mothers come, disrupting the generational racism passed via her maternal line.

Reading Miranda in relation to temporality in her article "The Spectral Queerness of White Supremacy," Amy King emphasizes the symbolic import of Miranda's consumption of time. Drawing on Edelman's concept of reproductive futurism, King interprets Miranda as a character challenging "white British societal expectations" so as to exist in queer time (66). Defining queer time as one in which "the present no longer pivots around the past and the future," Rebecca Fine Romanow's reading of queer time is instructive here as well (6). Miranda, in refusing to carry out the generational racist vampirism of her matrilineal line, refuses to "reproduce." She also refuses to live *in the right time* by wearing her mother's watch, which she leaves set to Haiti time, the place of her mother's death. A former colony that is the only country in the world to have established nationhood after a successful slave revolt, Haiti here contributes to the novel's interrogation of the historical horrors wrought by imperialism and enslavement. Miranda, in wearing the watch set to Haitian time, wears a small piece of revolution on her wrist. Ore, who buys her replacement batteries for this watch, figuratively provides Miranda with a means to extend this revolutionary sentiment. Rebelling against the house and its desires she be a "perfect person" that is "so white," she is "purer than crystal," Miranda ultimately swallows the watch batteries in an act of suicide that kills (white) time (73).

As the battery acid seeps through her, Miranda finds she has unknowingly descended to the bomb shelter of the bed and breakfast, the same place her Grand Anna hid from the bombs dropped over Dover during World War II. Becoming another casualty of imperialistic battles, Miranda, by novel's close, has vanished. According to Ore, she is "in the ground beneath her mother's house." According to her brother Eliot, she will return to reclaim her shoes, ones which mysteriously fill and refill with blood after her disappearance. The murderous house, on the other hand, claims she is dead, "stretched out inside a wall" because she "*wronged* me." Just as it not entirely clear whether Miranda inherited vampirism in addition to mental illness, Miranda's ultimate fate is left open at novel's close. Yet, given she reiterates "I am going down against her" several times near the end of the narrative—with "her" seemingly referring to the monstrous triad of Grand Anna, the goodlady, and the Silver House—Miranda's fate seems to be aligned with eating away at the legacy of generational racism, effectively ameliorating the trauma the house (and wider "Britannia") engender. In doing so, she erases herself from existence, leaving only a trace of her chalk-white body and ivory-colored mannequin inhabiting her former bedroom. Miranda thus does not overcome her PTVD. Instead, she chooses death/non-existence over spectral, blood-thirsty whiteness (1–4). In a similarly racially informed tale, another PTVD sufferer prefers death to his life in the projects.

Vampire Life in the Projects: *The Transfiguration*

An official selection at Cannes 2016, *The Transfiguration*, a brooding, philosophical take on the vampire, is set in the Queens Borough of New York. Focusing on aspiring vampire Milo, a young black teen, the film can be constructively compared to *Candyman*, another racially infused horror set in an urban housing project with a black monster at its center. Both films promote a problematic association between the inner-city and violent depravity. In her reading of the film, Robin Coleman argues *Candyman's* representation of "a fearsome housing project home to gang violence, filth, and a most violent monster" serves to celebrate whiteness, doing so through a *black man*, who, once *turned monster*, directs his rage at other blacks (188). In the film's back-story, said man is tortured and lynched in 1890 for impregnating a white woman. This framing story references America's historical obsession with "miscegenation," one which fueled the construction of black men as sexual beasts threatening white femininity. Yet, in *Candyman* this history is used not to condemn white male supremacy and its horrors, but rather to cast the black male protagonist as monstrous.

In the film proper, this man is brought back to life in 1990s Chicago to haunt the infamous Cabrini Green projects. Dubbed "Candyman," he murders some twenty-five residents. A housing project riddled with gang violence, Cabrini Green can be compared to the Rockaway Housing Projects featured in *Transfiguration*. However, this time around, the black monster is sympathetic and his relationship with a white woman is rendered in positive terms. Moreover, in *Transfiguration*, Milo, the main character, directs his violence at well-off white people, a narrative move that implies he has at least partially overcome internalized racism and instead projects his anger to those he sees as causing the problems that plague his neighborhood. Indeed, rather than relying on the stereotypical trope of the violent black man, *Transfiguration* mines racial and economic discord, the traumas wrought by gang-warfare and the continuing wars in the Middle East, and the attendant dysfunction of families marred by PTSD, suicide, and abuse.

The debut film of writer-director Michael O'Shea, *Transfiguration* opens in a public restroom. Milo is in a stall with a middle-aged white man. Another white man in the bathroom hears strange slurping noises coming from the stall and leaves hurriedly. It is unclear whether he flees as he suspects a sexual encounter, a violent one, or both. Close-cropped shots within the stall reveal the white man is bleeding from the neck. This initial segment suggests Milo is a vampire, yet we will soon see him eating cereal and then throwing up blood. Is he really a vampire? If so, is it white blood he can't tolerate? Is he a "crazy killer" (as his girlfriend later inquires) or merely a traumatized youth obsessed with vampire lore? Or, is he, like the black male monster of the earlier *Candyman*, a monstrous product of racism? Set in Queens, the largest and arguably most violent borough in New York City, Milo lives with his brother Lewis, an Iraq war vet. The always-on TV dominating their living room brings news of local murders and arrests. On the streets outside, Milo is regularly accosted by school bullies and local gang members. Lewis apparently opted to join the military rather than said gang, yet the film makes it clear this choice didn't afford a "better life" but leads to Lewis' PTSD. As we only ever see him watching TV from the couch, it is unclear if he is physically as well as mentally wounded. What is clear, however, is that he believes Milo's violent predilections pale in comparison to "the shit that goes on" in the world. As he puts it to Milo, "No matter how bad you think you done there's somebody doing a whole lot worse." His nihilistic view (and PTSD) is linked to witnessing "a lot of body parts" while on active duty in Iraq. Such details are culled from U.S. realities, not only of ongoing war and joining the military as a "way out" of poverty, but also via the real-world Rockaway Projects setting, one the *New York Times* deems "one of the city's most crime-ridden housing complexes" (Kilgannonaug).

Life in the projects eventually leads to Milo's murder after he lures a young white man seeking drugs into the basement of his building. Presumably seeing the man as another (white) source of blood, his vampire pursuits are thwarted when local gang members arrive on the scene. Milo hides as they approach, leaving the young man to assume the assembled black youths are drug dealers that Milo summoned. Taking his queries about cocaine and molly as a racial affront, one of the gang members retorts, "So you think everybody that live up in here is a drug dealer?" Asserting "Whoa, I'm not racist," the white man fails to recognize the racial dynamics of the situation. As the misunderstanding escalates, Little G, the youngest of the group, is encouraged to "Shoot this bitch." He does. Later, we see Milo being returned to the neighborhood in a police car, the indication being he has "snitched" on the gang, something he is soon accused of by the gang leader. Soon after, Lewis, worried about his brother, warns Milo, "I can't protect you from them. You know that right? … And don't trust the cops either, all right. They frame you for that shit just 'cause they can." Here, Lewis suggests the cops are corrupt, something that links to his insistence "people are doing [shit] all the time to each other," that they "just close their eyes to [this shit] and let it happen." News of nearby murders, familial violence, sexualized attacks, and chronic bullying are all part of "this shit," as is Milo's eventual murder. Traumatized by family factors (by his father who was "yelling and screaming all the time" before he died when Milo was eight, by his mother's later suicide, his brother's absence, and his girlfriend's abusive grandfather) as well as by realities of life in the projects (drugs, gang violence, poverty), Milo turns to vampirism as a means of escape. It is never made absolutely definitive, but the suggestion is Milo is not truly a vampire but only adopts a "vampire lifestyle" so as to cope with the traumas his life presents. What is clear, though, is he *believes* he is a vampire. As such, his vampirism acts as a mental break—one in which choosing vampirism is preferable to facing up to realities of his inner-city life.

That he directs all his vampiric violence at white people higher up the socio-economic ladder casts him as a far different monster to the traumatized *Candyman*, however. Rather than seducing a privileged white woman while murdering black inhabitants of the projects, as does *Candyman*, Milo directs his violence at better-off whites, taking not only their blood but also their money. After giving the money he has collected to his girlfriend Sophie so she can escape the "puncturing" of her body by prurient groups of white boys that use her for group sex, as well as move away from her sadistic grandpa who pierces her skin with cigarette burns, Milo orchestrates his own death. Having earlier told Sophie it is against vampire rules to commit suicide, he ruminates on whether he deserves to live at narrative's end. He writes in his journal, "I'm not sure vampires should ... be here. I mean I know they've always been here, but, I mean, if you can only exist to hurt people and you know better, then maybe it's better to decide not to exist at all." Though writing in this journal helped him deal with trauma, he ultimately decides it's best he not exist. As such, he does nothing to correct the local gang's belief he snitched on them, and, in so doing, courts what in vampire parlance is called the true death. Gunned down as he is walking through his neighborhood, voice-over narration from his vampire journal accompanies a tableau of his bullet ridden body being placed in a coffin. As suggested by the film's title, perhaps Milo's death will transform him into a divine creature—maybe a vampire even. Or, more nihilistically, perhaps his life as a young black male in the projects simply sucked more than death.

Read All About It: *Fangland*

Whereas *White Is for Witching* and *The Transfiguration* revolve around traumas wrought by racism, poverty, gang violence, and war, *Fangland* offers a media-focused take on historical atrocities. Centering on Evangeline Harker, an associate producer for the highly successful news show *The Hour*, and her encounter with the Romanian vampire, Ion Torgu, *Fangland* refashions the *Dracula* narrative into a tale of post–9/11 trauma.[8] Prompted by the conviction the world needs a "monstrous history lesson," the vampiric Torgu aims to "infect" the world with such knowledge by unleashing the spirits of those killed at sites of global atrocities. Described as "Two million years of murder in the form of a man," Torgu might be thought of *as* historical trauma (especially given his Romani identity and its association with enduring persecution) (202). Read as such, it is understandable why Torgu chooses New York City as a fitting place to bring "his armies into the world" so as to force humanity to reckon with historical injustice (327). Described as "a place where he can feel truly comfortable, a place beside a great hole in the ground where thousands died" that is "rich in death," the World Trade Center becomes "ground zero" for the traumatic memories Torgu seeks to leash upon the world (327). To put this endeavor in motion, when Evangeline travels to Romania to interview him, Torgu lets loose a plague of words upon her so that she will infect the news station and ultimately the news itself once she returns to New York. "His words had fangs," as Evangeline puts it, explaining they "poured into my ear like poison" (279). Plagued with visions of "every man and woman who had ever been forced to strip and stand before their own mass grave, every girl ever slaughtered before her parents' eyes, every village ever annihilated, every name ever extinguished for all time on the whim of a butcher, every single little massacred citizen … since the dawn of time," Evangeline turns decidedly vampiric herself (279).

Once the taped interviews arrive in New York City, they infect the news station of *The Hour* with a vampiric audio virus—"a force beyond comprehension" which incites several employees to go mad, kill themselves, and/or inflict violence on others (335). Ultimately causing a fire at the studio headquarters, the virus results in fifty-four deaths consisting of "some of the most famous names in the history of television news" (384). This is not any news staff, but that of "the top-rated news show on American television," one that "pioneered the magazine format in that ferocious year 1968, when assassination, race riots, overseas war and popular music conspired to overflow the banks of the regular time slot allotted to news" (130). In other words, *The Hour* was born in an era of social unrest as well as vigorous investigate reporting. In contrast, the post–9/11 milieu the novel takes as its setting is one wherein the show *The Hour* is framed as the "audible last gasp" of network news (136). Attributing this demise to a failure to "heed the dead enough," Torgu laments the U.S. has become a country "that cares nothing, knows nothing" of the "worst calamities of the twentieth century" (139).

By making the historical "book of slaughter" known, Torgu hopes that "the entire race" will have to "bear this unbearable burden" along with him (201, 292). "In the last century … 187 million people were destroyed by human hands, more than in all the previous centuries of murder, a tenth of the world's population, and in every corner," Torgu rails (291). According to one employee of *The Hour*, "the September disaster lies at the root of this entire thing" (293). In accordance with arguments put forth in works such as *Horror After 9/11*, *Fangland* suggests the date is "conterminous with terror itself" (Miller 4). Argued to bring about PTSD symptoms on a massive scale, even for those not in close physical proximity on the day, the symbolic import of 9/11 is utilized in *Fangland* to represent collective trauma on a mass scale (Miller 230). Framing 9/11 as an infectious event,

Torgu's primary form of vampirism is the release of a plague of memories. A "monstrous historian," Torgu seeks to erase the human "capacity to forget" so as to rectify "the spectacular murders that cry out for acknowledgment" (383, 328, 201). In rendering the vampire in this way, *Fangland* offers a unique contribution to the vampire canon, one that brings to mind the zombie-infection spread by words in the film *Pontypool*. Rather than choosing vampirism to ameliorate PTVD (as does Milo in *Transfiguration*) or inheriting it (as does Miranda in *White Is for Witching*) Torgu's vampirism penetrates the present with past traumas. With a Dracula-like abode in Romania and an appearance that rivals the hairy-palmed count, Torgu takes over memories *not* bodies, doing so to vampirically force historical reckoning.

Though *Fangland* was penned prior to pervasive rhetoric about "fake news," it's tempting to read it in light of the ongoing decimation of news media as well as to the increasing regularity of violence inflicted on investigative journalists. While Trump and company suck the life from democratic media with rampant accusations of "fake news," Torgu seeks to virally transmit facts about historical mass murders. Whereas Trump's "fanged words" call for "great big walls" to protect the dark heart of global capitalism, Torgu seeks to reveal that human trauma knows no borders. Torgu aims to force humanity to face up to the wounds history has wrought. As PTSD is depicted as something that need be actively addressed by individuals rather than buried if its sufferers are to heal, we might read Torgu's aims to virally spread traumatic memories as an attempt to alleviate collective trauma. In keeping with this line of argument, the vampire figures featured in *White Is for Witching* and *Transfiguration* are traumatized because they seek to forget the pain of their individual histories (for Miranda, her mother's murder, for Milo, his mother's suicide) instead of attempting to process them. Torgu, in contrast, benefits from remembering, something that releases him from torment at novel's close. Such ameliorative remembering also aids the vampires taken up in the next section who, unlike Miranda, Milo, and Torgu, are able to forge morally-based vampiric identities.

Section 3: Ethical Vampirism

Like the monster generally, which is, as Margrit Shildrick argues, "freighted with sexist, racist and ableist connotations which must be constantly challenged and undone," the vampires in the tales examined below "overrun the boundaries of the proper" (7, 11). Displaying that horror can in fact be an ethical project, the vampires in the texts that follow refuse the construction of (certain) humans as moral and (all) monsters as immoral/aberrant. Featuring ethical vampires seeking to redress various types of immorality (pedophilia, rape, greed, and so on), the narratives interrogate "who is due moral consideration and who is not" in their engagement with what Shildrick terms "the ethics of embodiment" (132). As a figure that emphasizes the corporeal nature of existence, the vampire provides an apt conduit through which to explore embodied ethics. Generally relying on proximal, healthy bodies to supply the blood necessary for their survival, vampires are part of bodily economy of exchange. If they are to survive, they cannot destroy their blood supply nor the planet that houses their "human blood banks.'"[9] And, just as a symbiotic, interdependent relationship between human and vampire is called for in order to forge a more ethical vampire life, so too is co-existing in mutually beneficial ways with other vampires (in romantic relationships, families, and networks)—something deemed necessary for *moral immortality.*

"Be Me a Little": *Let the Right One In*

John Ajvide Lindqvist's *Let the Right One In* (*LTROI*), published in 2004, is set in Sweden amidst the economic downturn of the 1980s. Made up of a series of intertwining narrative threads, the text includes news stories, police reports, and diagnostic case notes to bolster its examination of societal issues dominating the era (nuclear proliferation, mass unemployment, heroin addiction, etc.). With myriad types of violence percolating under the surface of the novel's nearly five hundred pages, Lindqvist's work deals extensively with morality and ethics. Troubling distinctions between good/evil, right/wrong, child/adult, and male/female, *LTROI* serves in part as a meditation on power and violence, implicitly posing questions such as: Do imbalances of power necessarily lead to violence? What justifies acts of violence, retribution, and/or vengeance? How are interpersonal violence and systemic, societal violence inter-related? And, most pertinent to the discussion that follows, can committing violence ever be ethical?

The novel circulates most prominently around the relationship between Eli, a two-hundred-year-old child vampire, and Oskar, a twelve-year-old boy.[10] The story opens as Eli and Håkan move into the same apartment complex as Oskar. While Håkan is presumed to be Eli's father by the outer world, in actuality, Håkan murders on Eli's behalf in exchange for being allowed to live with Eli. Eli fomented this arrangement as they are averse to the bloodshed their vampire survival requires. In contrast to Eli's reluctance to commit violence, Oskar is fascinated by it. He keeps a scrapbook of clippings about serial killers, treating the stories as sweet escape (tellingly eating candy as he studies his macabre collection of photos and news clippings). In an early scene, Oskar contemplates an image of a Swedish murderer known for butchering male prostitutes with a chainsaw and muses to himself *"Could be me in twenty years."* Using the scrapbook as inspiration, after studying its contents, Oskar goes to his kitchen, sharpens the biggest knife he finds, and makes a mock holster out of newspaper so as to play at being "a dreaded mass murderer." Heading outside with the knife, he imagines selecting his next victim. As he walks towards the forest "the fantasy gripped him and now it felt like reality" and he is said to see the world "through the eyes of a murderer. A world he controlled, a world that trembled in the face of his actions." Though Oskar fails to link his fascination with violence to the fact he is so often the victim of it, he clearly is drawn to this "game"—one that provides a means to envision himself as more powerful than his bullies. Through the friendship he forms with Eli, Oskar will not only be encouraged to defend himself (rather than live in a fantasy world), but also to rethink his romanticization of violence (18–23).

Soon after Oskar and Eli meet, Eli learns Oskar is being bullied and advises him "You have to strike back." When Oskar counters it is three against one, Eli insists "Then you have to hit harder. Use a weapon…. Hit them more than you really dare. Then they'll stop" (105–6). While not a proponent of violence generally, Eli knows the horrid consequences that can result from not being able to defend oneself. In Eli's case, their powerlessness led to them being castrated and turned into a vampire by a sadistic older male at twelve years old. As a result, Eli has had to kill (or rely on someone to kill for them). Yet, they are so averse to violence they toy with the idea of suicide, framing death as a "wonderful idea" (386). However, it is not until Eli is being pursued by Håkan in the latter half of the narrative that they seriously contemplate suicide. Said pursuit occurs after Håkan is infected with the vampire virus. Prior to this, Håkan viewed Eli as his "beloved," a designation resulting from their mutually agreed upon relationship—one in which in exchange for providing Eli with blood, Eli lives with Håkan, allowing him to look at, but not touch, their naked body. Before this arrangement, Håkan was fired from his teaching position after he was discovered to be a pedophile. After becoming Eli's blood provider, which involves murdering regularly on Eli's behalf, Håkan quenches his pedophilic desires by looking at and sleeping next to Eli's naked body. The situation, as Håkan characterizes it, provides "the best of all possible worlds"—one where he can be with a twelve-year-old child who is in actuality a two-hundred-year-old vampire (108). Their situation falters, however, after they move to a new area and Eli befriends Oskar.

Spending time with Oskar, a kindred twelve-year-old, results in Eli acting more like an adolescent, to move "in a loose-limbed way" and "use childish expressions" (109). This behavior on Eli's part heightens Håkan's sexual desires for them, but Eli continues to insist only looking will be allowed. Threatening to cease providing blood for them if they don't agree to more, Håkan's growing lust not only leads to him pressuring Eli for more contact, but also causes his murdering skills to falter. He botches a killing, fails to get blood for Eli as a result, and renders himself a police suspect in the process. As a result, Håkan devises a plan to continue murdering for Eli: he will pour acid over his face so as to make himself unrecognizable. At his next murder site, as he hears what might be police approaching, he pours concentrated acid over himself. When the police find him, his flesh has melted away, leaving one eye as the only recognizably human feature in a mass of glistening muscle and bone. Hospitalized as a result of his severe injuries, Håkan is soon visited by Eli. Håkan makes it known he wants Eli to bite him by pointing to his throat insistently. Eli informs Håkan he will have to kill him afterwards, then bites Håkan as requested, drinking from his neck. As Eli does so, a guard enters the room, necessitating Eli to escape out the window—something that results in Håkan being left alive but infected by Eli's bite.

Soon after, Eli contemplates suicide (partially fueled, presumably, by the fact they have been forced once again to return to killing after losing Håkan's blood-providing services). Feeling especially guilty after they attack one of Oskar's friends (even though they don't kill or turn him), Eli descends to the basement of the apartment complex and breaks a broom handle into a makeshift stake. Eli holds the point of the stake towards their chest, but is prevented from driving it into their flesh when they hear someone approaching. Eli realizes it is Håkan, who soon throws open the door, tearing it partially off its hinges. Unsure what his intentions are, Eli senses an "overpowering sense of threat emanating from Håkan." Håkan then pulls up his shirt, revealing his "stiff swollenness" and begins to masturbate. Relieved Håkan doesn't seem to plan on attacking them, Eli laughs, "All this. To be able to jack off." Envisioning Håkan sadly masturbating for eternity, Eli is taken by surprise when Håkan punches them with such force that part of their ear rips off. When Eli regains consciousness after Håkan's attack, their ankles are tied above their head. They feel something cold near their anus, trying "to force its way" inside them. Spying the broken broomstick handle lying within reach, they grab it and swing it towards Håkan, hitting him in the chest. Eli then manages to escape, leaving Håkan locked inside the basement. Håkan is apprehended by the police sometime later. The autopsy and resulting diagnostic report describe his cadaver as still showing signs of life. Likened to "the eel that dead and butchered jumps in the frying pan," Håkan has become a vampiric "meat stew" of phallic grotesquerie, an embodiment of his ever-slithering penis and its pursuit of young flesh (390–3; 444).

Although the young boys who bully Oskar are arguably less abhorrent than Håkan, they also prey on those weaker and smaller, getting pleasure from doing so. Together, Håkan's predation of children, the violence enacted on Oskar by bullies, and Eli's castration at the hands of a powerful vampire figure redolent of Gilles de Rais (suspected of murdering hundreds of children during the 1400s) convey a continuum of violence spanning the centuries, one linked to a refusal (or inability) to see others in terms of "the ethics of embodiment" that Shildrick links to collective notions of "who is due moral consideration and who is not" (132). Conventionally, of course, "monsters" are not framed as deserving of moral consideration. Further, in the case of vampires, their "bodily economy of exchange" is often not a reciprocal one but one based on dominance and control (especially where male vampires are concerned). However, in the case of the vampire Eli, they are far more ethical than the humans that surround them, including Oskar. Indeed, Eli's forgiving, empathetic nature is what prompts them to approach outsiders like Håkan and Oskar in the first place.

Oskar, though a more sympathetic figure than Håkan, dreams, as shared above, of becoming a killer. While his visions of becoming a mass murderer in a sense come to pass given that he becomes Eli's new partner (and as indicated in Lindqvist's later story, also a vampire), he is disabused of his glorification of violence through his relationship with Eli.[11] When they initially meet, Oskar is fascinated by Eli and the promise they hold out for ameliorating his loneliness. Yet, Oskar is nevertheless cruel to his new friend. For instance, at one point, he refuses to invite Eli in to his living room. He waves his hand mockingly around the door frame, asking what will happen if they enter without being invited. Perturbed, Eli indicates Oscar is being sadistic. Unmoved, Oskar responds, "Let's see it." Eli enters. Their skin flushes, blood oozes from every pore, and their mouth twists in pain. Oskar hastily shouts three invitations and Eli's bleeding halts. Though Oskar expects the blood to disappear, it does not, instead coagulating to stripe and clump on Eli's body. Here as elsewhere, Oskar does not think about the consequences of his actions or the impact they might have on others—conveying as much with his half-hearted apology "Sorry, I … I didn't think…" And herein is Oskar's key character flaw—he fails to *think* about consequences. Not tuned into the ethics of embodiment, he treats other bodies as objects to toy with, mock, and mutilate (as when he dreams of mutilating the body of one of his bullies while viciously stabbing hunks of bark from a tree early in the narrative) (343–5).

Eli, via their queer body and identity, forces Oskar to come to terms with the differing bodies—and feelings—of others. A key scene in this regard happens when Eli takes a shower to clean their body of blood. When they emerge from the shower, they drop the towel they are wearing and gesture towards their nudity, saying "Just so you know." Prodding Oskar, "You understand now that I'm not a girl," Eli calls upon his friend to confirm he has taken in Eli's bodily reality. Asking if he is disappointed, Oskar evades discussion of the matter. "Cut it out! You're sick. Just lay off," he blurts. Oskar wants to be friends with Eli, but also does not want to face up to Eli's difference. In contrast, Eli is keen to be honest about what/who they are. In response to Eli's attempts to help him understand their bodily reality, Oskar changes the subject to one he is more comfortable with: violence. "But you kill people!" Oskar rails, as if this truth makes Eli's gender identity and body facticity mute. "Yes, I kill people. Unfortunately," Eli admits. When Oskar proceeds to insist there must be some other way, Eli calls him out on his hypocrisy, reminding him that when they met, Oskar was stabbing a tree with a knife as he thundered "What are you looking at, idiot? Want to die, or something?" Although Oskar is affronted when Eli suggests his play-acting of violent scenarios suggests he would actually kill someone, he does, at Eli's insistence, admit that he would likely kill if he knew he could get away with it. "Sure you would." Eli replies, "And that would be simply for your own enjoyment. Your revenge. I do it because I have to. There is no other way." Oskar, still keen to differentiate his violence from Eli's, counters he would only commit violence in self defense. Eli disagrees, asserting he would do so "Because you want to *live*. Just like me." Eli then invites Oskar to "Be me a little" and pulls him in for a kiss. This kiss transports Oskar into Eli's mind, allowing him to experience Eli's 18th century violent vampiric transformation as if he himself were going through it. Oskar's re-living of Eli's forcible castration contributes to the continuum of violence Oskar experiences over the course of the narrative—one that allows him to experience Eli's torture and gives him more appreciation for Eli's bodily difference and gender fluidity as well as their ethical code (349–52). Just as Eli encourages Oskar to repudiate his fascination with violence, so too does Eli help him accept gender fluidity. Choosing to live a life "in between" the gender binary, or what Ahmed names the willful "refusal to be housed by gender," Eli's "queered view" helps Oskar to *see* things differently, something that differentiate him from his bullies who *see* things through the normative codes of society, or, in Ahmed's terms, the general will (*Willful Subjects* 149). This "queer vision" is, in effect, something Oskar's bullies threaten to annihilate when they threaten to blind Oskar's in the climactic pool scene, an attack that also seeks to *drown* his brand of alternative masculinity. In the scene, the bullies capture Oskar in the corner of the pool and inform him he will have to hold his breath for five minutes or they will cut out one of his eyes. Deciding death is better than losing an eye, Oskar gives in to drowning. The lead bully then pulls Oskar's head above the water and readies to stab him in the eye. Before he can do so, Eli arrives to save Oskar (and dispatch the bullies).

The epilogue to the novel, set three weeks later, revisits the pool scene. A detective gathering evidence recounts how witnesses described Oskar as being rescued by an angelic figure, one that, due to the copious amounts of blood at the scene, seems "Hardly one from heaven" (471). In the closing scene that follows, Oskar sits in a train car accompanied by an old-fashioned trunk (which presumably contains Eli). The fact Oskar exudes happiness (as noted by the conductor) indicates he has willfully chosen to depart the city with Eli. This accords with the reciprocal, interdependent relationship the two have formed. That they have done so across norms of age, gender, sexuality—not to mention via bridging the human/monster divide—indicates they have chosen to "become together," to use Bacon's terminology. Eli and Oskar, each queer characters in so many ways, have formed an ethical relationship, one built on disclosure, empathy, and understanding—and one which they will presumably provide what the other needs—be it blood, protection from violation, or love. Whereas *LTROI* focuses on the ethical relationship forged between two adolescents (albeit one of them has been an adolescent for a long time), the next novel up for discussion explores how attempting to live up to normative societal expectations results in dangerous levels of repression—including the repression (and rejection) of one's true identity. Much like Oskar, who eventually embraces his non-normative masculinity, the Radley family will come to accept that they are not an average middle class family.

Willful Families Versus Toxic Will: *The Radleys*

The best-selling 2011 novel by Matt Haig, *The Radleys*, offers a study in vampire *will* versus vampire *willfulness*. Recall that Ahmed frames *will* as driven by a power-over mentality and *willfulness* as about agency and resistance. In Haig's narrative, *will* results in violence and manipulation and is most associated with the character named—you guessed it—Will. In contrast, the Radley family of vampires, Helen, Peter, Clara, and Rowen, are ethical characters. Initially too afraid to own up to the reality they are vampires, the Radleys eventually stray from being upstanding middle-class citizens and willfully embrace the blood-drinking life. As their story opens, the Radley parents, Helen and Peter, have not told their children they are vampires. This conceit of a "normal" family allows for a vampire-infused critique of the "keeping up with the Joneses" mentality—one that links provocatively to Ahmed's casting of the family as a key component of the general will (aka the status quo). Noting how "family becomes another fantasy of the 'whole social body'" in her writing, Ahmed documents how normative family formations further the interests of heteropatriarchy. The family, as she characterizes it, upholds "the straight line of inheritance." Drawing on varied meanings of straight, including good, normal, hetero-sexual, and so on, Ahmed positions the "straight family" as "willing to re-produce the whole" and take "seats at the table" of the general will, and, in so doing, help keep social norms and systems in place (113–92). Haig's novel accord to such theorizations concerning the family as an oppressive structure. Set in the village of Bishopthorpe where "it is easy to believe the lie indulged in by its residents—that it is a place for good and quiet peo-ple to live good and quiet lives," the text depicts traditional middle-class suburbia and its "good families" as stultifying (5). Implicitly calling for a more queer concept of family and identity not reliant on repression, Haig utilizes the vampire to castigate restrictive moral codes regarding gender, sexuality, and class status. This condemnation of the repression required to "be normal" is furthered especially by *The Abstainer's Handbook,* a book within the book described as "an abstaining vampire's self help man-ual." Noting he is intentionally "satirizing overly puritanical moral struc-tures" through the handbook in the novel's afterward, Haig references such structures as particularly prevalent in the current era (379–80). The handbook encourages vampires to assimilate, integrate, and abstain from drinking blood—to, in other words, abstain from being different. Peter and Helen endeavor to accord to such "vampire abstinence," while Will, Peter's duplicitous brother, also a vampire, opts for hedonistic abandon and a wholesale rejection of morality—a stance that informs not only his heavy, irresponsible blood-drinking but also leads him to a life of violent crime. His *willingness* to commit harm is echoed in Harper, a human teen who sexually assaults Will's niece Clara.

The incident occurs at a party Clara attends, one where Harper pur-sues her doggedly even thought she makes it clear she is not interested in him. When Clara attempts to leave the party, Harper "plants himself in her path." Clara, noting Harper "looks suddenly dangerous, his drunken face revealing its potential for human evil," begs him to leave her alone. Harper refuses, saying "I know you fancy me. Just stop pretending." Herein, Harper frames his pursuit as "normal" and casts Clara as selfish for denying him. As Clara walks "with a new urgency ... toward the road," Harper catches up with her, again insisting "I know you like me." Comparing her situation to "how dogs and monkeys feel in the laboratory when they suddenly realize the scientists aren't there to be nice to them," Clara recognizes the precarious position she is in, but feels powerless against the "boy twice her size who could do anything to her." Harper proceeds to take Clara's phone, taunting "Come and get it," acting, as Clara puts it, like "a three-year-old blown up into a monster." Representative of a monstrous *will*, Harper construes Clara as his rightful prey. But, when Harper pushes Clara to the ground and places his hand over her mouth, she bites him, resisting this designation. The taste of his blood awakens her vampirism and she "lashes out in a wild, uncontrollable rage ... with sudden strength she pushes him, slams him into the ground." His blood then "floods into her, drowning the weak girl she thought she was and lifting someone new— her strong and true self—to the surface." When Clara's parents arrive on the scene, her dad finds Harper's body devoured, his lower intestines spilling out of him "like escaping eels." Reflecting that "once Clara started she wouldn't have been able to stop," Peter places no blame on his daughter (in sharp contradistinction to the blaming-and-shaming surrounding sexual assault in the real world) (52–64).

After this incident, the entire family is forced to come to grips with the reality they are vampires, something that in turn leads to revelations about the assault that led to their vampirism in the first place, one carried out by Peter's brother, Will. Akin to an older, more dangerous version of Harper, Will feeds on women, regularly blood-minding them with his vampire powers and then killing them for sport. In one such murder, Will targets a young female supermarket worker and lures her to his van, one riddled with blood stains from his former victims. This van brings to mind tales of abduction, particularly of women, both real and fictional. As in narratives such as *Silence of the Lambs* and *Room*, male mobility and capital makes their violent acts possible. Will, one such male body, is presented as a vector of the sexually-and-romantically dysfunctional culture of which he is a part. He embodies the negative, pathogen form of *male will*, that which Ahmed links to oppression and injustice in her study. The later revelation that Will turned Helen, now his brother's wife, *against her will*, furthers the representation of Will as having an evil *will*. According to the vampire lore of the novel, by turning Helen, Will binds her to him for life. Drawing on the common trope of the vampire as able to compel others desire, Haig presents Will as able to *will* Helen to want him. While Will feels "that deep joy that always came to him when killing another person's happiness," Helen does not break off her engagement to Peter as Will had hoped she would (280). Fighting the blood-minding Will forces upon her, Helen *willfully* refuses to become Will's lover. Herein, Helen's ethical behavior stands out in contrast not only to Will's, but to Harper's.

Condemning Harper—a human teen—and Will—a male vampire—for forcing their entitled, sexually violent will on others, the novel considers how culture encourages males to take pleasure in power, framing this encouragement as akin to being turned into a predatory monster. Using the previously noted *Abstainer's Handbook* as a vampiric commentary on dysfunctional moral codes, Haig's novel equates the policing of sexuality to the ubiquity of sexual violence, presenting these outcomes as different sides of the same coin which result in figures such as Will Radley, the vampire serial killer, and female victims, such as Clara and Helen. Framing sexual desire as the vampire within that turns villainous through the promotion of rampant repression on the one hand and a gross sense of entitlement on the other, the narrative implicitly calls for acknowledging individual agency—sexual and otherwise—and *abstaining* from forcing ones *will* onto others. If an ethical society is to be realized, the narrative suggests, everyone must learn to control their *will* but not sublimate it—they must, in short, become *willful*.

The Pen Is Mightier Than the Fang: *Byzantium*

The 2012 film *Byzantium,* adapted by Moria Buffini from her play *The Vampire Story*, and directed by Neil Jordan, features a mother and daughter vampire duo, Clara and Eleanor, as they navigate their blood-dependent lives. Opening in present day Ireland circa 2010, the film includes regular narrative flashbacks to the early 1800s, the era in which Clara and then Eleanor were each turned vampire. Ethics of immortality play out across the shifting time periods in a slowly unfolding narrative, one that meditates in particular on the female vampire life.

The film's evocative imagery points to several key motifs: socioeconomic decay, the dehumanizing effects of capitalism and war, the longstanding commodification of the female body. From nineteenth century bordellos populated with sick prostitutes to twenty-first century abandoned theme parks, derelict buildings, and seedy strip clubs, the film depicts depraved aspects of culture, ones wherein people die alone in gloomy hospital rooms, young sex workers are ill and/or strung out on drugs, and greedy bosses endeavor to stiff their workers. Along with images of visceral realism—murder by decapitation, bodies suffering from war wounds, incurable illness, and old age—the film proffers several artsy tableaus—waterfalls that flow with blood, horses galloping against the ocean's tide, flocks of birds bursting from dark caves. Juxtaposing images of violence and pain with ones of breaking free, the film's visuals echo the opposing viewpoints of its central female protagonists. On the one hand, Eleanor insists on a joyless vampire life and subscribes to the view pain, tragedy, and loss are inevitable. On the other, Clara, her mother, treats life as a rollicking adventure. Refusing to waste precious time on guilt, remorse, or trying to live up to societal standards, Clara is a lusty vampire renegade in contrast to her staid, brooding daughter. Yet, by film's end, the melding of Eleanor and Clara's viewpoints results in a far more sustainable—and ethical—vampire existence for each of them.

The film opens with Eleanor narrating, "My story can never be told. I write it over and over, wherever we find shelter. I write what I cannot speak—the truth." *Byzantium* does tell her story, though. In fact, her narrative makes up the bulk of the diegesis and serves to emphasize the immortal power of storytelling—something aptly summed up by Eleanor's creative writing instructor when he imparts, "Humans need to tell stories. It's a fundamental and uniting thing. It's through stories that we come to understand ourselves and we come to understand the world." Describing the story Eleanor turns in for his seminar "as if Edgar Allan Poe and Mary Shelley got together and had a very strange little child," this teacher inspires Eleanor to share her story rather than merely throw the pages she writes to the wind (as was her previous practice). The title of her work, "A true account of my making and my life and death from the year of my birth, 1804," accentuates the *making of a vampire* whereas the film as whole emphasizes the *making of female experience*. This making vampire/woman, echoing the famous dictum of Simone de Beauvoir, "a woman is made, not born," links to the focus on Clara and Eleanor as "made" by the social forces that surround them: phallocentric law, normative gender expectations, and sexualized violence. By highlighting women forced into sex work in both its respective time periods (along with the accompanying violence, addiction, disease, and economic insecurity that results), the narrative questions the dubious ethics of reigning conceptions of gender, ones in which women are "made" into replaceable commodities while males rule the human—and vampire—world.

In the film, the Brethren are the ruling vampire elite. An all-male organization, their primary code is that female vampires are not allowed to create other vampires. They want the vampire race to consist solely of males of noble birth and are thus displeased when they find out one of their own, Ruthven, turned Clara, a lowly harlot. "You were to find a man of good blood who appreciates this brotherhood and what we do," they scold him as they look over Clara with disgust. When they ask her how she will use "this gift" of vampire existence, she replies "To punish those who prey on the weak. To curb the power of men." This rebellious pronouncement leads the assembled Brethren to lament their code bars them from destroying the low-born woman unless she creates other vampires. As such, they banish her. Later, after Clara breaks this primary code by turning her sixteen-year-old daughter Eleanor, the two females are hunted by the Brethren. As a result, they must move from place to place regularly. They have survived in this fashion for two hundred years, though with very different ethical codes. Whereas Clara stays true to her conviction "those who prey on the weak" must be punished, Eleanor strives to live a non-violent life of the mind. In this, Clara's trajectory is more in keeping with a thirst for vengeance, while Eleanor hungers for finding meaning in a bleak world. Yet, both of them balk at the notion female vampires cannot create—Clara through creating Eleanor and Eleanor through creating a vampire mythos (and, as the end of the movie implies, by turning her ailing boyfriend).

Importantly, Clara was only able to turn Eleanor in the first place by stealing the Brethren's secret of immortality. Taking the map from Ruthven that details how to reach the nameless island where humans can be turned vampire, Clara prevents her daughter's pending death from syphilis. The island, described as "a sinister black thumbnail sticking out of the ocean," has waterfalls that flow with blood each time a vampire transformation takes place in the appointed underground cave. Such feminized imagery of vampire reproduction (invoking menstruation and the womb) suggests linkages between the Brethren's attempt to control vampire reproduction to patriarchal aims to control (female) nature and the reproductive female body. Echoing the notion of male god as creator, the Brethren's desires herein link to parthenogenesis. A myth bound up with "avoiding or short-circuiting the acknowledgment of one's origins in a woman's body," the evocation of parthenogenesis in the film is associated to the patriarchal vampire society (Braidotti 1994,184). In addition to outlawing the "birth" of female vampires, the Brethren aim to create a male-generated vampire race, one of god-like bodies able to live outside of time. Notably, this attitude of male superiority is tied to the male hand, one that delivers physical blows to Clara over her years as a prostitute and whose fang-like thumbnail is used as murderous weapon by Brethren vampires. Calling themselves "the pointed nails of justice," the Brethren act as the figurative "hand of god."

Though Eleanor views her mother and herself as ruthless monsters, it is the Brethren, as they themselves describe it, who steal time with blood. In contrast, via telling the story of her and her mother's lives, Eleanor writes the female vampire *into time*. Read in relation to the legacy of the vampire canon, one whose classics are largely written by men and position male characters as primary, Eleanor's "true account" serves as feminist corrective to the canon. Refusing to keep quiet, Eleanor wrests narrative control from the male hands that would deny her right to exist, let alone write. As for Clara, she wrests control from the male-led Brethren by surviving on her own terms. At film's close, as Clara and Eleanor prepare to part ways, Eleanor tells her mother "Your instinct is to hunt the powerful and protect the weak. I'd like to try and live that way." Eleanor's final words, "I throw my story to the wind and never will I tell it more. Another one begins," indicate she will craft a new life-story. That she and her mother survive positions them as fairly unique permutations of the female vampire. In contrast to Carmilla, the female vampire staked and beheaded in LeFanu's *Carmilla*, or the similarly dispatched of Lucy of *Dracula*, the female vampires of *Byzantium* live on—and will do so, one can presume, by their individual ethical codes—codes that are by necessity scripted by oneself for oneself. Or, as Clara's closing dictum phrases it, "Live your life how you choose." With this willful, ethical mother-daughter vampire duo, the story *genders* vampire agency differently. Redressing the male-dominated vampire canon, the film places primacy on female vampires who foment their own ethical code. In sharing their story, *Byzantium* births a new vampire mythos, one in which the female vampire (and her pen) is mightier (and far more ethical) than the phallocentric "nails of justice."

Moral Immortality: *The Ethical Vampire Series*

Condemning predatory male violence along similar lines as *A Girl Walks Home Alone at Night* and *The Radleys*, *The Ethical Vampire Series* (*EVS*), by Susan Hubbard, is a coming-of-age vampire saga centered on Ari, a half-vampire, half-human thirteen-year-old. The trilogy, which consists of *The Society of S* (2007), *The Year of Disappearances* (2008), and *The Season of Risks* (2010), tackles political corruption, greed, and scientific hubris in addition to charting what an ethical vampire existence might consist of. Like Amirpour's film, which equates male violence to the insatiable hunger for drugs, sex, and oil, Hubbard's series examines "the profound consequences of materialism and greed," in order to explore how "Mortals actions ... have immortal effects" (2010, 303). The series specifically links patriarchal violence done to women to violence done to the planet, a theme that echoes arguments made by eco-feminist Jane Caputi. A fictional extension of Caputi's claim that "the body of the female victim signifies the corpse of the earth," Hubbard's trilogy suggests females must claim agency so as to save and protect human and planetary bodies (1993, 146). In stressing that human actions have long-term, generational consequences—that, in short, we humans need to act *as if* we are immortal, *and moral*, vampires—the series contends everyone should try to live a life "worthy of eternity" (Preston 165). Such lives, according to *EVS*, should be attuned to a long-term view of existence based on ethics rather than profit. The main vehicle for studying what such an existence would look like is Ari, who is unaware as the narrative opens that she is half vampire. The books chart her journey from child to adult, equating her growing knowledge of vampire society to realizations the world is far more complex—and dangerous—than her sheltered upbringing led her to believe.

In the first *EVS* novel, after nearly being raped while hitch-hiking across the country in search of her mother, Ari learns she is part vampire. This discovery comes about after she accepts a ride from a dangerous male, described as wearing sunglasses though it is night, as having "long and stained" fingernails, and as obsessively clenching and un-clenching his jaw. We are cued to suspect the man is a vampire—but, in actuality, he is a sexual predator—and perhaps a serial killer (159). After stopping the car in secluded spot, he grabs Ari. Laughing as she struggles to get away, he forcefully unbuttons her pants. She bites him in response, unleashing her inner vampire (much the same as Clara's trajectory in *The Radleys*). Confessing her "crime" to her mother after they are reunited, Ari reprimands herself for killing her attacker. In response, her mother reminds her, "He would have raped you." Naming Ari's act self-defense, she insists, "From all you've said I doubt that you were the first girl he took out there. Be glad you're the last" (219). Here, Hubbard's work presents rapists as evil, and vampires—at least those like Ari and her mother—as ethical. Significantly, akin to Clara in *The Radleys*, Ari recognizes her monstrous proclivities only *after* she is sexually attacked. Via such representations, both *The Radleys* and *The Ethical Vampire Series* intimate that sexual assault is par for the course in a generally violent culture, one which necessitates that females *become monstrous* so as to be able to prevent attack. In so doing, narratives of this ilk meditate on the difference between *perpetuating* violence to enact power and *resorting to* violence in self defense (something also taken up in *LTROI*).

As the story continues, more females disappear and some are found dead, something that positions Hubbard's saga as part of the growing canon of millennial monster texts that condemn sexual violence. Teeming with progressive political sentiment, ethical vampires within *EVS* not only rail against interpersonal violence but also endeavor to put a stop to capitalist ruination of the planet. Particularly concerned with the ethical treatment of animals, the need to care for the earth, and finding sustainable ways to exist not based in exploitation or driven by profit, food, and so on, Hubbard's vampires are what neoliberals might call "vampire snowflakes." Such attempts to create a more just world via vampire activism, to overcome personal and collective trauma, and to forge more ethical relations with others and the planet not only shape the tales examined in the three preceding sections, but are also apparent in several post-millennial texts featuring viral vampires, the subject of the final portion of this chapter.

Section 4: Viral Vampires and Dystopian Futures

While viral vampires are generally presented as a scourge, the texts in which they appear sometimes deploy this vampire type in the service of critique—to castigate, for example, corporate capitalism, militarism, scientific experimentation, human exploitation, and societal violence. The best-selling trilogy *The Passage*, by Justin Cronin, is exemplary in this regard. Infused with a radical, progressive bent, the post-vampire world the series depicts is riddled by many of the same problems that plague our own. Like a vamped-up *1984*, Cronin's saga details dystopian horrors, although via a less overtly political narrative. The 2009 film *Daybreakers* and the 2007 adaptation of *I Am Legend* also utilize the viral vampire to imagine dystopian futures. *Daybreakers*, set in a post-vampire world beset by a dwindling supply of human blood, draws scathing conclusions about corporate capitalism and its seemingly ever-present, immortal offspring, militarism. The *I Am Legend* film, in contrast, champions a strong nation-state and lionizes militarized masculinity as the "true savior" of a post-apocalyptic New York. Other examples of this rabid vampire figure, one Stacey Abbott argues is "increasingly integrated and intertwined" with the zombie, are also in evidence in *The Strain* series, the *Stakeland* films, the *Blade* and *Underworld* franchises, the television show *Ultraviolet*, and the movie *30 Days of Night* (4).[12] Even *True Blood*, more known for its sexy vampires, takes up a viral vampire apocalypse arc in its seventh season. In some cases, the *Dracula* narrative is put in conversation with more viral permutations of the figure, as it is in the Showtime series *Penny Dreadful*. In what follows, I will consider three representative texts featuring viral vampires—the apocalyptic saga *The Passage* (and its 2019 Fox TV adaptation), the dystopian film *Daybreakers*, and the post–9/11 remake of *I Am Legend*.

The Passage: A Willful Girl Saves the World

The Passage trilogy provides a relatively unique iteration of the viral vampire narrative in that it has a female savior at its core. Cronin readily admits this depiction was intentional. In his closing comments included in the final book, he writes "Finally, special thanks to my daughter, Iris, who challenged me ten years ago to write a story about 'a girl who saves the world.' Darlin', here it is" (604). Cronin has widely shared that his daughter's request prompted him to develop the series—not only that, but he credits his daughter as helping him craft the saga, saying in a 2016 interview, "This was a project that was devised initially by a father and his daughter" (Watkins). His trilogy, a global best-seller adapted into a TV series in 2019, spans some 1,500 pages over three books. Cronin cites Orwell's *1984* as a key inspiration. The texts themselves draw extensively on biblical themes and narrative patterns pertaining to the hero's journey, the jungle quest, and the western, as well as tales of post-apocalyptic survival. A new form of vampire, called virals in the novel, are the central monsters. An admixture of traditional vampires (they are associated with bats, cannot abide sunlight, and feed on blood) and viral vampire (they are fast moving and highly infectious), Cronin's virals are spawned on an expedition in South America when members of a research team are infected with a virus transmitted by bats. Those who survive the infection have boosted immune systems and enhanced strength, speed, and longevity. The novels of the saga—*The Passage* (2010), *The Twelve* (2012), and *City of Mirrors* (2016)—chart what happens after the virus is inadvertently spread throughout the United States. Jumping back and forth over a one thousand year time-frame, the bulk of the narrative is told from an omniscient viewpoint and centers on several dozen interlinked characters. On the whole, the saga condemns oppressive social formations and frames a communalist, egalitarian society as the way forward. It also foregrounds females as world saviors. Cronin notes this aspect of his trilogy is not meant to imply that *only* women can save the world, but rather "the woman in all of us." Characterizing female strength as more world-building and healing than destructive, he affirms "the female characters in my trilogy are all designed to embody female strength" (Watkins). Many of the females in the saga are also survivors of sexual assault, something some read as problematic.[13] Yet, in my estimation, the grounding of this post-apocalyptic tale within stories of rape and assault is key to the progressive politics the series champions—a politics that is in keeping not only with socialist ideals, but feminist ones. The 2019 TV adaptation thankfully did not jettison this component of the book—in fact, in ways, it made it more prominent. Before delving into themes of female strength, sexual assault, and rape revenge, an overview of the series is in order.

Framed as the archives of Professor Miles, who carried out extensive research to accurately render the one thousand years since the viral appeared, the trilogy consists of multiple narrative threads and a huge cast of characters, all of which link back to Amy, the primary hero. Though traditional epics and the Christian bible they often invoke generally fail to feature female heroes, Cronin rights this wrong via his female-Christ figure. In addition to Amy, the primary female hero, the book features twelve apostle-figures, four of whom are women. Near the end of the saga, Amy carves the names of her twelve apostles in stone, solidifying their depiction as prophets, saviors, and messiahs of biblical proportion. This carving is then discovered by satellite image some nine-hundred years after the viral vampire outbreak, prompting Professor Miles to travel to the site and meet Amy, the part human, part vampire hero.

The first book of the series, *The Passage*, opens as the world is being decimated by virals. It spans ninety years in chronological time, documenting various pockets of humanity and their attempts to survive. The first section details Project NOAH, a top secret government initiative that involves transporting death-row inmates to a military compound for genetic testing. The inmates will be infected with the virus Jonas Lear encountered while on a research trip to South America, an infection that ultimately leads to their transformation into viral vampires. As the book moves forward in chronological time, readers are introduced to various characters related to Project NOAH, including government agents that are tasked with finding and transporting hand-picked prisoners back to the military compound in Colorado. The agents are also ordered to apprehend a six-year-old-girl from a convent, Amy, who will be infected with a mutated form of the vampire virus. As the narrative proceeds, Tim Fanning (the "patient zero" also known as "Zero") along with the twelve inmates infected with the virus, take control of the military compound and escape. These viral vampires rapidly spread their plague, destroying most of the U.S. population. Meanwhile, Amy is rescued by Wolgast, the special agent tasked with bringing her to Colorado. He becomes a surrogate father to Amy and the two survive in a mountain hideaway where Wolgast eventually dies of radiation poisoning caused by the nuclear devices that were detonated across the U.S. in hopes of eradicating the virus (another instance of the saga's castigation of a weaponized society). The narrative then jumps forward approximately ninety-five years to follow the human survivors of The Colony, a walled-in sanctuary in California. In interviews, Cronin refers to The Colony as a "lifeboat" in which survivors "have found a way to exist socially that's resilient." Pointing out most of those left surviving are "good people," Cronin notes he aimed to depict humans as gaining courage via "connection to other people" (Newitz). Cronin's work thus resists the individualistic and militaristic mindset of many other apocalyptic texts to instead focus on the power of communal ties. Notably, his work contrasts markedly to the pro-militarism, pro–America, individualist sentiment proffered in Max Brooks' viral zombie novel *World War Z*. Published four years before *The Passage*, the colony of survivors Cronin imagines reads like a socialist commune based on equal sharing of resources and work, something not only absent in Brooks' work, but openly mocked.

In the first book of Cronin's series, one of the primary crises of survival involves running out of the batteries needed to power lights lining the walls of The Colony which keep the light-sensitive virals at bay. At this point, our knight-in-shining-armor arrives in the form of a girl: Amy. She and several Colony inhabitants soon go in search of the military site in Colorado where another group of humans have managed to survive. On their travels, they come across The Haven, a settlement of survivors housed in a Las Vegas prison. The Haven is under the control of one of the twelve lead virals, Babcock, a ruthless leader who requires human blood sacrifices in exchange for protecting the Haven community. In order to continue to produce enough humans to provide necessary quantities of blood for Babcock, Haven females are treated as livestock and forced to bear children. After successfully escaping Haven, Amy and company proceed to the military compound, the location of the original viral infestation. There, they find Lacey, the nun who was Amy's caretaker when she was a child, and initiate a plan to lure the virals back to the compound in hopes of destroying them. As the original virals and all they have infected, known as their "many," communicate telepathically, Amy's group presumes killing any of the lead virals will kill their many as well. Their plan fails, however, and one of their group, Alicia, is infected. Sara, the lead medic of the series, treats Alicia with the modified virus that Amy and Lacey were infected with, resulting in Alicia's transformation into a human/vampire hybrid. Critically, all of the females infected with the modified viral virus—Amy, Lacey, and Alicia—become savior figures—putting them in stark contrast to the infected male figures who become the viral patriarchs of twelve different violent, human-destroying strains of vampire. In book two of the saga, Amy and company aim to hunt down and destroy the remaining twelve virals.

In *The Twelve*, the Colony sanctuary from book one is contrasted with the concentration-camp-like Homeland, ruled by virals and "Red-eyes" (who survive by drinking blood from other virals). Sexual abuse is a key theme in this part of the narrative. The blood drunk by Homeland leaders comes from the viral Grey, one of the titular Twelve. As a human, Grey was a convicted pedophile, something linked to his own childhood sexual abuse. This strand of Cronin's trilogy associates the generational "passing down" of sexual violence to the depraved, post-apocalyptic world of Homeland, a compound besieged by acts of sexual abuse and rape where captured slave-laborers serve totalitarian leaders in various ways. Many females and trans-folk are forced into sex work, deemed "tangible physical assets in an economy of scarcity"—or, in other words, disposable human commodities (343). Homeland is, for the most part, male-ruled and relies mainly on female labor, furthering the saga's exploration of gender inequity. Like Orwell's classic novel, this aspect of the series suggests top-down systems turn those in power into violent tyrants and those oppressed into dehumanized automatons. As will be discussed in more detail below, *The Passage* series offers a continuing interrogation of sexual violence as a key linchpin in the maintenance of hierarchy and oppression. That the strongest and most heroic females of the saga emerge from Colony, the egalitarian sanctuary featured in book one, is integral to the pro-communal, anti-violence stance of the series.

The third and final book, *City of Mirrors*, opens nine hundred years in the future at the Third Global Conference on the North American Quarantine Period. It thus circles back to the opening of book one, providing a narrative framework similar to that of *The Handmaid's Tale* (which is bookended by a similar conference). The narrative then picks up where the second book in the series left off, focusing on a colony of survivors in Kerrville, Texas. Meanwhile, the original viral vampire, Fanning (aka Zero), plans to destroy humanity and lies in wait at Grand Central Station in New York City. Concurrently, one of the twelve human apostle figures, Michael, is readying a large boat to travel to an island in the South Pacific rumored to be viral-free. When viral attacks re-emerge in Kerrville, hasty preparations for the lifeboat journey ensue. Once the boat is ready, some seven hundred survivors board. Amy stays behind with a few others to hunt down Fanning and destroy his many. After a climactic battle in which Amy prevails, the book jumps forward nine hundred years, circling back to where it started. Professor Logan Miles, Chair of Millennial Studies, is preparing for "humanity's long-awaited return to that feared and vacant continent," North America (569). The saga ends as the professor arrives in the U.S. and locates Amy. He asks her to tell him a story. She does so, "writing" the story the series imparts in the process. Hence, by its close, the narrative has gone back and forth in time repeatedly, over the span of a century. It closes some nine hundred years in the future to reveal that humanity has survived.

Significantly, the back-story of the saga's primary hero, Amy, involves a single mother, an abusive father, and an attempted gang rape. As such, interpersonal violence sets the dystopian narrative in motion. At the outset of the series, Amy's mother Jeanette turns to sex work to make ends meet, procuring a gun for protection. One fateful evening, a man picks her up and takes her to his fraternity house. When Jeanette refuses to go inside, a violent scuffle ensues and the man forces her to the ground. Realizing she will be gang-raped by him and his fraternity brothers if she doesn't take action, Jeanette puts her gun to his head, pulling the trigger. Panicked and pessimistic about her chances of survival following this incident, Jeanette opts to leave Amy at a church before taking to the road, something that ultimately leads to Amy's inclusion in Project NOAH. Amy is the first child and only female injected with the vampire virus as part of the project. In contrast to the other twelve subjects, all of whom are not only male death-row prisoners but are generally associated with death, Amy is cast as benevolent savior. A child for the majority of the saga due the ways the virus slows maturation, she, like Melanie of *Girl with All the Gifts*, is a heroic monster figure, one whose vampiric gifts will be used to protect humanity. Clearly the "girl who saves the world" that Cronin's daughter requested he write about, she is played by the young black actress Saniyya Sidney in the Fox television adaptation. This casting reflects a welcome change in the horror genre: the foregrounding of young black girls.[14]

Also of note are the changes the TV adaption makes regarding the racial and gender identities of a number of other characters. Giles Babcock becomes Shauna Babcock. Colonel Sykes, a male in the books, becomes Dr. Nichole Sykes. Amy spends far longer as her human self than she does in the book, proving herself to be, as her surrogate father Wolgast describes her, "wicked smart and strong and fast and funny and tough." As in the novel, the TV adaption presents her as fearless and heroic. Of most interest to me, however, are the changes made to Babcock's character and narrative arc. In the novel, Babcock, a male, is sentenced to death row after being convicted of murdering his abusive mother. Once infected, he manipulates humans to go on a three-day killing spree. With his many minions, he takes control of Haven, and, as referenced above, instigates human sacrifice rituals and forces females to act as human brood mares. He is, in short, a heinous villain. In the TV series, in contrast, Babcock is a charismatic, strong-willed female whose back-story involves being sexually abused by her step-father for nearly a decade. Years later, Babcock discovers her mother knew about the abuse but did nothing. This revelation leads her to stab her mother and kill her stepfather. For this, she is sentenced to a correctional facility. She is later taken by Federal Agents to the Project NOAH facility. Before being admitted, the guards transporting Babcock attempt to rape her while she is handcuffed. Richards (the operational overseer of the facility) witnesses the attack and fires a warning gunshot. Once in the proximity of Babcock's attackers, he asks, "What the hell is going on here?" "We were just having a little fun," Simmons, one of her assailants, replies.

Simmons continues to harass Babcock while she is being housed at the facility. During one of these incidents, Grey, another member of staff, tells Simmons to cut it out. Angered, Simmons grabs Grey and forces him up against Babcock's cell, kicking his phone underneath the bars in the process. Grey reaches carefully beneath the bars for his phone, worried Babcock might attack. She doesn't. This emboldens Simmons. He puts his face between the bars of her cell, taunting her. She grabs him and bites into his neck, draining him of blood in mere seconds. In the meeting about the incident that follows, various Project NOAH team members debate what to do with Babcock. Her murder of Simmons is the first such incident in the three years the

An advertisement for *The Passage,* the television adaptation of the trilogy of novels by Justin Cronin. The ad features Amy Bellafonte (Saniyya Sidney), the girl infected with the viral virus as part of Project NOAH (Fox, 2019–).

facility has been operational. Lear, the lead scientist, comes to her defense, arguing Babcock killed Simmons in an act of revenge. Though the team decide to euthanize her, she is ultimately spared when Richards, the man who thwarted her attempted rape, discovers she has had to deal with a lifetime of sexual violence. That much of this occurs during an episode entitled "That Never Should Have Happened to You" underscores the series' critical take on rape culture—one that suggests such violence is itself a virus, one that even super-powered female virals are not immune to. Via this more sympathetic version of Babcock, the TV adaptation humanizes the virals, making them tragic figures in the process. Further, by presenting virals as themselves victims of rape culture, sexual assault is depicted as a more dangerous virus than that which spreads vampirism—something that accords to Alicia's narrative arc in book two of Cronin's series.

Like Amy, Alicia is part viral and also a female savior figure. She is the strongest physical warrior of Amy's apostles. Also like Amy, her story is housed within a rape culture script. Captured by Guilder, head of Homeland (and a key antagonist of book two), Alicia is raped repeatedly. Guilder eventually turns her over to his minion Sod, a man who "would have raped the wind if it had a hole in it" (322). Sod tortures and assaults Alicia, as described here:

> ... through the days of his dark business, Sod left no part of her untouched.
> He had filled her ears and nose with the hot stench of his grunting exhalations. He had scratched her, struck her, bitten her. Bitten like an animal. Her breasts, the soft skin of her neck, the insides of her thighs, all embedded with the marks of his teeth [464].

Portrayed as "wearing a greedy, bestial smile," Sod eventually releases Alicia from where she has been chained to a bench, saying he wants so "try something new" (464). Once released, Alicia drives a blade "deep into the dark heart of him" in order to "feel him die," much like he drove himself into her body, wounding her repeatedly. Designating "Sod of the bench and the grunting exhalations" as similar to "all the men in all the years of history who had violated a woman in this manner," Alicia's disposal of him offers a viral vampire take on the rape revenge motif so prominent in millennial monster tales (549). In her rape revenging quest, Alicia also murders Martínez, a serial killer and rapist in his pre-viral life. *The Twelve* details this former life, focusing on his rape and murder of a woman named Louise whom he sees as "an organization of warm surfaces created only for his desire and dispatch." Once turned viral, Martínez has dreams in which he "was forever raping a woman named Louise" (10). Alicia, as part viral, is able to see these dreams and to feel "Louise's terror, and her pain, and then the dark moment when the woman understood that death was imminent, [that] the last thing she would feel as she departed the world would be Martínez, raping her" (231–2). Herein, both Alicia's and Louise's rapes are presented as eternal, as something that goes on forever, if not literally, then in the dreams of the rapist and the continuing trauma of the victim. Also significant is the fact that Martínez, before being turned vampire, had a very particular method for choosing his victims:

> He chose low women, those lacking learning or culture, not because he despised them or secretly wanted them but because they were easy to ensnare. They were no match for his beautiful suits and movie-star hair and silken courtroom tongue. They were bodies without name or history or personality, and when the moment of transport approached, they offered no distraction [311].

That Martínez recalls these days with "poignant fondness" and links them to "The days of blood and mayhem and the great unleashing of his kind upon the earth" links the viral epidemic to sexual violence. Moreover, the fact Martínez was an attorney and used his "silken courtroom tongue" in his rapist pursuits symbolically conveys a legal system that does little to end rape. In contrast, Alicia's killing of Martínez, whom she makes say Louise's name before he dies, figuratively gives voice to all the sexually violated women in history (313).

The closing book of the saga, *City of Mirrors*, continues the call for a society free from sexual violence via a focus on the first viral vampire, Zero, and his pre-viral life as Timothy Fanning. His story is one of heartbreak and unrequited love, one which leads to sexual assault and his eventual pursuit of Amy. Knowing that in destroying Amy, the Christ-like savior, he could destroy humanity itself, Zero's aim is prompted first by the loss of his mother and then his lover Liz, both to cancer. Robbed of the love of these primary females during his human life, Fanning became a cancer himself, one intent on infiltrating the world with his malignancy. His turn to primary villain is inaugurated after he encounters one of his former students, Nicole, as he is attempting to "drink himself into oblivion" (168).

In the scene, Fanning and Nicole taxi to her apartment after several drinks. Once they arrive, Nicole tells Fanning to wait outside, but he enters the building when another tenant departs. Fanning descends to Nicole's basement apartment, number zero (a nod to the monster he will soon become). Banging on the door frantically, he promises "I'll behave." Nicole relents and lets him in. Fanning then presses against her and kisses her neck, thinking "I wanted to drink her." "Tim, stop. I mean it," she responds, continuing "you're scaring me. I need you to leave." She tries to shove Fanning away as he lurches towards her railing "You bitch. You fucking bitch." In the scuffle that ensues, the kitchen knife she is holding penetrates her chest when Fanning falls on top of her. Nicole dies and Fanning proceeds to clean the apartment of clues. He hears a sound as he is doing so, a baby girl making joyful squeals in her crib. When he later recounts this story as justification for his misery, he pauses to ask "What is the worst thing? The deaths of millions? A whole world lost? No: the worst thing is the sound I heard." Recognizing this encounter as a turning point that led to his desire to destroy humanity, Fanning dubs himself the "great devourer of the world" and begins to refer to himself as "Zero." Later identifying Amy as the alpha to his omega, Zero evokes the New Testament's Book of Revelation, where God proclaims, "I am Alpha and Omega." In naming Amy as alpha (the beginning) and himself as the omega (the ending) he seems to imply that he will end existence/time, thus destroying her goal to keep humanity alive (171–173).

Ultimately, by defeating the virals with the help of her human apostles, Amy provides humanity a second chance—a dead end that kills the vampire scourge and births a new viral-free world. Via this Christ-like figure, the series runs counter to depictions of god as vengeful. Further, instead of a monotheistic conception, the trilogy promotes the notion of an all-encompassing oneness. "Everything had a soul," the final text of the saga imparts, referencing "a deeper reality that ordinary people could glimpse only fleetingly, if at all. A world of souls, both the living and the dead" (43). Crucially, the broken world that Fanning and others represent is linked specifically to the creation of two genders—a notion that accords with feminist thought, queer theory, and other socially justice minded formulations:

> It has been said that in ancient times there was only one gender; in that blissful state, humankind existed until, as punishment, the gods divided each of us in two, a cruel mitosis that sent each half forever spinning across the earth in search of its mate, so that it could be whole again [363].

Here, Cronin suggests one gender—or a world not divided by gender—would make for a better society. Moreover, via inclusion of non-hetero-sexual, non-binary-gendered characters, the saga calls for a recognition that humans deserve equity regardless of sex, gender, sexuality, race and other identity markers. Cronin also champions a *queering* of love in his narrative, one that is more expansive, inclusive, life-affirming, and *not* based in the ownership model that informs hetero-patriarchal-monogamy. Fanning, as Zero, is portrayed as the enemy of this type love, as someone who "wouldn't rest until the whole world was a mirror to his grief" (526). Yet, even he is awarded the saving grace of love at the saga's end, summed up in the following: "All things fell into the past but one; and what that was, was love" (524). Thus, while *The Passage* series is filled with devastation, sexual violence, and human exploitation, it ends not with nihilism and death, but with hopeful rebirth. The bio-engineering quest to weaponize humanity (aka Project NOAH) that sets the story in motion serves to castigate the power-over mentality shaping both patriarchy and militarism. The saga also presents violence as a continuum, one that runs the gamut from weaponizing infection to acts of sexual assault. This aspect of Cronin's work accords with Jane Caputi's insistence that our world is undergirded by "sexually political terrorism" based in the "interconnections between technology and sexual violence." Arguing the ideology of male supremacy and the resulting "destructive consequences of phallo-technology" will bring about the ruination of humanity if not replaced with a more equitable system, Caputi's theoretical stance accords to the arguments underlying Cronin's narrative—namely, that if we do not change our ways, humanity (and earth) will reach its end (*Gossips* xxi).

The Passage series relates particularly to the "willfulness archive"

Ahmed calls for, one that "wanders" away from established thought patterns of the general will in order to map new modes of being. Framing archives of this ilk as "premised on hope," Ahmed explains, "When you stray from the official paths, you create ... desire lines, faint marks on the earth ... traces of where you or others have been" (22). Cronin's work, made up of legal documents, personal diaries, emails, letters, and so on, serves as a "willful archive" of the viral apocalypse, one which centers on a bevy of willful wanderers who stray from traditional paths in their attempts to save humanity. Cronin also channels the political impetus of dystopian classics such as *1984*, acting as what Ahmed terms a "novelist of the will" by producing an archive of the future that resists militarism, totalitarianism, and the will-to-power (27). Recall that Cronin was spurred to write the series via his daughter's request for a story about "a girl who saves the world." That this girl's story is framed by a rape narrative—and that the series features numerous instances of sexual assault, forced pregnancy, and lack of reproductive choice—results in a willfully feminist saga, one that does not "kill joy" but that instead calls for the dead end of tyrannical power.[15] Thus far, the television adaptation echoes the political spirit of Cronin's saga. In turning Babcock into a female sexual assault survivor, the show extends the saga's critique of rape culture and frames the "good guys" as just as likely to commit sexual violence as the virals. In its casting of Amy the TV adaptation adds another important new twist—a young girl of color as the savior of humanity.

There Will Be Blood: The Corporate Vampires of *Daybreakers*

Set ten years after a vampire outbreak in a world where only five percent of humans remain, the 2009 film *Daybreakers* circulates around the dwindling blood supply threatening continued vampire existence (with blood standing in allegorically for oil). Reports about the surge in global blood prices, blood riots, and blood-related crime saturate the movie, as when, early on, Starbucks is revealed to hawk blood concoctions rather than lattes. Echoing the stark economic divides that animated the Occupy Wall Street movement, something Ahmed argues can be understood as a movement of "willful monstrosity," *Daybreakers* is set in a bifurcated world of haves and have-notes (164). The haves are the middle to upper class white vampires who live in gated communities and drive cars decked out with drive-by-day technology; the have-nots are the poor and homeless humans, as well as the "subside" vampires (whose blood deprivation has rendered them more animalistic and viral). In addition to the vampire

1 percent and their subside counterparts, an enclave of humans survive on the outskirts of the vampire-ruled city, hoping to find a way to turn vampires human again—a goal which will require putting a stop to the evil machinations of Charles Bromley, vampire CEO of Bromley Marks, a bio-pharmaceutical corporation aiming to rule the blood market which exemplifies what Abbott calls "disembodied vampire conglomerates" (*Celluloid*, 217). Significantly, *Daybreakers* brought this type of corporatized vampire to the big screen soon after the burst of the U.S. housing bubble in the first decade of the 21st century, a shift that heightened tensions surrounding socio-economic status. Intentionally invoking real-world tensions and nodding towards the economic crisis that informed the Occupy Wall Street movement, the film incorporates news reports and headlines within its diegesis, ones which speak specifically to cultural anxieties related to wealth inequity, (im)migration, dwindling resources, and escalating militarism.

The inequitable socio-economic system that informs the diegesis is established in early scenes set inside the Bromley Marks corporation. While privileged white male vampires discuss plans to create a viable blood substitute in their expensive suits, a vast blood-bank of naked and unconscious human bodies hang in an inner chamber of the building. Here, Ahmed's reading of capitalism as "the whole body" that good subjects must be "willing to reproduce" is particularly apt. Her naming of capital as "lifeblood" that "must be kept in circulation no matter what" is evocatively rendered in the transformation of humans into blood sacks fueling the vampiric capitalist machine (105). At the other end of the spectrum, Charles Bromley, the ruthless CEO, embodies corporate will. He does not wish to solve the blood crisis let alone find a cure for vampirism but to enact a blood(ied) commerce, one he admits has "never been about a cure" but "about repeat business." So ruthless as to have his daughter Audrey, part of a rebel faction of humans, caught and turned into a vampire against her will, he is the film's apex of villainy, something emphasized particularly when he chains his daughter and several soldiers to Hummers. Planning to have all of them turned so that they burn in the sun, he is here the figurative embodiment of blood-hungry corporatism. A corporate thug, Bromley seeks to destroy anyone and anything who gets in the way of his profit-reaping agenda. Relying on a militarized police state to do so, he treats soldiers as disposable commodities. Akin to a villainous combination of George Bush, Dick Cheney, and other hawkish military types, he is willing to sacrifice human lives to secure power. In the scene, after the chained soldiers are pulled into the sun, an infected soldier bites a human soldier. In quick succession, all amassed soldiers are infected as they turn to bite the soldier nearest them in a cannibalistic wave.

Herein, corporate militarism is rendered in vampire-industrial-complex form. The solution to such a system, the film suggests, is to turn vampires human again so as to destroy the fascist hold Bromley Marks has on society. To this end, Edward, a hematologist played by Ethan Hawke, takes up with the rebel human faction, hoping to find a way to reverse vampirism. Eventually discovering vampire blood can reverse the virus, Edward returns to Bromley Marks to rescue captured humans. When Bromley bites him in a nasty confrontation, he is turned human again. Attacked by his own now-vampire-army in the scene that follows, the corporate criminal is brought to his demise. As the film closes, Edward and other human rebels drive towards the rising sun as he narrates their plan to spread the cure to others. The recent adaptation of *I Am Legend* ends on a similar note (at least in the theatrical ending), with Neville driving towards a human enclave of survivors.

Will the Real Monster Please Stand Up?: *I Am Legend*

The 2007 adaptation of *I Am Legend* (*Legend*), starring Will Smith, transforms Robert Neville into an affable hero.[16] Released during the closing years of George W. Bush's presidency, this version of *Legend* speaks to the conservatism and xenophobia of the post–9/11 era. In the original novel, Neville was a lone white male surviving amidst a horde of vampires invading his California suburb, factors read by some as representing gentrification and associated fears of racially diverse neighborhoods.[17] The 2007 film departs from the racially segregated Compton of the original novel, however. Set in New York City, the change in location is accompanied by marked changes in Neville's character who is in this iteration depicted as an African American scientist and soldier (as opposed to the white suburb-dwelling lead of Matheson's text). In this modern adaptation, as noted by Sean Brayton, "the racialized body holds the key to 'national survival'" (67). Yet, as Brayton demonstrates, Neville's race is not foregrounded. Whereas whiteness is coded as infectious and threatening via "dark-seeking" vampires with light skin (as well as via the white female doctor whose medical discovery causes the viral outbreak), Neville's blackness is put under erasure. In effect, he functions as a "post-racial" protagonist—one who never mentions race—unless you count the fact he name-checks Bob Marley. An amorphous "good American man," Neville loves his family, his dog, and his country. A soldier first and foremost, his gun-savvy battle skills open the film as he races through post-apocalyptic NYC with his dog Sam in tow. He exits his car after spying deer bounding through the city, seemingly to hunt them. An imperial hunter in an un-civilized landscape, he refrains from killing any deer after lions enter the scene. Now human king of this New York jungle thanks to staying behind after the city was evacuated, Neville is not cast as villain but as military hero (who spares animals to instead hunt vampiric "Darkseekers"). Much as Neville's precision shooting and militarized body render him safe on the streets of the city, so too do the huge ships, planes, and helicopters that dominate the visual field in the evacuation scene suggest a well-honed military machine. In flashbacks to this evacuation, we learn Neville chose to stay behind in New York to research a cure, effectively becoming a mil-itary of one who will fight the vampire scourge. His status as military hero is further emphasized via a *Time* magazine cover on which he is featured in full military regalia and named as "Savior, Scientist, Soldier." Neville is, unlike the nation itself, impervious to vampire infection. Positioned as the savior of humanity, his closed and proper body stands in metonymically for the fortified borders sought by the U.S. after 9/11. In the film, such bor-ders are threatened by dark, infectious others, something Brayton reads as reinforcing "post–9/11 paranoia and anti-immigrant impulses" (74). Reading the adaptation as one that furthers reactionary sentiment, Bray-ton contends the film obfuscates its conservativism via its heroic black lead. This interpretation holds up given the movie's pervasive neoliberal sentiment wrapped in a desirable consumerist packaging wherein Nev-ille is just as much consummate consumer as he is military hero. With several scenes detailing his swanky brownstone, well-stocked kitchen, and not one, but two top-of-the line gym walkers (one for him, another for his dog), the movie is awash in desirable commodities. It also features scenes in which Neville visits a nearby video rental store, something that indicates that even after the apocalypse, Americans will be able to shop. Meanwhile, there is no reference in the diegesis regarding how Neville landed his prime real estate in central NYC on a military salary nor of how he came to prominence in the white dominated scientific field.

While Neville is positioned as an amalgam of scientific genius, mil-itary hero, and cool consumer, the women of the film are stereotypically cast. In a clip at the start of the film, one of the few female characters, Dr. Alice Krippin (played by Emma Thompson), is proudly discussing her discovery of a cancer vaccine on a televised news segment—the very one that will mutate and cause the viral siege. Furthering the notion women should stay out of science, this plot point also casts her as an overly confi-dent braggart with elements of the femme fatale, or the female who brings death. Along with Neville's wife and daughter, Dr. Krippin is removed from the narrative. This "active displacement of women," as Brayton deems it, is importantly a displacement of *human* females (73). Rather than sentient human women, the film features a female mannequins whom Neville flirts with, a female dog (Sam), and a female Darkseeker who lies unconscious in Neville's extremely well-appointed in-home laboratory. Here, the fact Neville's primary experimental fodder is a female Darkseeker cements women as objects to be moved around by the state (as when we see mothers and children being evacuated) or used in service of the state as virtual lab rats by men of science. Anna, the lone female character playing any significant role, enters the scene in the latter portion of the film and partially rectifies this male-fueled narrative. Replacing the character Ruth from the original novel, Anna is a Brazilian immigrant who (along with her son Ethan) is immune to the virus. Though she saves Neville from attacking Darkseekers partway through the film, she, by film's close, is cast as a damsel in distress saved by Neville (who rides her out of the city by way of a shiny SUV instead of a princely horse). In addition to positioning Anna as little more than a set piece (and having her see Neville as heroic in contrast to Ruth's viewing of him as ruthless killer and scourge in the novel), the female vampire Neville experiments on is also a damsel in distress figure. Lying dormant and bound to a gurney in Neville's basement laboratory for the entire film, she is ultimately rescued by her male vampire mate. Granted, her blood holds the cure to the mutated virus, but it is Neville's scientific dedication that has "infected" her blood and "invented" the cure. She is thus not so much a curative female body as an inert scientific experiment, one who is immobilized and unconscious in both the theatrical ending shown in cinemas and the alternative ending featured in the DVD.

In the theatrical ending, Neville locks himself, Anna, and her son Ethan in a fortified area of his lab. As the (male) vampire horde threatens to break in, Neville shouts through the glass "I can fix this, I can save everyone." When it is clear the lead (male) vampire does not believe him, Neville gives Anna a vial of the cured (female) vampire blood and instructs her to hide until dawn. He then detonates a grenade as he launches himself towards the gathered Darkseekers. Herein, his body acts as a sacrificial weapon that saves Anna, Ethan, and, by extension, all of humanity, something emphasized in the closing scene that shows a survivors' colony in Vermont. In voice-over, Anna says of Neville "he gave his life to defend [humanity] … we are his legacy … this is his legend." In a reversal of Matheson's original ending, Neville is not sentenced to death but cast as Christ-like. In the alternative ending of the 2007 film, Neville is also a savior figure, but one who survives. Stepping out of the secured glass area of the lab, he pushes the gurney containing the female vampire towards her male vampire mate. When the female vampire awakens, her mate transforms from murderous attacker into a romantic vampire prince, saving his vampire Snow White. As the reunited lovers nuzzle, Neville watches

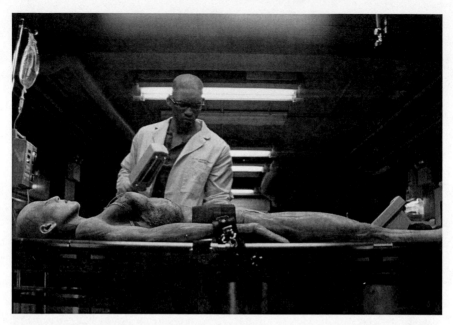

Robert Neville (Will Smith) inspecting the female Darkseeker (Joanna Numata) who serves as his experimental fodder in *I Am Legend* (Warner Brothers Pictures, 2007, directed by Francis Lawrence).

in amazement, realizing the Darkseekers are not the evil abominations he had presumed. Here, perhaps the loving vampire couple are meant to embody Bob Marley's "virologist idea" that "you could cure racism and hate ... by injecting love into people's lives" which Neville waxed poetic about earlier in the film. This ending softens Neville's gung-ho militarism, rendering him sympathetic to the Darkseekers' romance. Yet it also indicates the vampires chased Neville earlier in the film not due to bloodlust, but because they sought to rescue the female vampire he had abducted. While this ending humanizes the Darkseekers, it does not elevate the female vampire above the status of property to be bartered between Neville and her mate.

Importantly, both endings cast Neville as heroic. In the first, he gives his life to defend the human colony of survivors (one tellingly fortified by border walls); in the second, he returns his female captive to her vampire brethren, ending the battle between the two "races." This represents a departure from the original novel in which Neville is executed by the vampires aiming to form an improved society free of human violence. His famous last words from the novel, "I am legend," suggest not only will humans become the stuff of legend, but that he is not a "legendary hero," but rather a "terror to be destroyed" (159). In the 2007 adaptation, in contrast, in both the theatrical ending and the alternative ending, humanity survives *thanks to Neville*, framing him definitively as hero. In each version, the securing of national, racial, and gender boundaries/borders allows for a "happy ending." As such, this particular iteration of *Legend* accords with the conservative agenda of a strong military, strong border walls, and strongly demarcated concepts of what constitutes good Americans. That it does so via a black male lead is not a point of celebration—at least not in terms of how the casting obfuscates the film's regressive bent. By framing Neville as a hip, likeable hero, one played by a media darling and fan favorite, Will Smith, the adaptation hides its conservative underbelly with recourse to an uber-cool post–*Fresh-Prince-of-Bel-Air* aesthetic.

* * *

The majority of the texts discussed above feature vampires that offer visions of how we might, as put by Ted Preston, live lives "worthy of eternity" (165). Presenting vampires who bring down sexual predators, pedophiles, drug dealers, and bullies, who rally against the wider systems of patriarchy, white supremacy, heteromonogamy, and global capitalism, who refuse to accept slavery, imperialism, and socio-economic inequity, the narratives variously redefine what counts as a life worth living. In this regard, the political critique pervasive in zombie tales is arguably infecting the vampire canon.[18] Some of these politicized vampire engagements take rape culture to task, as with *A Girl Walks Home Alone at Night* and *The Passage*, and others feature vampires as champions for the marginalized—the enslaved, exploited, and bullied. Whereas some narratives draw on the viral vampire to challenge forces of the state, others utilize the creature to address personal trauma and the struggle to forge an ethical existence. In both the more sweeping societal critiques and those focusing on micro experiences within families, friendships, and romantic relations, the vampire *queers* dominant cultural logics. In contrast to the original framing of the vampire as a monstrous other threatening humanity witnessed in ur-texts like *Dracula*, 21st century tales repeatedly transform the figure, turning it into one with a thirst for justice, both personal and political.

3

Wicked Good

Witches of the New Millennium

"Unruly women are always witches, no matter what century we're in."—Roxane Gay

Although the witch as a figure is arguably harder to reclaim than either the zombie or the vampire for the precise reason witches are primarily coded female, many narratives are rewriting her horrific history, recasting her in the modern day, and sending her flying into a diverse range of texts across literature, film, and television. As yet another monstrous figure that refuses to die, the witch is often bifurcated into one of two camps—good or evil—as in the famous question posed to Glinda by Dorothy in *The Wizard of Oz*: "Are you a good witch or a bad witch?" Thankfully, the new millennium offers a plethora of witches who decline to live by the dictates of such restrictive binaries—who refuse good or evil and instead become wicked good. This feminist bent witnessed in recent witch texts will be the concern of this chapter. In the first section, four realist narratives—two of them set in Britain and two of them set in the United States—will be taken up in relation to the project of reclaiming the witch in (and for) history. The second section turns its focus to televised witches interested in smashing the patriarchy. In the third section, new iterations of fantasy and fairy tale witches in both film and fiction are considered. The fourth and final section discusses four films and one novel that revolve around witchy retribution.

Troubling the Witch

Accusations of witchcraft have plagued the globe on and off since the 14th century—even earlier if we include the ways women are cast as evil in religious texts, mythology, and lore. What was Lilith if not a witch that refused to bed down, missionary style, with Adam? Though witches arguably haunted the cultural imaginary most prominently between the years 1400 and 1800 (the height of the witch hunts), they currently inhabit the media and literary landscape in great number and variety. Just as many scholars have questioned why zombies have taken culture by storm, so too might we ask "Why witches? Why now?" Part of the answer certainly lies in the fact we are experiencing two contradictory impulses in relation to gender: on the one hand, a profound anti-woman, anti-feminist backlash, and, on the other, a heightened popularity and embrace of feminism and other social justice movements.

Given the witch has been deployed to denigrate women as well as to celebrate female empowerment and agency, it is no surprise the figure is looming large in our current era of gender trouble. Nor is it surprising— given the historical besmirching of feminism—that we are witnessing a heightened association between the feminist and the witch, something Kristin Sollee muses "might signal something deeper" in her 2017 book *Witch, Sluts and Feminists* (Loc. 1874). Calling the current era "generation witch," Sollee puts the witch in conversation with slut-shaming, rape culture, and liberatory feminist politics, framing language as a "spell" which through repetition can "transform intent into action" (Loc. 764–5). Such witchy theory is not unique to the present moment, however. Rather, Sollee's text contributes to the long-stranding feminist analysis of the witch. Suffragette Matilda Joslyn Gage, for example, insisted that misogyny drove the persecution of witches. Delineating the ways "witch" and "woman" are interchangeable constructions, Gage's theories informed those of her well-known son in law, L. Frank Baum, and his creation of the iconic good witch Glinda. Later along in the 20th century, as second wave feminism took culture by storm, the Women's International Terrorist Conspiracy from Hell, aka W.I.T.C.H., emerged as an important arm of the women's liberation movement.[1] Their first collective action involved a march on Wall Street so as to place a metaphorical hex on this linchpin of capitalism. Made up of a number of independent feminist groups active in the women's liberation movement, W.I.T.C.H. insisted feminism needed to encompass not just an attack on patriarchy, but on all systemic forms of oppression. Acting as a precursor to the now well established concept of intersectionality (one inaugurated by black feminist scholar Kimberlé Crenshaw), the organization held that in order to enact wider social change, they needed to aim their focus on all forms of inequity, not just those related to gender. Just as with the figure of the witch, who has been variously represented as dangerous seductress, old hag, Satan's minion, and so on, so too did W.I.T.C.H. have different guises. Changing the meaning behind the W.I.T.C.H. acronym to fit particular activist causes, e.g.,

"Women Interested in Toppling Consumer Holidays" and "Women In-censed at Telephone Company Harassment," the group grew largely out of socialist feminism and its dedication to revolutionary change. Drawing on guerrilla activist tactics, the group creatively used the witch figure and re-lated iconography to stage theatrical, attention-grabbing protests. Though some members went on to dismiss the impact and tactics of the group, they undoubtedly left a legacy in their witchy wake, one recently taken up in Portland, Oregon, in support of the Black Lives Matter movement and transgender rights, something Sollee argues "reaffirmed the witch's con-tinued role in feminist activism" (Loc. 768). Such positive deployments of the witch are also in evidence within the realm of governmental politics, as when Hillary Clinton supporters called themselves "Hags for Hillary" and donned "Witches for Hillary" buttons, or as when wiccan practitioners in the thousands united to perform a binding spell on Donald Trump. Gwen-dolyn Kiste, like Sollee, celebrates such acts, arguing combining the power of witchcraft with that of political activism has radical potential. "After all, during a protest, is chanting together not a form of magic spell, of hoping to change the world with the power of words?" she inquires. "It's not too late to reclaim our lost narratives," and "no longer ... accept the lies that have stripped us of our power," she asserts.

Alas, just as the witch is currently being deployed to support pro-gressive change, so too is the figure utilized to further misogynistic sen-timent. For example, Trump supporters decried Hillary Clinton as the "Wicked Witch of the Left." Bernie Sanders followers altered the "Feel the Bern" slogan to "Bern the Witch." Several prominent males have co-opted witch-hunt terminology to garner sympathy and/or outrage. For instance, Woody Allen claimed the sexual assault accusations against Harvey Weinstein have created "a witch hunt atmosphere" (West) while Don-ald Trump deemed himself, via twitter, the target of "the single greatest WITCH HUNT in American political history" (Bartash). Such usage is at odds with the usual deployment of the phrase, one which is associated with "hunting" those who threaten established authority. Further, pars-ing witch-hunt phraseology to condemn those attempting to bring about social justice while defending misogynistic, conservative, and capitalist impulses goes against the actual history—it was not those in power who bore the brunt of witch hunts (as Trump's and Allen's use of the phrase suggest), but most often the marginalized.[2]

Witch hunt history, though rendered inaccurately (if at all) in main-stream education and cultural memory, marks the witch as a uniquely monstrous figure—one that does not only haunt our pages and screens—but who was widely persecuted for over four centuries (and whose per-secution is undergoing a revival today in parts of Africa, India, and Saudi

Arabia).[3] Historically, calls to hunt the witch were solidified via the 15th century instruction manual for persecuting and killing witches *Malleus Maleficarum* (Latin for *Hammer of Witches*). Containing preposterous claims of witches gathering penises to keep them as disembodied pets, its tone is one of fire and brimstone. Widely disseminated thanks to the newly minted Gutenberg printing press, *Malleus* was instrumental in legitimizing the persecution of those accused of witchcraft. Significantly, it cemented the association between heretical practices, witchcraft, and the devil. Associating evil with women specifically, the screed based its allegations on women's supposed weaker nature and stronger propensity for lust. In addition to the religious underpinnings of texts like as *Malleus*, general societal shifts played a role in the persecution of those deemed witches, something cogently documented in Silvia Federici's *Caliban and the Witch: Women, The Body, and Primitive Accumulation*. Arguing witch-hunts were largely fueled by the transformation from feudalism to capitalism, Federici's work explores the connections between privatization (also known as the enclosure of the commons) and the solidification of key hierarchical systems related to gender, class, and race. As Federici details, for the top-down capitalist system to triumph, the relations that characterized the medieval world had to be destroyed. Among these were the views of humans' relation to the natural world, to each other, to their own bodies, and to their labor/work. As she and others document, women played a key role in various resistance movements and anti-enclosure struggles of the period. In response, the state fueled "a climate of intense misogyny that degraded all women" wherein the monstrosity of the woman/witch was intricately associated with the female body, its reproductive capacity, and its associations with nature, the healing arts, and the private/domestic world (Federici 48). Herein, Adrienne Rich's well-known quote regarding the female body as "the terrain on which patriarchy is erected" is particularly apt (55). The body of the witch is a specific construction of such terrain, one that sowed seeds of distrust within families and communities while promoting a distrust of women—even amongst women themselves.

Over-turning this historical designation of the witch as a variously dangerous, evil, destructive, and over-sexed, many millennial texts positively recast the figure. Ranging from narratives celebrating female power to ones that cogently attack the curtailing of reproductive justice, this "witch renaissance" encompasses myriad types of texts, including novels, films, short stories, television series, web series, graphic novels, and video games. More specifically, in keeping with Alice Hoffman's best-seller *Practical Magic*, which serves to, as Heidi Breuer puts it, "provide strategies for defending against, avoiding, or otherwise mitigating the aggressive violence of men," many recent narratives put the witch in conversation with male violence, sexual and otherwise (51). This is the case in historical novels such as *The Witchfinder's Sister* as well as fantastical, fairy tale infused texts like *Tender Morsels* and the 2014 film *Maleficent*. Dealing pointedly with rape culture, such narratives posit that the targeting of the witch is part of a continuum of violence fueled by the demonization of female power, the disparagement of female sexuality, and the construction of woman as rapeable object. This type of insistence is in evidence in *The Daylight Gate, The Diary of a Witch, American Horror Story: Coven, Sisterhood of Night*, and *All Cheerleaders Die*, all discussed in what follows. Myriad contemporary witch texts also condemn associations between evil and racial, sexual, and class based difference (as in *I, Tituba, Black Witch of Salem, Red Clocks, The True Story of Hansel and Gretel, A Secret History of Witches*, and *The Black Witch*). Focusing on the derision of the witch in various periods and locations, narratives of this ilk link the fear of the witch to patriarchal formations and capitalist imperatives. The witch is reviled, as numerous texts suggest, because she flouts societal norms, because she threatens male control of the family and industry, because she claims her body as her own. To begin our consideration of this wickedly appealing figure, let's turn to four contemporary realist-based narratives.

Section 1: Revising Witch History

A number of fictional books shine incisive light on the periods in which the witch-hunts occurred in both Europe and the United States. This is especially important given the documentation of witch-hunts comes from the persecutors, not the accused. Indeed, there are no primary sources penned by women (let alone women accused of witchcraft).[4] As such, narratives told from the female perspective provide a voice denied to women historically—something that accords with one of the acronyms of the second-wave feminist W.I.T.C.H. collective: "Women Inspired to Tell their Collective History." This sharing of witch history is enacted in Louisa Morgan's *A Secret History of Witches* as well as Beth Underdown's *The Witchfinder's Sister*. Novels set in more recent times, for instance, Alice Hoffman's *The Rules of Magic*, Ellen Herrick's *The Sparrow Sisters*, Mira Grant's *Into the Drowning Deep*, and Brunonia Berry's *The Lace Reader*, similarly shed sympathetic light on witches past and present. Such works turn the witch into a positive figure not deserving of persecution. Meanwhile, those who hunt the witch, whether figuratively or literally, are presented as villains. In fact, so many millennial era texts feature positive witch figures located in real world settings and epochs that discussing them all would be a book in itself. Rather than a summary overview of this corpus, in what follows I will focus on four novels that place willful witches in specific historical contexts. Through evocative tales that render the witch—and her persecution—all too real, these novels each depict sexism, violence against women, and the curtailing of reproductive rights as horrors spanning the centuries.

Alice Nutter and the Pendle Witch Trials: Rape as Witch-Hunt Weapon in *The Daylight Gate*

The Daylight Gate, by Jeanette Winterson, explores the Pendle Witch trials of 1612 with an emphasis on the gruesome acts carried out against those accused of witchcraft. Commissioned by Hammer (of horror film fame) to write a novel for their new imprint, Winterson delved into the religious, capitalist, and patriarchal underpinnings fueling the trials, incorporating various trademarks of Hammer horror along the way. Centered on Alice Nutter and the Pendle witches, the novel serves as a corrective to texts like the *Wonderfull Discoverie of Witches*, written by county clerk Thomas Potts in 1612. Potts, along with judges associated with Britain's infamous witch trials of the 17th century, sought personal career gain and royal favor from King James, who had himself authored *Daemonologie* in 1597, a dissertation that set out to justify the execution of women accused of witchcraft. According to Stephen Pumfrey, Potts and his ilk penned such works so as to "protect and advance their careers," at the cost of women's lives—something that adds credence to claims made by Federici, that the hunts were about solidifying and advancing male power (32). Though Winterson's novel adds supernatural elements and hallmarks of the horror genre to her take on this time in British history, her account is arguably more accurate in its portrayal of the power machinations—and sexual violence—informing the witch hunt era.

The opening of *Daylight Gate* introduces Alice Nutter. Based on the real historical figure, Alice serves as the protagonist. Depicted as a strong-willed, independent thinker, and sexual dissident, Alice protects those accused of witchcraft. Early on, she comes across two men raping a local woman, Sarah Device, in an attempt to coerce a confession she is a witch. Alice intervenes. Reminding them "The Magistrate decides what woman will be proved witches. Not the mob," she orders the men to untie Sarah (15). In response, the men endeavor to have Alice accused of witchcraft. They convince the area magistrate, Roger Nowell, to charge

Nutter. Significantly, he charges Alice not because he believes she is a witch, but because he holds a grudge against her for winning the lawsuit in which he claimed part of her land belonged to him. Here, the novel alludes to one of the impetuses for the larger witch-hunts that shaped the period: the fear regarding women's growing property rights. Alice, one of the women with such growing rights, is not of noble birth, which further raises the ire of local men. When she allows the Demdike family (who are assumed to be witches) to stay on her property, she is targeted by Nowell and eventually executed. Importantly, Winterson's account of this time and place presents witch trials and their resulting executions as a deliberate attempt to nullify resistant peasants, stamp out any religion other than Protestantism, and attack land-owning women like Alice. In her account, the real historical figure—Alice Nutter—becomes a hero, a self-made woman who sleeps with whom she pleases (she is depicted as bisexual), who has compassion for the poor, and who intervenes on behalf of sexual assault victims.

Incorporated into the tale are various hallmarks of horror: rats, severed heads, torture devices, cut-out tongues, purported deals with the devil. Such tangible frights act as manifestations of the more nebulous reign of terror against witches the text references. The female body is particularly targeted in these pursuits, something evidenced when the imprisoned Alice has metal spikes driven into her back. Bloody and blindfolded, she is led through a macabre dungeon, replete with thumbscrews, Iron Maidens, and dungeons. Her captors show her "the rat room," which is "piled with rats about three feet deep, eating each other," and gleefully explain how there are slots "where we can push through an arm or leg" (194). When her blindfold is removed, she witnesses a particularly brutal form of agony: a prisoner being skinned alive. To ease her resulting fears, her captors tell her, "We're not going to rape you," as if doing her a kindness (one that likely results from her status as a rich landowner) (194).

Framing rape as weapon utilized against poor females in particular, the text not only opens with a scene of attempted rape, but presents nine-year-old Jennet Device as a child born of rape. In her take on Jennet's life-story, Winterson depicts the lead accuser of the Pendle witches as a man who rapes Sarah Device over a matter of years, and then rapes the daughter born of those rapes, Jennet. Adding a rape-revenge twist to the close of the narrative, Winterson has Jennet retaliate against her father, something that provides welcome relief from some of the misogynist horrors the text documents. In the scene, Jennet is alone when she hears her father Tom break in. "She didn't want the hard thing tonight. She was sore," the text relates (207). When her father lunges at her, she dodges his advances, causing him to fall through the trapdoor that leads to the cellar.

Jennet then seals this door shut, sentencing Tom to death by starvation. Here, a young girl takes vengeance on her father and rapist, one who also is responsible for locking up her family on charges of witchcraft.

The execution scene similarly provides some catharsis via providing Alice with the ability to die on her own terms. As she and the Demdike women are prepared for hanging, the gathered mob throws "Cow dung and blood, urine, vomit and human feces" in their direction (219). In response, Alice holds her arms up towards the sky and shouts, causing the crowd to riot as they try to protect themselves from what they assume is the curse of a witch. Some of the assembled crowd are trampled to death, an ironic reversal. Meanwhile, Alice smiles and lifts her neck towards the heavens, calling her pet falcon to her. Understanding her request, the bird swoops onto her shoulders and severs her jugular vein. Herein, though condemned to death, Alice still finds a way to assert her agency, choosing to die via her familiar's beak instead of the executioner's noose.

The Witch's Pen: *Diary of a Witch*

Published just a few years after Winterson's novel, *Diary of a Witch* (*Diary*), by Colleen Passard, tells a similar historically inflected tale of female persecution. Set roughly within the same period of history in Scotland (rather than the North of England), the novel presents the story of Elspeth, a midwife charged with witchcraft. The diary, written as Elspeth awaits execution, details her life story and the persecution she endures while incarcerated within a small, frigid cell. Pervaded with rich historical particulars and a decidedly feminist undercurrent, *Diary* provides a corrective to the lack of women-authored works from the witch-hunt era. As with Winterson's narrative, the villains of the text are not the witches but their accusers. Some of the women featured in the novel are midwives and healers; others are battered wives, prostitutes, barmaids, peasants, and widows. By incorporating details of so many different women's lives, *Diary* frames witch persecution as part of the continuum of female oppression. Emphasizing the strangling of women's intellect wherein females had to hide any proof of being "quick of mind," *Diary* also characterizes marriage as a crushing system wherein "the tying of the nuptial knot" is described as akin to "the tightening of a noose around a woman's neck" (Locs. 79, 2323).

Painting a stark picture of Elizabethan times, the text details the pervasive misogyny that shaped the era as well as the poor working conditions, massive levels of poverty, and various diseases that marked one for death. Referring to *Malleus Maleficarum* as a "witch-hunter's manual birthed out of ignorance and fear," Passard's work unearths the religious, land, and labor battles that fueled witch-hunts. The novel, akin to the scholarly work of Federici, suggests the changing ideological landscape led to the vilification of women. For instance, in one scene from the novel, we witness Elspeth join a group of women workers in their protest against intolerable working conditions only to be threatened with "Fie on thee, witch! I'll have thee hanged!" In another scene, a woman is drowned for questioning a tax imposed on fishermen. As news of "gruesome tortures and human burnings" spreads, the women featured in the narrative come to realize that "without the presence of a man we were susceptible to attacks both on our virtue and our lives." These attacks force Elspeth and her mother to flee their home. Here and elsewhere, the novel links witch persecution to a wider pursuit to wrest power and property from certain segments of the female population (Locs. 818, 5225, 3424, 3545).

As Elspeth's story continues, an Elizabethan version of rape culture becomes apparent—one in which prostitutes are beaten and young girls commit suicide after being raped by their fathers. Elspeth is sexually assaulted as well, first by a wealthy aristocrat that gives her and her mother shelter and later when she is locked up awaiting trial after being accused of witchcraft. Refusing to confess despite undergoing an onslaught of barbaric provocation, Elspeth uses her final hours to write, proclaiming that her pen "like a sword, is drawn against this massacre of truth." Hoping her diary might help to cure the "patriarchal plague" and "poisonous pedagogy" of her era, Elspeth's voice offers vociferous resistance denied to women accused of witchcraft historically. Noting near the close of the tale that "[the] only justice I have left is in my pen," Elspeth sees her pen as a mighty weapon that just may bring an end to the "war of extermination" which she characterizes as one "waged against all passionate women." Significantly, Elspeth contends dualistic thought animates this war, naming "good/bad, right/wrong, light/dark, saint/sinner, misery/joy, God/Devil, Heaven/Hell, man/woman, pleasure/pain" binaries as undergirding the inequitable systems of her world. Arguing that "the fallacious thinking that splits the Oneness of everything into opposites" is one linchpin of inequity, Elspeth serves as an early incarnation of post-structural feminist thought, who, one imagines, would get along very well with the likes of Donna Haraway, Judith Butler, and Gloria Anzaldua (Locs. 317, 314, 3642, 3997–8).

Meanwhile, the detailing of the array of violence within the narrative as a whole furthers feminist claims that the female body is "the terrain on which patriarchy is erected" (Rich 55). Importantly, as the novel emphasizes, it is not only through torture and execution the female body is targeted, but also through everyday realities of the marriage system, the working world, and educational practices. Elspeth suffers because of all of these forces, as do many other women, including her mother and grandmother. Such cross-generational oppression allows patriarchy to remain "erect," something further witnessed in the fictional imagining of another historical witch proffered in a novel by Maryse Condé.

Rape, Lynching and Witchcraft: *I, Tituba, Black Witch of Salem*

I, Tituba, Black Witch of Salem (*I, Tituba*), though published some 30 years ago, is very applicable to the post-millennial canon this study takes as its focus, especially in regards to its foregrounding of the intersections between gender and race.[5] Angela Davis, in her foreword to the novel, contends the work is one of great political import that "furnishes Tituba with a social consciousness" (xi–xii). While details of Tituba's life are embellished by Condé, something necessitated via the scant details of her life, figures from the Salem witch trials provide a realist backdrop. Like Winterson, Condé uses historical facts to bolster a tale that fuses the natural and the supernatural in order to focus on gender and racialized inequity. Noting how gender intersects with "oppositions created by social class, education, ideology, and environment," Condé is clearly interested in giving voice to the matrix of oppressions that undoubtedly shaped Tituba's life.

The novel opens as Tituba's mother is raped on a slave ship headed for Barbados. Several years later, when another man attempts to rape her, Tituba's mother responds by striking him with a blade and is shortly thereafter hung for murder (8). After her mother's execution, Tituba is taken in by an old witch, Mama Yaya, and taught magical arts. Believing witches should be "cherished and revered rather than feared," Tituba is proud of this training (17). Alas, when she is sold to Samuel Parris and taken to Massachusetts, her association with witchcraft inaugurates her persecution. As a black woman, she is assumed to be one of the "visible messengers of Satan," because of the color of her skin, something emphasized when young Betsey Parris asserts "You're a Negress, Tituba! You can only do evil. You are evil itself" (65, 77).[6] Soon after Betsey's pronouncement, men wearing black hoods break into Tituba's quarters and pin her down. Functioning akin to a Salem era KKK, the men beat Tituba and penetrate her vagina with a sharp stick, taunting "Go on, take it" (91). After this attack, Tituba and other accused witches are shackled and taken to prison. While there, Tituba meets Hester from *The Scarlet Letter*. This intertextual "subversion of history," as scholar Ann Armstrong Scarboro calls it, places the novel in conversation with a classic heroine, one that, like Tituba, suffered due to her refusal to kowtow to norms of gender and religion (216). In a striking portrayal, Condé depicts Hester as a feminist witch figure and "yet another ... victim being branded as guilty" (98). In so doing, the novel offers a new take on Hester, imagining her as an ally to the historical figure Tituba and, in the process, equating the evils of sexism to those of racism.

Within the narrative, Tituba foresees that she will only be "a footnote in history," her story comprised of "a few lines in the many volumes written on the Salem witch trials" (xi, 149). Asking "Why was I going to be ignored? ... Is it because nobody cares about the Negress and her trials and tribulations? Is that why?," Tituba's enquiry prompts readers to question such historical silences and misrepresentations (149). Further, details of more and more slave ships arriving on American shores and references to "Indians ... wiped off the map and reduced to roaming the land that once was theirs" emphasize America as a country founded on enslavement and genocide (170). "Via an active, constitutive voice, Tituba leaps into history, shattering all the racist and misogynist misconceptions that have defined the place of black women" according to Davis' foreword (x). Within the novel, this enduring oppression is not only placed within the colonial and religious contexts of Tituba's era, but also linked to twentieth century persecution, as when Tituba is referenced as "strange fruit" and thereby connected to more recent lynching of African Americans.[7] These various elements shape the narrative's examination of the injustice of the Salem witch trials while giving intersectional attention to how sexism, racism, religion, and colonialism fueled them. *Re-presenting* Tituba as a trained, powerful, and rebellious magical woman, Condé, as argued by Kelli Randall, "critiques and ultimately rejects pejorative definitions of the word 'witch' in order to definitively give Tituba an identity as a life-giving sorceress."

Ending not with execution, but with Tituba's return to her Caribbean island home, the text is one of many that argues the witch does (and should) live on. Figuratively reborn once back on the island, Tituba is poised to rebel against the imperialist forces that have ravaged her homeland. Fittingly, her story in this iteration closes as she joins local revolutionaries in hopes of birthing a better future. In this regard, the novel feels far more relevant than the Fox television series *Salem* that ran from 2014 to 2017. In contrast to the sympathetic portrayal of Tituba that Condé's novel enacts, *Salem* depicts her as a duplicitous seductress. As critic Shoshana Kessock puts it, "Tituba's historical role as an African slave who was scapegoated and victimized by the white townsfolk is blatantly disrespected in this retelling of the witchcraft hysteria." In other words, *Salem* blames the witch figure rather than recuperating her. Thankfully, a bevy of texts counter this type of negative portrayal of witchy women, as does the novel taken up next.

Mending Reproductive Wrongs: *Red Clocks*

The 2018 dystopian novel *Red Clocks*, by Leni Zumas, consists of four intersecting narratives detailing the lives of Ro, a high school teacher and writer; Mattie, a teenager trying to end an unplanned pregnancy; Susan, an unhappy mother and wife; and Gin, a queer modern witch put on trial for a crime she didn't commit. Set on the Oregon coast in the near future, the novel's horror is not that of imagined monsters, but of draconian laws enacted by a "fetus-loving" president (Loc. 2254). As such, though set in the future, the novel is decidedly realist. Within the text, extreme anti-choice laws have made abortion illegal, outlawed in vitro fertilization, and rendered it impossible for single people to adopt with the "Every Child Needs Two" act. Clearly a fictional projection of terrors that may become all too real given the current cadre of politicians seeking to curtail reproductive freedom, *Red Clocks* is, as noted in *The Atlantic*, set in a United States "so familiar as to be almost unremarkable."

While the narrative arcs of all four main characters are intriguing for what they reveal about the ways female lives are circumscribed under current patriarchal powers, the one featuring Gin, a local witch known as "The Mender," is the most pertinent to this study. Descended from a line of magical women, Gin's *mending* remedies are described as "thousands of years in the making." Her potions, "fine-tuned by women in the dark creases of history," help heal wounds inflicted by abusive husbands as readily as they aid females in carrying out their reproductive choices (Loc. 832). Accused of medical malpractice for helping her girlfriend Lola, Gin is put on trial after providing Lola with a potion to heal a burn inflicted by her husband. Symbolically, this burning links Lola and Gin as similarly threatened—one by her husband, the other by a figurative witch-hunt. As the narrator imparts, "This predicament is not new. The mender is one of many. They aren't allowed to burn her … though they can send her to a room for ninety months" (Loc. 3161). Gin is found innocent in her trial, however, and returns to her cottage in the woods to continue with her "mending." Her time spent in court prevented her from aiding Mattie, however, a local teenager seeking Gin's help in terminating an unplanned pregnancy. This in turn results in Mattie's attempt to cross the "Pink Wall"—the Canadian border that now allows police to detain and forcibly test females suspected of being pregnant. After escaping arrest at the border, Mattie secures help from Ro, her high school teacher, who helps her find an underground feminist organization, a modern midwife-witch-collective of sorts.

Featuring a number of female characters harmed by gender norms, repressive laws, and heteromonogamous family imperatives, *Red Clocks* reflects all too real possibilities. It also hints that magic is more than just herbal remedies, as when Gin warns her prosecuting attorney about the true powers of witchcraft. Part of these powers, as we discover, comes from making potions from the bodies of the dead. For this purpose, Gin has kept her dead aunt's corpse in the freezer. Gin's mentor in the ways of witchcraft here continues to be a curative body, even in death. Moreover, by linking Gin's queer sexuality to her ostracization, the novel implies her isolation in a forest cabin may be not so much a choice as a necessity. The inhumane treatment Gin receives is further equated to the beached whales that lie dying on the shores of her Oregon locale, their decaying bodies evoking the toxicity of capitalism in massive mammalian form. Through these explorations of the ways the oppression of women ties to the ruin-ation of the natural world, this speculative work of fiction monsterizes ruling ideologies rather than the female body. Real-world challenges to fracking, pipelines, and nuclear power are figuratively challenged via the female bodies the novel features—ones which are harmed by the polic-ing of their sexual desires and reproductive capacities as much as they are by societal injustices. Characterizing this not-too-distant future as "a land-snatching, resource-sucking, climate-fucking imperialist machine," *Red Clocks* insists female persecution is the bedrock upon which patri-archal capitalism builds itself, framing the control of the planet and its resources as part and parcel of an exceedingly destructive continuum.

Section 2: Patriarchy Be Damned

As with the four texts discussed above, the witches to be examined in this section resist normative identity formations and ruling ideologies. Instead of drawing on individual figures from history (Alice Nutter, Ti-tuba) or specific historical contexts (17th century Britain, the near future U.S.), the chosen texts revolve around fictional witch families, covens, sisterhoods, and Wiccan collectives. In the two most recent narratives, *The Chilling Adventures of Sabrina*, the 2018 *Charmed* reboot, there is an overt focus on gender inequity. Framing witchcraft as a patriarchy-busting practice, the narratives have light, comedic tones and scripts featuring knowing winks to popular culture. Though more serious in tone, *Penny Dreadful*, *Coven*, and *Sisterhood of Night* similarly broach issues of feminist import while the campy teen-flick from Lucky McKee, *All Cheerleaders Die*, fuses the witch with the zombie in order to eviscerate the male gaze and the rape culture it fosters. Admittedly, some of the featured witches in these narratives quite happily use witchcraft for selfish—sometimes extremely violent—purposes (as with Fiona, the "Supreme Witch" of *Coven*)—but the majority of the magical women use their powers in service of subverting dominant paradigms. Though set in a range of locations and time periods, the narratives share a common message: the persecution of witches stems from a prejudicial logic that aims to oppress all those deemed a threat to so-called order. Rather than castigating witches and witch-identified women for their "wickedness," the texts analyzed in the forthcoming section instead point to sexist, racist, ageist, classist, and heteronormative formations as forces of evil.

The Willful Witches of *Penny Dreadful*

John Logan's *Penny Dreadful*, which aired on Showtime from 2014 to 2016 in a three-season arc, courted critical acclaim and a dedicated fan base. An intertextual smorgasbord drawing on *Frankenstein*, *Dracula*, *The Picture of Dorian Gray* and *The Strange Case of Dr. Jekyll and Mr. Hyde*, the Gothic infused series puts various characters and figures from classical horror in conversation with one another. For my purposes here, what I am most interested in is how the show rectifies the absence of witches (and women) in the classical horror texts it takes as inspiration—ones which are primarily driven by male characters and monsters. As I will offer a more extended analysis of *Penny Dreadful* in Chapter 4 in relation to female monstrosity, I will touch on it only briefly below, doing so to highlight how it deploys the figure of the witch via Vanessa Ives and Joan Clayton as well as through the depiction of "Daywalker" and "Nightwalker" witches (the former being witches of the herbalist/midwife variety and the latter those who act in consort with the devil).

In one of the primary story arcs, Vanessa, the lead female protagonist, is reluctant to acknowledge her magical abilities as she views them as a sign she is cursed. Presented as possessed and/or insane for much of the three seasons, Vanessa undergoes exorcisms, imprisonment within mental institutions, and bodily persecution (including forced feeding, electric shock therapy, water torture, and trepanning). The seeming linchpin for bringing about "the eternal night"—the series' terminology for an apocalyptic shift that would allow for demonic forces to overtake the world—Vanessa is targeted by vampires, demons, malevolent Egyptian gods, as well as by the devil-serving Nightwalker witches. Believing her psychic powers, fluency in "verbis Diablo" (the language of the devil), spell-casting abilities, and monster-hunting prowess mark her as demonic, Vanessa suffers a great deal of self-loathing. Rather than blaming the Victorian mind-set that casts powerful witchy women such as herself as a threat to order, she instead chastises herself. Sometimes trying to pray-away her proclivities and other times giving in to the powers these abilities afford, she is ultimately a sympathetic character whom the series presents as hampered by the strictures of late-Victorian society. Vanessa is linked to a witch hailing from the 16th century, Joan Clayton, an herbal practitioner and skilled sorceress who helps the poor and downtrodden, particularly women seeking abortions, which affords her the nickname "the Cut Wife." Living on land in Ballantrae Moor given to her centuries ago by Thomas Cromwell, her narrative arc nods to the import of being granted land when the enclosure of the commons was pauperizing whole swathes of Britain.

Through her dealings with Joan, who trains her in the ways of witchcraft, Vanessa learns to embrace her "ungodly" difference. Insisting that "people in this world hate what is not them ... fear all they don't know ... hate themselves most of all for being weak, for being old, for being everything all together that is not godlike," Joan calls upon Vanessa to

Vanessa (Eva Green) holding a knife to Sir Geoffrey's (Ronan Vibert) throat after he threatens to rape her in the first season of *Penny Dreadful* (Showtime, 2014–2016).

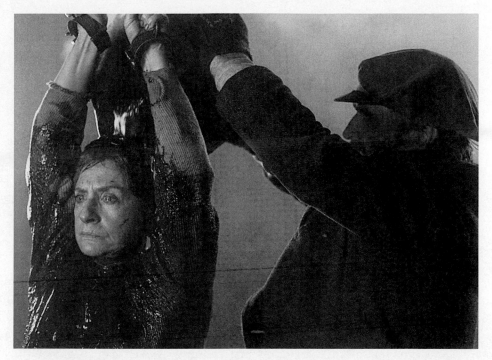

The Cut Wife (Patti Lupone) being prepared for execution in *Penny Dreadful* (Showtime, 2014–2016).

embrace her powers. The rhetorical question she poses to Vanessa, "Monsters all, are we not?" asserts the divide between the monstrous and the non-monstrous does not hold. Together, the two form a willful witch duo who use their magic in patriarchy-defying ways.

One of their primary targets is Sir Geoffrey Moore, a man intent on amassing wealth and violating women. First threatening to rape Vanessa and then instigating Joan's execution, Sir Geoffrey is an apt embodiment of misogynist sentiment and aristocratic hubris. Notably, his narrative arc reflects capitalism's reliance on the designation of women as witch, something that accords with Silvia Federici's claims about the figure. Though Frankenstein creatures and vampires are more prominent than witches in the series, the story arcs of Vanessa and Joan importantly recast the witch as a progressive force railing against the inequities patriarchy fosters.

The Semi-Woke Witches of *American Horror Story: Coven*

American Horror Story: Coven features modern-day witches living in New Orleans. Over the course of thirteen episodes, the third season of the *AHS* franchise engages with New Orleans history, the slave system, the Salem witch-hunts, and post–Katrina Louisiana. Set primarily at Robicheaux Academy, a school for witches, *Coven* centers on mother and daughter witch-duo "The Supreme" (Fiona Goode, played by Jessica Lange) and her daughter, the headmistress of the academy (Cordelia, played by Sarah Paulson), and their cadre of student witches—Madison, Nan, Zoe, and Queenie. Two other primary characters, each based on figures from New Orleans' past, Marie Laveau (a "Voodoo Queen" played by Angela Bassett), and Delphine LaLaurie (an infamous murderess played by Kathy Bates) round out the narrative. Instead of furthering the notion of witches as demonic as does the recent Fox series *Salem*, *Coven* presents witches as chosen women born with special powers. These powers, however, provide abilities easily misused. Although the witches of *Coven* commit various wicked acts (including murder), their wickedness pales in comparison to the horrors of racism and sexism the series engages with. Widely lambasted for what critics deemed problematic depictions of women of color, *Coven* admittedly treads a precarious line between critiquing racism versus furthering stereotypical racialized tropes. This season of *AHS* nevertheless manages to put race in conversation with gender in ways that show the enduring power of white supremacy and misogyny, something that makes it, in my estimation, more "woke" than some viewers claim.

Opening with an episode featuring Delphine LaLaurie, *Coven* houses its deployment of the witch in historical legacies of bodily torture. The initial scenes feature LaLaurie holding a party in her palatial home circa 1834. After we hear her attempt to auction off her daughters to assembled male guests, the narrative cuts to LaLaurie in front of her bedroom mirror. With her fierce visage taking up the entire frame, she vigorously paints blood on her face. Reminiscent of the evil queen from Snow White and her magic mirror, LaLaurie draws not on magic but on white privilege to "milk" slaves imprisoned in her attic as she believes their blood can render her aging face youthful. Concerned with her husband's roving eye as much as with her aging appearance, LaLaurie soon accepts a potion from voodoo-practitioner Laveau. Though Laveau claims her potion will ensure fidelity on the part of LaLaurie's husband, it instead renders LaLaurie unable to die. Herein, Laveau takes revenge on LaLaurie for her disfigurement of Bastian, Laveau's lover. While this narrative arc between Laveau and LaLaurie embellishes historical facts, LaLaurie brutal torture of slaves is based in reality. So too is Laveau based on the infamous voodoo queen, one who worked as a healer, led occult ceremonies, and, as in *Coven*, was a sought after hairdresser catering to white and black clientele alike. Framing these two women from history as immortal, the show brings them vividly to life in modern New Orleans. Whereas LaLaurie is resurrected by supreme witch Fiona to become a servant at Robicheaux Academy, Laveau runs a hair salon in the 9th ward. Unfortunately, in its depiction of Laveau, the series relies heavily on the representation of voodoo as a "dark art" associated with snakes, zombies, demons, and sacrifice (including of babies). It also presents Laveau as harboring an undying prejudice against Fiona's coven and the "white magic" they represent. These factors, along with the ways her character accords to the "angry black woman" stereotype, rightly garner the show criticism.

In addition to its admittedly flawed engagement with race and racism, *Coven* also interrogates female beauty imperatives, obsessions with fame/power, constructions of female sexuality as evil, and the pervasiveness of sexual violence. Fiona is most pertinent in regards to the first, beauty imperatives. Ruthless in her pursuit of power, status, and a youthful appearance, Fiona is introduced in the first episode by way of a plot point emphasizing her willingness to do anything to prevent aging. Having traveled to Los Angeles to seek out the scientist she paid to develop an age-reversing serum, Fiona learns the serum won't be ready for two more years. Insisting she cannot wait, Fiona drains the life from the scientist, consuming his youth in a vampiric form of age-defiance. After doing so, she gazes admiringly at her revitalized face in the mirror. But her skin quickly wrinkles and sags. In her resulting fit of rage, Fiona smashes every mirror in sight. Unwilling to live without the "beauty and influence she has curated and leveraged throughout her life" she serves, as Erin Harrington argues, as an "articulation of the toxic veneration of normative female sexuality," a veneration dependent on the young and beautiful female body (262). Fiona's lust for youth continues to play a role throughout the season, even prompting her to contemplate sacrificing babies in order to secure immortality. She also kills Madison, a young starlet and witch, and chases vitality through a dangerous affair with the Axeman, a serial killer. Reluctant to give up her role as supreme witch, Fiona is power-hungry, vengeful, and exceedingly vain. Primarily a wicked character, she is ruthless in her dealings with her daughter Fiona, pits the witches of Robicheaux Academy against one another, and refuses to follow the dictates of the ruling Witch Council. As a character who "conflates youth, beauty, and desirability with raw power," Fiona, akin to LaLaurie, takes particular pleasure in having power over others (Harrington 261).

Fiona's wickedness is echoed in Madison, the Robicheaux witch-in-training who is similarly obsessed with beauty and acclaim. Early on, we see Madison kill a Hollywood director when he scolds her for missing a cue. Enslaved to notions that beauty equals power for women, Madison's wickedness is linked to her vacuous, celebrity status. Like Fiona, she covets power and is willing to harm others to get it. Yet, the audience is encouraged to sympathize with Madison's enslavement to beauty norms, norms that are also shown to court violent male desire. In Madison's case, said violence occurs first at a college party and later via the Robicheaux butler. Regarding the first incident, when Madison attends a fraternity party with fellow witch-in-training Zoe, she is deemed "prize tuna" by one of the frat brothers in attendance who ultimately drugs her and orchestrates her gang rape. Kyle, apparently the lone fraternity member with a conscience, intervenes. Evidently, Madison's power was not able to prevent sexual assault (something that alludes to "untouchable" hegemonic male power). After her rapists retreat to their waiting party bus, Madison emerges from the frat house and uses telekinesis to crash the departing bus, killing her attackers in a fire-fueled act of rape revenge. Herein, she is able to avenge the violence done to her but not prevent it (much like the many avengers populating the rape revenge genre). Following her rape, Madison feigns normality. As she sits crying and bruised in a bathtub, she narrates,

> I am a millennial. They call us the global generation. We are known for our entitlement and narcissism. Our one defining trait is our numbness to the world, our indifference to suffering. Hell, I was gang raped. Two days later, I was back in class like nothing happened.

Despite these claims, Madison is clearly traumatized by the sexual violence she experiences. Eventually murdered by Fiona, she is also sexually violated by Spalding, the Robicheaux butler who absconds with her corpse, moving it to his upstairs quarters. Dressing her up like a doll to fuel his sexual fetishes, Spalding's acts serve as a continuation of the violence Madison experienced while alive.

Although the witches of the series sometimes use their magic to inflict harm, they generally do so in response to wrongs wrought by patriarchy, white supremacy, and top-down systems of power. Exploring the way women are associated with wickedness through the figure of the witch and then interrogating this conflation, *Coven*'s "evil" women are driven to their acts via the social systems in which they must function. Herein, as Harrington argues, the show provides "a subversive challenge to misogynistic accounts of female worth and value" (20). Moreover, through what Harrington names "some of the most interesting and nuanced representations of older women in horror," the show importantly undercuts the far more common representation of aging women as undesirable, no longer sexually viable, and waning in intellect (258). With Jessica Lange, Angela Bassett, Kathy Bates, and Frances Conroy making up the cast of witches, all of whom are in their 60s and 70s, *Coven* features vibrant, intelligent, witty older women that exude agency, sexual and otherwise. In addition to its refreshing incorporation of actresses across the age spectrum, the series points to the ways gender, race, class, body-image, (dis)ability and geographic location all intersect to inform women's life experience. Linking witch bodies burned at the stake to black bodies forced into slavery, suggesting violence against women shares commonalities with violence done to the planet and its creatures, and highlighting "non-normative" bodies as ones which matter, *Coven*—though not an unabashed feminist triumph—is definitely a witch show worth watching.[8]

Covens Are Doing It for Themselves: *Sisterhood of Night* and *All Cheerleaders Die*

Sisterhood of Night and *All Cheerleaders Die* each feature witch figures in relation to our current social-media, selfie-obsessed age—*Sisterhood* to castigate cyber-bullying and sexual assault and *Cheerleaders* to mock the toxic-jock and appearance-obsessed culture perpetuated in the to-be-seen high school world. While *Sisterhood* circulates around teens deemed wicked due to the witch-infused rituals they perform, *Cheerleaders* features a group of females who seek vengeance against the jocks that did them wrong. Sharing a common focus on the invasive gaze levied at females, both films present witchy young women actively subverting norms of gender and sexuality, sometimes murderously so.

Sisterhood, a 2014 independent film adapted from a short story by Steven Millhauser and directed by Caryn Waechter, centers on a group of outcast female friends. Mary, the most overtly rebellious, creates a makeshift coven in response to the frustrations she experiences with high school culture. Defying dress codes and refusing to take part in the popularity contests her peers deem so important, she (shock, horror, gasp) eschews social media. Taking to photography instead, her female gaze refutes the bodily surveillance females undergo as readily as it does the policing news cameras intent on framing her sisterhood as an evil coven. Though they are mainly interested in sisterly solidarity (much of which is carried out at night in the forest), the fact Mary and her coven cohorts insist on keeping their group secret courts ire from the community. They are not, in other words, allowed to keep secrets in a world that frames their bodies as public fodder nor, of course, to cavort in the night without boys or parents to "protect" them. Set in a media-saturated world much like our own, their antics spark gossip and eventual hysteria (fueled by salacious news coverage as well as a jealous classmate's popular blog).

A modern retelling of Miller's *The Crucible*, *Sisterhood* positions news and internet media as fueling the contemporary witch-hunt that infuses the film. Opening with voice-over narration that informs the audience "It was in an atmosphere of furious accusation and hysterical rumor that this story takes place," the movie repeatedly circles back to news coverage of the sisterhood. In so doing, it emphasizes news media as a prurient force more intent on garnering audience attention than investigative journalistic pursuits. Internet culture is also indicated as a similarly negative rumor mill. When a classmate's blog inadvertently becomes an online meeting ground for women to share their stories about abortion, sexual assault, and bullying, the positive potential of the medium is made clear. Most evocatively, in a pivotal story arc in which a shy member of the sisterhood, Lavinia, is targeted by a group of sadistic teens, interconnections between real world violence and cyber violence are highlighted. In this sub-plot, a few female schoolmates target Lavinia. First convincing Travis, the boy she has a crush on, to invite her to a Halloween party, they then foment a plan to catch her on film in an incriminating act. Travis thus asks her to leave the party and go into the woods with him, where, unbeknownst to her, the other girls are filming. Feigning interest in her, Travis asks her to remove her top. Though the full extent of what occurs is never made clear, the resulting video captures a topless Lavinia in the forest, wearing a Halloween witch hat while shouting "No!" and begging to be let go. Lavinia is understandably traumatized when the group posts the footage online. Not long after this incident and its subsequent online airing, Lavinia takes her own life, chewing up pills like trick-or-treat candy. Here, the emphasis on the filming and broadcasting of the violence done to Lavinia echoes the mean-spirited news coverage of the sisterhood. One way to redress such negative media and online culture, the narrative suggests, is the creation of safe online and real-world spaces for females to share their histories of abuse as well as their culturally induced self-hatred. Framing such spaces as modern covens, *Sisterhood* closes with a throng of young women defiantly dancing down the street in wild costumes of their choosing. Via this updated version of "taking back the night," the film closes by celebrating the willful, lived female body rather than the mediated, digital self.[9]

All Cheerleaders Die, directed by Lucky McKee, is similarly critical of school culture and its fostering of mean-spiritedness. One of a number of recent contemporary teen horror forays that Martin Fradley argues reflect the gender inequities faced by females, *Cheerleaders* plays with notions of female wickedness through a delightfully wicked group of characters—a lesbian wiccan practitioner, a would be documentarian that uses her camera to castigate the school and its prurient culture, and a bevy of "slutty" cheerleaders. Opening with a film within a film that consists of lead character Maddy's footage of a typical student day, we are led to view high school as a place for females to "look hot" so as to secure the interest of male students and teachers alike. At first documenting the vacuous conformity of high school life and the mind-numbing lack of education therein, Maddy's film soon moves from halls and classrooms to the football field where her camera captures her friend Lexi's limb twisting death—the result of a cheerleading stunt gone horribly wrong. After said death, Maddy is enraged when Terry, Lexi's star football player boyfriend, quickly supplants his now dead girlfriend with another cheerleader. In order to be better positioned for revenge, Maddy infiltrates the cheerleader/football social circle. Later in the film, we will learn this endeavor was fueled by the fact Terry attempted to rape her after Lexi died. Before we learn this important bit of history, however, we watch as Maddy successfully tries out for the cheer team, one which she knowingly frames as "out of her league" due to her low socio-economic status. Donning the guise of "hot rich heterosexual girl" though she is actually a working class lesbian, Maddy's invasion into the echelons of high school popularity soon find her attending a jock party.

At the alcohol-infused gathering, Terry punches his new girlfriend in the face, knocking her to the ground. Violence quickly escalates among the group, pitting cheerleaders against jocks in what ultimately becomes a fight to the death—one that comes about as a result of jock versus cheerleader car chase. In the resulting crash, the car full of cheerleaders is launched into a roadside river. As luck would have it, Leena, Maddy's ex-girlfriend and a practicing Wiccan, witnesses the accident. Still harboring a torch for Maddy, Leena climbs down to the river bank only to find Maddy and the other cheerleaders dead. Casting a spell to save her ex-girlfriend, she unwittingly reanimates the entire group. Once reawakened, the teens morph into flesh-hungry creatures with heightened sex drives. Soon dispatching a lewd man to satiate their newly undead hunger, they proceed to deploy their hot-zombie-witch-bods to teach the prurient males populating their high school some lessons. Principally targeting the football players who are all too eager to "cash in" on the pleasure their reanimated bodies promise, this "coven of hungry succubi," as one reviewer calls them, sends-up various female tropes—the vapid cheerleader and the femme fatale prime among them (Seibold). Similar to *Jennifer's Body* (discussed in Chapter 4) the narrative joyously skewers female stereotypes and, though campy, has a decided undercurrent of rightful feminist rage. The movie, which "cycles from indie romance, to feminist polemic, to genuine horror, to horror satire, to titillating B-picture," closes on a gloriously bloody battle between the cheerleader witches and soon-to-be-dead jerkish jocks

(Seibold). After Maddy dispatches Terry, her would-be rapist, she rides off via motorcycle with her ex-girlfriend Leena in a triumph of Wiccan lesbian love. Part of a growing canon of teen horror films taking on gender inequity in deliciously unique ways, *Cheerleaders'* fun-fueled gore glee-fully castigates the dark side of high school. Two other witchy television series proffer similar takes on coven-culture, each also circulating around young females and "gendered discontent."

Witches Rebooted: *Chilling Adventures of Sabrina* and *Charmed*

The Netflix original series *Chilling Adventures of Sabrina* is a wick-edly fun watch. Focusing on the half-mortal, half witch Sabrina Spellman as she navigates the tricky terrain of teenage life, the show positions itself as in conversation with feminism and the "witch sisterhood."[10] As schooled in horror as she is in witchery, Sabrina is described as "nuts" for monster movies—so too is show runner Roberto Aguirre-Sacasa and author of the *Sabrina* comics, as is made apparent via the show's many nods to the hor-ror canon.[11] From the hay maze that invokes the famous icy end met by Jack Torrance in *The Shining* to the demon-possessed uncle who spews green vomit redolent of Regan from *The Exorcist*, the series incorporates myriad scenes that reference iconic films. Set pieces and visuals further add to the horror homage the show enacts, as with the puzzle box Sabrina solves, unwittingly unleashing a demon (a plot point echoing Clive Bark-er's *Hellraiser*), Sabrina's attack by birds (a Hitchcock nod), or the heavy reliance on red costuming (as witnessed in classics such as *Suspiria* and *Rosemary's Baby*).

Such references are inaugurated in the first few moments of the pilot episode. Opening as Sabrina and friends watch a screening of *Night of the Living Dead*, the pilot cues savvy viewers to expect a deliciously intertex-tual show. Even more rewarding for the horror fan, the teens soon discuss *Night* at the local bookstore-cum-coffee-shop. Naming the film as only nominally about zombies, the friends deem Romero's classic as a medita-tion on war, civil rights, and the nuclear family's demise.

Season two is also informed by a myriad of horror references. In one scene, Theo (formerly Susie) is bullied in a high school locker room after making his trans identity public—a sequence that calls to mind similarly fraught scenes in classics such as *Slumber Party Massacre* and *Carrie*. In another, a sheet-clad creature passes itself off as a ghost bringing to mind the infamous scene from *Halloween* in which Michael disguises himself as a ghost. Adding to the intertextual feel are verbal quips (as when Ambrose

Sabrina (Kiernan Shipka) of *Chilling Adventures of Sabrina* (Netflix, 2018–) wearing a red dress like that worn by Rosemary (Mia Farrow) in *Rosemary's Baby* (Paramount Pictures, 1968, directed by Roman Polanski).

approaches a pensive Sabrina with "a Penny Dreadful for your thoughts" variety) and numerous name-checks to the genre—Ambrose Bierce, Faustus Blackwood, Shirley Jackson and Daniel Webster among them.

The narrative arc of the first season charts Sabrina's decision regarding whether or not to go through her "dark baptism" on her pending 16th birthday, one in which she is expected to sign her soul over to the devil, or, as he is termed in the show, the Dark Lord. As Sabrina informs the audience in voice over narration in the pilot, she must "choose between two worlds: the witch world of her family, and the human world of her friends." Ultimately, Sabrina, a character heavily doused with feminist chutzpah, resists normative expectations of both worlds, each of which are decidedly patriarchal. In addition to navigating relationships with her boyfriend Harvey, her best friends Roz and Susie, her cousin Ambrose, and her aunts, Zelda and Hilda, Sabrina fights the feminist good fight against bullies, ineffectual school principals, and the duplicitous Faustus Blackwood, high priest of the Church of Night. Her battle against evil continues in the second season, one that finds her battling the misogyny of the warlock movement and fighting the religious hypocrisy of the so-called "Order of the Innocents."

Season one, set more in the human world, presents Sabrina's high school as decidedly hellish (à la *Buffy*). When one of her best friends is deemed an "abomination" and "sick girl-boy" by a gaggle of "troglodyte football players," Sabrina vows to take on such "Puritanical masculinity," deeming patriarchy as the foundational devil informing such acts. To address this malady and its effects, she proposes a club for young women, to, as her friend, Roz, puts it, "topple the white patriarchy." Naming the aims of their intended club as to "come up with proactive solutions.... To mobilize and protest if we need to get political, to fight when we need to fight, to defend each other," they dub their organization WICCA, The Woman's Intersectional Cultural and Creative Association. In addition to battling deleterious gender norms, WICCA takes up the cause of banned books and the "fascism afoot at Baxter High" that results in classics like Toni Morrison's *The Bluest Eye* being removed from library shelves. Via these allusions to consciousness raising groups of second wave feminism and the second-wave feminist organization W.I.T.C.H., the show grounds itself not only in the horror genre, but also within feminist ideology.

In addition to trying to foment change in the real world, Sabrina challenges witch world norms. Somewhat akin to Hermione Granger and her fight for house elves, Sabrina insists picking a familiar from a catalog of choices is dehumanizing, proposing instead that a familiar choose her. Later, after Salem approaches her in the woods and she brings him home, her aunt Zelda is aghast. "You'd rather a feral familiar than one bred for service," she rebukes, to which Sabrina replies, "Salem doesn't serve me, Aunt Zee. We're in a partnership. He'll protect me, I'll protect him." As for balking the expectations related to her dark baptism, Sabrina questions why she should remain a virgin, noting she has "reservations about saving myself for the Dark Lord." A so-called "half-breed," Sabrina refuses to cut off relationships with her human friends. As with her familiar Salem, whom she treats as an equal, Sabrina looks upon humans not as inferior, but as kindred creatures, regardless of their race, sexuality, class, and so on. Most significantly, she refuses to accept the notion she must give up her freedom so as to be granted power from the Dark Lord, asserting instead "I want both. I want freedom and power." Revealing her own views on gender, her aunt Zelda replies, "He'll never give you that ... he's a man." Faustus, the Dark Lord's minion, proves this to be true, telling Sabrina that if she signs the "Book of the Beast," she is swearing "to obey without question." Sabrina, in keeping with her character, refuses this expectation, choosing to run full speed from the "dark baptism" that would render her full witch (and a servant of Satan). Rather than choose the witch world as expected, she proclaims she will follow "another path ... a third way" in a markedly feminist, queer declaration. After being accepted into the Academy of Unseen Arts despite her choice to remain half-human, her cousin promises her she will meet "witches and warlocks from all over the world," many of whom, he promises, "will be hot." She retorts "I'm not going to the academy to hook up.... I am going to the academy to learn how to defeat the Dark Lord. I'm going to learn how to conjure him, bind him, banish him. That's my only agenda" And what a patriarchal smashing agenda it is.

The witches of CW's *Charmed* share a similar feminist agenda. The original series, which first aired in 1998 and ran for eight seasons, also took on gender inequality. However, as documented in a post from *The Marie Sue*, the content was generally played for laughs and included "very little outside the cliché and obvious." Although it's too early to tell if the reboot will ultimately end up taking feminism more seriously, so far this new iteration has broached the #MeToo movement, sexual harassment, rape culture, cis-heteronormativity, and the necessity of boots on the ground activism. In their promotional materials for the show, CW names the show a "feminist reboot" in which the featured witches are not only interested in "vanquishing supernatural demons ... and maintaining familial bonds" but in "tearing down the patriarchy." Kelsea Stahler of *Bustle* agrees, deeming the show refreshingly more intersectional and less chaste than its predecessor. Lauding the reboot's treatment of sex as "just another part of life," she enthuses of *Charmed*, "it's basically as if witchcraft, the CW, and a women's studies class had a fantastically entertaining lovechild."

In this post-millennial re-take on *Charmed*, the three charmed ones are witches of color. Maggie, the youngest, is an undergraduate and sorority hopeful. Middle sister Mel is a lesbian graduate student and ardent feminist. Maggie, the oldest sister, is a genetic scientist. Their mother, Marisol, chair of the university women's studies department, is killed in the pilot episode under mysterious circumstances after aiding a young woman with charges of sexual harassment against a tenured white male professor. On the phone as the pilot opens, Marisol asserts, "This is not a witch hunt. It's a reckoning, and I want him out!"[12] The "he" she refers to is Professor Thaine, who is protesting his academic suspension. The insinuation their mother was killed at least partly as a result of her outspoken condemnation of Thaine is what inaugurates the sisters into their charmed role as witches. That their mother is replaced with a white cisgender male department chair (something Mel vociferously protests) not only alludes to entrenched privilege, but also accords with post-gender-essentialist thought given this particular cis male is a feminist who has "been published twelve times by respected feminist journals and re-tweeted by Roxane Gay." As it turns out, he is also "an advisor to witches," otherwise known as a White-lighter.

With narrative arcs dealing with growing up POC in a white-privileged world, the justifiable fear of police, the importance of consent, and work-place harassment, the true demon of the 2018 *Charmed* world, is, as Stahler puts it, "the patriarchy, straight up." In contrast to the original show, which limited the sisters' agency and associated them primarily with domesticity, romance, and self-sacrifice, the reboot—at least thus far—places the three witches in relation to ills of the contemporary world—sexism, homopho-bia, racism, and rape culture among them.[13] No longer does the sisters' magic mainly circulate close to home (and to romantic pursuits)—instead, it is tied specifically to social unrest and housed largely within the familiar world of Trump-merica. This, as well as the fact their mother was wom-en's studies chair up until her untimely demise, places the academic arm of feminism in conversation with the contemporary witch revival—a magical move to be sure. Along with *Sabrina, Charmed* contributes to the witch re-naissance that is taking both film and televisual landscapes by storm. One is set in a colorful admixture of old and new (of the moment references colored with '50s fashion and old school cigarette holders), the other is located in a university town replete with dorms, sorority houses, and coffee shops. Both lean more towards the comic than horrific, but both also fea-ture their fair share of demons and other beasties. *Sabrina* and *Charmed* sometimes overdo it in their knowing winks to popular culture, yet their takedowns of the patriarchy nevertheless roil with real-world issues.

Section 3: Post-Millennial Fantasy and Fairy Tale Witches

Populated with various monstrous figures, the fairy tale is oft infused with elements of horror. Likewise, the horror canon quite regularly draws upon fairy tale imagery and motifs, something witnessed, for example, in Guillermo del Toro's *Pan's Labyrinth* and the more recent M. Night Shyamalan film *The Visit*. Alison Littlewood names fairy tales "the first horror stories"—ones she notes are populated with willful characters such as Little Red Riding Hood. Sue Short takes a similar view in her book *Misfit Sisters*, declaring "fairytales are an integral influence upon horror" (5). Noting that both genres "have been claimed as reactionary in their intentions yet radical in their possibilities," Short laments how often horror upholds traditional gender norms—a sentiment Littlewood shares (11). The current flowering of fairy-tale imbued horror leans more towards "radical possibilities." Building on the established tradition of revisioning fairy tales for feminist purpose, the arguably witchy mothers of which are Angela Carter and Margaret Atwood, several 21st century authors are adding to the canon—Neil Gaiman, Kelly Link, Emma Donoghue, Helen Oyeyemi, and Naomi Novik among them. I explore three such authors in what follows—Margot Lanagan, Angela Slatter, and Laurie Forest. In their witch-heavy narratives, no longer is the witch cast as evil queen or poison-apple wielding crone, instead she is—among other things—a powerful sorceress, a recalcitrant "old maid," a renegade hedge-witch, and a racism-defying, religious-dogma questioning witch leader in training.

Delectable Feminist Witches in a Not-so Dainty Tale: *Tender Morsels*

Tender Morsels, published in 2008, refashions elements of "The Ungrateful Dwarf" and "Snow White and Rose Red" to tell the story of Annie, a midwife and witch; Liga, a young girl sexually abused by her father; Branza and Urdda, Liga's two daughters; and Miss Dance, a powerful sorceress. Via inter-woven narratives that celebrate female sexuality and agency on the one hand and condemn rape and sexual violence on the other, the novel presents witchcraft and magic as able to redress the wounds patriarchy inflicts upon female bodies. Opening when Liga is a young teen being abused by her father, *Tender Morsels* is unflinching in its depictions of pregnancy gone wrong.[14] Soon after we meet her, Liga miscarries in the snow, where "so much of her boiling self fell away that she felt quite undone below the waist" (9). Impregnated by her tyrannical father, who, like "a great water snake," rapes her again and again after her mother dies, Liga is an exceedingly tragic figure (11). In another instance of unplanned pregnancy, her father shouts at her "Bleed, girl, bleed!" He then proceeds to purchase a foul-tasting concoction from the midwife/witch Annie and forces Liga to take it (13). After more miscarriages and birthing a stillborn child, Liga determines to hide her next pregnancy from her father, something that leads him to call her a "deceiving witch" (27). When he goes to Annie again to purchase more spells to end yet another pregnancy, the midwife realizes he has been raping the girl. As a result, a "curse stirred deep" within her, one which ends with Liga's dad being trampled to death by a horse (28).

After her father's death, Liga struggles to survive on her own. Attempting to live on what she can salvage from the forest, she is targeted by a young woodchopper who tells her she has no right to forage. Looking her over "as if she were a beast he was assessing the conformation of, in a market stall," his attack calls to mind the enclosure of common lands that forced peasants into starvation during the era of capitalist accumulation (46). In this fairy tale version of a newly capitalist world, the woodchopper casts Liga as a "thieving witch," one who—we will soon find out—the woodchopper is all too willing to steal happiness from. Along with four other males, he comes to Liga's cottage to rape her. When the group break in, Liga crawls up the chimney to hide. They soon find her, one proclaiming, "I can see right up her. Right up the crease of her" and another ordering her, "bring down that little purse to me! I shall count every coin you have in it!" Here, Liga's body is nothing but a "crease" for the males, a monetized treasure they feel entitled to take as they please (54).

Liga initially sees no way to escape such atrocities and contemplates suicide. As she prepares to die, a magical apparition appears and gives her two magic stones to plant by her cottage, stones which transport her to a near-perfect fairy tale world. There, she raises two daughters in peace, free from male violence. Later in the narrative, her head-strong daughter Urdda—one who finds her mother's created world "terribly dull"—crosses over into the real world after venturing into a cave (252). This fairy tale within a fairy tale framing suggests there is but a thin border between fantasy and reality, one which allows the violence of one world to cross into another. Yet Urdda, who is made of "such material that worlds will move for her," easily breaches the membrane between the "real" world and the "fairy" one (198). Arriving on "Bear Day," a time of lawlessness where men dress as bears and "run, and kiss and roar and paw and smash" women, all who "must be touched and marked," Urdda soon discovers both worlds are marred by animalistic male violence (135, 141, 225). Though Bear Day is "supposed to be about civilizing men" and curbing sexual assault, lack of male civility is the norm in this bear-chase-women world (275). When three men are unable to remove their furry costumes after an annual Bear Day celebration—something that alludes to male sexual predation as problematically permanent—Annie, the midwife/witch, goes with Urdda to consult Miss Dance, a powerful sorceress. Miss Dance asserts that these occurrences reflect "someone practicing outside their abilities" and agrees to puzzle out how to set things right (302). A pro-education witch, she soon takes Urdda on as an apprentice to learn the ways of magic. In the meantime, Liga is brought over to the "real world" and called upon to face-up to the abuse she endured from her father, something the old witch Annie helps her to process. Sharing she has been "quite oft acquainted with men tekkin what they will from me without my say-so," Annie's admission reveals that sexual violence has a long history in their world, one that extends far beyond Bear Day activities (356).

Naming the messages behind Grimm fairy tales as an "irritant" that spurred *Tender Morsels*, Lanagan, the author, describes the moral message for young women such tales impart as "[you] must expect men to behave like animals sometimes. If you just keep on being sweet, nice, obliging and helpful in the face of this poor behavior, you will be rewarded." Instead crafting stories that affirm "there is some animalistic behavior that is not forgivable and shouldn't be tolerated," Lanagan recasts the fairy tale for feminist purposes. Significantly, despite the magical power women hold within the narrative, they are still controlled by a patriarchal script, one wherein their stories are shaped via the violent men that surround them. At the level of form, this is emphasized via the use of a third person point of view for the females' stories versus first person for the male stories. Referring to the female characters of the novel, Lanagan explains "I wanted to give the sense of them being pushed around by the story, being pushed around by life, not being in control of their fates." As for the male characters, the author imparts, "I wanted to sound as if they took it for granted that their story was the central story, that they were at the centre of their universe. It was a statement about the sense of entitlement the men carried around with them, that the women didn't have" (Macalpine). Making the feminist intent of her work apparent, Lanagan evocatively speaks to the centering of male stories and voices. Staying true to this intent in *Tender Morsels*, Lanagan supplants the double-marriage witnessed in *Snow White and Rose Red* with an all-female happy ending. By replacing the romance at the core of so many tales, her haunting fantasy illuminates the horrific consequences of constructing women as prey (something emphasized through the Bear Day tradition). With nary a prince in sight, the novel's topsy-turvy world of monstrous fathers, predatory rapists, and bear-men unable to control their lust upends the male-as-hero-and-female-victim-or-villain fairy tale tradition. Instead of females endangered by their own wickedness, vanity, or tendency to marry widowed patriarchs and then mistreat their step-daughters, Lanagan provides contemporary readers delicious morsels of feminist sentiment wrapped in a not-so-tender story of rape, revenge, and redemption.

Rocking the Marriage Boat:
The Brides of Rollrock Island

The Brides of Rollrock Island, also by Lanagan, tells the story of Misskaella Prout, a female shunned by her community. Deploying the mythological selkie in order to critique marriage as system, Lanagan again deploys witch figures to castigate patriarchal formations. In the novel, the damsel-in-distress-defying Misskaella makes her living by trapping selkies in their human form so as to sell them as brides to local men seeking compliant wives. As one man who will undoubtedly be no peach of a husband puts it, "they'll go where they're pushed, these women" (118). Opening years before Misskaella turns to selkie-dealing, readers meet her as a young, churlish girl. Mercilessly teased as a child and treated as an ugly duckling by her family, Misskaella realizes her "fat bottom" and rebel temperament make her unmarriageable. Coming to recognize marriage as a racket, Misskaella is akin to a fairy tale Emma Goldman, as when she drops wisdom like "they set us against each other as you set chickens at a market, comparing their feathers' gloss and the brightness of their eye, their temperament and general breeding" (51). She refuses to do anything with her "thickset, unpromising shape" and instead turns to magic, amassing a fortune in the process (45). Herein, Misskaella is presented not as monster but as savvy businesswoman. A female who has been treated "like a broom or dishrag that anyone might pick up and use," she is described as "nine parts sympathy, one part pure wickedness" (11, 291). Eventually moving to her very own mansion filled with treasures, she takes on a female apprentice, Trudle. Similarly maligned for her lack of beauty, Trudle and her children provide Misskaella with a family that loves her. Though she maintains her purported goal is to train Trudle in "the art of being terrifying," in actuality, Trudle becomes like a daughter to the prickly Misskaella (278). Closing as Trudle readies her witchy mother figure for burial, Trudle takes solace in the fact "Nothing can tease her now" (294).

In the denouement to Misskaella's story, Trudle opens the parcel Misskaella requested to be buried with and finds three sets of baby-clothes—those of Misskaella's three selkie children, all of whom died prematurely and whom Misskaella never told anyone about. Readers learned about her first child early in the novel, but the existence of the other two is not revealed until the very end. Her first selkie child incited excessive shame and fear in Misskaella lest she, an unwed young woman, was discovered to be a mother—and of a seal-child no less. In so doing, the narrative not only overturns the witch as anti-mother, but also gestures towards the tragedies that befall unwed mothers in societies ruled by strict codes of sex, gender, and marriage. Trudle's wish that closes the text, that Misskaella and her three children be tossed into the wind so as to land "nearby ... not caring a jot who knew," suggests that only in death can queer families like that which Misskaella forges free themselves from societal censure (302). Ending this exposé of "the terrible life a witch must lead" on a more somber note than *Tender Morsels*, Lanagan nevertheless remains true to her intent to rework the irritating messages found in fairy tales, myths, and lore (302). Here is hoping we encounter more of her willful witches in the years to come. Until then, there is no shortage of sassy sorceresses in recent fiction, some of whom are found in the works of the author next up for discussion.

No Patience for Women-Hating: *Of Sorrows and Such*

Of Sorrows and Such, by award-winning author Angela Slatter, depicts the sorrow of living in a male-dominated world within a female body. Set in Edda's Meadow, a place named after "yet another woman lost to history," this millennial fairy tale features a church-led, witch-hating society—one that reads like a fantasy version of the Puritanical world depicted in *The Scarlet Letter*. Opening with narrator and protagonist Patience Gideon reflecting on the fact "Females are seldom remembered once they've gone beneath the earth; indeed, many go unremarked while they're still upon it," Edda's Meadow casts women as caught within the vices of a dogmatic society. Despite the fact she is the witch "Edda's folk turn to for everyday remedies," Patience has a precarious position within the community. Contrasting herself to the doctors who "spout fancy terms" and "hand out tablets that give a little relief, but no cure," Patience is nevertheless fiercely proud of her magical abilities and refuses to give up her witchy ways, explaining "it would have been easier to stop breathing." On "the wrong side of fifty" as she sees it, Patience is akin to a fairy tale version of Gin from *Red Clocks* (discussed in the first section of this chapter). Like the patriarchy-defying happy-to-stay-single Gin, Patience has opted for an unwed life on the outskirts of society, one that affords her the freedom to house witches on the run and mother her adopted daughter as she sees fit (10–13).

Though Patience claims "we bosomed creatures are not important enough for menfolk to concern themselves with," the male leaders of Edda's Meadow are in actuality very keen to control women and eradicate witches (53). One such man, Pastor Alhgren, is slowly poisoning his wife, as one does when it's time for "a newer, younger, prettier wife" (123). Described as "a man who preaches fire and brimstone at adulterers and fornicators, drinkers and usurers, gamblers and gluttons, yet is determined to be the cause of his wife's demise," the pastor's wife-ridding goal is thwarted by Patience. Imparting that "no witch would have put up with this sort of husband," Patience uses her powers to free women from staying (or entering into) bad marriages (72). With all the "injuries that would be done to women who did not conform" percolating in the background of the text, it's not long before Patience's marriage-defying ways lead her to be captured by town leaders (121). This is set in motion when a shape-shifting witch named Flora comes to Patience for help. Having been attacked while in animal form, Flora is now bleeding to death. Knowing she does not practice the kind of magic that can aid Flora, Patience calls on Selke, one of the "intermittent stream of wandering witches" seeking refuge in her home (22). Patience implores Flora and her sister Ina to cease their shape-shifting ways, reminding them "many have been turned to ash for what we can do" (37). Soon facing this exact fate, Patience is arrested on charges of being a witch, beaten, starved, and nearly killed. Thankful she is not raped, she likens herself to "a cow kept in a byre or a pig in a sty," and takes solace in the fact that even if her male jailers find her mother's book of magic—hidden away in her basement—they will not be able to decipher it as it is "written in the language of witches" (116, 118). After Selke helps her escape, Patience takes to the road so as to avoid further persecution. Framed as "sowing seeds ... of discord, seeds of hope" in so doing, her escape from the village where women are treated "as if they are a meal of some kind" seems a wise choice. Though "a witch's life is made of sorrow and such" according to Patience, her rebellious patriarchal-smashing-magic will surely find a new location to be of use (123, 50). In the next book under consideration, a young witch seems a kindred spirit to Patience, albeit one that sets her sites on prejudice more so than misogyny.

Teaching Tolerance: *The Black Witch*

The Black Witch courted pre-publication controversy on social media when Shauna Sinyard, a blogger focusing on YA, called it "the most dangerous, offensive book I have ever read" (Rosenfield). This resulted in an intense backlash that found author Lorie Forest castigated for writing a book about race (she is a white woman), called a Nazi sympathizer, and widely condemned on Twitter. This virtual witch-hunt is ironic given the content of her novel calls for tolerance of all beings, including witches, fairies, werewolves, selkies, dragons and various otherworldly beings. The call for tolerance *Black Witch* instigates is housed within a tale that addresses racism and systemic injustice through a fantasy lens—a housing that admittedly simplifies very complex issues with the promise that an anti-racist education can solve endemic prejudice. Yet, *Black Witch* nevertheless constructs justice-minded witch figures that serve as a corrective to the many evil hags and one-note seductresses so often featured in tales of the witch. Somewhat akin to *Wicked* in its exploration of magical species brought together in a tolerance-teaching setting, Forest's novel houses much of its story at a school—Verpax University.

Centered on Elloren, a teenager who does not yet realize she is a witch, the narrative is set in Earthia, a world populated by numerous species, each with cultural practices and religious beliefs of their own. A "Glendorian," Elloren believes she hails from a "pure-blooded race" (Loc. 182). Once she attends college, her supremacist views give way as she befriends different "races"—winged Icaruls, shape-shifting panthers, warrior elves, sexually trafficked selkies, and so on. As she learns more about the injustice that saturates the starkly species-stratified world in which she lives, Elloren seeks out a scholar of history, Professor Kristian, who disabuses her of the belief "The Book of the Ancients" is true. His name serving as a mocking indictment of Christianity and its tendency—especially of late—to lean towards fundamentalism, Kristian informs Elloren her beloved book is "complete fiction." Noting that when "stripped of its religious underpinnings" the sacred book tells the story of a madman hungry for power, Kristian insists the racial purity on which the Book of the Ancients relies "is probably the greatest myth of all time." Learning that her grandmother was "a cruel, religious zealot who wanted to wipe out every race in the Western Realm," Elloren is led to question everything she thought she knew. Here, the novel frames religion as a dangerous weapon, one that spreads xenophobia and homophobia in like measure. It also places Elloren's growing awareness within the context of an impending war—one wherein the rumored "Black Witch" will triumph. Though the narrative closes before we discover if Elloren is the Black Witch, the novel hints at her great powers throughout. Becoming part of the resistance movement that aims to bring down the tyrannical power system governing Earthia at the novel's close, the stage is set for Elloren to realize the full potential of her powers in the second book of the series (Loc. 5233–5326).

In this first book, not only are readers introduced to a group of characters chafing against the stratified society of Earthia, but also to "wand-fasting," a practice in which young girls are "magically bound to young men for life," to child laborers who are "beaten if they protest," and to heinous military practices that rely on imprisoning and torturing dragons (Loc. 216, 5117). Casting a wide net in its presentation of various forms of injustice, *The Black Witch* rallies against those like the power-hungry male courting its main character, one who un-charmingly claims "you have to dominate or be dominated" (Loc. 5368). Elloren willfully refuses such hierarchical codswallop in this YA series, one that uses species-ism as a metaphor for racism in much the same way as *Wicked* some 25 years ago. Thus, *The Black Witch,* along with Lanagan's novels and Slatter's *Of Sorrow and Such,* bode well for post-millennial readers who like their fairy tale and fantasy witches feminist.

Section 4: Conjuring Retribution

Whereas the narratives in the first three sections reclaim the witch, turning her into an historical renegade, a wickedly willful rebel, and a re-imagined fantasy/fairy tale figure, the witches featured in the final section of this chapter are arguably harder to rehabilitate. Their witches destroy entire towns, kill innocents, ruin families, and possess souls, making a case for executing witches in ways reminiscent of *Malleus Maleficarum*. Although they don't steal penises to make fleshy bird nests, they do incite violence, drive men to insanity, kidnap babies, pollute communal water sources, and hang out with devils of color.[15] However, they do so within oppressive contexts that don't allow many—if any—other options. Jane, from *The Autopsy of Jane Doe*, tortures and kills the father and son performing her autopsy, doing so as retribution for being burned as a witch. *Hex*, the best-selling novel by Thomas Olde Heuvelt, features an undead witch who harms the living in response to the violence done to her body over the course of 300 years. *Autopsy* and *Hex* each revolve around females who are not imbued with identifiable character traits or personalities. Instead, the tales focus on the *body* of the witch in ways that proffer metaphoric "every witches"—ones whose experiences stand in for the general abominations done to women assumed to be witches. The other three narratives present females who take up take up the "bad witch" mantle to redress what they endure in a woman-hating world. While Thomasin from Dave Eggers' *The Witch* chooses to "live deliciously" rather than succumb to the stark dictates of her puritanical family, Elaine from Anna Biller's *The Love Witch* turns to witchcraft to heal the trauma her father and husband have inflected upon her. In *The Woods*, directed by Lucky McKee, a group of persecuted witches overtake an all girls boarding school. Though this group of texts includes a number of stereotypical wicked witch figures, their narratives also hint at the redemption and joy choosing the witch path can proffer.

A Toe-Hold on Villainy: *The Autopsy of Jane Doe*

"Everybody has a secret" intones the father in *The Autopsy of Jane Doe*. In this 2017 film, the secret is that the primary body being autopsied belongs to a witch. Documenting one harrowing night in a family mortuary where father (Tommy) and son (Austin) are tasked with discovering the cause of death of an unidentified female corpse, the film initially reads

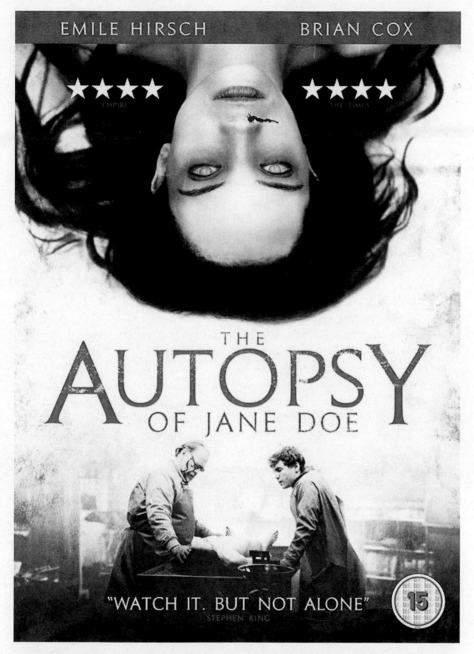

The top of the poster for *The Autopsy of Jane Doe* shows Jane's (Olwen Kelly) dead face from the perspective of a coroner, while the bottom shows Austin (Emile Hirsch) and Tommy (Brian Cox) inspecting Jane's corpse (IFC Films, 2016, directed by André Øvredal).

much like a crime procedural. However, as the autopsy proceeds, the discoveries Tommy and Austin make become increasingly inexplicable. The claustrophobic setting and preponderance of slow, tracking shots through dark hallways contribute to the mounting terrors—ones which accelerate once Tommy and Austin conclude Jane Doe is a witch—or at least was accused of being one. After discovering pulverized bones, blackened organs, and various strange items inside her body (a tooth wrapped in cloth, string, peat moss), the two conclude she was buried alive, possibly after being lit on fire. Though Tommy and Austin sympathize with the horrors her body has undergone, the camera shows no such sentiment. Like a relentless scalpel, it hones in on gory details of dissection and excavation. Each cut, each layer of skin, each removed organ is disassociated from human suffering. Meanwhile, Jane's pale skin, thin figure, and blank expression construct her as an inert and passive object. Via camera angles repeatedly positioned from above her corpse, viewers experience her autopsy in all its flesh-peeling, bone-cutting intensity. Yet, beneath the surface of this seeming glorification of bodily excision lies a more ameliorating—if vengeful—tale.

Incorporating typical horror film elements—mysterious noises, a worsening storm, failed electricity, a sinister basement, ghostly apparitions, a dead girlfriend—the dread mounts apace. Father and son soon repeat what was apparently done to Jane in the past, perhaps more than once—they burn the witch. The ceiling and walls catch fire when they do so, but Jane's corpse remains untouched, causing the two to flee from the morgue. A corpse, presumably animated by Jane, chases after them. Tommy is attacked by a hag-like figure before he and son barricade themselves back inside the morgue. Once there, the two take up the mystery of Jane's corpse with renewed determination, cutting into her scalp to take a sample of brain tissue. Upon discovering live cells in the tissue, they decide Jane is still alive and is torturing them, something described as "her revenge … her ritual." Although initially encouraged to empathize with Jane, she is villainized in the latter part of the film. Taking out her reign of terror on the affable father and son, a duo appalled by what was done to her, Jane doesn't allow Tommy and Austin to escape her clutches alive. If she, a purported witch, could not be suffered to live, why should others carry on unscathed?[16] Tommy and Austin are perhaps—in Jane's estimation—representative of the many men who hunted and executed women like her. As retribution, they are sent to early graves, a fate unheard of for witch hunters historically.

After Jane dispatches the father and son who invaded her body with their scalpels and rib saws, her eyes turn from milky white to brown. The mortuary lights come back on. Sheriffs arrive on the scene only to find Jane's corpse free of incisions. As the film closes, we see Jane's body in the back of an ambulance being driven to another mortuary. Once there, one can presume, she will continue to avenge her death. Fittingly, Jane's monstrous female body has the last laugh: her toe twitches in the closing shot, sounding the bell tied to her foot, a signal her *toe-hold* on witchy vengeance is just beginning.

The Witch's Revenge: *Hex*

Hex, lauded as one of the best horror novels of late, is set in Black Spring, home of a three-hundred-year-old reanimated witch. Sentenced to death in 1664 after she was charged with raising her nine-year-old son from the dead, Katherine Van Wyler's rotting corpse has been shuffling catatonically through the town ever since. With chains around her body and her eyes sewn shut, Katherine roams through Black Spring on a pre-determined path. While believed to be relatively harmless as long as she is left alone, local leaders insist "we have every reason to believe that if her eyes open and she starts uttering her spells we will all die" (66). Terming her a "paranormal time bomb," the book's nearly four hundred pages do not go beyond basic elements of Katherine's history (67). Instead, the mistreatment she undergoes by the paranoid inhabitants of Black Spring and a handful of its teenage sons are front and center.

One of the main characters, Steven, is sympathetic to Katherine's plight. His son Tyler, a technological whiz-kid and vlogger, is not as compassionate, at least not when his bullish friends encourage him to treat Katherine as fodder for their teenage pranks. Their witch-bullying agenda is impeded by the "HEX Control Center," a surveillance complex that monitors the town's "containment policy"—a mandate that the existence of the witch must be kept secret (76). Though forced to live under the gaze of some four hundred cameras, Tyler and his friends are most put out by limited internet access (necessitated by the need to keep Black Spring off the [Google] map). In response, the teens launch "Open Your Eyes: Preachings from the Witch's Nest" with the mission to gather enough evidence about Katherine's existence to make knowledge of Black Spring's witchy inhabitant go viral. What the project morphs into, however, is escalating instances of bullying Katherine. Their first act against the witch, moving a town lamp-post in her path that causes her to fall down, is deemed a triumph. Gleeful that the blinded Katherine provides them with a "vaudevillian pratfall," the adolescent males are cast as merry pranksters (378). Sometime later the teens put Ray-Bans on Katherine and taunt her by rapping lyrics from a Jay-Z song: "Who's my bitch now? Take that witcha, hit ya, back split ya..." (98). To their excitement, after she flees, they discover the sunglasses have been melted and covered in a sulphuric goo, something they believe to be ectoplasm. The group then connive to carry out a "whisper test" to discover what powers Katherine's endless, near silent mutterings contain.

Later, Tyler and Lawrence, the most-mild mannered of the group, head to Philosopher's Creek in hopes of finding Katherine in one of the few locations out of reach of control center cameras. Once there, they find their three compatriots poking Katherine with branches. Tyler shouts at them to stop, but they refuse to do so, insisting they are carrying out scientific research. This interaction leads Tyler to muse on Jaydon's history of violence, wherein Jaydon "wasn't stingy about passing along the punches he had received at home" (103). Recalling an incident when Jaydon kicked a ball full-force into Katherine's face, Tyler remembers becoming frightened "not of the witch, but of Jaydon" and asks himself, "If a boy of twelve had been able to kick a soccer ball at the witch with so much pent-up rage, what would the same boy be capable of at nineteen?" (104). As it turns out, Jaydon is capable of sexualized attacks, ones where he moves from attacking Katherine with a branch to asking her, "You want me to touch your boobies?" When he does so, some of the other boys "doubled over and shrieked with laughter," as Jaydon "bumped and ground his hips obscenely" at the witch. "You haven't got the guts," one of the teens mocks. Jaydon retorts, "I'd fuck her all right." He then bellows in her face, "You filthy whore! You'd like that, wouldn't you?! Dirty cunt!" and offers twenty bucks to whoever "takes a picture of her tit." As Katherine "endured the humiliation silently," Tyler wonders if she is just "waiting for her moment" (102–6). Two more attacks on Katherine, one in which Jaydon duct-tapes an X-Acto knife to a stick, cutting open her nipple and surrounding breast tissue, and another in which he corners Katherine, stones her, and beats her with a broomstick, hurtle the narrative towards its terrifying conclusion.

In effect, Jaydon's actions are a continuation of the violence done to Katherine some three-hundred years prior when she was wrongly accused of killing her son and put to death. This time, however, the violence done to her is spurred by Jaydon's abusive childhood, one no one talks about, just as they don't discuss his mother Griselda's abuse at the hands of her husband and Jaydon's father, Jim Holst. Instead, amongst this "conspiracy of silence" Jim went missing some seven years prior (86). Whereas Jaydon responds to his father's former abuse and subsequent disappearance by later abusing Katherine, Griselda makes meek offerings to Katherine in hopes she might protect her from further harm. Both responses fail to confront the familial violence they experienced, let alone break the silence around it. The same can be said of the trauma Katherine endures. Remaining relatively placid for hundreds of years, Katherine's fury is unleashed in the final third of the novel. Presented as having "irreversibly bewitched" the inhabitants of Black Spring and leading "the soul of the town" to self-destruct, Katherine causes the town to descend into chaos, something she instigates "with her degenerate whispering" which "brought out the very worst in all of them as part of some diabolical plan" (239, 255). Going Sissy Spacek on the town, she makes the local creek bubble with blood, bringing a Carrie-like "Red Death" to the citizens that incites many to commit suicide. By turning Katherine "into an abomination," Black Spring has, according to the narrator, "brought this on themselves" (224). Via this claim, the novel continues its condemnation not of the witch, but of the violence done to her. Additionally, by emphasizing the acts of a gaggle of teen boys, at least one of them a survivor of abuse, *Hex* positions atrocities done to women accused of witchcraft to century-spanning male violence. In this post-millennial tale of witch retribution, the last we see of Katherine, she is making "druidic arm gestures toward the heavens, murmuring corrupted words and sounds" in an "underworld incantation to the skies" (351–69). Perhaps she, like the young heroine of the next tale, will soon ascend skyward.

Delicious Ascendancy: *The Witch*

Deemed "a new horror classic," "the best witch movie ever," and "one of the year's best researched and most historically accurate offerings," *The Witch* garnered a Sundance award for Robert Eggers, a first time director, and was critically celebrated in a way horror movies rarely are (Hutchinson, Faraco, O'Falt). To make this exquisitely bone-chilling film, Eggers spent several years researching America's witch-hunts. The resulting narrative, an admixture of painstaking attention to historical detail mixed with shocking scenes of brutal, super-natural violence, is a tale that seems part documentary, part scary movie. Shot mainly using natural light with a cast of relatively unknown actors, the documentary aura imparted by the film suggests witches are just as factual as other elements of the narrative. In so doing, witchery is put in conversation with religious doctrine and early American colonialism, depicting each as having the capacity to do great harm. Implicating religious dogma and the patriarchal nuclear family in the tragedy that ensues, the film also relies on magical explanations for what occurs. Though many view Eggers' movie as a fiercely powerful feminist statement,[17] it is not, I contend, quite so straightforward. Yes, the over-bearing father is condemned and the cruel mother is portrayed as duped by social systems that name her daughter as a potential slut, but so too are young females depicted as susceptible to the devil's charms, who is, by the way, *black*—a depiction that both genders and racializes evil. Nevertheless, *The Witch* includes, as one reviewer puts it, "80 minutes of patriarchal dysfunction" (Halperin). In this "nightmare from the past," as Eggers describes his movie, the harsh environment of early colonial life is captured expertly, but so too is the fear of witches that suffused the era. However, though this fear is tied to gendering the witch female, racializing the devil as black, and construing indigenous people as savage, it is ultimately associated most prominently to the notion the witches are real and they are evil. While settler colonialism and Puritanical belief provide background framing, the blighted crops, abducted babies, and ill children are linked to polluting, demonic femininity—something that within the diegesis destroys the family and, in turn, threatens to destroy the white patriarchal colonial project. Herein, the film circulates around a family that is representative of what Ahmed names "the whole social body" and its linkages to the preservation of the social order. Significantly, Ahmed links this notion of family to the "reproductive duty" placed on women and the "Protestant tradition that views the child's will as that which must be broken" (*Willful* 5, 63, 114). As we will see, Thomasin functions in the film as a "willful child" who refuses to abide by the expectations thrust upon her by her family.

The film opens as said family stand before an austere council decreeing their banishment. That this banishment might equal death is made plain via large gates that close with chilling finality as the family depart (as "savage" Native American traders watch them go, no less). After traveling by rickety wagon across a vast, barren wilderness, the father, William, gathers his wife and children to pray at a clearing facing a dense forest. Mysterious music plays in the background, sounding much like wailing women. William holds his arms aloft to the sky, supplicating to the heavens. The narrative then jumps forward. Thomasin, the oldest daughter (played by then unknown Anna Taylor-Joy) is fervently praying, "O most merciful father, I here confess I have lived in sin. I have been idle of my work, disobedient of mine parents, neglectful of my prayer. I have, in secret, played upon thy Sabbath and broken every one of thy commandments…. Forgive me." Shot in close-up, her large eyes dominate the screen. Soon after, she will cover and uncover these eyes as she plays peek-a-boo with her baby brother Sam. After a few rounds of the game in which the baby giggles with delight, Thomasin removes her hands from her eyes to find him gone. She screams as she looks towards the forest, the place William has forbidden his family to enter. She runs towards the woods but stops short, seemingly too frightened to go on. It is unclear if she spies the red-cloaked figure stealing into the forest with a bundle in her arms, presumably baby Sam.

In the next scene, Sam lies on an outdoor table, his naked, chubby body set in sharp relief against wrinkled hands touching him greedily. Soon crooked fingers hold a knife above Sam's belly. The camera cuts away. In the shot that follows, a naked old woman sits stirring a macabre cauldron of blood and guts. She then rubs herself with the gory mixture and rhythmically spreads some on the handle of her broom.[18] The scene closes with a shadowy image of her aloft in the sky. Apparently feeding on the family's youngest has given her the power of flight. Back at the farm, Thomasin drops a lone egg from the henhouse. In it lies a dead, bloodied chick. Soon after, the twins, Jonas and Mercy, sing riotously to the family's escaped goat, Black Philip. Tensions within the family mount. Thomasin, in a fit of annoyance at her chore-defying younger sister, convinces Mercy she is a witch, an interchange instigated when Mercy startles her sister as she is cleaning clothes at the edge of a nearby stream with Caleb, their brother. Emerging from the surrounding bushes, Mercy, in the put-on voice of a witch, cackles "I be the witch of the wood ... and I have come to steal thee ... clickety clackety!" Angered, Thomasin retorts, "I be washing father's clothes ... and thou are playing idle!" Mercy retorts, "Because mother hates you," adding "Black Philip says I can do what I like." Thomasin then draws on the lore of witches, claiming she abducted baby Sam: "Aye, it was a witch, Mercy. It was I ... 'twas I that stole him. I be the witch of the wood! I am that very witch. When I sleep my spirit slips away from my body and dance naked with the devil.... I signed his book. He bade me bring him a babe, so I stole Sam." Thomasin closes by threatening she may steal Mercy too, boil and bake her, and then instructs, "Swear thy silence."

As Caleb and Thomasin are in the woods the next day, their dog spies a rabbit and runs off, spooking their horse. Thomasin is thrown to the ground. Caleb, searching for the dog, finds the pet dying, its entrails spilling out in a fleshy mass. Much like the bloodied chick Thomasin saw earlier, the eviscerated dog evokes the family itself, which is being ripped apart and gutted by the fear their religion fosters and the barren environment exacerbates. Shortly after this, we see Caleb crawling through dense branches, following a hare. He spies a cottage almost hidden by its covering of moss, branches, and mulch. A barefooted women in a red cape steps out and walks towards him. Presumably the same red-caped old woman that killed Sam, she has transformed her appearance into that of a buxom young beauty. As she approaches Caleb, she bends forward, her cleavage bursting towards his hungry eyes. He is afraid but drawn to her. She touches his face gently as she pulls him in for a kiss. Her hand, suddenly aged and gnarled, forcefully grabs the back of his head before the camera cuts away.

Later that evening, as Thomasin is putting the goats in the barn, she finds Caleb propped against it. He is naked and seemingly near death. Katherine wonders if it could be "Indian magic" that has cursed Caleb or "unnatural providence," asking, "Does this not look like witchcraft?" Caleb dies in a harrowing scene that follows. William, presuming his other children played a role in their brother's death, locks them in the barn, thundering "Think upon thy sins!" As they huddle in the dark, Thomasin asks Jonas and Mercy, "Are you witches?" They ask the same of her. We see William praying desperately outside the barn door. Meanwhile Katherine, upstairs in her bedroom, envisions Caleb sitting on a nearby chair, holding baby Sam in his lap. "I have brought a book, mother," Caleb tells her, clearly referencing Satan's infamous book of signatures. The camera then cuts back to the barn. Mercy and Jonas hear sounds upon the roof and then at the barn door. Just after, we see a crouched naked woman, similar to the crone figure that killed Sam, sucking on one of the goat's nipples. She turns her head and cackles, her mouth dripping with blood. Thomasin, who has fallen asleep, wakes and screams. The camera cuts back to Katherine, laughing wickedly in her bedroom. Caleb and Sam are gone and she holds only an empty red cape in her lap. A large black raven flaps at her breasts, pecking away at her nipple.

The next morning, William finds Thomasin lying at the edge of the barn, the goats dead and eviscerated, and Thomas and Mercy nowhere to be found. In shock, William stands as if a statue. Black Philip gores him. In the bedroom, Katherine is again lured by apparitions of her sons and agrees to sign the devil's book. Soon after, she attacks Thomasin. Pushing her viciously, she excoriates "You reek of evil ... proud slut! Do you not think I saw thy sluttish looks to him [Caleb] ... and thy father next?" As Katherine sees it, Thomasin is the cause of the family's ruin. After a brutal scuffle that results in Thomasin killing Katherine to prevent being choked by her, Thomasin falls asleep. When she wakes, it is night. She walks out to the barn with a candle. Black Philip enters the barn. "Black Philip, I conjure thee to speak to me ... speak as though dost to Jonas and Mercy" she commands. "Dost though understand my English tongue ... answer me." She turns, seemingly deciding he cannot speak, but then we hear a deep, sultry voice ask "What dost though want?" Thomasin responds, "What's canst thou give?" "Wouldst thou like taste of butter ... a pretty dress, wouldst thou like to live deliciously?" the voice asks. "Yes," she responds, inquiring, "What will you from me?" "Dost thou see the book before thee?" Black Philip whispers. The camera cuts to the book (the very same Katherine signed earlier), its pages filled with signatures. We then see Black Philip for the first time in human form—though only fleetingly. "Remove thy shift," he purrs, standing behind Thomasin. Significantly,

Black Philip in his human form is a *man of color*, or, as Eggers' script defines him, "a beautiful bearded man with a dark complexion." To be sure, the devil in animal form accords with historical iconography of the devil as a black goat, but in making the devil in human form a person of color, the film perpetuates a problematic racial construction. In a similar vein, Eggers' script describes the indigenous traders we see at the outset of *The Witch* as savage with painted faces while Katherine blames Caleb's death on "Indian Magic" within the diegesis.[19] Unfortunately, the movie does not interrogate these racialized underpinnings of its horror nearly as well as it engages with gender, religious practice, and the nuclear family. Instead, Black Philip transforms into *a black man* meant to represent the devil and then takes *a virginal white girl* into the woods to join the Sabat.

In the closing moments, Thomasin, now naked, walks towards the forbidden forest. Black Philip, returned to his goat form, runs after her. In a clearing in the woods, we see naked women encircling a fire. They hold long sticks redolent of broom handles as they dance spasmically. They then rise from the earth, free of gravity. Thomasin soon rises to join them. Her face, shrouded in shadows and evoking that of a skeleton, variously shows joy, pain, abandon, hilarity. The final image is her body aloft before a tree, her arms held skyward, echoing the pose of prayer so often taken up by William. In this ending, one deemed an "ecstatic post-patriarchal conclusion," Thomasin is finally free of the suffocating weight of her family and their traditions (Halperin). *The Faculty of Horror* episode dedicated to the film, "Season of the Witch," emphasizes the import of the closing image, noting Thomasin ascends rather than descends (which overturns Christian perceptions of hell/damnation). Deeming the film a "high-minded feminist liberation tale," the episode accords with interpretations proffered by other scholars of horror. For instance, Dawn Keetley also heralds the film, naming it as "one of those rare horror films that will, without a doubt, enter the canon of important and enduring horror films." Though I agree with the preceding sentiments, I also wish to point to Jeffrey Jerome Cohen's discussion of the gendering and racializing of devils and witches:

> The narratives of the West perform the strangest dance around the fire in which miscegenation and its practitioners have been condemned to burn. Among the flames we see the old women of Salem hanging, accused of sexual relations with the black devil; we suspect they died because they crossed a different border, one that prohibits women from managing property and living solitary, unmanaged lives [16].

Referencing the sexism and racism on which the West builds itself, Cohen here also nods to the role played by capitalist ideology, one that insisted females had to be "managed" to keep the existing socio-economic wheels turning in favor of white male rule and its "taming" of the American landscape. In the same way the frontier was characterized as "a place of danger waiting to be tamed into farms," so too was the female body a wild place that needed to be "fenced in" (Cohen 16). In relation to such constructions, *The Witch* makes a convincing case for Thomasin's attraction to "living deliciously." Two other films, one set in the late 1960s and another with a decidedly retro '60s/'70s feel, likewise utilize the witch to call for such delicious living.

Foul Born Females: *The Woods*

The Woods, from 2006, is led by a strong and rebellious female protagonist, Heather. Toying with the burgeoning female freedom of the '60s era, the film tells a part radical, part reactionary story about witches, and by extension, about females and the female body. The opening line "feet off the seat," a curt directive from Heather's mother, inaugurates this story in which women are often bitches. Her mother, along with the witches that run the all-girls boarding school Falburn Academy, where Heather will soon attend, falls into stereotypical representations of the shrewish older woman. In contrast, Heather's father, Joe, played by Bruce Campbell (Ash of the *Evil Dead* franchise), is kind and supportive, including of his rebellious daughter Heather. Henpecked by his bossy wife, he will later be targeted by the lead witch, Miss Traverse (played by Patricia Clarkson). As *The Woods* opens, Heather is being sent to Falburn as a result of burning down a tree in her yard (itself an act evoking witch execution). As this opening segment portends, Heather will soon be "hunting" witches at Falburn. Though she never hangs them from a tree or burns them, she does, at film's end, destroy the coven that runs the school.

The Academy, meant to rectify Heather's rebellious behavior, is led by Traverse, who, like Heather's mother, tries to "tame" her new student. When she arrives at Falburn, her mother, by way of goodbye, instructs Heather, "Don't let your nails get out of control." This command, along with the prior "feet off the seat," targets Heather's unruly body and frames her as "improperly" feminine. The same is true of the first snide comment made to Heather by Headmistress Traverse: "Do you like athletics? You look as though you might"—an observation which suggests Heather is not only a rebel, but possibly a lesbian. As a breaker of sex/gender rules, Heather is soon targeted by Traverse, who hopes to turn her recalcitrance into something more productively witchy.

As the film proceeds, we learn Traverse and her sisters took over Falburn Academy when they walked out of the woods a century ago. Taunted and bullied by existing students, the sisters *traversed* norms of gender by overtaking the school, corrupting its students, and eventually inhabiting a succession of the student's bodies as their own bodies age. Rendering the students compliant by tainting the communal well water and infecting the school's milk supply with tree bark and blood, the witches' acts herein call to mind the "polluting female body" and the "bad breast."[20] As a result of ingesting these female-poisoned fluids, Heather begins to experience nightmares and hallucinations. Then, when her parents retrieve her from the school, their car is overturned by the "evil woods" on the return drive home. As Alice, Heather's mother, is dragged out of the car by a vine, she inadvertently kicks Joe, Heather's dad, in the head. Admitted to a hospital as a result, Joe is soon attacked by Headmistress Traverse who slices open her hand and forces her black blood down Joe's throat, causing him to go into a catatonic state. Later, Joe throws up the blood, breaking Traverse's hold over him. Sometime later, he arrives at the school with an ax in hand, one which he and Heather wield to kill the witch faculty, including Traverse. Father and daughter then hug, emphasizing that all is now "right" in the world: the coven of teachers have been killed, the infectious tree roots have been forced back into the woods, and Heather can return home, freed from the curse of foul-born witches.

Although punctuated with the girl-power ballad of 1964, Dusty Springfield's "You Don't Own Me," and featuring the rebel-girl Heather at its center, *The Woods* plays into a number of androcentric tropes. Similar to *Suspiria* from 1977, *The Woods* centers on a school run by evil witches intent on "polluting" various female innocents. In both movies, witches are categorically evil, endanger "normal" females, and enact violence against good men. Each also feature plucky, young female protagonists at odds with older, authoritative women. In so doing, *Suspiria* and *The Woods* each further the notion that power is dangerous in an older woman's hands. Nevertheless, the focus on a rebel girl who uncovers centuries of bad deeds allows a girl to win—something all too rare in cultural narratives. In the next film considered, a young woman also triumphs, though in contrast to Heather, she uses witchcraft to do so.

True Love as Patriarchal Nightmare: *The Love Witch*

Drawing inspiration from George Romero's 1972 *Hungry Wives* (also known as *Season of the Witch*), Anna Biller's sumptuous 2016 movie centers on Elaine, the titular "love witch." Elaine, like Joan from Romero's film, suffers from expectations placed on women to be obedient, passive, and beautiful. Also like Joan, Elaine uses witchcraft to rail against such

Elaine (Samantha Robinson) of *The Love Witch* pictured with writer and director Anna Biller standing behind her.

strictures. Whereas *Hungry Wives* opens with Joan being abused by her husband, Elaine's abuse happens off-screen. Though traumatized by memories of her abuse, Elaine is determined to start a new life. As the movie opens, she is relocating to a new town by way of a beautiful coastal drive in a red convertible, Tarot cards by her side. When she reaches her new Northern California digs, we meet Trish, the woman renting Elaine an apartment. Trish invites her to lunch and we soon witness the two women dining in a lavish, aggressively pastel tea room (one of many symbols of hyper-femininity within the film). Admitting to Trish she is "addicted to love," Elaine is taken aback by Trish's critical response. "A husband isn't a prince, Elaine, and life isn't a fairy tale," she imparts, sternly closing with "We have to face that fact." Elaine, hardly a poster child for feminism, quips in her typical la-dee-dah manner, "Maybe life could be a fairy tale if you pleased your husband more."

Regularly immersing herself in prince-filled daydreams, Elaine clearly desires a happy ending of the fairy tale variety. Insisting at one point, "We may be grown women, but underneath we're just little girls dreaming about being carried off by a prince on a white horse," she basks in "girly things"—fantasy, fashion, bodily pruning. Intent on nabbing a "prince," she turns to magic. Disappointed by being treated as no more than a bit

A promotional poster for *The Love Witch* (Oscilloscope Laboratories, 2016, directed by Anna Biller).

The tearoom scene in *The Love Witch* as Trish (Laura Waddell) reminds Elaine (Samantha Robinson), "life isn't a fairy tale" (Oscilloscope Laboratories, 2016, directed by Anna Biller).

of flesh, she works to manipulate men into loving her (sometimes with hexed tampons, other times with bewitched chocolate cake). Yet, rather than condemning Elaine for such acts, the film upbraids society. As Trish indicates early in the movie, Elaine is "brainwashed by the patriarchy" and her "whole self-worth is wrapped up in pleasing a man." Her desire to find a man to please is not only a result of the wider patriarchal world in which she resides, but instigated via the mistreatment heaped upon her by her father and husband. Whereas her husband rails at her, "You need to take better care of yourself and of the house," her father calls her "a crazy bitch for a daughter," telling her things like "you could lose a few." Such invectives clearly shape Elaine into the woman we meet in the film—one who is obsessed with maintaining a beautiful, pleasing exterior. Indeed, Elaine decorates her body as lavishly as she does her multicolored apartment. Painting on make-up and donning sexy lingerie, she treats her body as art, albeit art she construes as *for* male consumption. Dedicated to finding love, she uses witchcraft to manufacture herself into a fantasy woman. Alas, when the men she targets don't fall in love with the fantasy, she kills them.

As writer/director Anna Biller explains it, "The main character's life is completely destroyed because she tries, and fails, to be a man's perfect fantasy, the type of fantasy pushed on women in men's magazines and pornography." Noting "the real seed of destruction lies in men's almost religious awe of the female naked body," Biller captures such destruction not only through Elaine's self objectification but also via various scenes of nearly nude women gyrating at a local stripper bar. Though Biller refers to her film as "almost didactically feminist," *The Love Witch* is far from patronizing or preachy.[21] Rather, its rich color palette, fairy-tale tableaus, and death-by-tampon narrative arcs are devilishly enjoyable. With a vibrant retro aesthetic that takes viewers back in time so as to convey gendered relations are stuck in the past, Biller's work characterizes patriarchy and its demeaning gazes—not women and witches—as the illness to be cured.

* * *

Similar to the Roxane Gay quote that serves as epigraph to this chapter, "Unruly women are always witches, no matter what century we're in," the article "The Contemporary Witch, The Historical Witch and the Witch Myth" insists "women will remain witches for as long as their oppression endures" (Bovenschen et al. 119). Yet, as the texts examined in this chapter exemplify, oppression need not always endure, and the witch is one figure that can help us envision a more tolerant world. Although the witches discussed above exist in patriarchal worlds, they help us to imagine a post-patriarchy in which young women might get the abortions they need, older women can still be mighty (and mighty sexy), and women as mothers, daughters, lovers, grandmothers and so on, hold the power to recast the world into something more magical. In such a future, women would not be accused of witchcraft—as they are today in India, Saudi Arabia, and Ghana. Female politicians would not be called witches as a form of insult, but as compliment. The witch would be venerated—much as males in power (as well as males in fictional tales) have been for centuries. Perhaps in such a future, we can, as Madeline Miller puts it, "at last celebrate female strength, recognizing that witches—and women—are not going away." For, like the women of the 2016 novel *The Power*, by Naomi Alderman, who reassemble the world into a matriarchy via the electrical power surging from their hands, unruly women offer not dead ends, but enduring hope.

Flying through our cultural narratives with increasing regularity, the witch is currently being called upon to foment change, not only in fiction, but in the real world. In her continued appearance in the public sphere, she carries signs proclaiming *"Witches for Black Lives," "Trans Women Are Women,"* and *"Thou Shalt Not Suffer the Patriarchy to Live."* Notably, the witch is also flying her feminist flag via the contemporary revival of W.I.T.C.H., an organization that draws on its five-letter name to create endlessly permeable acronyms, a key one being "Women Inspired to Tell Their Collective History." Significantly, during one of the group's first collective actions, they passed out leaflets proclaiming "You are a Witch by being female, untamed, angry, joyous, and immortal" (Adler 208). Such a proclamation is evident in the wicked good witches of numerous narratives of the post-millennial moment—a proclamation that does not only exist in fiction, film, and television but one that, right now, is likely gathering in a town or city near you, casting incantations, hexing patriarchy, and conjuring the will to resist.

4

Woman,
Thy Name Is Monster

"...the monstrous is produced at the border which separates
those who take up their proper gender positions from those
who do not"

—Barbara Creed

Across film, television, and fiction, post-millennial narratives are taking female monstrosity seriously. Exploring the various ways females coded as monstrous inform texts of the new millennium, my objective in this final chapter is to explore how the monstrous feminine serves as a powerfully political metaphor for our times. The first section addresses Gothic Monstrosity in relation to the New Woman, the Frankenstein figure, the female ghost, and the woman as author. Examining the domestic world of monstrous mothers and demonic children, the second section contends that social systems and historical legacies instigate horrors found within recent "home horror" narratives. In the third section, millennial iterations of the Creature Feature are taken up. The fourth section draws on the figure of Medusa to read contemporary permutations of the femme castratrice, the succubus, the female slasher, and the final girl. On the whole, the narratives analyzed in what follows champion willful monstrosity, doing so via a range of modes (Gothic, monster movie, slasher) and positive reconfigurations of common tropes (the damsel in distress, the femme fatale, the madwoman in the attic, the ghost bride).

Re-Making Female Monstrosity

As Simone de Beauvoir puts it, "One is not born, but rather becomes, a woman" (1949). So too are monsters made, not born. Shoring up fears of the other, the monster has projected upon it all culture wishes to repress, oppress, and control. Women, located not in the far reaching environs depicted in maps of old, but in our communities, families, our very beds, provide a proximal conduit for such projections. Aligned with the irrational, the grotesque, the abject, the polluting, the natural world, and the body (rather than the soul), linkages between the female and the monstrous have imbued the patriarchal imaginary throughout recorded history. Spanning mythology, folklore, and religion from around the globe, the woman as monster is called upon to explain original sin, blamed for disease and species mutations, accused of corrupting man, birthing degenerates, and unleashing evil upon the world. "All human societies," Barbara Creed writes, "have a conception of the monstrous-feminine, of what it is about a woman that is terrifying, horrific, abject" (1). Cristina Santos similarly references "cross-cultural similarities that construct women as monstrous irrespective of language, geography and religion" (xv). This woman equals monster equation is evident in biblical women like Eve and Lilith, in the mythological Medusa, in figures such as the witch, the succubus, the lamia.[1] Women are so regularly allied with the monstrous, in fact, that they are often not depicted in exaggerated form in horror texts, their mere female bodies being enough to construe monstrosity. As Bram Dijkstra explains, "Since women, being female, were, as a matter of course, already directly representative of degeneration, there was no need to find a symbolic form to represent their bestial nature; their normal and perfectly naked, physical presence was enough to make this point" (275). In other words, women became the representation of difference writ large, a difference grounded in their fecund bodies that, as Kristeva famously posits, are allied to the abject and its associations with the leaky, shape-shifting, bleeding and birthing female body.

In *The Monstrous Feminine*, Creed explores the more deleterious aspects of this woman as monster conception. She argues the "ideological project of the horror film" is "designed to perpetuate the belief [in] woman's monstrous nature" (71). Questioning "Why has the concept of woman as monster been neglected in feminist theory?" in her 1993 monograph, she was writing on the precipice of a great and varied feminist outpouring on this very concept (152). The monsterization of woman (as well as the feminization of the monster) was soon to be explored in Clover's *Men, Women, and Chain Saws* [1993], Caputi's *Gossips, Gorgons and Crones* [1993], Lykke and Braidotti's *Between Monsters, Goddesses and Cyborgs* [1996], Grant's *The Dread of Difference: Gender and the Horror Film* [1996], and Pinedo's *Recreational Terror: Women and the Pleasures of Horror Film* [1997]). Such work draws on various disciplines and methodologies—queer theory, disability studies, sociology, critical race studies, and psychology among them. Resisting the notion there is any "ideal" human or identity, monster theory of this ilk provides a *different* way to approach *difference*—one that is not based in stark divides such as female/male, monster/human, queer/(hetero)normative.

Alas, female subjects that challenge the obedience, passivity, and purity expected of them are still cast as monsters in the popular imaginary. Such woman are "framed as the locus of both disease, and of impending social disaster" (Jones, 2011, 40). This is particularly true in times of large-scale societal change, as with, for example, the shift from agrarianism to capitalism. At such times, the woman becomes a primary vessel at which to direct societal discontent as well as a vehicle for inciting fear so as to harness power, something that Sylvia Federici documents at length in *Caliban and the Witch.* Rendered suspect in this era via an association with heretics, pollution, radicalism, and economic turmoil, females were executed in the thousands. In our current era of corporate capitalism, neo-liberalism, and techno-globalization, women are once again being hunted as witches. So too are they being encouraged to return to the home, please their partners, eschew birth control, avoid getting raped, raise good consumer children, take "me time," have "aha moments," and practice "mindfulness," all while making sure to keep their bodies tight, trim, and beautiful. As for women who exhibit *too much* agency, or—heaven forbid—any whiff of feminism—they are dangerous creatures indeed.

Such agentic women in contemporary times are what Sara Ahmed names feminist killjoys—women who "kill joy" in their questioning of societal norms and structures. This killjoy, a twin to the willful subject, is a monster in the eyes of normative society. Too loud, lusty, opinionated, and obstinate, not white enough or chaste enough or heterosexual enough, following the wrong religion or no religion at all, refusing to buy into consumer capitalism and disputing the oppressive ideologies strangling the world, the killjoy is the "monstrous feminine" of the quotidian world. She refuses to abide by limiting binarisms and seeks to tear down the master's patriarchal, white supremacist, heteronormative housing project. She won't just rain on your parade, she will bleed on it. Yet, surprisingly, wonderfully, she is gaining positive traction in our new millennium. She is behind Black Lives Matter, Dakota Pipeline Resistance, #MeToo, and #TimesUp. Although the continuing relevance of feminist politics is sometimes co-opted into a "feel good feminism" (one enacted more through consumerism than political activism), make no mistake—the monstrously willful feminist killjoy is here to stay.[2]

Most pertinent to my study, the current embrace of feminism (albeit a tenuous, complicated one) is bleeding into the horror genre and its engagements with the monstrous. As evidenced above, horror scholarship has long engaged with the politics of gender.[3] However, feminist readings of the genre have often tended to "underestimate its subversive potential," instead focusing on negative gendered depictions, the eroticization of violence, the paucity of positive or heroic female characters, and so on (Pinedo 71). Yet, recent work by the likes of Natasha Patterson, Alexandra West, Elizabeth Aiossa, Kinitra D. Brooks, and Robin R. Means Coleman suggest valorization of horror's subversive abilities is on the rise. Indeed, much scholarship of late specifically mines the feminist potential of the genre, proving not only that "overlaps between the feminine and the monstrous can be highly productive" (as Shildrick claims), but that horror itself is doing feminist work (29). Such productive overlaps between the feminine and the monstrous are in evidence in textual foregrounding of zombie girls of color, female Frankenstein creatures, queer vampires, rebel witch covens, and fearless final girls. Notably, perhaps more than any other mode, texts of the horrific and monstrous from the post-millennial period present females as fully human, heroic, powerful, wise, and complicated as their male counterparts—and as flawed.[4]

As the previous chapters have maintained, post-millennial texts featuring zombies, vampires, and witches not only provide rich ground for feminist political critique, but also *include* overtly feminist concerns within their narratives. Engaging with legacies of colonialism, slavery, and white supremacy, critical of corporatism, sexual violence, and marriage as an institution, calling for less militarism, more ethical scientific practices, and better relations with the planet and its creatures, monster narratives regularly call upon their audiences to fear the darker sides of humanity rather than embrace the call to render others monstrous. Such a rendering, one that includes "The making monstrous of particular types of bodies," profoundly informs real world injustices (Halberstam 4). Yet, the flip side of this is that embracing the monstrosity of existence (and embodiment) has the capacity to undo such injustices. What might be possible if we admitted the monster is the self? That "the other" is but a comforting—if violently hierarchal—fantasy? That the foreign and the alien hold the power to frighten only in so much as we allow them to do so? Such admissions would involve rethinking what has heretofore been thought of as an exterior monstrosity existing outside the borders of the self. If we were to let this monster in, to see its reflection in our own, might we be able to move towards undoing the hierarchies that bind us to oppressive models of gender, sexuality, class, race, and power? If we let this monster in, might we be able to step beyond the restrictive conceptions that place the "normal" and "ideal" in one box, and the aberrant, non-human, and deviant in another? This type of deconstruction of the boxes bounding our identities and relations would surely be *scary* in the way most unknown things are, but, we surely would be better to, as the saying goes, feel the fear and do it anyway. In this vein, let's begin such a rethinking of the monstrous by taking a look at a handful of millennial Gothic narratives featuring the New Woman, female Frankenstein creatures, and that devilishly frightful monster, the female author.

Section 1: Gothic Monstrosity in Feminist Guise

The Gothic mode, a genre defined by the impetus "to uncover the unfamiliar beneath the familiar," has long provided a fictional housing with which to examine the politics of gender (Palmer 172). In this regard, many Gothic tales of the Victorian era showcase New Woman characters, a figure that circulated in the popular press, the consumer world, and theoretical treatises, most often in ways that depicted her as a social menace associated with the "dangers" of female emancipation.[5] In advocating for female educational equity, expanded professional opportunities for women, and a more egalitarian approach to marriage/family, the New Woman posed a threat to the prevailing Western social order and the gender hierarchy it depended upon. In contrast to the woman as "angel of the house," one integral to the cult of "true womanhood" which characterized the Victorian era, females who resisted such roles were framed as monsters who sought to destroy "the scripturally sanctioned rule of male over female in marriage" (Poole, *Monsters*, 77). The New Woman was cast not only as a figure that would destroy traditional marriage/family, but as one with the potential to bring about apocalyptic shifts that may destroy society itself. Cast as "a monstrous aggressor" in the Victorian imagination, the New Woman was an especially common figure in literature of the era, something Sally Ledger's *The New Woman: Fiction and Feminism at the Fin de Siècle* attests to (P. Murphy 2).[6]

Patricia Murphy, who also addresses the feminist work carried out via fictional New Women, argues characters of this ilk spoke to the "suffocating weight of tradition" that imprisoned females in a choking patriarchal embrace, something she reads in relation to the live burial motif imbuing Gothic texts (144). This "entry into a premature grave" experienced by female characters provides a haunting reflection of real world oppressions, ones which the New Woman railed against (144). The three post-millennial Gothic narratives discussed in this first section of the chapter, *Penny Dreadful, Crimson Peak,* and *I Am the Pretty Thing*

That Lives in the House, deliver a similar reflection as their Victorian era predecessors, one in which lead female characters breech convention in ways both dangerous and pleasurable, something Fred Botting names a hallmark of the genre. In Showtime's *Penny Dreadful*, two New Woman protagonists, one a powerful female hunted by Dracula (Vanessa) and the other an avenging Frankenstein creature (Lily), play integral roles. As for the 2015 film *Crimson Peak*, it has a female author at its narrative center—one who encapsulates the ambitious, career minded New Woman of the early 20th century. Lastly, *I Am the Pretty Thing That Lives in the House* features several iterations of the New Woman—a murdered newlywed come back as ghost, an aging female author, and an in-home-nurse turned detective.

A Monster Like No Other: *Penny Dreadful*'s Vanessa

Penny Dreadful's Vanessa Ives has all the markings of a New Woman. Intelligent, independent, and willful, she eschews marriage, sleeps with whom she pleases, and ultimately prevents the "eternal night" Dracula seeks to launch in London. At various points throughout the three season run, Vanessa acts to protect outsiders such as herself. A social justice warrior of her time—one whom Trump might find "a nice bit of ass"—she is importantly not pilloried for her New Woman attributes but celebrated for the very things that make her "new"—her agency, her power, her insistence she could "never be happy sitting by the fire" in a "loveless mansion." Though relentlessly pursued by a nefarious Egyptian god, by Dracula, by villainous Nightwalkers, and by the devil himself, Vanessa remains true to herself and her convictions. While she is presented as conflicted about her faith in Catholicism as well as her penchant for divination, Vanessa ultimately forges a self-identity not ruled by her church, by the patriarchal figures that surround her (as with her quasi-father Malcolm), or by societal convention (particularly in relation to her sexual agency and disinterest in marriage).

When we first witness her character, she kneels in front of a crucifix, her head bowed, fervently praying. The over-the-shoulder shot hides her bowed head, making it appear as if she has been decapitated—the fate of many a female monster.

The following front angle shot then reveals a mass of spiders crawling across her skin. Her shadowed face is tortured, frantic. The religious iconography here, along with later exorcism scenes, aligns Vanessa to the demonic female. Wedded to this is another trope, that of madwoman.

An over the shoulder shot of Vanessa Ives (Eva Green) from episode one of *Penny Dreadful* that makes it appear as if she has been beheaded. Dressed in black, Vanessa's dark figure contrasts with the light cast over the crucifix she fervently prays towards (Showtime, 2014-2016).

Sequestered in her room and chained to her bed at multiple points over the show's arc, Vanessa frequently spends time locked up as doctors and priests try to cure what is variously deemed demonic possession, hysteria, and insanity. But Vanessa rallies against the people and institutions that corset her, something that is played out with particularly delicious wickedness when she attends a party with Malcolm in the second episode of season one. When the assembled upper class guests take part in a séance while at the party, Vanessa begins to channel the voices of Malcolm's dead children who accuse him of being a bad father and an even worse husband. She then rails, "You filthy man, you man, you animal, betrayer," her face contorted with rage. Herein, Vanessa turns the tables and presents Malcolm, a wealthy, upstanding British gentleman, as monster. After crawling atop the table to writhe, convulse, and arch her body impossibly backward (in the pose typical of demon possession), Vanessa runs into the street, leaving the partygoers dumbfounded.

Part Gothic New Woman, part madwoman, part demon, part angel, Vanessa has a lust for life and the inquisitive, courageous demeanor to suck the marrow from it. Yet, she is the character that struggles the most with her inner monstrosity, believing herself to be cursed. Following in the footsteps of her mentor, the Cut-Wife (discussed in the previous chapter), Vanessa eventually comes to accept she is "like no others." Embracing her monstrosity by the series' close, she successfully defeats the Nightwalker witches as well as Dracula—and maintains control of her own soul to boot. In the final episodes, she prevents the "eternal nigh" threatening London when she willfully chooses to die rather than join forces with Dracula. This sacrifice positions her as a newfangled Gothic daughter, one who escapes her life in Sir Malcolm's gloomy patriarchal mansion as well as successfully shrugging off the confines of mental asylums, rest cures, and myriad psychological attacks. Not only that, she rebukes the devil and stands firm against the lure of the immortal power Dracula promises.[7] Though her capitulation to death can be placed amongst the many Gothic heroines, femme fatales, and "fridged" females who die within their narrative moorings, it can also be allied to resistant female figures such as Joan of Arc, Medusa, and Lilith. Further, her unwillingness to live in a world which seeks to hold her captive in its oppressive norms, much like that of the protagonists of *The Awakening,* or, more recently, *Thelma and Louise,* functions as a symbol of the "suffocating weight of tradition" referenced by Patricia Murphy, one that makes it nearly impossible to survive as a fully empowered female agent within a patriarchal society that does not grant full inclusion to women (144). Choosing death over continued existence as a wanted, hunted woman, Vanessa's demise is at least partially positive— she willfully chooses a dead end so as to allow London a new beginning.

Finally, a Feminist Frankenstein Creature: *Penny Dreadful*'s Lily

To turn to Lily, the other primary New Woman figure of *Penny Dreadful,* she, like Vanessa, is targeted by malevolent males culled from Gothic classics such as *Frankenstein, Dr. Jekyll and Mr. Hyde,* and *The Picture of Dorian Gray.* She is first introduced to viewers as a saucy and quickwitted sex worker named Brona Croft, an Irish immigrant afflicted with consumption. Unafraid of revealing details of her life when she meets sharpshooter-cum-werewolf Ethan Chandler, she explains to him she formerly worked in a factory, imparting "it was a dispiriting endeavor. One by one we were all replaced by new machines." After a horrible coughing fit, she jokes to Ethan, "I'm off to look for work that a machine can't do, not yet, anyway." In this instance, Lily aptly compares factory work to sex work, emphasizing the mechanization and dehumanization capitalism brings—

particularly to female, immigrant bodies such as hers. Here, her status as a sex worker also speaks to the blurring between the New Woman and the prostitute discussed by Murphy in *The New Woman Gothic*—a blurring that links the sexual agency of the New Woman with the woman-as-body-for-hire.

For Brona the blurring between prostitution and marriage is particularly pronounced. Told by her mother she had better tie the knot as her only choices are "marriage or whoring," Brona refuses to marry, describing her fiancé as a "brittle man with brittle hands." Alas, after Victor Frankenstein murders her so as to "make" a wife for his first creature, she is reanimated as undead wifely material. Victor's targeting of Brona reeks of both classism and xenophobia—she is, in his (and society's) view, a "lowly" Irish prostitute, a sick one at that, and her life is worth less than will be her revived corpse. After Victor suffocates her with a pillow as he pretends to be administering to her as doctor, he submerges her corpse in a watery grave at his lab to wait for a storm powerful enough to produce the needed bride-reanimating juice. Once a storm hits, Victor performs his brand of science with Caliban (his first creature). Brona reawakens naked and unable to speak, her memories gone. Renamed Lily and told she is Victor's cousin and Caliban's fiancée, she eventually regains her voice and much of her memory. Initially naive and tractable, she becomes less so as she remembers more and more from her former life as Brona. These memories fuel her refusal to marry Caliban, something she voices in no uncertain terms when he returns to "collect his goods." Calling him a hypocrite given he wants to live as a "real man" yet trap her as domesticated wife, Lily likens him to "all other men" and launches into a rousing feminist-fueled invective:

> We flatter our men with our pain. We bow before them. We make ourselves dolls for their amusement. We lose our dignity in corsets and high shoes and gossip and the slavery of marriage. You force us onto your beds. You drag us into the alleys, cram yourselves into our mouths for two bob when you're not beating us senseless.

Shoving the cowed Caliban to the ground, she continues, "Never again will I kneel to any man. Now they shall kneel to me. As you do, monster!" His stricken visage soon softens her outrage, though, and she is reminded he too is a product of Victor's corpse-electrocuting-agenda. She then kneels next to Caliban, calling him "My monster. My beautiful corpse." Declaring that Victor "brought forth not angels but demons, thee and me," she asks, "What should we do with this power?" Informing him, "I want a man unlike all other men. My brother. My equal," she suggests the two of them "create a do-over" where "the blood of mankind will water our garden, us and our kin, and our children." Herein, her feminist-inflected desire for an equal partner is undergirded by a more radical, vengeance-fueled aim. Eventually drawing on the history of female oppression to rally other women to her cause, Lily's quest leads to one of the most delightfully rebellious narrative arcs of *Penny Dreadful*.

Later encapsulating her hopes for future women via comments shared with a mother mourning her lost child at a cemetery, Lily proclaims: "Please know that the day a good woman will have to undergo such indignities are almost past. We will not have to suffer our children to starve, and freeze, and die dishonored on cold hills. We will not be hungry forever, we will rise."[8] Significantly, Lily's aims are linked to the women's liberation movement of the time in a scene featuring a group of suffragettes carrying placards as they chant "Votes for woman. Rise up for equality!" Lily initially scoffs that "all this marching around in public and waving placards" is not how to foment change, instead insisting change is acquired "By craft. By stealth. By poison. By the throat quietly slit in the dead of the night. By the careful and silent accumulation of power." Her initial vision thus frames domination as the goal. Yet, by the series' end, she understands that strident militism is not the answer. Before coming to this realization, she recruits an army of fellow sex workers to her cause, rallying them with speeches that call for vengeance. "We are not women who crawl. We are not women who kneel. And for this we will be branded radicals, revolutionists," she tells them, continuing, "Women who are strong and refuse to be degraded and chose to protect themselves are called monsters. That is the world's crime."

Eventually realizing the futility of a revolution that will supplant one type of tyranny with another, Lily ultimately tempers her views. She no longer seeks to master men, but rather to live life on her own terms without the weight of patriarchy hanging like an albatross around her neck.[9] Her narrative arc, as Megen de Bruin-Molé argues, marks her as the most subversive figure in *Penny Dreadful*. As she writes, "the female Creature speaks, and lives to speak another day. She is allowed to escape into the world, with all her anger and violence and emotion. With all her monstrous femininity…. Who knows what delightful, irrational, and monstrously *female* things she will do in the world" (emphasis in original). At the series' close, Lily is poised to continue her aims to politicize other women, to perhaps join suffragettes in the streets of London, carrying a "Rise up for Equality" placard. As Lauren Sarner posits, the show makes "militant feminism compelling," turning Lily's radical call for retribution into an understandable reaction to female oppression. Indeed, the "personal is political" mantra is brought to monstrous life via Lily's trajectory. In so doing, *Penny Dreadful* provides audiences with a Gothic New Woman who lives up to the feminist sentiment bubbling under the surface of Shelley's original novel. Crucially, Lily transforms from the stereotypical man-hater mainstream culture is so fond of associating with feminism. Though understandably driven to radicalism by the horrible things that have been done to her, Lily ultimately adopts an equity-based view, one grounded in female independence and agency. A *Bride of Frankenstein* for the new millennium, she, much like the bride in James Whale's 1935 film, is horrified by the suggestion she should marry the men foisted upon her.[10] "I need no man to save me," she insists, a declaration that just as well could have come from Vanessa, her kindred Gothic New Woman.

New Woman as Author of Her Own Fate: *Crimson Peak*

Guillermo del Toro's *Crimson Peak* is set just after the pivot to the 20th century, in 1901 (or some 10 years later than *Penny Dreadful*). Dramatizing tensions between the past (associated with dead parental figures and decaying mansions) and the future (associated with Edith, the film's New Woman protagonist), the story opens in New York City. Early scenes emphasize the modern workplace, the changing roles of women, and the aspirations of our heroine as she tries to publish a manuscript. This strand of the narrative reflects what Stephanie Green references as "the rising importance of female authorship and authority within a fast expanding publishing industry." As Green notes, "The emergence of the Gothic New Woman can be seen as closely associated with the rise of mass print media consumption at the nineteenth century fin de siècle." This rise in the demand for print media is just what Edith hopes to capitalize on, yet such hopes are dashed when an editor compliments her for her handwriting rather than her writing itself, telling her she should focus on penning love stories if she wishes to have a chance at publication. Edith balks at this, declaring that in the future she will type her work so as to disguise that she is female.

More interested in the working world than in courtship, Edith is warned near the outset of the film she will likely die a spinster like Jane Austen, something that she takes as a compliment. Likening herself to Mary Shelley, Edith realizes the dangers inherent in marriage. Such exchanges make up some of the many writerly moments in *Crimson Peak*, ones which ultimately muddle Edith's life story with the fictional story she has penned. In fact, her status as a writer bookends the narrative, one that opens with her trying to secure publication for her manuscript and ends with an image of a book entitled *Crimson Peak* (with Edith listed on screen as author). This prompts one to wonder: is the film Edith's ghost story, one edited to include the romance a prospective publisher insisted upon, or is it the story of her transformation from an ambitious writer immersed in the modern world of New York to a confused, haunted heroine confined in a dilapidated mansion after marrying a rakish man with a decidedly sinister sister? I prefer the former—one wherein Edith never leaves New York and the narrative proper is but a fictional tale of her making. Said tale features our heroine (Edith) moving to a crumbling Gothic estate in North England where she is positioned between an aloof husband (Tom) and his jealous sister (Lucille), each of whom hopes to capitalize on Edith's inheritance money.

In contrast to the sympathetic Edith, Lucille acts as a gender traitor of sorts, serving her brother Tom's interests (and the patriarchy by extension). Via this relocation to England, Edith is placed within a traditional gendered script; she is no longer an authoress but a meek wife, confined in an attic bedroom and plied with cups of poisonous tea by her vindictive sister-in-law. Lucille's campaign against Edith is not one of mere mean-spiritedness but instead is informed by her family legacy, one of abusive fathers and bedridden mothers in which Lucille's only role was that of nursemaid. When Edith arrives, she is another person for Lucille to watch over, one whom Lucille will poison and try to kill, much as she did her brother's prior wives. The story here takes a cleaver to the horrific results of imprisoning females within domestic roles of mother, wife, daughter, and sister, suggesting it is time for women to step into the promises of the new century, to become the type of New Woman figure Edith is prior to being sucked into life at Allerdale Hall, a decaying façade with moldering walls and a collapsing roof where red-tinged ghosts stalk the corridors. Positioned more as victimized women than malevolent entities, these female ghosts work to alert Edith to the malicious intentions of Tom and Lucille. Rather than menacingly haunting the living, the ghosts warn Edith the bloody history of Allerdale Hall and the "crimson peak" upon which it sits. Herein, *Crimson Peak* re-envisions the Gothic female ghost, turning her into an ally.

Meanwhile, Edith refuses to play the part of damsel-in-distress or madwoman and instead acts as female detective. She doggedly pursues the secrets the house conceals, riding its rusty elevator into its unsafe spaces and, at one point, stealing Lucille's hefty assortment of keys so as to better search the mansion for clues. In effect, she is a New Woman making her own choices, one in keeping with the characters she references as the type she likes to create as an author. Lucille, on the other hand, acts as female villain, one seemingly trapped within the role of dark-haired vixen. A femme fatale figure, her brilliant piano skills symbolize her as one who *plays* the role of "proper woman." Seething with jealousy and rage, Lucille turns savage, much like the butterfly-eating moths she warns Edith about.

Given she is unable to draw wealth into the estate via her own actions (as marrying would require her to move to her husband's location), she is left with the option of manipulating her brother's actions. Though a villain, she is at least partially a sympathetic one—a monstrous woman caught in the web of patriarchy whose only path to power is through a male. Herein, the information the tale offers about Lucille's father is key. "Our father hated our mother," Lucille informs Edith, telling her how he broke both her mother's legs, forcing her to be bedridden. Lucille clearly wants to avoid such an immobilized state so takes instead to disabling other women. Acting as her father once did, she throws Edith over a banister late in the film, breaking her leg. Such avarice and cruelty is perhaps what caused her to be labeled mad in her earlier years, a past obliquely hinted at within the narrative.

Just as Edith is expected to play the angel in the house, so too is Lucille conscripted to play the part of demonic madwoman. Yet, the fact the house is collapsing upon itself intimates that such spaces and subject positions cannot hold. Red clay slowly seeps up through the basement as white snow falls through a hole in the roof—figuratively, the house cannot escape the blood of its past, something Edith, a figure associated with light colors and clothing, sheds light upon. Serving as an architectural double for the bodies of the women it has imprisoned within its walls, the mine the house sits atop seethes red clay into the lower floors. In contrast, the white snow that falls through the roof intimates the possibility of over-writing the hall's blood-soaked past—something Edith achieves in the film's visually arresting ending. Set outside rather than in the dark foreboding spaces of Allerdale Hall, this skull crushing final scene features Edith braining Lucille with a shovel, an ending which changes the tradition of a male stepping in to save the day. Tom and Lucille are both dead by movie's end. Gone too are the black moths and red skeletal ghosts—each of which emphasized the old house, based on an old societal structures and norms, was rotten. The last we see of Edith, the aspiring young female writer is limping across the snow, a symbolic blank page, ready and waiting for her next story.

The Umbilical Ties That Bind: *I Am the Pretty Thing That Lives in the House*

I Am the Pretty Thing That Lives in the House (*Pretty Thing*), directed by Oz Perkins, is a deliciously Gothic tale circulating around three female characters. A veritable nesting-doll of bookish plots, the three primary characters of *Pretty Thing* consist of a widely published horror author,

Iris Blum (Paula Prentiss) a (purported) fictional character from one of Iris' books, Polly Parsons (Lucy Boynton), and Lily Saylor, (Ruth Wilson) a hospice nurse hired to take care of Iris. The surface plot spans roughly one year, with Lily continuing to serve as nurse to Iris, and neither of them ever leaving the house. This framing story soon gives way to the revelation that Polly is not a fictional character created by Blum, but a real woman murdered in the home, one built in 1812 by Polly's bridegroom. Mainly told through Lily's perceptions and voice, the film serves as a meditation on storytelling/authoring as well as upon aging/death. Iris, a renowned author, has dementia, something that has robbed her of her memories, her writing, and her books. Distanced from reality, she thinks her new nurse Lily is Polly, the heroine from her best-selling book, *The Lady in the Walls*. Meanwhile, Lily hates books and movies, especially scary ones, and is a generally nervous, unnerving character. She talks to herself regularly in variously scolding and mocking tones. Both she and Iris are recluses, neither of them communicating with the outside world or taking visitors. Characterizing death as an enveloping darkness that closes around one "like a claw," Lily and Iris will each be dead within a year. As for Polly, she is dead when the story begins.

That things are not as they seem is a prominent theme throughout, something heightened by blurred camerawork and eyes/faces/bodies reflected in mirrors, windows, and television screens. In the first shot, a ghostly woman glides in a shadowy blur across black space. Fuzzy shots such as these mirror the unclear vision of the characters, two of whom wear (but regularly remove) thick glasses. This hazy visual landscape adds to the film's blurring of time, one wherein each of the three protagonists hearken from different eras (the early 1800s, the 1960s, and the contemporary moment). At the start of the narrative, Lily is delivered to the home by Mr. Waxcap, the estate manager. Her opening monologue, spoken as she looks into the camera, introduces several key motifs:

> I have heard myself say that a house with a death in it can never again be bought or sold by the living. It can only be borrowed from the ghosts that have stayed behind, to go back and forth, letting out and gathering back in again. Worrying over the floors in confused circles. Tending to their deaths like patchy, withered gardens. They have stayed to look back for a glimpse of the very last moments of their lives. But the memories of their own deaths are faces on the wrong side of wet windows, smeared by rain. Impossible to properly see.

Revealing the house is "The staying place of a rotted ghost," Lily continues: "From where I am now, I can be sure of only a very few things. The pretty thing you are looking at is me. Of this I am sure. My name is Lily Saylor. I am a hospice nurse. Three days ago, I turned twenty-eight years old. I will never be twenty-nine years old." This prophetic revelation gives way to a dark and twisted Gothic tale, one whose ambiguities are never fully resolved. Are all three women ghosts? Is the story only in Lily or Iris's imagination? Is Iris mentally impaired or does she have the ability to see and communicate with ghosts? Is the house itself malevolent? These and other unresolved questions contribute to *Pretty Thing's* mysterious plot—one in which the three women are not only trapped in the house, but also within staid expectations of femininity. Iris and Lily, their names evoking flowers and gardening, are stuck within the molderous home. Whereas Iris is "planted" within her decaying mind, Lily grows into quite the detective, digging through the home's secrets, primary among them whether Polly is real, how she died, and why she still haunts the house.

Not long after Lily arrives, she discovers a mold spot growing in the wall of the front hallway and reports the problem to Mr. Waxcap. When he arrives, his mild-mannered timidity does not prevent him from arguing the estate cannot pay for any mold-related repairs. They are "cosmetic" not "structural," he explains. When Lily avers that the problem is not cosmetic, he clarifies "cosmetic as opposed to structural. The flesh and not the bones." His choice of words here indicates that "flesh" is not important, only structure or bones, implying the fleshy, pretty things that live in the house are not integral to its structure (unlike the husband who built the house or Waxcap, who controls its funding). The description also invokes Polly's skeleton which, unbeknown to Lily at this point, is buried behind the molding wall. She is, in effect, a replaceable pretty thing not integral to the edifice (unlike the hammer, pliers, and planks of wood used in the home's construction and witnessed in various imagery throughout the film). Perhaps female presence is a thorn in the side of this "masculine structure" and the money/tools that keep it in shape.

Lily, desirous to "open up the wall" (as she tells the handyman), searches the house, traverses its floors, and gets into the guts of its secrets. She rips at the home's structure while beautifying it with vases of flowers, tending to its "flesh." Having arrived long after the home was built, she is not part of its "structure." Rather, as various images convey, she is attached to it as if by an umbilical cord. The first time we see such a cord, Lily is on the phone to a friend. An unseen force lifts and pulls on the phone cord, eventually causing the phone to fly out of Lily's hand, figuratively pulling her back into the home/womb and cutting off contact with the outside world. This will be the only time Lily interacts with people not attached to the home (whether as ghost, estate manager, or handyman). Later, in images of her where she appears as if a blurred ghost, Lily is chewing/ingesting something that appears to be a cord. Polly, the house's primary ghost, is likely the entity that lifted the phone cord when Lily first arrived. To her, cords are sinister. Telling of her birth, she narrates:

I'm not more than a few minutes old and my mother is already dead, her forehead slick with sweat, and cool with the pallor of icebox butter. I am tied to my mother's body by a terrible rope that is a shiny, twisted midnight blue-black.... But now I am dead. And yes, I left the world just as I came into it. I am wearing nothing but blood.

Here, the blue-black umbilical cord is tethered to Polly's mother who died only a few minutes after Polly was born. As for Polly, she will die soon after getting married at the hands of her husband. After bringing her to the house, he kills her with hammer blows to the head. He then buries her in the front hall, and, according to Iris, leaves her "Carelessly concealed in a grave too shallow to be rightly called a grave at all. Better to call it a hiding place." Her name is a seeming reference to the eighteenth century murder ballad, "Pretty Polly," implying that Polly may have been pregnant by another man at the time of her murder (as was the woman in the song). The recurring umbilical cord imagery also suggests a pregnancy. When Lily later finds Polly's burial place in the wall, dark twisting cords cover her shallow, womb-like grave. She is effectively "roped" to the house with umbilical cords, a symbolic parallel to her mother's death from childbirth as well as to her own murder that results in, as she puts it, "leaving the world just as I came into it ... wearing nothing but blood." Tied to the house she was murdered in, Polly has perhaps also ensnared Iris and Lily, or perhaps the house itself—a male built structure—entraps all three of them.

At one point, Iris warns Lily: "Learn to see yourself as the rest of the world does, and you'll keep. But left alone, with only your own eyes looking back at you, even the prettiest things rot. You fall apart like flowers." In other words, learn to view yourself from a circumscribed position where you accept being a pretty *thing*—a kept flower—or you will end up alone, to wilt and die. This is a fitting warning for the New Woman figure—one that can be associated with Polly due to her willfulness, to Iris as Gothic female author, and to Lily as nurse (the latter two being professions particularly associated with the New Woman). Given the ending of the film indicates both Iris and Lily are dead, they will now "rot" like Polly. But will their ghosts leave the house alone? Will their stories, like Polly's, continue on loop even when others inhabit the home? As much is indicated in the closing shot of the home's interior. The camera pans over one of the bedrooms, now peopled with two children who are inexplicably startled awake as Lily's voice narrates, "I have heard myself say that a house with a death in it can never again be bought or sold by the living. It can only be borrowed from its ghosts." Explaining the trauma of death persists "pressed deeply in place like type on paper," Lily closes her narration with "I think I'll stay for one more look at her." Given that she has been "looking at" Polly and Iris throughout *Pretty Thing*, as well as her own face in the mirror, which "her" Lily wants to get another look at is unclear. What we are left with, though, is the indication that these three women, all of them blurring the bounds of "proper femininity" and refusing to see themselves "as the rest of the world does," are left to rot, to "live" in the house but only as "things"—not as independent New Women, but as kept flowers, pressed within the walls of a man-made home.

As the above section contends, *Penny Dreadful, Crimson Peak* and *Pretty Thing* revolve around New Woman figures rendered monstrous due to their refusal to abide by gender norms. They are too opinionated, independent, free-thinking, and intractable. They use their talents to weave spells, author books, unearth buried secrets, and incite rebellion. They breach the boundaries of family and home, working as supernatural sleuths, writers, and nurses. Yet, their commitment to new ideas, new professions, and new models of what it means to be female make them "unwomanly" in the eyes of their respective time periods. The women featured in the two films examined in the next section are similarly viewed as aberrant—particularly in relation to how they perform (or, in the eyes of society, fail to perform) their familial roles and womanly duties.

Section 2: Get Out of My House! Banishing Systemic Monsters

The domestic space of the home has long been a favored horror setting. Where better to explore all the various monsters in the closet that haunt our imaginations? Populated with sinister fathers, malevolent mothers, and demonic children, the genre—from the Gothic to contemporary "house horror"—often suggests homes themselves are monstrous. Quite regularly, a bad home is associated with a bad mother. Sometimes, when the mother is bad, her children follow suit. Positioned in the "private" world of the home according to traditional conceptions of the family, mothers and children are linchpins to what Sara Ahmed terms the "straight line of inheritance," the line that calls for willing wombs, obedient children, and deference to (male) authority. When mothers and children don't toe this straight line, (patriarchal) order is lost, as films such as *The Exorcist, The Brood,* and *Carrie* exemplify. While we see examples of renegade mothers and children in the two films taken up in this section, subversive takes on family life are still relatively rare within the horror canon. Much more widespread are continuing insinuations that bad mothers and their bad children destroy the family unit, wreak economic havoc, and unleash demonic forces. This is the case in *Goodnight Mommy*, a film where two back-from-the-grave twins torment their appearance-obsessed mother as she recovers from cosmetic surgery. It is also the case in *Paranormal, The Conjuring, Mama*, and the TV reboot of *The Exorcist*, all of which associate mothers and children (especially female ones) with the demonic. Most recently, we can witness it in the much-hyped *Hereditary* wherein a strange daughter, her mentally unstable mom, and her demon-worshipping grandmother are associated with familial destruction.

In contrast, two recent takes on domestic horror blame societal ills rather than mothers and their children—*The Babadook* and *Housebound* (27). Speaking to one of the few aspects of horror that Creed names as subversive, each of these films challenge "rational discourse and the symbolic order" by championing the "non-rational" discourse of women and children (38). In *Babadook*, Amelia's "irrational" grief and Sam's monster-talk are cast as the by-products of a neglectful society, not as evidence of their personal defectiveness. In *Housebound*, Kylie's caustic complaints and her mother Miriam's ditzy ghost stories turn out to be far more "rational" than the words of judges, psychiatrists, and police officers. Instead of framing the refusal to "recognize the paternal order" as "what produces the monstrous," *Babadook* and *Housebound* construct the paternal order dysfunctional (Creed 38). Further, by refuting mothers/children as more prone to evil (one proffered in much horror) *Babadook* and *Housebound* suggest we should be wary of father figures (who exert deleterious power even after divorce/death within the narratives).[11]

Neither film frames the single mother (whether divorced or widowed) as to blame for the tragedies that ensue (as she is, for example, in *The Exorcist, Carrie, Psycho, Friday the 13th*, and so on). Rather, *Babadook* and *Housebound* each address—albeit in far different registers—the negative impact of phallocentric culture. Telling stories of women and children trapped in domestic roles and spaces, these films contribute to Gothic depictions of the home as prison while also positioning such homes as part and parcel of punitive societal structures. As with the acclaimed televised adaptation of *The Handmaid's Tale*, which frames the large, gloomy home the main character is trapped within as a symbolic condensation of an inequitable society, so too do *Babadook* and *Housebound* address societal horrors via locking their characters in prison-like homes. Yet, in contrast to *Handmaid's*, they position the home as a space partially outside of—and thus at least somewhat immune to—a punitive society. Serving as apt examples of what Erin Harrington names "gynahorror," they interrogate "the underpinnings of the social, political and philosophical othering of women," an othering that results in mother-blame and child guilt-by-association, as well as one that casts the domestic space as one of insanity, repression, and rot (1).

Who's Afraid of the Big Bad Pop-Up Book? *The Babadook*

The critically acclaimed 2014 independent horror film, *The Babadook*, written and directed by Jennifer Kent, focuses on the isolation and grief of Amelia, a widowed mother, and her rambunctious, preternaturally odd son, Samuel. An international success, the film transports Gothic themes into present day Australia. Set within a dreary mausoleum of a house, *The Babadook* draws on themes of mental instability, social ostracization, and debilitating grief. The dark, gloomy interior, claustrophobic bedrooms, and sinister basement space of Amelia and Sam's home all contribute to the aura of demonic domesticity. The first scene, which features Amelia having a horrible nightmare about the night her husband died, sets the tone for the horrors that follow, ones linked particularly to her experiences as a widowed mother. The initial shot, a close-up of Amelia, her face stricken with fear, gives way to images of a harrowing car crash. Amelia's body is violently tossed and turned in the dream until she is eventually summoned awake by Sam's desperate plea, "mom … mom … mom…. I had the dream again." To appease his crippling fear that a monster is in the house, mother and son look under beds and into wardrobes. Amelia assures Sam the house is monster-free and then cuddles Sam in bed while reading to him about the big bad wolf. Here, the juxtaposition of loving mother and scary story foreshadows Amelia's turn to "wolf" as well as the coming of the Babadook monster that will "blow the house down."

After mother and son fall fitfully asleep, Amelia detaches Sam's grasping hands and feet from her body, retreating to the edge of the bed. A prelude to the hold the Babadook will achieve over her person, this early assertion to break her body free from the physical and psychological hold others wield over it becomes the primary battle the narrative chillingly documents. Set in motion after Amelia reads Sam the *Mister Babadook* book, this battle "pops" into their lives seemingly as a result of this black-and-white pop-up story and its titular monster who insists "Let me in!" A dark-clothed, sunken eyed creature with large pointy teeth, pale skin, and black lips (redolent of a cartoonish Bela Lugosi), the Babadook leaps off the page to infiltrate their home. Emerging from various spaces (a coffin-like wardrobe, the basement, the dark corners of Amelia's bedroom), the Babadook shares traits with the vampire: it has to be invited in, wears a black cape and top hat, has long fingers replete with claw-like nails, uses shadows to invoke its presence, and crawls, insect-like, across ceilings. Further, once invited in, it does not leave. As the story-book warns "If it's in a word or it's in a look, you can't get rid of the Babadook." As well as emphasizing the staying-power of this vampiric baddie, the phrasing here also foregrounds the monstrous power of words and looks—a power that mother and son will soon be wielding against one another as they try to survive within their newly monster-infested home.

While the house is the primary location the horrors manifest, the "words and looks" of the surrounding community are the true culprits casting a pall over their lives. School officials, family welfare representatives, Samuel's doctor, and local police construe mother and son as profoundly dysfunctional. Those outside the home fail to address the physical, psychological, and material hardships of Sam and Amelia's single family. Instead, they enact a panoptican-like surveillance of the two, one that first ejects Sam from school and then invades their home-space to determine if Amelia is a "fit mother." The pair are similarly surveyed by Amelia's uppity sister. Asking when Amelia is going to "get over" her husband's death, the sister implies their fatherless family is abnormal and codifies Amelia's ongoing grief as pathetic. Via a focus that begins in the home and then expands to include the social landscape, the film's Suburban Gothic feel places its tale of horror within a social milieu defined by, as Amanda Howell puts it, "the suburbanisation of poverty"—one she argues puts "single parent families with female heads of household especially at risk." Noting that Amelia's widowhood "has altered her social status for the worse," Howell frames Amelia as a struggling not only with motherhood and grief, but with a culture that censures women in particular. Amelia's monstrous transformation is caused by, as Howell sees it, the patriarchal expectation put on women "to be effective and tireless careers"—a pressure we see Amelia struggling with not only at home, but at her nursing job (194–5).

Whilst most mothers in horror fall into good mother/bad mother depictions, Amelia is importantly a complex amalgam of both. She alternates between the good mother and the monstrous mother repeatedly (as signified not only in her quickly changing behavioral modes but in her different voice registers—one sweet and kind, the other deep and demonic-sounding). At one point telling Sam to "eat shit," she is associated with abjection, decay, and waste. She is the devouring, incorporating mother, one that threatens to absorb Sam, something intimated particularly in the scene where she pulls a reluctant Sam into the bathtub with her, a figurative representation of his re-absorption into her womb. Further, as the Babadook seemingly takes over her identity, she plies Sam with tranquilizers, kills the family dog, and serves up gruel riddled with glass shards. Simultaneously, Sam is depicted as an exceedingly bizarre child.

Amelia (Essie Davis) purging the Babadook, symbolized here as black vomit, from her person (*The Babadook*, IFC Films, 2014, directed by Jennifer Kent).

Giving the impression of being beyond human in various scenes (as when he stands impossibly balanced high above the earth on the top of a swing set) and as possessed in others (via hysterical screams and bodily fits), Sam's fondness for magic links him with the occult. A more benign version of the Babadook, he parasitically clings to Amelia, chipping away at her sanity and sense of self, his persistent wails redolent of the cavernous, devouring mouth of the bookish monster. Hence, while the Babadook is partly a monstrous manifestation of Amelia's grief and rage, so too is it a semi-doppelganger for Sam. Importantly, the malevolence the Babadook infects their lives with is inextricably tied to outside forces. It only shows up after Sam is turned away from his cousin's home and suspended from school. It then insinuates itself more forcefully when a doctor insists Sam's fear of monsters is normal and the police discount Amelia's claims someone is out to get Sam and her.

Despite the lack of support from the outer world, Amelia and Sam eventually quell the Babadook. Yet, when the monster first takes over Amelia's body, she sleeps for days, sits zombie-like in front of the television, and loses track of time/reality. At one point pulling a rotting tooth from her mouth, she remains persistent in her attempts to extract the putrefying monster from her person. Her attempts to exorcise the Babadook are eventually achieved when Sam ties her up in the basement late in the diegesis. Once captured thus, Amelia vomits out a viscous wave of black fluid, effectively ejecting the Babadook from her person.

This eruptive scene expels the monster from her person. Is it possible, however, that this is not the first time Amelia has ejected the Babadook? Did she initially spew out the monster in book form? Is she in fact the author of the *Mister Babadook* book? Given she authored "some magazine, some kids' stuff" before becoming a nurse (as she tells her sister's friends), it is plausible she composed the pop-up book. Perhaps she did so to contain the monster safely between the covers of a book. Yet, it manages to burst into their lives. She at one point tears the book to pieces and burns it, but this does not destroy the monster. Recall also the Babadook uses words and looks as its monstrous weapons—the very same instruments used by the judgmental school officials, the stern sister, the dismissive doctors and police. An outsider, the Babadook knocks loudly, demanding to be let in. It conveys none will be "left off the hook" and warns "do not tear up this book." So, while the Babadook monster seems to be a (writerly) manifestation of Amelia's consuming grief, so too might it be viewed as a judgmental interloper, a policing presence inside the home. It does not want tears or hugs or kind words, it wants control. When Amelia forcefully shouts near the end of the Babadook's reign of terror, "You are trespassing in my house!" this monster is deemed an invading outsider. She may have "invited" the Babadook in by creating/reading the book, but so too might she have distilled outside forces into a single entity—one that she and Sam will nullify together.

Critically, the end of the film, one whose happy ending is rendered in fairy tale form, suggests Amelia and Sam have successfully revised this monster story by sequestering the Babadook in the basement. In the closing scenes, mother and son relax in their back garden on Sam's birthday. Sam uses his homemade monster-killing gun to shoot at a dartboard. "Good shot!" Amelia congratulates him, a sharp contrast to Amelia's angry reprimand when one of Sam's contraptions broke a window at the film's outset. Now, the two are all sweet voices and hugs. Amelia gazes at a blooming black rose as she digs in the dirt. Sam finds a worm, adding it to a bowl already full of the wriggling creatures. "Wow, you've got a lot today," Amelia coos. They take the bowl of creepy-crawlies inside. Standing by the stairs that lead to the basement, Sam inquires about the Babadook, asking "Am I ever gonna see it?" to which Amelia replies, "One day, when you're bigger." Once in the basement, Amelia fends off the growling Babadook, forcing it back into the shadows after it attempts to take over her body again. She keeps it outside her person, yet she also locks it in the basement. She is, in other words, not going to let it out of her control to police them from without. When she returns to the garden, Sam asks, "How was it?" She assures him, "It was pretty quiet today." One day, when Sam is bigger, perhaps he will join his mother in keeping the monster fed. Until then, they will presumably tend to their grief by feeding the symbolic monster, keeping the tyrannical power it presents safely buried in the basement. As Sam pronounces in his magic trick that closes the film, "life is not always as it seems." And neither are mothers always monsters and children always bad. Sometimes, in fact, the words and looks of "well meaning" outsiders make life unbearable. When such monstrous outsiders knock at the door, *The Babadook* warns, don't let them in.

Not So Sunny Realities of Post-Colonial Suburban Life: *Housebound*

Housebound, a 2014 New Zealand film that has already garnered a U.S. remake, sizzles with comedic horror thanks to marvelous turns by actresses Morgana O'Reilly (Kylie) and Rima Te Wiata (Miriam). Made on a shoe-string budget by first-time writer-director Gerard Johnstone, the movie holds a 97 percent rating on *Rotten Tomatoes*, its appeal surely being due to its over-the-top hilarity, surprising twists and turns and finely executed jump scares. The majority of *Housebound* takes place in a decidedly Gothic home, one that imprisons the rebellious Kylie and haunts her paranormally-minded mother, Miriam. A former halfway house and cite of various murders, the house—like so many in horror—hides a plethora of secrets within its walls. Before the film is over, Kylie, the "hilariously antisocial leading lady," will have to delve into its basements and crawl-spaces, effectively turning the house inside out in order to right her upside-down life and heal her dysfunctional relationship with her mother (D'Angelo). Kylie is in the process of robbing an ATM as the movie begins. After her inept partner-in-crime knocks himself out with a sledgehammer, she hotwires a getaway car. Captured by the police, she is soon charged with an eight month house-arrest. Her freedom curtailed by probation officers and an ankle monitor, Kylie would prefer jail-time to her mother's blathering. Though Kylie initially scoffs at Miriam's claims their house is haunted, as time passes, a number of strange occurrences incite her curiosity. Taken aback when a hand grabs her ankle in the basement, Kylie fears an intruder (rather than ghosts) may be in the home. But, when an animatronic teddy bear keeps coming to life and strange, unexplained noises persist, she is forced to entertain the idea her mother is right, that the house is indeed haunted. Keen to reveal rational rather than paranormal explanations, Kylie launches an investigation of the home, searching its basement and digging into its floorboards to excavate the truth. Finding paperwork that divulges the home's former incarnation as a halfway house where multiple murders took place, Kylie confronts her mother. "You knew a girl was murdered in my room and you still let me live in it!" she accuses. Responding drolly "It wasn't an ideal situation," her mother goes on to allude to the money and marital problems that led to their

current housing situation. Exasperated, Kylie continues her quest to unearth the home's secrets. After discovering an orthodontic retainer in her
sleuthing pursuits, she is determined to identify the killer. She tampers
with her ankle monitor so as to allow herself more freedom of movement,
an act that results in Amos, the security contractor monitoring her probation, to enter the scene. To her mother Miriam's delight, Amos moonlights
as a paranormal investigator and agrees to bring his ghost-hunting equip-
ment to their home. Meanwhile, Kylie remains convinced a murderer is
at the heart of the weird goings-on and entices Amos to help her find the
killer. The two soon decide the odd next door neighbor is likely the culprit,
a suspicion furthered by the glee said neighbor takes in butchering and
skinning possums. Alas, nothing is as it first seems in this twisting tale,
and the seemingly monstrous neighbor in actuality provided safe haven to
one of the halfway home's escapees, Eugene, an eccentric tinkerer-genius.

As Kylie is trying to piece together the sordid history of the house as
well as the cause of the strange occurrences continuing within its walls,
Dennis, the court-ordered psychologist assigned to her case, visits a number of times, insinuating both she and her mother are delusional. Referencing Kylie's history with mental illness, Dennis maintains Kylie needs
to be institutionalized. Joined by a string of police officers and probation
officials, these confrontational incursions into the home serve as con-
densed representations of the state's attempts to "control" Kylie via legal
and medical means. Kylie is here cast as a thorn in the side of "proper
society." So too is her erratic mother, one who cannot control her daughter and lost Kylie's father to capitalist pursuits. Kylie later learns from
Graeme, her mother's not-macho-or-rich-enough new partner, that her
biological father now runs "a boat brokerage on the Gold Coast" and has
"Done quite well for himself." Alluding to an ugly divorce that resulted in
economic hardship for Miriam and a fatherless life for Kylie, it is revealed
her dad bought the house they now reside in on the cheap with plans to
subdivide it and double his investment. A metaphor for their fractured
family, the dilapidated home on the wrong side of town also implicates
New Zealand's colonial history and the resulting pressures to assimilate
to the (white) capitalist ethos of "moving up." The monetary aspirations
of Kylie's father, a man now residing on the Gold Coast, named for the
area's 1860s era gold rush, furthers such sentiment. Abandoning Kylie in
much the same way "mother countries" ditch the inhabitants of their col-
onies, this narrative thread provides a twist on the gold-digging woman
trope. Importantly, Kylie's father tries to strike gold by buying a cut-rate
home so he can relocate to a richer, whiter environ. Though these details
only lurk underneath the surface of the film, the history of New Zealand
and the resulting forced assimilation of the indigenous Maori is arguably

presented in "monster house" form. That this house is inhabited by Miriam and turned inside out by Kylie and Amos, all of whom have Maori roots, speaks to the continuing economic disparity and disenfranchisement of certain segments of the population. Formerly a halfway house called Sunshine Grove, the home was used to keep similarly "unwanted" types out of the mainstream—and, as it turns out, to kill at least ten of them. As such horrors further unfold, it becomes apparent Dennis, the psychiatrist now treating Kylie, was Sunshine Grove's director. Upon discovering he wears an orthodontic retainer (something linked to the killer) Kylie turns her suspicions towards Dennis, the shifty-eyed doctor who wants to erode Kylie's freedom as much as her sanity. In other words, Dennis, a symbol of patriarchal colonialist domination, *retains* power by keeping the poor, the female, and the aberrant "housebound."

This filmic admixture of Suburban Gothic, house horror, and family drama gives way to a zany comedic ending, one that makes hilarious use of domestic spaces and items, figuratively making the "crazy" women of the home the (domestic) heroes and the upstanding doctor the villain. In the action packed last twenty minutes, Dennis sets his murderous sights on Kylie and Miriam in order to prevent them from bringing to light his serial-killing past. As mother and daughter attempt to evade him, they discover Eugene, a former halfway house inhabitant with wild hair and an exceedingly odd demeanor, living in the walls of their home. With Eugene's help, Kylie and Miriam fend off Dennis, reclaiming their home and bonding in the process. Miriam initially distracts Dennis with idle chatter, proving female chit-chat to be a worthy weapon. Kylie later takes a cheese grater to Dennis' face before immobilizing him in an oversize laundry basket. After he frees himself from the hamper, he attempts to strangle Miriam with a phone cord (a nod to the "need" to silence chattering women). Ultimately electrocuted with a meat fork (perhaps the same one he committed his murders with), Dennis' head explodes into a waterfall of blood. Separated from the "manly bite" to "fork over" the home's current inhabitants, his demise is a symbolic blow to the economic and state forces that have hindered the women's life trajectories (and invaded their domestic space). Irreverently checking off many staples of the horror genre, the film gleefully imprisons its viewers in a comedic romp rendered scary not by monstrous women, but by abandoning fathers and creepy doctors. Helmed by a mother-daughter duo that triumph over the variously hostile, ineffective, and violent men in their lives, *Housebound* renovates haunted house motifs, overturning both "woman in peril" and "madwoman in the attic" tropes along the way. It, along with *The Babadook*, provides progressive alternatives to the mother-hating, child-demonizing narratives that still circulate in our contemporary media landscape.

Section 3: Gendered Discontent in 21st Century Creature Features

Creature Features of the 1950s and 60s draw on technology gone wrong, alien invasions, and mutated life forms run amok. These B-movies dominated the expanding U.S. drive-in theater market of the mid-twentieth century with campy, over-the top monstrous figures that tapped into societal anxieties. The giant, infectious, and/or quickly multiplying creatures featured in film and televisual examples of this horror/sci-fi sub-genre are most often linked to cultural fears surrounding new technologies/discoveries, especially as they pertain to "alien" life and threats of invasion, war, and human extinction. What will be my primary interest in what follows are the gender politics of the sub-genre, something that has informed the Creature Feature since its inception. For instance, the female protagonist in *The Creature from the Black Lagoon* (1954) helmed the boat transporting the scientific team and questioned the necessity of marriage—both factors that distance her from the damsel-in-distress trope.[12] Later forays like *Attack of the 50 Foot Woman* (1958), *The Wasp Woman* (1959) *The Leech Woman* (1959), and *Invasion of the Bee Girls* (1973) addressed gendered discontent, contributing to what Pam Keesey dubs "drive in feminism." In her article "The B-Movie Mystique," Keesey examines such movies in relation to Betty Friedan's landmark 1963 book, *The Feminine Mystique*. Noting the gendered monsters in films of the late '50s deal with the very conventions Friedan's book critiqued, Keesey contends the Creature Feature genre expresses "women's dissatisfaction with unfulfilling home lives and careers." She argues the for-profit genre was able to address such issues due to its low brow status, something that allowed the films to fly under the critical radar. In addition to depictions of mutating female bodies and female characters of the heavy-drinking, vain, and presumed-to-be-insane variety, some forays had males exhibiting what is now referred to as toxic masculinity. Husbands were often patronizing, domineering, and quick to discount their wives. Meanwhile, mad scientists were happy to experiment on women (much like their later counterparts witnessed in the recent series *The OA* and *Stranger Things*). Though the mad scientist figure was a common genre baddie, Creature Feature films oft represented "common men" as heroic while simultaneously exhibiting marked concern regarding female empowerment and agency. As Dara Downey parses it, the portrayal of emasculating females within the genre spoke to fears of a "dangerously feminised society." Via mutated women, some of them giant and some of them hybridized with other creatures, the genre, Downey posits, provided "the perfect excuse for indulging in violent, homosocial adventure" wherein "killing the [female] beast" was deployed to bolster the sentiment male dominance was necessary for a healthy world.

Thankfully, sentiments like these are overturned in many contemporary examples of the Creature Feature. In some such films resourceful women escape domineering males and fight alien invasion (as in *10 Cloverfield Lane*); in others, mutated animals are employed in ways that feature the female as hero and/or the male as lout (*The Shallows*, *Zombeavers*). Some instances explore what mad science has led to, often championing "mutants" rather than (male) human heroes (as in *Orphan Black*, *Morgan*, *Ex Machina*, and *The OA*). Creature Feature tropes have also made their way into the horror genre generally, as with *Coven*'s Fiona and her hunt for an age reversing serum, a plot arc that echoes similarly youth-seeking endeavors in movies like *Wasp Woman*. Other hallmarks of the genre—alien invasion, robotic incursion, technology run amok, and threatening, amorphous entities among them—are in evidence in *V*, *Westworld*, *The World's End*, *It Follows*, and *Bird Box*. Further shows such as *Lost in Space* and *Dr. Who* reboot earlier Creature Feature inflected narratives for a post-millennial audience.

The following section will take as its focus four narratives that illustrate recent iterations of the Creature Feature, each of which include hallmarks of the genre: invasive creatures, mutant humans, science gone wrong, "too powerful" females, and/or characters rendered into mindless automatons. Especially pertinent to this particular study, these tales provide much feminist food for thought. Interrogating the dark underbelly of society in formats that provide vicarious pleasure when bad creatures are taken out and good creatures (human and otherwise) prevail, *Stranger Things*, *The OA*, *A Quiet Place*, and *The Shape of Water* each contribute to the Creature Feature tradition in politically progressive ways.

Strong-Willed Resistance: *Stranger Things*

Stranger Things (ST), set in 1983 Hawkins, Indiana, took popular culture by storm in 2016. With a second season airing in 2017 and a third scheduled for release in 2019, the show's admixture of horror, sci-fi, and Creature Feature elements foregrounds willful characters rallying against strictures of 1980s suburbia while fending off mad scientists, corrupt officials, and voracious beasties. Will Byers, his mother Joyce, his brother Jonathon, and his three best friends, Mike, Dustin, and Lucas, are joined in the first season by Nancy, Mike's sister, her best friend Barb, her boy-friend Steve, and the local sheriff, Hap. In addition to the human cast of characters, Eleven and the Demogorgon, one a supernaturally powered young girl and the other a toothy mouthed monster, play key roles. Trou-bling the human/monster and good/evil divides, Eleven is heroic in spite of her monstrous otherness whereas the human male leader of Hawkins Lab, Dr. Brenner, is the primary villain of season one.

In the season, the human-eating Demogorgon (brought into the world via Dr. Brenner's nefarious experiments) abducts Will, taking him to the "Upside Down," the sinister world lying beneath Hawkins Lab. The search for Will is the motivating crisis of the season. In the second sea-son, more forces from the Upside Down, including the Mind Flayer and the Demodogs, infiltrate Hawkins. The season's big bad, the Mind Flayer, takes control of Will's mind as Demodogs threaten our beloved Hawkins cast of characters. Meanwhile, Eleven runs away from Hap, her newfound father figure, to hone her telekinetic powers with a group of similarly super-powered teens. Nancy and Jonathon continue their sleuthing pur-suits, working to expose the sinister agenda of the Hawkins Lab with the help of a conspiracy theorist as Joyce continues her efforts to ensure her son Will is protected from the dark forces pervading Hawkins. Max, a female skateboarder and video game master, joins the cast, along with her mean-spirited brother Billy.

In both season one and two, *ST* pays homage to a smorgasbord of iconic films, *E.T., The Goonies, Alien, Gremlins, Firestarter, Carrie, The Fury, The Evil Dead* among them. Evocative of the over-the top feel of many Creature Features, the show, like its B-movie predecessors, doesn't take itself too seriously. Yet, underneath the numerous metatextual horror references, the show radiates with socio-cultural anxieties haunting the contemporary U.S. imagination. Anchored by a number of complex, mon-strous female protagonists (the super-powered Eleven among them), *ST* has as much fun skewering gender norms as it does taking down mutant beasties. In its more serious moments, it also addresses domestic abuse, bullying, homophobia, scientific experimentation, and governmental corruption.

The pilot episode opens in Hawkins Lab as a male scientist runs for dear life down a long, dim corridor. Frantically entering an elevator, he is soon snatched up by an unseen force. The narrative then cuts to four *Dungeons & Dragons*–loving boys: Will, Mike, Dustin, and Lucas. After wrapping up their game, the boys say their goodbyes and head home on their bikes. As he rides towards his home on the outskirts of town, Will is startled by something unseen and falls off his bike. He runs home only to find an empty house. Aware he is being pursued, Will looks out the front window and sees a monstrous figure approaching. He hastens to the backyard shed and gets a rifle. The light in the shed flickers then goes out. When the light comes back on, Will has disappeared. Meanwhile, Eleven, a young girl with a shaved head wearing only a hospital gown, has escaped from Hawkins lab. Later wandering the forest after escaping capture, she encounters Mike, Luke, and Dustin as they search for their missing friend Will. By the close of this first season, Will is happily reunited with his family thanks to a multi-pronged effort to rescue him carried out by his mom Joyce, his brother Jonathon, Jonathon's friend Nancy, his three best friends, and the strange new inhabitant in town, Eleven. However, Will's return to the "right side up" world is soon tempered when he coughs up a strange, slimy slug-looking creature into his bathroom sink after a holiday meal with his family. This ejection foreshadows the Upside Down's infiltration of the "right side up" that season two takes as its focus.

Though Dr. Brenner and the Demogorgon monster are successfully dispatched within the final episode of season one, in the second season it quickly becomes apparent even more dreadful forces are poised to penetrate the small, sleepy Indiana town. Much as with the 1956 film *Invasion of the Body Snatchers*, set in a similarly mundane town, Hawkins is under siege in season two. Whereas in *Invasion* space pods take root on earth, in *ST*, a hive-mind monstrous force, led by season two's big bad, the Mind Flayer, takes hold of Will's brain while its root-like tentacles spread beneath the town. Soon, an army of voracious Demodogs will rampage through Hawkins. These monsters enter the narrative in the form of a small slug-like creature that Dustin, the comedian of the friend bunch, discovers—perhaps the very same slug that Will vomited up at the end of season one. After finding it in the forest, Dustin names the creature Dart and takes it home to be his pet. Little does he know his newfound friend will soon devour his cat and proceed to grow to the size of a horse before joining the Demodog pack rampaging through the town. As with the first season, the second closes with triumphs for our heroes. Eleven closes "The Gate" to the Upside Down, trapping all the Demodogs inside (and seemingly the Mind Flayer too). Given season three is due for release in 2019, we can presume such monsters are not entirely slain. In the discussion that remains, I would like to look at motifs of season one more closely, particularly in relation to the female heroes of *ST* and the series' engagement with strange, queer outsiders, many of which flout normative codes of gender.

During the first season, harrowing flashbacks to Eleven's treatment in the lab reveal Dr. Brenner is carrying out a covert study into mind control, telekinesis, and sensory deprivation, something that echoes real life operations like MK Ultra.[13] In the *ST* version of such an operation, the aim seems to be the creation of super-spies. However, after encountering the shadowy underworld known as the Upside Down, Dr. Brenner turns his attention to unearthing and controlling the forces therein. Eleven blames herself for opening the portal to this world, something that results from her first encounter with the Demogorgon—an encounter that positions her as strangely connected to the creature. Though the creature eats humans, it does not attack Eleven when she reaches out and touches it. As she does so, her fingers sink into the monster's body. Via this fleshy penetration, Eleven apparently imparts her ability to cross into different dimensions to the Demogorgon, making it possible for the monster to leave the Upside Down and enter the everyday 1980s world of Indiana. Eleven's encounter with the Demogorgon and the resulting portal soon result in (1) locals being hunted by the monster, (2) increasingly strange happenings within the town, and (3) Dr. Brenner's crew venturing through the portal, some of them becoming bodily hosts for whatever lurks within. The portal to the Upside Down world Eleven opens, represented as a pulsing, fleshy red opening, evinces your garden variety "monstrous womb." However, rather than promoting fear of feminine bodily monstrosity, the narrative instead encourages being wary of shady scientists and the corrupt establishments for which they work. Significantly, though the Demogorgon and the Demodogs are decidedly fearsome creatures, they are not cast as inherently malevolent, nor or they associated with stereotypical notions of female monstrosity.

Notably, the primary females of the series, Joyce, Nancy, and Eleven undercut the damsel in distress trope, acting instead as queer heroes. Eleven, the queerest of the bunch, is ambiguously gendered when we first meet her. After her escape from the lab, she sneaks into a restaurant to gobble down french fries by the fistful. She is discovered by Bennie, the owner, who presumes she is a boy thanks to her shaved head and "masculine" hunger. When Mike and company meet her, they are similarly confounded by her gender presentation. Later in the season, she will allow them to "properly gender" her so that she can pass as "normal." In the scene, her androgynous baggy clothes are replaced with a pink dress and her shaved head is covered with a girlish blonde wig. We don't hear her consent to this costuming, though she does deem it "pretty." However, she soon discovers the "real girl" drag to be irritatingly restrictive. Throwing off the itchy wig just before she stomps into a grocery store to steal all the frozen waffles she can carry—her nourishment of choice—she makes it clear she is far from the "pretty" doll-like and compliant girl society desires. Her fashion-eschewing aesthetic, unconventional diet, and refusal to be a "good consumer" further render her a rebelliously strange creature, albeit a highly sympathetic one. Additionally, her capacity to enter into different dimensions, to control and read others' minds, as well as her strong telekinetic abilities, equate her not only to the beyond-human but also to time jumping, border crossing, and boundary breaking. She performs humanity—and more specifically—gender—otherwise. Not one for "normal" human interaction, Eleven largely forgoes speech and is most comfortable alone. Far from the girly persona the boys hope she will adopt, she seethes with anger and despair in equal measure. Haunted by horrible memories of being Dr. Brenner's lab rat, she acts as a "queer avenging angel," one driven by her seeming goal to put an end to his monstrous research agenda (Reynolds).

This agenda, in keeping with the tradition of "scientific racism," uses marginalized bodies and alien others as non-consenting experimental fodder. One such other, the Demogorgon, is encountered by Eleven after she is sent into a sensory deprivation tank. Crossing into another dimension as a result, Eleven encounters the Demogorgon. As noted above, when she reaches out and touches the lizard-skinned creature, her fingers sink into its body, visually capturing on-screen Kristeva's concept of the abject as well as Bakhtin's formulations of the grotesque, open body. Here as elsewhere, Eleven and the Demogorgon are associated with one another, leading some to wonder if they are one and the same.[14] That Eleven overtly claims "I'm the monster" late in the first season gives credence to this claim. Further, when she destroys the Demogorgon at the close of the season, both she and the monster dissipate into hundreds of disembodied fragments. Before this happens, the two reach their right arms towards one another, mirroring the other's stance.

Eleven (Millie Bobbie Brown) facing the Demogorgon in the closing episode of season one of *Stranger Things* **(Netflix, 2016–).**

This monstrous doubling links to the two-headed depiction of the Demogorgon in *Dungeons & Dragons*. Associated with the underworld in mythology and cast as a demon from hell by Christian writers, the Demogorgon is also associated with revolutionary sentiment.[15] In *ST*, though Eleven is hardly a hellish demon, she is associated with the Upside Down and is characterized as a rebellious, rule-flouting figure. While undeniably cast as heroic in the series, she is not without her more negatively monstrous aspects—she murders several people and violently attacks others, as with the boys bullying her friends, one of whom she almost kills. In season two, she is exceedingly churlish with Hap, her new and improved father figure, and exhibits petty jealousy regarding Max, the new girl Mike, Dustin, and Lucas have befriended. Thus, although Eleven is positioned as savior at the close of each season, she is also depicted as (at least part) monster—one who wields her powers recklessly and cannot control her rage. In this regard, she queers the hero/monster divide, or, to look at it another way, she erases the border between the two, even erasing the borders of her own body—a reading visually encapsulated via her dissipation into a confetti like cloud at season one's close.

Eleven's association with both heroism and monstrosity is echoed in the narrative arcs of two other female renegades of the series—Joyce (Will's mother) and Nancy (Mike's sister). Joyce, a working class single mother, is characterized as an off-her-rocker woman who refuses to believe Will is dead. Receiving a distorted telephone call in the pilot episode, she is convinced Will is trying to reach her, especially so after a strange substance begins to seep through the walls of her home. Shortly thereafter, Joyce spies something or someone attempting to break through her living room wall. Following more strange phone calls, she proceeds to hang Christmas lights around the home to communicate with Will. Using electricity in order to "spark" further communication with Will, she is here "lit up" by "an electric thought" in a way redolent of Ahmed's naming of willfulness as "an electric current … switching us on" (55). When she later tears through one of the living room walls to try and get to her missing son, her drunken cad of an ex-husband (Lonnie) seeks to extinguish her willful spark. Here, much like the "mad woman" of *The Yellow Wallpaper*, Joyce buts up against the walls of patriarchal forces. Lonnie, like the husband from Gilman's tale, discounts her experiences. As argued by Hannah McCann, Joyce's hanging Christmas lights as a means to communicate with Will and her husband's resulting mockery can be linked to gaslighting, a term referencing an abusive tactic wherein the target is manipulated into questioning their own perceptions. Joyce is treated (and told) by others she is losing her grip on reality, not only by Lonnie, but by several Hawkins inhabitants. Herein, she is cast as unstable and delusional—

a queer mother who refuses to abide by "good mother" decorum let alone allow herself to be silenced. As will eventually be revealed, however, Joyce was right all along. Thanks to her "crazy" and willful tenacity, her son is returned to the right side up (in season one) and released from the clutches of the Mind Flayer (in season two). This is made possible not only by Joyce's absolute refusal to give up or give in, but also via her own affinity with the supernatural (something that allows her to transgress the walls between dimensions and perceive what others cannot). Whereas Eleven is the super-powered girl, Joyce is a super-mom, albeit one her community views as a freak. Rallying against a local populace that too easily buys into the narrative her son is dead, Joyce fights tenaciously for her "queer boy," one whom Lonnie deems "a fag." In contrast to the carefully coiffed mother Mrs. Wheeler (Mike and Nancy's mom) with her home-cooked family meals, Joyce brings to mind the hard-drinking, opinionated females (oft accused of insanity) in films such as *Attack of the 50 Foot Woman*, *Whatever Happened to Baby Jane*, and *Hush Hush Sweet Charlotte*. A divorcee with bedraggled, baggy clothing, unkempt hair, and a penchant for chain smoking, she is far from the "ideal" 1980s suburban wife/mother, much like many a female character in the Creature Feature genre.

Nancy, Mike's sister, likewise refutes "proper" femininity. In season one, she is mocked by her boyfriend Steve when he finds her practicing fighting skills with a bat. Steve suggests she forget about monster-hunting, the implication being she should return to his protective, horny arms. Though a cad in season one, Steve does not slut-shame Nancy as do the local sheriffs when her friend Barb goes missing. Meanwhile, the more edgy Jonathon (who is Will's older brother) frames Nancy as just a boring suburban girl who is going to end up like her parents. However, Jonathon is disabused of this notion when the two band together to practice shooting skills in preparation for their monster-hunt. Crawling into the Upside Down on one of their hunts, Nancy, like Joyce, is able to straddle dimensions. A fearless female, she is instrumental in luring the Demogorgon, willingly slicing open her palm to do so in one instance. Admittedly, she is cozied up to Steve in the concluding episode of the first season—a presentation that disappointed many fans, myself among them—but, during season two, her rebellious spirit returns. Launching an attack against Hawkins Lab, she secretly records the lab's new director, Dr. Owens. Along with Jonathon, she seeks out Murray Bauman, a journalist turned conspiracy-theorist, and the three agree to make it known to the public what is really going on at the lab. A Nancy Drew/Erin Brockovich type figure, Nancy's acts are importantly not framed as vengeful or individualistic (something the more common rape revenge narrative oft presents). Along with Joyce and Eleven, she helps bring an end to the Mind Flayer's hold on Will in the second season. These two indefatigable females, one a tenacious working-class single-mother and the other a suburban daughter flouting middle class normality, embrace the stranger side of life. They, along with Eleven, are key heroes of the show, ones which are both *willful* and *monstrous*.

Whereas these resistant, angry, powerful females overturn the fear of female agency that bubbled under the surface of classic Creature Features, the show's male characters serve to rebuke the type of toxic masculinity films of this type tended to excuse or applaud. Herein, instead of merely rebuking common culprits (mad scientists, corrupt government officials, ineffectual police) *ST* also mocks "macho" norms while being critical of the objectification/oppression of others such a notion of masculinity relies upon. Framing much of its engagements of masculinity in comic guise—Steve and his poufy hair secrets, Dustin and his toothy purr, Billy's mullet-muscled bravado and shameless flirting with Mrs. Wheeler—*ST* queers masculinity and femininity alike, suggesting human society would benefit from the demise of these restrictive cultural logics. Further, by having Mike fall for the monstrous Eleven, the show overturns the much more common narrative of a female falling in love with a monster (as witnessed in *The Shape of Water* which itself has echoes of *Beauty and the Beast*). Via such representations, the show celebrates the queer, the strange, and the monstrous so as to question family formations, gendered identities, and romantic alliances. Science, technology, and authority figures of various stripes are also positioned as suspect. The next series discussed similarly celebrates the strange, drawing on Creature Feature elements to do so.

A Death-Defying Angel: *The OA*

The OA, following on the 2016 summer phenomenon *Stranger Things*, debuted in December of the same year. Like its strange predecessor, *The OA* combines elements of science-fiction, mystery, horror, and the Creature Feature. The show centers on a willfully monstrous female with three overlapping identities, that of Nina Azarova, who nearly drowned as a child in her home country of Russia, Prairie Johnson, the adopted daughter of a Midwestern couple who has been missing seven years as the show opens, and OA, the "original angel" able to travel between dimensions.

Though primarily a supernatural mystery imbued with science fiction and fantasy components, *The OA* also incorporates many horror conventions. Imprisonment, sinister experimentation, hallucinations, nightmares, multiple realities, and supernatural occurrences are prominently featured. Abandoned buildings, spiral staircases, bewitched mirrors, sinister crawl spaces, a macabre underground club replete with a choir of blind children, and a door behind which lies something unspeakable further contribute to the creep factor. Several plot points of the series echo those featured in classic texts—*Frankenstein's* exploration of the life/death divide, *The Island of Dr. Moreau's* focus on experimentation/mutation, the split self motif at the heart of *Dr. Jekyll and Mr. Hyde*, the house as a place of female haunting/imprisonment prominent in *The Haunting of Hill House* and "The Yellow Wallpaper." OA, the imperiled female at the show's center, is part Gothic heroine, part inter-dimensional final girl.

In addition to being imbued with elements of classic horror motifs and modes, the series draws on several elements of the Creature Feature genre. As with the *Attack of the 50 Foot Woman*, the show circulates around a larger than life female—one who is similarly presumed to be mentally unstable. Indeed, OA embodies many of the "monstrous female" traits and tropes as envisioned in Creature Features of the mid-twentieth century. Within the genre, females are regularly associated with the alien and non-human. They are often represented as primitive, predatory, and murderous. They turn into animals (*Cat Woman, Face of the Screaming Werewolf, The Snake Woman*) and cavort with aliens (*I Married a Monster from Outer Space*). Responsible for luring monsters into the civilized world (*King Kong*) they are often insect-like or reptilian (*Invasion of the Bee Woman, The Deadly Mantis Girls, The Leech Woman, The Reptile*) They are at the center of many scientific experiments gone wrong (*The Blood Beast Terror, The Brain That Wouldn't Die*). OA speaks to many of these genre building blocks. She is either more-than-human or not human at all. She is associated with snakes and aquatic creatures. She is able to communicate with the space-angel-cum-magic-woman Khatun and cheats death multiple times. She serves as translator for a massive telepathic octopus. Yet, unlike many a female in classic Creature Features, she is not a dangerous monster or alien bent on destruction. Nor is she a damsel in distress. Though others attempt to control, police, medicate, and imprison her, she escapes repeatedly, as creatures are wont to do. As with other tormented creatures hailing from the B-movie era, she is tortured, drowned, choked to death, shot. In season one, she is trapped in a sinking bus and nearly drowned. Years later, she is abducted and imprisoned by a mad scientist figure. Season two finds her imprisoned multiple times over—in a straitjacket, strapped to a chair at a nightclub, ensnared in the branches of a giant tree, put in solitary confinement.

Near the close of the second season, OA explains her crushing experiences as follows: "I was pressed down like coal. I suffered. That's what an angel is. Dust pressed into a diamond by the weight of this world." As will be revealed over the course of two seasons, OA is not the insane girl her parents assumed her to be, not an eternal victim, not a compliant wife/ daughter. Instead, she is the "original angel," one who seemingly cannot be destroyed. As conveyed in the most Creature-Feature-laden scene of the series—one in which OA communicates with a clairvoyant giant octopus in front of an assembled audience—she is a savior figure. Whereas the octopus indicates OA is the medium through which humanity will be saved, her tripartite identities—as Nina Azarova, Prairie Johnson, and OA—link her to the triple goddess (often described as Maiden, Mother, Crone and the holy trinity).

Echoing OA's three identities at a structural level, season one involves three timelines—the recent past in which Prairie was held captive with four others in a subterranean lab, the more distant past in which Nina nearly drowned in Russia, and the present timeline in which Prairie, now deemed OA, befriends a group of teens and their eccentric teacher, telling them stories of her past lives. As part one opens, OA runs across a busy freeway bridge before jumping into the water below. She wakes up in hospital three days later. After being reunited with her parents and taken back home to the desolate Michigan suburb where they reside, she gathers regularly with her five friends, all of whom hail from the local high school. Believing they can help her travel across dimensions, she meets with them in an abandoned neighborhood home to share stories about her past and to teach them "the movements"—a series of five dance-like configurations that, when done in sequence, make inter-dimensional travel possible. She also extensively details the seven years she was kept captive in a subterranean basement by Hap.

Hap is studying near death experiences (NDEs) in hopes of revealing details of the afterlife. In contrast to OA's angelic, peace-loving affect, Hap, whose full name is Dr. Hunter Piercy, is *hunting* for answers and is not averse to *piercing* multiple bodies to do so. A modern day Perseus, he hunts OA, and he is clearly willing to metaphorically behead his prize subject. After happening upon OA in Grand Central Station, he lures her with oysters and false promises, ultimately taking her to his isolated home and imprisoning her with his other human specimens—Homer, Scott, Rachel, and Renata.

Hap sequesters these captives in a terrarium-like prison in an underground basement, forcing them to live in conditions that warp them into compliant, weakened creatures. He plies them with sedating gas and feeds them with small pellets, similar in appearance to plant food. As OA describes it, "we were like the living dead, right next to each other, but alone." Repeatedly bringing each of them to the point of drowning with a quasi-medieval water torture contraption, Hap is an amalgamation of Dr. Faustus (who similarly views medicine as only useful for what it can reveal

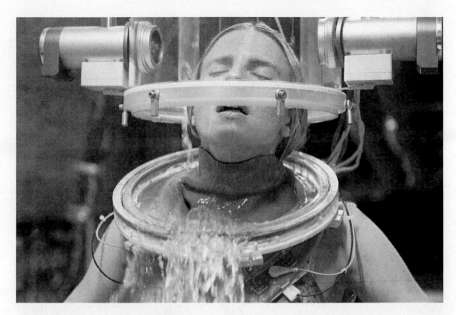

Prairie/Nina/OA (Brit Marling) in Hap's water torture device from season one of *The OA* (Netflix, 2016–).

Prairie/Nina/OA (Brit Marling) communicating with a giant telepathic octopus in season two of *The OA* (Netflix, 2016–).

about death/immortality), Victor Frankenstein (who also sought to pierce the life/death divide), Dr. Moreau (who carried out exceedingly gruesome experiments similar in scope), and Dr. Jekyll (who, like Hap, is defined by evil urges). His human captives, in contrast, are akin to the many tortured and misunderstood monsters that populate the Creature Feature canon. OA, like many such creatures, is strongly associated with the natural, the alien, and the beyond human.

In the segments featuring OA as the child Nina, she is particularly associated with water. After nearly drowning when her school bus careens into a river, she is transported to a seeming afterlife where she meets Khatun, a mystical inter-dimensional figure who seems part gypsy-witch, part angelic wise-woman. Khatun informs OA she can return to life but will have to give up her eyesight to do so. When OA next meets Khatun, after an NDE brought on by Hap's drowning machine, she is sitting near a pond in an otherworldly space. Khatun croons, "I see you're hungry. I'll fish for you." She then snatches a fish from the water which transforms into a bird, instructing OA, "Swallow it. It's the seed of light. If you grow it, all you need to know will be inside you." OA swallows the bird, which turns into a ball of light as she does so. She later refers to this fish/bird/light as "a gift ... like a living riddle, alive inside my body."

During this same encounter, Khatun, speaking of OA's fellow captives, informs her, "All five of you must work together as one to avert a great evil." To do so, Khatun conveys, they must learn "the movements"—five bodily positionings that flow one into the other like a choreographed dance. As the five captives will eventually discover, the movements have healing powers, make inter-dimensional travel possible, and can be utilized to defy death. Linked to the mysteries and magnificence of the natural world, the movements are "gifted" by swallowing "life" and "flight" (OA swallows a bird, Homer a fish). At the same time, the movements themselves echo animal postures and gesticulations—pulsating fingers, undulating arms, hissing sounds, one-legged stances. In addition to furthering the series' nature motif, the movements point to the central role the body plays in the series—one that show creator Brit Marling (who plays OA) describes as "a call to returning to the body" (*Hollywood Reporter*). In addition to framing the body as a site of resistance, the series condemns acts of violence against the body—not only those undertaken by Hap, but also those saturating contemporary society. OA's Michigan friends, for example, are abused and threatened by family members, chased by military police, subjected to bullying, dead-named by parents who refuse to accept them as trans. In a continuation of these interconnected types of violence, the first season culminates with a mass shooting attempt at the high school. In the scene prior, OA is gardening with her father before taking a bath. Submerged peacefully in water, she suddenly sits up in shock, bleeding from the nose (a classic symbol of telepathy/telekinesis she shares with *Stranger Things'* Eleven). Next we see her, she is running frantically towards the school. Through the glass walls of the cafeteria (an apt fish in a barrel reference), we see a gunman approach. He fires several shots before entering the cafeteria. OA's group of five make eye contact with one another and begin to perform the movements. The shooter holds fire, perhaps under the magic sway of the otherworldly dance. As a cafeteria worker tackles the shooter, a shot is heard. The camera cuts to OA, standing outside the glass, her hands over her heart. She has been shot. Whisked away into an ambulance, she pulls off her oxygen mask to tell her friends, "You did it, don't you see?" Continuing, "I have the will, can't you feel it?" she indicates their performance of the movements afforded her the ability to cross into another dimension—something season two affirms.

Halfway through the opener of season two, we return to the final moments of season one. OA is in the ambulance. As she loses consciousness, she sees Homer's face surrounded by stars. When she regains consciousness, she is being unloaded into a hospital in San Francisco. Disoriented, a nurse informs her name is Nina Azarova. "I did it. I jumped," she proclaims. She is not the only one that has jumped into the new timeline. As we later learn, Hap forced the four remaining captives to do the movements with him and, as a result, the five of them travelled to an alternative timeline, the same one as OA. Whereas OA wakes up in a hospital bed after being shot, Hap and company wake up in a mental institution. Hap is the director of the facility, Homer is his assistant, and Scott, Rachel, and Renata are patients. OA is soon admitted to the facility after being deemed a combative patient and put on psychiatric hold. When reunited with Scott, Rachel, and Renata in the common room, OA points out the massive aquarium they are standing beside is a replica of the one Homer recounted in one of his NDEs. The aquarium also resembles the glass prison Hap sequestered all of them in.

Intimations Hap's former captives will again be used as virtual lab rats become especially pronounced in the second episode of season two. This time, rather than drowning his human subjects, he turns them into virtual terrariums, believing "a seed inside every brain" holds the secret to multi-dimensional existence. He became convinced of this after learning of the so-called "dream house," one designed in the early 1900s by a psychic medium and her husband, an engineer. Built on a spring said to have mystical powers that made journeying to other realities possible, the edifice has many haunted house elements—it is abandoned and decaying, has bricked up windows, doors that lead to nowhere, a secret entry. In *Poltergeist* fashion, it is built on sacred indigenous land. Some go missing from the house, others jump to their death from its precipice. Hap later has one such dream-house-jumper named Liam transported to the mental facility. He will provide bodily fodder for Hap's experiments. Later, in a private laboratory, Hap stands over Liam, who is laid out on an examination table with the back of his head immersed in water. A visible sprout grows from his right ear canal. Hap grasps the sprout with pincers. Once exposed to the air, tiny leaves unfold.

Not until the final episode of season two are the dark secrets Hap's lab contains revealed. The audience witnesses the reveal at the same time as OA, who Hap invites to take a look at his latest experiment. In a shallow pool within, several bodies lie like lily pads. Branchlike roots grow from their ears, sprouting leaves, moss, and succulent flowers. "These flowers offer a glimpse into other dimensions. I've made a crude map of the multi-verse. Grown it, really," Hap boasts. OA is mortified. "I know this is hard to see, and it is a terrible sacrifice," Hap allows. He holds up a petal, telling her ingesting it will transport her to another destination in the multi-verse. "Just try it," he implores. Irate, she refuses. Noting the damage he did to her by holding her captive for seven years, she rails, "You crushed me. But you didn't destroy me. I died and came back to life with something you'll never have. You have violence, and terror, and loneliness." As she closes with "I have power" in Russian, an angelic glow surrounds her. The lights in the lab, as well as in the surrounding mental facility, flicker on and off.

In this epic battle between a mad scientist and an otherworldly angel, the show pits aspects associated with traditional masculinity—rationality, intellect, science, dominance, individualism—against those associated with femininity—irrationality, spirituality, embodiment, nature, communalism. Show co-creator Zal Batmanglij suggests as much in an interview addressing audiences' visceral reaction to "the movements." Noting "we have a real hard time with women in our society; we have a hard time with the feminine," he suggests people are critical of the key role the movements play in the series due to the fact they are "a more feminine thing." Describing the meeting between the mass shooter and OA in the final episode as symbolizing "hypermasculinity meets hyperfemininity," Batmanglij argues the vitriolic reactions to season one's finale can be put down to the fact most don't believe "the feminine can stand a chance against the normalized masculine." The triumph of the feminine in our culture, he argues, is viewed as a "ludicrous idea" (*Hollywood Reporter*). OA, symbolic of the feminine, is able to survive in season two as well. Not only that, but her rag-tag gaggle of friends also survive—minus two—and they, like OA, represent the marginalized—as do several characters first introduced in season two. Hap, an embodiment of toxic masculinity, also survives—but he will, the show indicates—never triumph.[16]

Making America Tolerant Again:
The Shape of Water

Guillermo del Toro's *The Shape of Water*, the Academy Award winner for both best picture and best director in 2017, examines humans' propensity for hatred and violence, doing so via a take that is part fairy tale, part monster movie, part homage to the Hollywood musical, and part civil rights polemic. Lauded as a "queer, race-aware, MeToo masterpiece," the film expertly proves the monster movie has plenty of life in it yet (Day). With overt links to *The Creature from the Black Lagoon*, del Toro's latest outing tells the story of Elisa, a strong-willed deaf woman who falls in love with an amphibious creature housed at Occum, the ominous government facility where she works as a janitor. Akin to *Black Lagoon's* Kay, Elisa (Sally Hawkins) is independent, confident, and forward-thinking. Like Kay, who drives a boat through the Amazon in the 1954 film along with a team of scientists hunting the "Gill Man," Elisa steers her own course. With Cold War sentiment and the burgeoning civil rights movement brewing in the background, *Shape of Water* is set in a divisive atmosphere of United States vs. Russia, whites vs. people of color, and heterosexuals vs. queers. Displaying that such binaries do not hold, the film depicts its Russian scientist/secret agent as a good guy, the creature as an affable romantic, and the U.S. military men as caught in the vise-grip of toxic masculinity. Even the seemingly friendly, down-home waiter at Doug's Pie Shop is revealed to be a racist-homophobe, one whose Southern accent is as fake as the bright green hue of the key lime pie he hawks. Via narrative details of this ilk, del Toro deftly crafts the tale in a way that evokes both the movie's 1962 setting and the current moment in what John Richardson rightly describes as "a poetic critique of Trump and hollow promises of his 'Make America Great Again' philosophy."

A film-maker with feminist values, del Toro's dedication to complex, strong female characters is a long-standing one, and Elisa (Sally Hawkins) of *The Shape of Water* is no exception. Like other heroines from his oeuvre, she is trapped within a patriarchal script, one that in her specific case is linked to militarism, sexism, heteromonogamy, and ableism. From her close friendships to her neighbor, Giles (Richard Jenkins), an aging gay artist, and Zelda (Octavia Spencer), her black coworker, to her distrust of the military men that run the lab where she works, Elisa is, as del Toro puts it, "the driving engine of the movie" (Russell). Likening herself to the creature, she knows her disability sets her apart but disagrees with others' view of her as damaged.[17] She may be a "princess without voice" (as Giles refers to her), but she still makes herself heard.

The Shape of Water's primary baddie is Strickland (Michael Shannon), the military leader in charge of Occum. Strickland not only sadistically tortures the captured Amazonian aquaman, he also harasses female workers, insinuates he would like to rape Elisa so as to make her "squawk a little," and treats his wife like a sex robot. In addition to belittling the workers at Occum, especially Elisa and Zelda, Strickland gleefully tortures the creature with a cattle prod—a practice which results in the creature biting off two of his fingers, which, once sewn back on, fester and rot, serving as an apt signifier of Strickland's putrescent nature. Though Strickland is deemed "a man of the future" by the salesman encouraging him to buy a Cadillac in the diegesis, he is in actuality a man of the past, one who espouses sexism, racism, and xenophobia. In a symbolic destruction of his outdated views, his new Caddy, described as akin to a "clean and crisp ... dollar bill" is dented late in the film as Giles and Elisa, in a van disguised as a laundry truck, escape Occum's lot with the creature in tow. In the scene, Strickland's "Taj Mahal on wheels" has its gleaming exterior besmirched, an event that reveals his jingoistic claim that "the future is bright" to be a faulty one—at least for men like him. Undone by film's end, just as his commander General Hoyt warned he would be, Strickland's demise is contrasted to the creature's triumphant return to the sea. Joined in his watery home by Elisa, who is now able to breathe underwater thanks to his magical touch, the queer amphibian is the prince, Strickland the toad. In this "fairytale for troubled times," as del Toro calls it, queer desire triumphs.

Maternal Fortitude Meets Daughterly Ingenuity: *A Quiet Place*

A Quiet Place, directed by John Krasinski, the sleeper hit of Summer 2018, is part monster movie, part post-apocalyptic survival tale, with heavy doses of Creature Feature elements. The film opens in 2020, three months after huge, freakishly fast-moving beasties have munched their way through most of humanity. Using echolocation to find their victims, the creatures' presence necessitates that humans make as little noise as possible if they are to survive. Concentrating on the Abbott family as they attempt to evade becoming snacks for the insatiable creatures, *Quiet Place* opens with the family making their way through a post-apocalyptic ghost town seeking supplies. After the family enter a grocery store, the youngest Abbott, Beau, is drawn to a space shuttle toy. His dad, Lee (John Krasinski), indicates he can't keep it. Taking pity on him, his sister Regan (Millicent Simmonds) sneaks the toy to him as they depart the store. On their precarious walk home, Beau is killed when the battery operated sound emitted by the toy draws a nearby creature. Here, the technology and space travel the toy represents advance the film's negative take on the modern world—one whose militarism and scientific advances are framed as failing to save humanity from the beasts such "progress" likely discovered or created. As indicated in a newspaper headline we witness flapping in the wind which declares "U.S. Military Defeated: We Can No Longer Protect You," the Abbott family will have to save themselves. This survivalist component of *Quiet Place* led some to dub the film a "fantasy of survivalism" with regressive messages at its core (Brody). Such claims obfuscate the fact the narrative is more nightmare than fantasy—a nightmare that notably animates 1950s era fears of nuclear fallout, catastrophic war, and environmental devastation for contemporary audiences.

In its housing of apocalyptic themes as they pertain to one nuclear family, the film has a more intimate focus than do most Creature Features. Championing family unity and fortitude over weaponry or governmental intervention, the film suggests neither societal institutions nor their leaders will save humanity. At the same time, the film's creatures, with their decidedly machine-like qualities, evoke the techno-science of advanced capitalist culture, one whose tentacle-like incursion into daily life is now threatening to eat humanity out of existence. In contrast to the many mid-twentieth century Creature Features that deployed insectoid monsters to address fears of monstrous femininity (as in *Wasp Woman*, *Leech Woman*, and *The Shrinking Man*), the beasties of *A Quiet Place* are more aptly linked to an invading army characterized by traits more associated with masculinity (strength, speed, stealth, tactical know-how). Meanwhile, suggestions of monstrous femininity are absent. Yet, as is the case in many a classic creature feature, females seem strangely connected to the monsters that threaten humanity (as with two of the genre's most iconic films, *The Creature from the Black Lagoon* and *King Kong*).

Championing the nuclear family over and above (nuclear) science, *Quiet Place* presents domestic, everyday items and spaces as saving the Abbotts (a kitchen timer, a bathtub, a basement-level laundry room). The family home is a bastion of domesticity and natural rhythms. It is not immune, however, to the dangers that lurk if the quiet is broken, something which happens early on when Regan and her brother Marcus inadvertently spill a candle over the board game they are playing. The ensuing noise results in creatures soon scuttling over the rooftop. Though clearly anxious to break in and eat the human morsels within, they are unsuccessful in this instance. Later, they are again drawn to the house as Evelyn (Emily Blunt) is home alone. Heavily pregnant, she steps on a nail protruding from the basement stairs, dropping the glass picture frame she is carrying as a result. Drawn by the sound of shattering glass, the creatures breach the home. To add to this harrowing turn of events, Evelyn goes into premature labor. Successfully quelling her need to scream out as contractions ripple through her—an act of super-human fortitude in and of itself—she manages to creep upstairs without a sound to deliver her child—sans assistance let alone pain killer—in the bathtub. Figuratively, the offending (phallic) nail punctures the "quiet place" of the home, yet the (womb-like) tub provides protection. These scenes, some of the most terrifying of the film, overturn the many representations of the monstrous mother and abject pregnant body. Instead of devouring womb or murderous mommy, Evelyn is the picture of maternal fortitude—one who is willfully monstrous in her battle against the murderous creatures invading her home. Though both she and her daughter view themselves as horrible monsters who contributed to Beau's death (Regan because she gave him the toy, Evelyn because she did not carry him on their walk home), the film positions them as *willful* heroes—ones who draw upon their bodily monstrosities (pregnancy, disability) to protect each other and their home.

The nerve-racking, action-packed ending finds Regan discovering her father's research materials and several versions of the cochlear implants he was designing. Reminded how the high-pitched noises emitted from one of these implants successfully scared off an attacking creature in a prior altercation, Regan foments an ingenious plan. Boosting the sound of one of the cochlear implants by positioning it next to one of Lee's microphones, Regan's strategy leads to the successful annihilation of the creature that has breeched the home. When one exposes the myriad ears and teeth that lie beneath its exoskeleton in response to the noise, Evelyn shoots it in the head. Alas, the sound from this shot draws more creatures. Armed with knowledge about the debilitating effect of high-frequency sound and the vulnerable flesh that lies beneath the beasties' exoskeletons, the family ascend to the porch. Ending with Evelyn cocking a gun as numerous creatures approach, the closing moments indicate mother and daughter are ready to take on the predators. In contradistinction to the more common ending where "male military or scientific experts successfully ... defeat the monster and restore the normative order," the movie champions female ingenuity (not to mention a birthing mother's ability to silently endure pain so as to save herself and her family) (Pinedo 14).

A Quiet Place, along with *Stranger Things, The OA, and The Shape of Water*, reveals the Creature Feature is alive and well in our 21st century world. Granted, taking in a B-movie at the drive-in is a thing of the past, yet the thrills, chills, and nervous laughter induced by monster movie consumption are still readily available to contemporary audiences. Indeed, thanks to various technological advancements, including much larger home television screens, one's own quiet place arguably offers one of the best spaces to consume contemporary mutations of the Creature Feature. And, if the latest trends in this sub-genre are any indication, we just might witness the birth of a more feminist-friendly monster movie trend, one hinted at not only by the narratives above, but also by recent films such as *Honeymoon* (where an alien-like entity takes over the body of a newly pregnant female), *Annihilation* (in which four women navigate a creature-feature filled landscape), and *Bird Box* (with Sandra Bullock playing tough-as-nails Malorie as she saves herself and two young children in a post-apocalyptic world).

Section 4: Medusa Figures in Post-Millennial Horror

While the witch is so pervasive a figure as to deserve a chapter all her own, monstrous females that share affinities with Medusa are also in abundance, particularly if we read the Gorgon from the lens of rape revenge, the male gaze, and/or the femme castratrice.[18] Although Medusa does not circulate as a literal character very often in the horror genre, the fears associated with the infamous Gorgon often do. Typical elements of her myth go as follows: She is one of three Gorgon sisters. Her beauty catches Poseidon's eye and he rapes her in Athena's temple. As punishment, Athena changes Medusa's hair into snakes and gives her a face that turns those who look upon it to stone. Perseus is sent to kill the Gorgon. Using a reflective bronze shield to avoid Medusa's treacherous gaze, he beheads her, eventually delivering her head to Athena.[19] This myth contains a number of key themes—the power of looking, the female body as treacherous, rape/murder of a powerful woman as justified. An embodiment of female rage and power, a symbol of divine (albeit monstrous) femininity, and a powerful muse for feminist thinkers, Medusa is a particularly enduring female monster. Yet, her name is used as shorthand to designate women as monsters. As a case in point, during the 2016 presidential race, Trump campaign merchandise featured him as a would-be Perseus holding the decapitated head of Hilary Clinton rendered in the guise of the snake-haired gorgon. Elizabeth Johnston documents how this "Trump that Bitch" campaign is a contemporary example of the ways powerful women, akin to Medusa, are presented as monsters deserving of punishment, banishment, rape, or death. Classics scholar Mary Beard argues, "It's no accident that we find her decapitated, her head proudly paraded as an accessory," naming Medusa's tale "the classic myth in which

An image used on Donald Trump campaign t-shirts depicting Trump as Perseus holding the decapitated head of Medusa, here illustrated as Hillary Clinton. The t-shirt is still on sale online: https://www.zazzle.com/donald_trump_slays_hillary_clinton_perseus_medusa_t_shirt-2355593497 97313547).

the dominance of the male is violently reasserted against the illegitimate power of the woman" (71, 73).

To be sure, fear of female power has long animated patriarchal nightmares (not to mention Freudian theory). Such fear infuses myth, lore, and religious texts via murderous mothers, vampiric lamia, and would-be-Adam-usurpers. From Medea to Lilith, the harpy to the witch, the soucouyant to La Llorona, the supposed monstrosity of the female is tied to their willful resistance to be "good" mothers, wives, or servants as well as to the corrupting power they wield over "innocent" men (as with the sirens who deployed their enchanting voices to lure sailors to their demise). Understood as "a particularly nasty version of the *vagina dentata*" by many scholars, Medusa is a representative figure of female monstrosity, one whose "visage is alive with ... toothed vaginas, poised and waiting to strike" (Creed 111). According to Joseph Campbell and Sigmund Freud, Medusa's head of snakes serves to represent vaginal monstrosity. Campbell speaks of the castrating vagina in *The Masks of God* whereas Freud reads her "horrifying decapitated head" as representative of the "terror of castration" that makes males "stiff" (273). The prototypical femme fatale, sexy but deadly, Freud understands her as encapsulating the terrifying truth: women have no penis!

As she embodies fears associated with the mythic vagina dentata, Medusa is often deployed in ways that bolster notions of woman as monstrously other. A figure akin to the half snake, half woman lamia as well as to the demonic succubus, she is evoked in misogynistic guise in works such as *The Lair of the White Worm* by Bram Stoker and "The Likeness of Julie" by Richard Matheson. In H.P. Lovecraft's story, "Medusa's Coil," anti-woman strains take a decidedly racist turn. At the story's close, it is revealed the story's Medusa figure, married by the protagonist's son, is not only the immortal snake-woman, *she is black*! This story herein reflects the racist sentiment imbuing much of Lovecraft's work, an author who described real-world immigrants of New York as "slithering and oozing in and on the filthy streets," a depiction that intriguingly invokes Medusa's head of snakes (qtd. in Poole, *Monsters*, 97). Though tales such as Lovecraft's "Medusa's Coil" and films such as *Clash of the Titans* (both the original and the remake) continue the tendency to cast Medusa as abhorrent monster, various post-millennial Medusa figures reclaim monstrous feminine figures (and their powerful gaze) to castigate systemic sexism. As of yet, however, such Medusa-inflected narratives have not engaged in any extensive way with systemic racism. This is true of the four films discussed below, ones which feature a teenage incarnation of the vagina dentata, a cheerleader turned lamia/succubus, a female slasher, and a final girl figure whose weapon of choice is a turkey-baster filled with semen. While these narratives variously cast the predatory male gaze, toxic masculinity and rape culture as monstrous, they do not hone in on white supremacy as part of the matrix of oppression. Yet, they do enact important feminist revisionist mythmaking. By rendering their Gorgonesque protagonists sympathetically, they justify the violence of their protagonists (Dawn, Jennifer, Needy, Rocky, and Mandy)—framing their vengeance against raping Poseidon's and murderous Perseus's figures as not only understandable, but necessary.

Abstinence Bites: *Teeth*

The 2007 film *Teeth*, directed by Mitchell Lichtenstein, introduces audiences to the teen purity enthusiast Dawn, first encountered during an opening flashback scene. In the scene, a young Dawn, playing in a kiddie pool, is instructed by her step-brother Brad to "show me yours." When she does, Brad loses the tip of his finger to Dawn's toothy nether regions. Fast forward a decade or so, and Dawn is a proud speaker for "Promise," an abstinence-only organization. Announcing that virginity is "the most precious gift of all" at a Promise assembly, Dawn advises those in attendance to keep their "gifts" tightly wrapped. Soon after departing the stage, Dawn meets Tobey, a new boy in town. Her awestruck demeanor upon their encounter suggests her own gift might soon be "unwrapped."

Some days later Dawn joins Tobey for a swim at a nearby lake. The t-shirt Dawn wears for their rendezvous, emblazoned with the pronouncement "Warning! Sex changes everything," foreshadows the tragedy to come: Tobey rapes her. Though their interactions begin consensually, once they climb into a secluded cave, things progress too quickly for Dawn's liking. She announces her desire that they stop. Tobey, now on top of her, doesn't stop. She is rendered unconscious in her struggle to extract herself from beneath him. As Tobey is raping her, Dawn resumes consciousness and begins screaming. Tobey begins screaming as well. He stands up, bleeding from his crotch. The camera cuts to his severed penis on the cave floor—a flaccid bit of flesh that Dawn's mind-of-its-own vagina has rendered inert. Dawn shrieks, shielding herself from looking at Tobey's dismembered member.

The scene draws on black humor and what Pamela Robertson deems "feminist camp practices," doing so in service of cultural critique, particularly as it pertains to gender (9). Such critical camp informs a scene that comes soon after the one at the lake: Dawn visits a male gynecologist in hopes of finding reassurance that her genitals are normal. By way of "examination," the sleazy doctor shoves his fist inside of Dawn after removing his protective glove, enacting a medicalized assault that "represents the routine but painful erosion of sexual and reproductive agency within the American health care system" (Kelly 96). As his offending fingers penetrate Dawn, we hear a chomp. Dawn pushes at the doctor with her feet, eventually dislodging his hand. Four bloodied fingers fall to the floor. "It's true!" he screams, "Vagina dentata!" This scene, though including over-the-top reactions and cartoonish gore, lobs a serious critique of the medical (and legal) invasion of the female body. As the film proceeds, the mocking depiction of an "abstinence-only culture" mainly interested in policing female sexuality while allowing rape culture to thrive continues.

Dawn, still eager to figure out why her genitals have castrating ability, studies redacted textbook images of the nude female and Googles "female genital mutation." Upon discovering references to the vagina dentata, she reads the following: "A toothed vagina appears in the mythology of many diverse cultures all over the world. In these myths the story is always the same. The hero must devour the woman, the toothed creature, and break her power." As this verbiage suggests, "vaginal mutation" is powerful—something Dawn realizes as she transforms from a passive body to a willfully avenging female. Though her vagina is at first presented as having a figurative mind of its own—as when it castrates Tobey and bites off the fingers of the gynecologist—Dawn later controls her castrating capability, consciously turning her teeth against sexual predators.

Significantly, the film equates sexual violation to the pollution of the natural world via two nuclear cooling towers that spew sinister plumes into the sky throughout the movie. These phallic monstrosities metonymically represent the nuclear family of which Dawn is a part—one where her step-brother is a misogynistic cad and her mother is dying of cancer (another nod to the *pollution* of female bodies). The radiation from the towers could certainly be the cause of Dawn's "vaginal mutation"—a healthy response, some might say, to a toxic world. Yet, Dawn initially casts her toothy genitals as criminal. Convinced she must confess the deeds her vagina has wrought, Dawn seeks out a neighborhood friend, Ryan, for solace. After Ryan gives her a handful of his mom's Xanax, Dawn passes out. After she wakes, as the two are about to have sex, Dawn warns Ryan about her weaponized vagina. Undeterred, he insists he will "conquer" her teeth, stating "I am the hero." Clearly referencing the myth wherein a conquering male hero must "unfang" the vagina, Ryan will instead become victim when he and Dawn have sex a second time. As they do so, Ryan gets a phone call. He answers it. The conversation reveals he made a bet with a friend that he could bed Dawn. Appalled at this discovery, Dawn castigates him as he continues with his thrusts. He responds "your mouth is saying one thing ... but your sweet pussy is saying something very different." Then we hear the fateful chomp. Here, the indication is that when Dawn consents, her nether teeth don't bite. But, when others sexually violate her, her teeth act accordingly.

Apparently emboldened after this incident with Ryan, Dawn proceeds to seek revenge against her prurient jerk of a step-brother. As she prepares to seduce her creepy step-brother Brad, a Medusa movie plays in the background, allying the toothy-teen to the snake-haired monster. So as to turn Brad to "stone," she climbs on top of him. She severs his penis in one fell bite then stands up, dropping it from between her legs. Brad's dog, aptly named Mother, grabs the severed penis from the ground.

Echoing an earlier scene in which Brad forced a dog bone into his girlfriend's mouth, Brad has become "the chomped bone" thanks to Medusa/Mother. Narrative arcs such as this, where the white, heterosexual male body is rendered vulnerable and bloody—and where severed penises fall to the ground—are exceedingly rare in film. This is perhaps why *Teeth* was met with accusations of misandry. However, when we think of how commonly women's bodies are bloodied and dismembered—in real life as well as in fiction—claims like this are exceedingly hypocritical. *Teeth* rectifies this double-standard through its delightfully vengeful protagonist.

The closing segment hints Dawn will continue her toothy quest. While hitch-hiking, an elderly man picks her up. Stopping for gas, he smiles at her lecherously. She tries to get out the car, but he has locked the doors. He sticks his tongue out at her, making licking noises and suggestive faces, clearly intending to "get some." Dawn looks into the camera knowingly, her sly smile hinting at what is to come. Putting on a seductive stare which we can presume will soon turn the letch to stone, Dawn has clearly embraced her excising ability. This delightful story of an empowered toothy teen, one Felix Morgan aptly describes as a "genital superhero origin story," is followed two years later by a film helmed by another modern Medusa.

Bombshell Bodies and Needy Avengers: *Jennifer's Body*

Jennifer's Body, written by Diablo Cody and directed by Karyn Kusama, provides another avenging monstrous Medusa figure. As the film's title indicates, Jennifer's body is the most salient thing about her. The males that surround Jennifer certainly agree, treating her as consumable product. In turn, she performs sexy femininity, treating her body as a prop. Actively pursuing sexual encounters and not much else, Jennifer recognizes her curvaceous form and pretty face give her power. She is less savvy, however, about the dangers wielding such power can lead to. Insisting to her best friend Needy "We have all the power" in a scene at a club, she grabs Needy's breasts, declaring "these are like smart bombs." All one need do, Jennifer claims, is "point them in the right direction." Here, she frames the female body as sexy weapon. Yet, when members of the band she and Needy have been watching lure her outside, an actual weapon is turned against her. Believing sacrificing a virgin to the devil will guarantee their musical success, the band members stab Jennifer, leaving her for dead. Instead of staying dead, however, she transforms into a succubus/lamia figure with a huge, cavernous mouth lined with several rows of razor sharp teeth.

Rendered monstrous as a result of her sexualized murder, Jennifer takes to succubi-ing with aplomb and is not particular about whom she targets. It seems that being male, from the standpoint of the monster Jennifer becomes, makes one guilty by default. Hinting at the pervasiveness of rape culture and framing those who do nothing to prevent sexual violence as accomplices, Jennifer's murderous body functions as a vampiric version of the vagina dentata, one that eats men—and only men—whole. Though it seems particularly unjust that her best friend Needy's sweet, non-violent boyfriend becomes a target, his death sparks Needy's own turn to a final girl/femme castratrice.

By film's close, Needy has morphed from meek best friend to avenger. Locked in a detention center for her aberrant violence (something that points to a contrasting lack of formal punishment of Jennifer's male killers), she is unwilling to stay imprisoned. Eager to finish off her vengeful pursuits, Needy levitates off her cell floor before karate kicking her way to freedom. Throwing social decorum to the curb, the formerly mousy good-girl seeks out the members of the band that sacrificed Jennifer in their fame-seeking ritual and knifes them all. Although one reviewer condemns this closing as depicting "that, in order for a girl to 'take back the knife,' she has to grow a dick," I would counter that instead the film shows females *need* to take back the knife so as to *cut* out the violent heart of patriarchy. Akin to its campy predecessor *Teeth*, *Jennifer's Body* mocks notions of feminine monstrosity while gleefully castigating male sexual entitlement and the violence it leads to. Contemporary interpretations of the Medusa myth, each film suggests the monsterization of the female body results from the (rape-happy) patriarchal imaginary. In the next movie to be considered, the rage of Medusa and her deathly stare is embodied by a young woman who refuses to be impregnated against her will.

Don't Breathe, Just Baste: Rethinking Home Invasion Horror in *Don't Breathe*

Don't Breathe, the summer hit of 2016 directed by Fede Alvarez, offers a unique permutation on the home invasion film and features a determined, quick-witted final girl at its narrative center. Said girl, Rocky, along with her two friends, Money and Alex, rob swanky domiciles to address their economic troubles. After hearing that a local veteran purportedly has $300,000 stashed in his home, the teens plan to make him their next target. Awarded said money after a woman killed his daughter in a car accident, the veteran, known only as "Blind Man," lives in an extremely fortified house with his attack dog. When the teens learn by chance that he is blind, they make a disastrous assumption: it will be a piece of cake for them to break in and rob his place while he sleeps. Ultimately revealed to be the bad guy of the tale, Blind Man turns the tables on the robbers. Over the course of the narrative, Blind Man hunts the teens through his fortified home, one replete with guns, barred windows, an intricate alarm system, a sinister basement that doubles as a solitary confinement cell, and a menacing Rottweiler. Rocky, the only teen to survive, is also the only one given a back-story. Flashbacks reveal her harrowing childhood, neglectful mother, and a younger sister whose care largely falls on Rocky's shoulders. In hopes the monetary haul robbing Blind Man promises would allow her and her sister to move out of the economically barren Detroit and away from their abusive mother, Rocky is the film's most sympathetic character. Though some critics argue Blind Man is at first an empathetic victim, this ignores the opening aerial shot in which we see him dragging Rocky's (presumably dead) body through a barren Detroit neighborhood. As this shot conveys, he, not the robbers, is the true villain.

When the three teens break into his home, they search for the money on the ground floor but fail to locate it. In order to look further, Money releases sleeping gas in Blind Man's upstairs bedroom. Presuming he has been rendered unconscious, Money shoots the lock off the basement door so they can continue their search. However, due to an immunity to noxious gases resulting from his time in the Gulf War, Blind Man is not in fact unconscious. After killing Money, who insists he is the only intruder, Blind Man discovers three pairs of shoes by his back door and realizes Money was not acting alone. In the meantime, Rocky, hidden in a closet, finds a safe holding millions of dollars. After Money is shot, she and Alex retreat to the basement to hide. Once there, they find a female restrained and gagged in a padded cell. As will be revealed, it is the young woman charged with vehicular manslaughter for killing Blind Man's daughter. As payback, he has impregnated her so as to "replace" the daughter he lost. After releasing her from her restraints, the three try to escape through a storm door, but Blind Man arrives and shoots at them, killing the woman. He breaks down sobbing, explaining "my baby." If there was any sense he was a victim, this scene undoes it. Revealing he has what one reviewer aptly calls a "rape dungeon," it frames Blind Man as sadistic and vengeful (Faraci). This characterization is soon ramped up when he turns off the electricity to impede Alex and Rocky's escape. After a harrowing chase scene in the now pitch-black basement (filmed in night vision format), Alex is cornered by Blind Man and attacked with pruning shears. Meanwhile, Rocky scrambles to escape through ventilation ducts as she is pursued by Blind Man's Rottweiler. She then suffers

Rocky (Jane Levy) constrained by a hanging harness made of seat belts as Blind Man (Stephen Lang) prepares to forcibly impregnate her (*Don't Breathe*, Ghost House Pictures, 2016, directed by Fede Alvarez).

a brutal, bone-crunching fall when the ducts open out onto the floor far below.

Waking up sometime later restrained and gagged within a seatbelt contraption in the basement's padded cell, Rocky watches as Blind Man mysteriously transfers liquids between glass beakers then sucks some of the viscous fluid into a turkey baster. He is here preparing to impregnate Rocky since his first "baby incubator"—the captured woman Rocky and Alex encountered earlier—is now dead. As Rocky frantically attempts to release herself from the harnesses entrapping her, he insists, "I am not a rapist." Apparently interpreting his acts as a "legitimate" brewing up of another child to replace his dead daughter, Blind Man, much like many an anti-choice Republican, views the female body only in terms of its birthing potential.[20]

As he approaches Rocky with the semen-filled baster (in what became a heavily debated moment in the film), Rocky's horror is rendered visceral via her frantic, wide-eyed stare and her desperate, flailing attempts to get out of the harness that imprisons her. Once she manages to do so, she plunges the offending baster down Blind Man's throat, forcing him to swallow his own semen. An example of the monstrous phallic woman discussed by Creed, Rocky gives Blind Man the dreaded evil eye, her face contorted with rage as she fills his mouth with his own raping fluid. Though critic Devin Faraci condemns this arc as "a pointless rape subplot" that isn't "thematically related to the rest of the movie," I would counter that the segment is a logical extension of the class and gender power dynamics *Don't Breathe* circulates around (Eggertsen). Writer/director Fede Alvarez readily admits the segment was meant to shock, but it does more than that—it positions Blind Man as ruthless attacker and Rocky and the other woman as victims of his male entitlement stance—one that can surely be linked to his time in the military—an institution hardly known for its lack of misogyny and sexual violence. He may be a veteran, but his time at war has not made him more humane, instead it has blinded him (literally and figuratively) to anyone's grief and pain but his own (underscored by his hoarding away of money while Detroit crumbles around him).

With his weaponized sperm locked and loaded into the barrel of a turkey baster, Blind Man is a raping vigilante, one who fails to see he has not only lost his daughter, but his humanity. Rocky, in contrast, morphs into a unique iteration of a rape avenger. Of the trio of thieves, she is the only one to survive, something that undercuts the opening shot's suggestion she is dead. Seemingly one of the many female victims populating the horror genre at the film's outset, she in fact turns out to be a bad-ass final girl. Her wide-eyed stare, featured in *Don't Breathe* promotional materials and posters, acts as a Medusa-like gaze, allowing her to triumph over Blind Man and his misogynist ethos that "there's nothing a man can't do." As Rocky reveals, there are things a man can't do, even a basting wielding uber-soldier like Blind Man.

Don't Look Now: *All the Boys Love Mandy Lane*

The 2006 film *All the Boys Love Mandy Lane* overturns the common slasher subtext wherein women are killed for having (or wanting) sex. Though slashers have resulted in much feminist condemnation of the sub-genre, some argue slashers provide cathartic viewing for female viewers.[21] Pointing out that "a substantial portion of the violence that the slasher film celebrates is female-on-male retaliatory violence," Isabel Pinedo, for example, insists on the import of the genre's featuring of "women using self-defense effectively" by taking on a "controlling gaze" (80, 77, 76). The female protagonist adopts such a controlling gaze in the film, aligning herself with the monstrous attacker rather than the female victims. Yet, the motivation behind her killings differs from the likes of Norman, Jason, Michael, and Freddy. She is not dealing with mommy issues (Norman), not born bad (as suggested with Michael), she did not drown at the hands of randy camp counselors (as with Jason), nor is she trying to punish those who punished her (as with Freddy). To be sure, the fuel for killers of this type is more nuanced than these quick summations indicate, but it's fair to say many slasher figures kill as a result of something which happened in their past. Mandy, in contrast, kills based on what is happening in the present—in short, being framed as "eye candy" for high school boys.

Herein, the typical slasher focus on watching/being watched plays a key role, something made evident in the opening moments of the film wherein Mandy is being ogled as she makes her way down a high-school hallway. Soon after, she is invited to a pool party by a popular senior, Dylan, who tells her "you look fucking hot this summer." Once at the party, Dylan watches Mandy obsessively, crooning "let me see what color those panties are." At the party, Dylan and Emmett (Mandy's best friend) drink on the roof. After Dylan boasts about how he will be hooking up with Mandy, Emmett encourages him to jump. Shouting "Mandy Lane!" as he launches himself towards the pool below, Dylan's head meets cement rather than water as he lands. An interesting inversion wherein male desire rather than female desire results in death, this early scene furthers the film's primary equation: the uninvited gaze courts death—something we might think about in relation to Medusa who turns the men who gaze upon her uninvited to stone.

Following Dylan's skull-crushing demise, the story skips forward to the following school year. As Mandy runs the track during P.E., males watch from the bleachers. "There she is, boys," one of them intones, "Mandy Lane. Untouched. Pure…. Men have tried to possess her and to date all have failed. Some have even died in their reckless pursuit of this angel." Such pursuits soon result in Mandy being invited to a weekend get-away at a ranch owned by the father of one of the teens. The males going on the trip, we soon learn, all have "the exact same goal"—having sex with the "untouched" Mandy. Along with Mandy, two other females, Chloe and Marlin, take the trip. Positioned as pawns for the males to use as they please, these two female teens viciously tear one another down in their battle to be deemed the most desirable. Calling each other fat and mocking one another's pubic-hair grooming choices, they are contrasted to Mandy who cares not a jot for male attention. When the group drive out to the ranch and make the obligatory stop at a backwoods gas station and proceed to steal a beer keg out of a man's truck, Marlin flashes her boobs at the man by way of distraction. Mandy then takes the driver's seat, a subtle nod to the fact she will "drive" the film. As the group travel towards their destination, one of the males ogles Mandy from the backseat while being given a hand job by Marlin. Witnessing as much in the rear view mirror, Mandy moves the mirror out of his line of sight. She will continue to enact such obfuscation of the male gaze as the narrative proceeds.

When the group arrives at the ranch, the teens are killed off one by one. While it seems Mandy is being spared as she is (virginal) final girl material, she has actually master-minded the killing, recruiting her friend Emmett to "slash" for her. Thus, rather than punishing sexually active teens as do many a slasher, the film castigates prurient males and mean-spirited females, all of whom treat one another abysmally. Mandy is the instigator of said punishment. Initially making a pact with Emmett, he acts as primary killer until the two disagree over their suicide pact and battle it out in a pit filled with rotting cattle carcasses. After killing him, Mandy formally dons the slasher mantle, turning her murderous gaze on those that objectify/judge her with their covetous/jealous stares. Furthering these "to-be-looked-at" motifs, characters assess themselves in the mirror throughout the film. But not Mandy. Instead, she uses the mirror to transform her reflection. Just before she attacks the remaining teens, she effectively trades in her "pretty girl" status for that of stone-cold killer. With her long blonde locks slithering around her, she becomes Medusa in the mirror, fortifying herself for battle.

Tellingly, the only person Mandy spares in her murder spree is the ranch hand, Garth, an Iraq war-vet who is critical of the teens' reckless partying and ruthless disregard for the ranch-house. Less privileged and entitled than the feckless teens, he recently had to kill the ranch's infected herd of cattle. Sharing with Mandy a distaste for superficiality, Garth also is presented as the likely slasher for much of the film. Alas, it is not the wounded war vet that masterminds the killing, but the "untouched" Mandy. Her time in the pit of cattle carcasses battling Emmett results in her body being covered with rotten cattle flesh; she is thus far from "pure." Evocative of her status as a piece of meat within heteropatriarchy, her visual alignment with the bloodied, decaying animals makes her less a heartless slasher than a creature infected by the violent, dehumanizing strains of the modern world. More complex than her beautiful blonde "angelic" status suggests, she refuses to be the "hot" victim and opts for murderous "savior" instead. The film's closing line, spoken by Garth, indicates as much. "You did it," Garth says, "you saved us." Maybe she has done more than save herself and the charming ranch hand, though; maybe she is in fact saving the collective "us" from the infectious "herd" and its rotten, polluting gaze. Along with the other females discussed in this final section—Dawn, Jennifer, Needy, and Rocky—Mandy adopts a controlling gaze, one aligning herself with the monster so as not to be the victim.[22] In effect, these females prevent the "beheading" that patriarchy favors for its women. With vaginal teeth, succubi hunger, weapon-wielding vengeance, and final girl panache, these are not your dutiful Athenas, but rather gloriously gutsy Gorgons.[23]

* * *

From Gothic New Woman figures that smash Victorian mores to telekinetic young females that take down mad scientists, the fierce females in the texts discussed above indict everything from rape culture to nuclear pollution. Intent on slashing the male gaze matrix, these complex, rebellious characters bring about transformative dead ends via their actions. Defying tropes of the damsel in distress, the madwoman, the happy housewife, and the maniacal mother, they harness their monstrous abilities to save not only others and themselves, but to redress the evils patriarchy, science, medicine, heteronormativity, and militarism unleash upon the world. Joined on horror's stage by numerous other willful female monsters, these feminist badasses of horror are much like the immortal head of Medusa—potent, powerful, and ready to strike in a theater, book store, or streaming service near you.

Conclusion:
The Monster's Tools

The story entitled "The Green Ribbon" from the children's book *In a Dark, Dark Room* features a girl named Jenny who keeps a mysterious ribbon tied round her neck. She is, the narration imparts, "like all the other girls" except for the ribbon. She meets a boy named Alfred who asks her relentlessly why she wears the ribbon. After they eventually marry, Alfred commands, "Now we are married, you must tell me about the green ribbon." She still refuses, saying she will tell him "when the right time comes." On her death bed, she tells Alfred he can untie the ribbon, declaring "you will see why I could not tell you before." After the ribbon is untied, Jennie's head falls to the floor.

There are many versions of this tale but the big reveal of the tale is always the same: the woman's head is not attached to her body. She is a monster. Or so the story would have us think.

Those of us not put off by Gorgon types know the male suitors/husbands are the cads. They assume the ribbon suggests something untoward. Like Alfred, they won't stop going on about it. They order the woman to remove the ribbon. If we read the ribbon as a symbol of virginity—an uncut ribbon as intact hymen—the insistence that it be removed equates to sexual coercion. When the husband removes the ribbon as the wife sleeps—the case in many iterations—the act is a metaphorical rape. It also suggests murder. The more common name for such ribbons—chokers—equates the husband's act to real world domestic violence: when abusers kill their partners, they often do so via choking them.[1]

If the woman of the story was choked prior to the narrative's start, if she has come into the story as the survivor of prior choking/murder, her willingness to put up years of incessant pestering about her ribbon are more understandable. Given the confines of femininity, the expectation she wed and have children, she might be trying to make the best of bad options. Better a man that nags about your choker than a man that

"Those of us who knew have been waiting for a Carmen Maria Machado collection for years. Her stories show us what we really love and fear."
—Alexander Chee

HER BODY AND OTHER PARTIES

STORIES

CARMEN MARIA MACHADO

The cover of *Her Body and Other Parties* features a green ribbon floating suggestively around the skinless musculature of a female throat (Graywolf Press, 2017).

chokes you. Better, of course, would be a decent partner—or no partner at all.

Her refusal to remove the ribbon or divulge anything about it conveys a strong will. She is viewed by the world (and her lover) as freakish, for her ribbon, but she cares not. She is monstrously willful—so much so she is able to keep her dismembered head attached to her body with no more than a ribbon!

In Carmen Maria Machado's contemporary retelling, the woman narrates the story. "In the beginning, I know I want him before he does," the story starts. It is thus the female that does the wanting. Yet, the man she desires is both selfish and violent. Their first sexual encounter is described with violent language: takes, breaks, locks, nipple knotting, blood slicking. Made aware of "the concrete sense of his need," she hears "something that sounds like a banjo being plucked," a depiction that brings to mind the infamous banjo scene from *Deliverance* and the equally infamous scene in which Bobby (Ned Beatty) is raped.

Though one of the first things she tells her eventual husband is that he can't touch her ribbon, that it is hers, touch he does. Just before they marry, he pushes her against a wall and puts his hands round her throat, his thumb against the ribbon. Another time, he "touches the bow delicately," which she characterizes as "massaging my sex." She tells him multiple times "Please don't," but he acts as if he doesn't hear. She says no again, her voice "cracking in the middle." Checking her ribbon frantically in response—as she does multiple times in the story—she finds "the bow is still tight."

The violations the husband commits are not the first she has endured nor will they be the last. A school teacher assaulted her in a closet. The doctor who delivers her son will surgically assault her, giving her the "husband stitch" the title of the story references, that one meant to tighten the vagina for male benefit, to return her to a "virginal" state, to make her, as the doctor says, "Nice and tight."

In addition to making the sexual violence that other versions only skirt around explicit, Machado adds another key element—ribbons become the symbol of being female. This is made clear when the husband asks "Will the child have a ribbon?" after she tells him she is pregnant. When the child is born, he has his answer: "No ribbon. A boy." Later in the tale, the narrator joins another woman for coffee. She mentions her young daughter, only saying "Eleven is a terrifying age." The two women do not discuss "the specific fears of raising a girl-child," though the narrator does reference that adolescence for girls is "too frightening to forget." It is so, the story indicates, because women are trapped within their ribboned bodies, because their voices are not heard.

Near the story's close, after years of marriage, the woman wakes up to find her husband "probing the ribbon with his tongue." "My body rebels," she relates, "bucking hard against betrayal." Her husband yet again does not listen to her pleas to stop. She wedges her elbows into him, refusing with her body. Afterwards, he looks at her "confused and hurt," not recognizing himself as rapist. "He is not a bad man," she explains, naming this "the root of my hurt." He is not "bad" in the sense he is like all the other men in her life—her father, her teacher, the doctor. Ending her revelation with an ambiguous "And yet—" indicates he is, in fact, bad. Finally worn down by her husband's haranguing her about the ribbon—which is woven into the many incidences of sexual violence the story documents—she tells him "do what you want," speaking of the ribbon. Her head falls to the floor, as in all the other versions. He finally has what he wants. Her body. Without a head. Without the mouth that can say no.

* * *

If we take the origins of these tales of ribbon-necked women into consideration, the ribbon reflects violence done to the female body by the state and its so-called masters—and, more specifically, to the cut of the guillotine. Two nineteenth century tales make this plain—Alexander Dumas' *The Woman with the Velvet Necklace* (1850) and Washington Irving's "The German Student" (1824). In each, a man visiting Paris becomes obsessed with a beautiful woman.

Dumas' take focuses on a young man, Hoffman, and his pursuit of Arsene, an opera singer. Upon first seeing her, Hoffman notices a velvet ribbon round her neck held together by a tiny diamond guillotine. Associated with death from the moment of her entry into the narrative, she is described as pale and ice-cold, likened to a marble statue, and said to move like a snake (a figurative Medusa of the French Revolution era). Near the novel's close, Hoffman finds his way to the infamous Parisian square where thousands were beheaded. Drawn to the "blood-stained" guillotine "by a magnetic force," he caresses the "ghastly machine" and its blade, which is described as having a "mouth, wet with blood." He spies a woman crouched on the scaffold. Her black velvet ribbon reveals her to be Arsene. She speaks as if "an automaton" in "a strange voice" from lips "which opened and closed as if by a spring." Though seemingly a ghost or a strange embodiment of the automatic beheading machine, Hoffman insists she join him at a hotel. Later, as she drinks champagne, "several red drops [roll] from beneath the velvet necklace." Hoffman is a bit taken aback. When her foot rests upon a log from the fire yet does not burn, he is quite sure something is not right. This does not deter him, however, from "devouring her with kisses." The next morning, Hoffman wakes to find Arsene dead. The doctor called to the scene informs him she was beheaded the day before. By way of proof, the doctor releases the diamond clasp holding the velvet necklace. When Arsene's head falls to the floor, Hoffman runs from the room screaming "I am mad!"

In Irving's shorter version of the tale, a similarly "passionate admirer of female beauty" finds himself at the execution square during "the height of the reign of terror." Referencing the guillotine as a "dreadful instrument of death ... continually running with the blood of the virtuous," he too finds a "shadowy figure" on the steps of the scaffold—one who also wears a black band round her neck fastened with a diamond clasp. Recognizing her "ravishingly beautiful" face as the one which has been haunting his dreams, he insists she come home with him. After leaving the apartment for a short while the next morning, he returns to find her "pallid and ghastly" corpse. He summons the police which, like the doctor in Dumas' tale, inform him the woman was guillotined the day before. When her choker is removed her head rolls to the floor. The student shrieks "the fiend has gained possession of me!" The last line tells of his fate: "He went distracted, and died in a madhouse."

In both of these iterations, the male protagonists come to a bad end. Some might blame the ribbon-necked woman. Yet, the blame rests on the men's shoulders—or, more aptly, their heads. While they are each profligate, they, unlike Machado's male characters, are not explicitly associated with sexual violence, though the specter of such violence lurks beneath the surface of both tales.

In the real world, the murderous guillotine was colloquially referred to as "the lady" and "the widow"—something that both feminized the guillotine, and, at the same time, further monsterized women. Such historical details are rendered all the more macabre by the guillotine's "birth"—to ensure its viability, designers tested it on multiple female corpses before ever doing so on male ones (Klein). Though most guillotined were men, many women were also beheaded by the device. Olympe de Gouges, a 18th century French feminist, was one such woman. Her execution—and that of other women agitating for race, class, and gender parity—was presented as a just reward. Two weeks after de Gouges' execution, Pierre Gaspard Chaumette, a prominent politician, expounded: "She died on the guillotine for having forgotten the virtues that suit her sex."[2] If we put such claims in conversation with the many tales of ribbon-necked women, the ribbon becomes a symbol of rebellion, one that defies the notion "upstart" women deserve beheading. Holding their heads on their bodies in defiance of the guillotines cut, they are dangerous, their monstrous bodies living beyond death. Lady guillotines of sorts, they cut their relentless male suitors down to size, driving them to obsession and insanity. Though

sentenced to death by the state, the woman, much like Medusa, their decapitated forebear, live on.

As with the rebellious *tricoteuses* of the French revolution, these
ribbon-necked women use female tools as weapons of resistance. The
tricoteuses (literally knitting women), though first respected as "mothers
of the revolution," were eventually disparaged and called viragos, whores,
and monsters.[3] Their successful march on Versailles forgotten, they were
banished from government proceedings, effectively told to go back to the
kitchen. The women took to gathering at the guillotine. Knitting red caps
of liberation as they sat amongst the crowds, their acts, though characterized as heartless villainy, can be more accurately read as a rebellious.
Later deemed "the furies of the guillotine," Dominique Godineau argues
their actions were particularly abhorred because, by knitting in proximity
to executions, they juxtaposed "delicate tenderness with the most extreme
violence." Taking a tool of home and hearth and turning it into a weapon
"tinged with bloody tips," they effectively deployed a traditional feminine
skill in a very public, politicized space (xviii). An early example of turning
women's work into public act, their acts are part of a long history of revolutionary knitting. Moreover, in knitting, they are using womanly tools—
monster's tools—to resist entrapment in the house of patriarchy.[4]

The *tricoteuses* and their kindred sisters, the ribbon-necked women,
refuse the demands of their self-appointed masters. Using velvet ribbon,
yarn, and knitting needles to do so, using womanized tools, they seem to
recognize, as Audre Lorde's famous dictum imparts, "the master's tools
will never dismantle the master's house." In the paradigmatic text intro-
ducing this notion, Lorde emphasizes that in order to infuse the "personal
is political" with the radical potentiality the concept names, the ways racism, sexism, ageism, and homophobia intersect must be taken into account. In contrast, if the tools of patriarchy—one of which is the denial
of privilege and its intersectional components—are relied upon, "only the
most narrow parameters of change are possible and allowable." This reality is made apparent in the actions of *tricoteuses* of the French revolution. Before and since, such resistance has chipped away at the "master's
house"—a house which has its foundations in patriarchy, white supremacy, imperialism, enslavement, and genocide.

In the realm of horror, resistance is often fomented using the tools
of the marginalized—the tools of those deemed monstrous. Sometimes
these tools are those associated with females—as with the mop water Dorothy uses to destroy the wicked witch. Other times cooking know-how or
knowledge of roots, herbs, and plants comes into play—as those are associated with "kitchen witches" and "hedge witches." In many instances, skills
presumed to be demonic, fabricated, or ineffectual are utilized—telekinesis,

clairvoyance, telepathy. Specific examples of using "monster tools" in contemporary horror narratives are many: the granny in *The Crazies* wields a knitting needle, Lori Strode uses a clothes hanger against Michael Meyers in *Halloween*, Big Daddy deploys gas-station-attendant-know-how in *Land of the Dead*. In texts this monograph specifically addresses, monster tools are repeatedly employed. Queenie takes down a racist with a deep fat fryer in *American Horror Story: Coven*. The mother-daughter duo of *Housebound* use clothes hampers, telephone cords, and an electric meat fork against the serial killer who has invaded their home. Carol disarms domestic abusers with cookies in *The Walking Dead*. In *The Love Witch*, Elaine "hexes" male cads with tampons and chocolate cake. The witchy girls from *Sisterhood of Night* draw on their fashion know-how to foment a new kind of take back the night. In *Us*, The Tethered use scissors as their weapon of choice. In these and many other examples, those marginalized—those monsterized—draw on tools "the master" considers lowly, unimportant, useless. Perhaps most often, such monstrous types use their very bodies to rebel—that fleshy tool masters associate with unruly nature, construct as lesser than mind, and align with those "meant" to serve.

Such monster-tool-wielding renegades are kindred spirits to the willful girl introduced at the outset of this study—the one who animates Ahmed's theories of willfulness. Recall the girl of the Grimm tale is deemed incorrigible and sentenced to an early grave, one she refuses to stay within. Though she is repeatedly covered with earth, "it was all to no purpose, for the arm always came out again" (Grimm Brothers, 125). Her arm is much like the head of the ribbon-necked women. It is like the tethered masses who refuse to be sequestered underground. Like the gothic new women of *Penny Dreadful* and *Crimson Peak*. Like the defiant vampires and zombies of *Let the Right One In* and *The Girl with All the Gifts*. Like the rebel outcast of *Stranger Things*, *The OA*, and *Shape of Water*. Like the many willful monsters that refuse to be relegated to the margins. Such monsters, like the girl's arm, resist. They rise up. They return. Until they tear down the master's rotten house for good, let's hope they always will.

Chapter Notes

Introduction

1. The title of the monograph takes its name from Ahmed's conception of willfulness, something I take up in the introduction. For Ahmed's conception of the feminist killjoy, see "Hello feminist killjoys," located at https://feministkilljoys.com/2013/08/26/hello-feminist-killjoys/.

2. As so cogently displayed in The Black Lives Matter movement, one that responded to racialized police violence and was founded by Alicia Garza, Opal Tometi, and Patrisse Cullors.

3. For further discussion of these and other tales, see Sarah Alison Miller's "Monstrous Sexualities: Variations on the *Vagina Dentata*."

4. For a reading of the *Twilight* saga as conservative, see Wilson, *Seduced by Twilight*.

5. Here I am drawing on the conception of "becoming vampire" as explored by Simon Bacon.

Chapter 1

1. For a thorough overview of this zombie iteration and its ties to Haiti/voodoo, see Bishop's *American Zombie Gothic*, especially chapters 1 and 2.

2. This zombie type is covered at length in Stacey Abbott's *Undead Apocalypse.*

3. McNally's Introduction to *Monsters of the Market* references the ubiquity of terms such as "zombie economics." Notably, the vampire has infiltrated culture in similar ways, as with the characterization of Goldman Sachs as a "great vampire squid wrapped around the face of humanity" (quoted in McNally p. 1).

4. Though the zombie originated primarily as a racialized Other (as in William Seabrook's *The Magic Island*), the figure came to be closely associated with females and femininity. As noted by Anthony Marsella, Haitian beliefs present females as more likely to be "zombified."

5. Intriguingly, one of the beliefs regarding Haitian zombies is that seeing the ocean can awaken them from their zombie status. See Brent Swancer, "The Mysterious Real Zombies of Haiti."

6. For an insightful consideration of *The Stepford Wives* and its influence on *Get Out*, consult Episode 67 from *Faculty of Horror*, "Where Is My Mind: The Stepford Wives (1975) and Get Out (2017)."

7. For a notable exception, see Caitlin Duffy's "*Get Out* and the Subversion of the American Zombie."

8. As critics such as Robyn Wiegman and Elizabeth Young argue, the hypersexual beastly black male trope served to validate lynching in the real world. Robyn Wiegman, *American Anatomies: Theorizing Race and Gender* (Durham and London: Duke University Press), 1995.

9. Here I am drawing on the conception put forward by Audre Lorde in her 1979 essay, "The Master's Tools Will Never Dismantle the Master's House."

10. In his excellent and incisive "This Is Us: Deconstructing Race, Identity and Sexual Trauma in Jordan Peele's "Us," Max Gordon discusses the film's "Thriller" and Michael Jackson references.

11. For further consideration of Native American symbolism in the film, see Emmy Scott.

12. A line that echoes Romero's jocular insistence that he fashioned the ghouls to

be like "us" is "there's nothing scarier than the neighbors!"

13. For details regarding the low prosecution rates of rape and sexual violence, see, for example, Kate Harding, *Asking for It: The Alarming Rise of Rape Culture—And What We Can Do About It.*

14. Harding, for example, names the phrase "the Zeitgeist of the twenty-first century" (7).

15. For further discussion of the normalization of sexual violence, see Buchwald Roth's *Transforming a Rape Culture.*

16. Bishop argues early films engage with "symbolic rape" (*Zombie Gothic* 88). Steve Jones offers extended examinations of rape within zombie texts. See also Wilson's paper on *The Walking Dead*, "Rules for Surviving Rape Culture."

17. Ames's readings of Carol in "The Zombified Body as a Metaphor for Motherhood?: The Walking Dead's Cultural Commentary on Gender Norms & Parenting Expectation" and "The Trauma of (Post-Apocalyptic) Motherhood: *The Walking Dead*'s Social Commentary on Gender Roles" are particularly instructive here.

18. For a feminist reading of Romero's zombie films, see Patterson's "Cannibalizing Gender and Genre: A Feminist Re-Vision of George Romero's Zombie Films."

19. See Abbott, *Undead Apocalypse,* Chapter 5, for an insightful analysis of such hybrids.

20. Decker's reading of Pandora as a monstrous mother and femme fatale who "releases all the evils into the world" can be usefully applied to Carey's depiction of a zombie child associated with Pandora—one who ultimately does not bring on the zombie apocalypse but serves as symbol of hope. See Decker, "Monsters as Subversive Imagination: Inviting Monsters into the Philosophy Classroom."

21. Here, I am drawing on Judith Butler's concept of "unworthy lives" versus "lives worth grieving" developed especially in *Bodies That Matter* and *Precarious Lives.*

22. See Luckhurst and Hayton for instructive readings on the politics of *World War Z.*

23. For example, Clint tells Rickie "In this world, you can't let other people fight your battles for you. It's called TCB, Rickie, huh? Taking care of business."

24. For a reading of the film *Jaws* in relation to vagina dentata symbolism, see Caputi, "*Jaws* as Patriarchal Myth" in *Goddesses and Monsters.*

Chapter 2

1. Several studies further this conclusion. See, for example, Abbott's *Celluloid Vampires,* Day's *Vampire Legends in Contemporary American Culture,* Williamson's *The Lure of the Vampire,* and Bacon's *Becoming Vampire.*

2. Such is the case, for example, in *The Gilda Stories, The Moth Diaries, The Transfiguration,* and *Penny Dreadful. Dracula,* of course, also finds Mina as a documentarian and writer. See Bedore for more on Mina, and Bacon for further discussion of the "writerly bent" of the vampire canon.

3. See Abbott's *Celluloid Vampires* for a useful examination regarding the influence of western and road movie traditions on vampire films.

4. In the excellent "Taking Back the *Night of the Living Dead*: George Romero, Feminism, and the Horror Film" Grant draws on a similar invocation of this feminist practice, providing a reading which argues the women of *Night* are more feminist/rebellious than oft given credit for.

5. Goodwin reads the girl's more villainous acts as refuting the "'good Muslim' trope," noting the girl is "neither good nor bad."

6. See Halperin for a summation of the "multivalent meanings" of the chador.

7. For further consideration of the racialized vampire, see especially Arata and Winnubst.

8. The post–9/11 era as one steeped in the idea "danger can happen at any time, in any place" is crucial to the novel's reading of the era through the lens of the vampire. (Rosenberg, 116).

9. The characterization of humans as "blood banks" also occurs in *Daybreakers* and *True Blood,* although in the latter narratives synthetic blood is created as an alternative to "the real thing." Other narratives, such as *Twilight,* suggest animal blood is able to sustain vampires.

10. As Eli is gender fluid within the text, wherein both "he" and "she" language designates their character, I will use them/they to reference Eli.

11. The story, "Let the Old Dreams Die" is set twelve years after the close of *Let the Right One In.*

12. For further discussion of viral vampires, see Abbott and Weinstock.

13. See for example, the reviews by Emmet O'Cuana and Stuart Kelly.

14. For more on such characters/castings, see Bacon's "The Girls Have all the Gifts."

15. I am drawing here on Ahmed's conception of the "feminist killjoy" developed extensively in *Willful* Subjects. See also https://feministkilljoys.com/2013/08/26/hello-feminist-killjoys/.

16. This depiction sharply contrasts to portrayal of Neville as anti-hero in Matheson's novel. See Abbott, *Undead Apocalypse,* Chapter 1 for an extended reading of *I am Legend.*

17. Reading Matheson's text as engaging with "anxieties around race relations in the lead-up to the Civil Rights movement," Bedore emphasizes the novel is "told entirely from the perspective of the lone able-bodied, middle-class man who kills vampires by day and holes up in his fortified home by night" (39). Lane addresses the topic of gentrification specifically, arguing the vampires "represent the unwanted foreign influence that threatens our borders with disease, breaks down the hierarchy of our sexual/marriage economies, and eventually turns everyone in the village into vampires. The dominant culture is lost, or conquered by the invading foreign parasite. This parasite wants our women, our land, our wealth, and eventually our blood. See any parallels between vampires and the racial other? Matheson certainly did."

18. This type of critique accords to that proffered, for example, in the racially charged, consumer capitalist, and militarized environs of Romero's films.

Chapter 3

1. For further discussion of W.I.T.C.H., see Sollee and Adler. Also of use is Episode 60 from *Faculty of Horror,* "Season of the Witch."

2. See the insightful piece "Yes, This Is a Witch Hunt. I'm a Witch and I'm Hunting You" by Lindy West for more on the appropriation of witch-hunt terminology.

3. Documentation of contemporary witch hunts can be found in Federici's *Witches, Witch-Hunting, and Women.*

4. This lack of primary sources authored by women is documented by several scholars, Breuer, Purkiss, and Sollee among them.

5. Of note is that in some cases Tituba is presented as Native American and in others as African. Paddison argues these differing representations reflect shifting politics of race. He writes, "Puritans viewed Indians as in league with the Devil, and they placed the blame for the Salem witchcraft outbreak on Indian woman Tituba. Two centuries later, Tituba became transformed in public memory as African rather than Native American to fit the racial needs of the 19th century" (166).

6. Here, the novel circulates around the framing of African peoples as in league with the devil as well as the association between sorcery and African peoples. Interestingly, West African mythology views the witch as a kidnapping creature. As Poole documents, this led to the view of slavers being associated with witchcraft. Citing the work of John Thornton, a Jesuit priest and historian, Poole notes the widespread belief among slaves that their transport to the "new world" was made possible via sorcery and witchcraft. See Poole chapter 1.

7. This reference surely is drawing on the classic song. See "Strange Fruit: The First Great Protest Song."

8. The story arcs of Misty Day, Queenie, and Nan are particularly instructive in this regard.

9. Notably, Ahmed, in *Willful Subjects,* relates her conception of willfulness to Take Back the Night actions. She writes "To reclaim the streets as a reclaiming of night is to enact what we will: a world in which those who travel under the sign of women can travel safely, in numbers: feminist feet as angry feet" (163).

10. In enacting spells, Sabrina opens and closes her incantations with "Visit us, Sisters. Intercede on our behalf," calling upon Morgan le Fay, Circe, Hecate, Tituba, Marie Laveau and numerous others for aid.

11. See Shelton for a comprehensive list of these references.

12. Here, the show is clearly referencing

recent examples of powerful men claiming they are the targets of a witch hunt, as with Donald Trump, Harvey Weinstein, Woody Allen, for example. See Bartash's "'Witch Hunt' and Other Top Trump Twitter Phrases" and West's "Yes, This Is a Witch Hunt. I'm a Witch and I'm Hunting You."

13. For further analysis of the original series, see O'Reilley and Breuer.

14. Depictions such as this led to the removal of *Tender Morsels* from *Bitch Media*'s recommended list of feminist YA novels. See McDermott's "*Tender Morsels* not for Feminists?"

15. *Malleus Maleficarum* infamously includes various claims regarding witches collecting penises.

16. I am here referencing the infamous Bible quote "Thou shalt not suffer a witch to live" (Exodus 22:18).

17. As do Subassati and West in Episode 67 from *Faculty of Horror*.

18. For a discussion of broom symbolism in relation to the witch, see Sollee.

19. As Paddison documents, "Puritans viewed Indians as in league with the Devil," a view that was widespread during the era (166).

20. My formulation here draws on Melanie Klein's notion of the bad breast and Julia Kristeva's conception of the abject.

21. Biller's quotes are drawn from personal correspondence.

Chapter 4

1. Mythological female figures, especially those who exhibit agency, are regularly cast as monstrous. See Beard and Decker for extended discussions of women in Greek myth.

2. Ahmed's writing on the feminist killjoy in *Willful Subjects* and *Promise of Happiness* discusses the misreading of feminists as unhappy. She writes in *Promise*, "feminists are read as being unhappy, such that situations of conflict, violence, and power are read as about the unhappiness of feminists, rather than being what feminists are unhappy about" (Loc.1266).

3. For instance, Linda Williams' exploration of the woman's look, Carol Clover's formulation of the final girl, and Barbara Creed's monstrous-feminine, arguably the most foundational feminist readings of horror, mined horror for its gendered components, digging into psychoanalysis, visual pleasure, and the gaze. The lesser known *Recreational Terror*, by Isabel Pinedo, focused specifically on the pleasures horror can afford feminist viewers.

4. For consideration of gender parity behind the camera, see Kermode. Other useful sources for feminist reads of contemporary horror include *Bitchflicks*, *Faculty of Horror*, *Horror Homeroom*, and *Graveyard Shift Sisters*.

5. For images of this ilk, see Lafrance's "The Weird Familiarity of 100-Year-Old Feminism Memes."

6. Mina Harker notably insists she is not a New Woman, something well-documented in writings on *Dracula*. See, for example, Bedore.

7. Here, the show circulates around what Bram Dijkstra names the "cult of invalidism" which romanticizes "the notion of woman as a permanent, a necessary, even a 'natural' invalid" (*Idols* 25).

8. Notably, Lily's representation as mother angered by societal injustice contrasts starkly with Stoker's representation of motherhood as a female responsibility and "good mothers" as those that adopt (proper) domestic roles.

9. The fact Mary Shelley was purportedly haunted by the albatross imagery from *The Rime of the Ancient Mariner* seems particularly apt given Lily's positioning as a female Frankenstein creature.

10. Elizabeth Young, "Here Comes the Bride: Wedding Gender and Race" in *Bride of Frankenstein*.

11. Poole similarly notes the representation of patriarchal fathers in *Babadook* in the introduction to *Monsters in the Classroom* (6).

12. For a feminist analysis of *The Creature from the Black Lagoon* see Davidson.

13. See Drell for more on the MK Ultra program.

14. For example, see Jackson's "Is Eleven Actually the Monster on *Stranger Things*?"

15. In *Prometheus Unbound*, Shelley links the Demogorgon to political revolutions. See Foot's *Red Shelley* for more on this line of argument.

16. Karim, Mo, and Michelle add to the already racially diverse cast, while Dr. Rhodes, played by Liz Carr, extends the series' engagement with disability. The two friends that do not survive the season

are Jessie, who dies by suicide, and Rachel, whom Hap murders.

17. Of note here is the criticism the film garnered regarding what some characterized as an ableist depiction. See, for example, Wall's "The Shape of Ableism."

18. As does Creed in *The Monstrous Feminine*.

19. For feminist readings of Medusa, see Beard, Creed, and Decker.

20. Notably, Blind Man here serves as a twisted movie version of conservative Republicans such as Todd Akin who claim pregnancy doesn't occur in cases of "legitimate rape."

21. See, for example, Booth, Clover, Pinedo, and West.

22. An alignment that brings to mind Williams' foundational essay "When the Woman Looks."

23. Decker names Athena "the champion of patriarchy," a designate here (77). In contrast, Creed argues that Medusa and Athena are one and the same figure (166).

Conclusion

1. As documented in Snyder's *No Visible Bruises*.

2. For an extended discussion of de Gouges, see Bar's "Olympe De Gouges, the Radical French Feminist Who Was Murdered Twice."

3. As in, for example, Chaumettes's 1793 speech denouncing women's political activism. The speech appears in full in *The French Revolution and Human Rights: A Brief Documentary History*.

4. See Segal for a useful overview of knitting as a form of activism.

Bibliography

Abbott, Stacey. 2007. *Celluloid Vampires: Life After Death in the Modern World.* Austin: University of Texas Press.

_____. 2016. *Undead Apocalypse: Vampires and Zombies in the Twenty-First Century.* Edinburg: Edinburgh University Press.

Adler, Margot. 2006. *Drawing Down the Moon: Witches, Druids, Goddess-Worshipers and Other Pagans in America.* New York: Penguin.

Ahmed, Sara. 2013. "Hello Feminist Killjoys!" *feministkilljoys.* Retrieved from https://feministkilljoys.com/2013/08/26/hello-feminist-killjoys/.

_____. 2010. *The Promise of Happiness.* Durham, NC: Duke University Press.

_____. 2014. *Willful Subjects.* Durham, NC: Duke University Press.

Aiossa, Elizabeth. 2018. *The Subversive Zombie: Social Protest and Gender in Undead Cinema and Television.* Jefferson, NC: McFarland.

Ames, Melissa. 2015. "The Trauma of (Post-Apocalyptic) Motherhood: *The Walking Dead*'s Social Commentary on Gender Roles." Paper presented at *The National Women's Studies Association Conference.*

_____. 2016 "The Zombified Body as a Metaphor for Motherhood?: The Walking Dead's Cultural Commentary on Gender Norms & Parenting Expectation." Paper presented at *Mid-Atlantic Popular Culture Association Conference.*

Andermahr, Sony. 2015. "Decolonizing Trauma Studies: Trauma and Postcolonialism." *Humanities* 4.4: 500–505.

Aparjita, Nanda and Peter Bray. 2013. *The Strangled Cry: The Communication and Experience of Trauma.* Oxford, United Kingdom: Inter-Disciplinary Press.

Arata, Stephen D. 1990. "The Occidental Tourist: 'Dracula' and the Anxiety of Reverse Colonization." *Victorian Studies* 33.4: 621–45.

Armistead, Claire. 2009. "Book of the Week: White Is for Witching by Helen Oyeyemi." *The Guardian.* Retrieved from www.guardian.co.uk/books/audio/2009/jun/18/helen-oyeyemi-white-is-for-witching.

Auerbach, Nina. 1996. *Our Vampires, Ourselves.* Chicago, IL: University of Chicago Press.

Bacon, Simon. 2017. *Becoming Vampire: Difference and the Vampire in Popular Culture.* Bern, Switzerland: Peter Lang Inc., International Academic Publishers.

_____. 2018. "The Girls Have All the Gifts." *Peter Lang.* Retrieved from https://medium.com/peter-lang/the-girls-have-all-the-gifts-83f259bf505a.

_____. 2015. "Hyde and Seek: The Changing Face of the Monster as seen in Stevenson's *The Strange Case of Dr. Jekyll and Mr. Hyde.*" In *The Monster Stares Back: How Human We Remain Through Horror's Looking Glass,* edited by Mark Chakares and Marcia Goncalves, 17–40. Oxford, United Kingdom: Inter-Disciplinary Press.

Balmain, Colette. 2007. "The Enemy Within: The Child as Terrorist in the Contemporary American Horror Film." In *Monsters and the Monstrous: Myths of Enduring Evil,* edited by Niall Scott, 133–479. Amsterdam: Rodopi.

Bar, Roni. 2017. "Olympe De Gouges, the Radical French Feminist Who Was Murdered Twice." *Haaretz.* Retrieved from https://www.haaretz.com/world-news/europe/.premium.MAGAZINE-the-radical-french-feminist-who-was-murdered-twice-1.5462530.

Bartash, Jeffrey. 2017. "'Witch Hunt' and Other Top Trump Twitter Phrases." *Market Watch.* Retrieved from https://www.marketwatch.com/story/in-trump-tweets-witch-hunt-now-all-the-rage-2017-06-15.

Beard, Mary. 2017. *Women and Power: A Manifesto.* London: Liveright.

Bedore, Pamela. 2017. "Gender, Sexuality and Rhetorical Vulnerabilities in Monster Literature and Pedagogy." In *Monsters in the Classroom: Essays on Teaching What Scares Us,* edited by Adam Golub and Heather Richardson Hayton, 35–56. Jefferson, NC: McFarland.

Bell, Alden. 2010. *The Reapers Are the Angels.* New York, NY: Holt Paperbacks.

Benshoff, Harry M. 1997. *Monsters in the Closet: Homosexuality and the Horror Film.* Manchester: Manchester University Press.

Bishop, Kyle William. 2010. *American Zombie Gothic: The Rise and Fall (and Rise) of the Walking Dead in Popular Culture.* Jefferson, NC: McFarland.

_____. 2015. *How Zombies Conquered Popular Culture: The Multifarious Walking Dead in the 21st Century.* Jefferson, NC: McFarland.

Booth, Rebecca. 2018. "Slasher, Sex and Sisterhood in the *Slumber Party Massacre.*" *Horror Homeroom.* 12 November. Retrieved from http://www.horrorhomeroom.com/slashers-sex-and-sisterhood-in-the-slumber-party-massacre/.

Botting, Fred. 2007. "Gothic Culture." In *The Routledge Companion to Gothic,* edited by Catherine Spooner and Emma McEvoy, 199–213. London: Routledge.

Bourke, Joanna. 2007. *Rape: Sex, Violence, History.* Berkley, CA: Shoemaker & Hoard.

Bovenschen, Silvia, et al. 1978. "The Contemporary Witch, The Historical Witch and the Witch Myth: The Witch, Subject of the Appropriation of Nature and Object of the Domination of Nature." *New German Critique* 15: 82–119.

Braham, Persephone. 2019. "The Monstrous Caribbean." In *The Ashgate Research Companion to Monsters and the Monstrous,* edited by Asa Simon Mittman and Peter J. Dendle, 17–47. Farnham, UK: Ashgate.

Braidotti, Rosi. 1994. *Nomadic Subjects: Embodiment and Sexual Difference in Contemporary Feminist Theory.* New York, NY: Columbia University Press.

_____. 1996. "Signs of Wonder and Traces of Doubt: On Teratology and Embodied Differences." In *Between Monsters, Goddesses, and Cyborgs: Feminist Confrontations with Science, Medicine, and Cyberspace,* edited by Nina Lykke and Rosi Braidotti, 135–52. Zed Books.

Braun, Michelle. 2011. "It's So Hard to Get Good Help These Days: Zombies as a Culturally Stabilizing Force in *Fido.*" In *Race, Opression, and the Zombie: Essays on Cross-Cultural Appropriatons of the Caribbean Tradition,* edited by Christopher Moremon and Cory Rushton, 162–173. Jefferson, NC: McFarland.

Brayton, Sean. Spring 2011. "The Racial Politics of Disaster and Dystopia in I Am Legend." *The Velvet Light Trap* 67: 66–76.

Breuer, Heidi. 2009. *Crafting the Witch: Gendering Magic in Medieval and Early Modern England.* New York, NY: Routledge.

Brody, Richard. 2019. "Review: Jordan Peele's "Us" Is a Colossal Cinematic Achievement." *New Yorker.* Retrieved from https://www.newyorker.com/culture/the-front-row/review-jordan-peeles-us-is-a-colossal-cinematic-achievement.

_____. 2018. "The Silently Regressive Politics of *A Quiet Place.*" *The New Yorker.*

Retrieved from https://www.newyorker.com/culture/richard-brody/the-silently-regressive-politics-of-a-quiet-place.

Brooks, Kinitra D. 2017. *Searching for Sycorax: Black Women's Hauntings of Contemporary Horror*. New Brunswick, NJ: Rutgers University Press.

Brooks, Max. 2010. "Steve and Fred." In *The Living Dead 2*, edited by John Joseph Adams, 203–10. San Francisco, CA: Night Shade Books.

_____. 2006. *World War Z: An Oral History of the Zombie War*. 1st ed. New York, NY: Three Rivers Press.

Brown, Sherronda J. 2017. "'Listen to the Ancestors, Run!': *Get Out*, zombification, and Pathologizing Escape from the Plantation." *Racebaitr*. Retrieved from http://racebaitr.com/2017/03/07/listen-ancestors-run-get-zombification-pathologizing-escape-plantation/.

Brownmiller, Susan. 1993. *Against Our Will: Men, Women, and Rape*. New York, NY: Fawcett Columbine.

Buchwald, Emilie et al. 2005. *Transforming a Rape Culture*. Minneapolis, MN: Milkweed.

Butler, Judith. 1993. *Bodies That Matter*. New York, NY: Routledge.

_____. 2016. *Frames of War: When Is Life Grievable*. New York, NY: Verso.

_____. 2006. *Gender Trouble: Feminism and the Subversion of Identity*. New York, NY: Routledge.

_____. 2006. *Precarious Lives: The Powers of Mourning and Violence*. London: Verso.

Byers, Thomas B. 1988. "Good Men and Monsters: The Defense of Dracula, Dracula." In *Dracula: The Vampire and the Critics*, edited by Margaret L. Carter. 149–57. Ann Arbor, MI: UMI Research Press.

Campbell, Joseph. 1970. *The Masks of God: Primitive Mythology*. New York: Viking Press.

Canavan, Gerry. 2010. "We Are the Walking Dead: Race, Time, and Survival in Zombie Narrative," *Extrapolation* 51.3: 187–204.

Caputi, Jane. 2004. *Goddesses and Monsters: Women, Myth, Power, and Popular Culture*. Madison, WI: University of Wisconsin Press.

_____. 1993. *Gossips, Gorgons and Crones: The Fates of the Earth*. Rochester, VT: Bear & Co.

Carey, M. R. 2017. *The Boy on the Bridge*. New York, NY: Hachette Book Group.

_____. 2015. *The Girl with All the Gifts*. New York, NY: Hachette Book Group.

Carroll, Noel. 2003. *The Philosophy of Horror: Or, Paradoxes of the Heart*. New York, NY: Routledge.

Case, Sue-Ellen. 1997. "Tracking the Vampire." In *Writing on the Body: Female Embodiment and Feminist Theory*, edited by Katie Conboy, Nadia Medina, and Sarah Stanbury, 380–400. New York, NY: Columbia University Press.

Casey, Caroline. 1998. *Making the Gods Work for You: The Astrological Language of the Psyche*, New York, NY: Harmony.

Charnas, Suzy McKee. 1997. "Meditations in Red: On Writing." In *The Vampire Tapestry*. *Blood Read: The Vampire as Metaphor in Contemporary Culture*, edited by Joan Gordon and Veronica Hollinger, 59–67. Philadelphia, PA: University of Pennsylvania Press.

Chekares, Mark. 2015. "Devoloping Co-Dependence Between Monsters and Children in Animated Feature Films." In *The Monster Stares Back: How Human We Remain Through Horror's Looking Glass*, edited by Mark Chakares and Marcia Goncalves, 3–16. Oxford, United Kingdom: Inter-Disciplinary Press.

Christie, Deborah. 2011. "And the Dead Shall Walk." In *Better Off Dead: The Evolution of the Zombie as Post-Human*, edited by Deborah Christie and Sarah Juliet Lauro, 61–65. New York, NY: Fordham University Press.

_____. 2011. "A Dead New World: Richard Matheson and the Modern Zombie." In *Better off Dead: The Evolution of the Zombie as Post-Human,* edited by Deborah Christie and Sarah Juliet Lauro, 67–80. New York, NY: Fordham University Press.

Cixous, Hélène, and Catherine Clément. 1986. *The Newly Born Woman.* Minneapolis, MN: University of Minnesota Press.

Clover, Carol J. 1993. *Men, Women and Chain Saws: Gender in the Modern Horror Film.* Princeton, NJ: Princeton University Press.

Cohen, Jeffrey Jerome, ed. 1996. *Monster Theory: Reading Culture.* Minneapolis, IL: University of Minnesota Press.

Coleman, Robin R. Means. 2011. *Horror Noire: Blacks in American Horror Films from the 1890s to Present.* New York, NY: Routledge.

Collins, Margo and Elson Bond. 2011. "'Off the Page and Into Your Brains': New Millennium Zombies and the Scourge of Hopeful Apocalypses." In *Better Off Dead: The Evolution of the Zombie as Post-Human,* edited by Deborah Christie and Sarah Juliet Lauro, 187–204. New York, NY: Fordham University Press.

Condé, Maryse. 2009. *I, Tituba, Black Witch of Salem.* Charlottesville, VA: University of Virginia Press.

Cousins, Helen. 2012. "Helen Oyeyemi and the Yoruba Gothic: White Is for Witching." *Journal of Commonwealth Literature* 47.1: 47–58.

Craft, Christopher. Autumn 1984. "Kiss Me with Those Red Lips: Gender and Inversion in Bram Stoker's *Dracula.*" *Representations* No. 8: 107–33.

Creed, Barbara. 1993. *The Monstrous-Feminine: Film, Feminism, Psychoanalysis.* New York, NY: Routledge.

Crenshaw, Kimberle. 1989. "Demarginalizing the Intersection of Race and Sex." *Feminism in the Law: Theory, Practice and Criticism,* Special Issue, pp. 139–68.

Cronin, Justin. 2016. *The City of Mirrors.* New York, NY: Ballantine Books.

_____. 2011. *The Passage.* New York, NY: Ballantine Books.

_____. 2016. *The Twelve.* New York, NY: Ballantine Books.

Cross, Stephanie. 2012. "Justin Cronin: 'It's not the end of the world, you know...'" *The Independent.* Retrieved from www.independent.co.uk/arts-entertainment/books/features/justin-cronin-its-not-the-end-of-the-world-you-know-8229142.html.

Cuklanz, Lisa M. 2000. *Rape on Prime Time: Television, Masculinity, and Sexual Violence.* Philadelphia, PA: University of Pennsylvania Press.

D'Angelo, Mike. 2014. "*Housebound* Devises a Novel Solution to a Common Haunted-House-Movie Problem." *The AV Club.* Retrieved from www.avclub.com/tag/housebound.

Davidson, Sabrina. 2016. "Feminism and Semiotics in '*The Creature from the Black Lagoon.*" *Medium.* Retrieved from medium.com/@1005696/feminism-and-semiotics-in-the-creature-from-the-black-lagoon-e03a72b2ef6c.

Davis, Angela. 1992. Introduction. *I, Tituba, Black Witch of Salem,* by Maryse Condé, Trans. by Richard Philcox, xi-xiii. Charlottesville, VA: University of Virginia Press.

_____. Spring 2002. "Joan Little: The Dialectics of Rape." *Ms. Magazine.*

Davis, Lennard J. 1995. *Enforcing Normalcy: Disability, Deafness, and the Body.* London: Verso.

Day, William Patrick. 2002. *Vampire Legends in Contemporary American Culture: What Becomes a Legend Most.* Lexington, KY: University Press of Kentucky.

Debruge, Peter. 2016. "Why *The OA* Is One of the Year's Most Important Films." *Variety.* Retrieved from variety.com/2016/tv/columns/the-oa-netflix-brit-marling-film-critic-appreciation-1201948242/.

Decker, Jessica Elbert. Fall 2016. "Hail Hera, Mother of Monsters! Monstrosity as Emblem of Sexual Sovereignty." *Women's Studies: An Inter-Disciplinary Journal* 45.8: 743–757.

_____. 2017. "Monsters as Subversive Imagination: Inviting Monsters into the Philosophy Classroom," In *Monsters in the Classroom: Essays on Teaching What Scares Us,* edited by Adam Golub and Heather Richardson Hayton, 70–86. Jefferson, NC: McFarland.

Dendle, Peter. 2007. "The Zombie as Barometer of Cultural Anxiety." In *Monsters and the Monstrous,* edited by Niall Scott, 45–58. Amsterdam, NL: Rodopi.

DeRosa, Robin. 2009. *The Making of Salem: The Witch Trials in History, Fiction and Tourism.* Jefferson, NC: McFarland.

Dijkstra, Bram. 1996. *Evil Sisters: The Threat of Female Sexuality and the Cult of Manhood.* New York, NY: Knopf.

_____. 1986. *Idols of Perversity: Fantasies of Feminine Evil in Fin-de-Siecle Culture.* New York, NY: Oxford University Press.

Doherty, Lillian E. 2001. *Gender and the Interpretation of Classical Myth.* London: Duckworth.

Douglas, Susan. 2010. *Enlightened Sexism: The Seductive Message that Feminism's Work Is Done.* New York, NY: Times Books.

Downey, Dara. 2011. "Seven Legs My True Love Has: Fantasies of Female Monstrosity in American Horror Fiction." In *The Horrid Looking Glass: Reflections on Monstrosity,* edited by Paul L. Yoder and Peter Mario Kreuter, 25–45. Oxford, United Kingdom: Inter-Disciplinary Press.

Doyle, Sady. 2013. "Double, Double, Race and Gender Trouble." *In These Times.* December. Retrieved from http://inthesetimes.com/article/15992/american_horror_story_coven.

Drell, Cady. 2016. "*Stranger Things*: The Secret CIA Programs That Inspired Hit Series." *Rolling Stone.* Retrieved from https://www.rollingstone.com/culture/culture-features/stranger-things-the-secret-cia-programs-that-inspired-hit-series-249484/.

Drezner, Daniel W. 2015. *Theories of International Politics and Zombies.* Princeton, NJ: Princeton University Press.

Du Coudray, Chantal Bourgault. 2006. *The Curse of the Werewolf: Fantasy, Horror and the Beast Within.* New York, NY: I.B. Tauris.

Dudenhoeffer, Larrie. 2014. *Embodiment and Horror Cinema.* New York, NY: Palgrave Macmillan.

Due, Tananarive. 2016. "The H Word: On Writing Horror." *Nightmare Magazine.* Retrieved from http://www.nightmare-magazine.com/nonfiction/h-word-writing-horror/.

Duffy, Caitlin. 2018. "*Get Out* and the Subversion of the American Zombie." *Horror Homeroom.* Retrieved from http://www.horrorhomeroom.com/get-out-subversion-of-the-american-zombie/.

Dumas, Alexander. 2002. *The Woman with the Velvet Necklace.* Amsterdam, NL: Fredonia Books.

Dyer, Richard. 1997. *White.* New York, NY: Routledge.

Edelman, Lee. 2004. *No Future: Queer Theory and the Death Drive.* Durham, NC: Duke University Press.

Eggertsen, Chris. 2016. "'Don't Breathe's' Most Disturbing Scene is Also One of the Year's Most Controversial." *Uproxx.* Retrieved from uproxx.com/hitfix/the-offensive-power-of-dont-breathes-controversial-turkey-baster-scene/.

Ehrlich, David. 2016. "*Train to Busan* Review: This Electric Korean Zombie Movie Goes Off the Rails." *IndieWire.* Retrieved from http://www.indiewire.com/2016/07/train-to-busan-review-korea-zombies-yeon-sang-ho-1201706829/.

Eisler, Riane. 1988. *The Chalice and the Blade: Our History, Our Future.* New York, NY: Harper and Row.

Faraci, Devin. 2016. "*The Witch* Director Robert Eggers on Black Philip, Folktales, and His Overhyped Film." *Birth, Movies, Death.* Retrieved from http://birthmoviesdeath.com/2016/02/19/the-witch-director-robert-eggers-on-black-phillip-folktales-and-his-overhyp.

Federici, Silvia. 2014. *Caliban and the Witch.* New York, NY: Autonomedia.

_____. 2018. *Witches, Witch-Hunting, and Women.* Oakland, CA: PM Press.

Fiedler, Leslie A. 1993. *Freaks: Myths and Images of the Secret Self.* New York, NY: Anchor Books.

Foot, Paul. 1995. *Red Shelley.* London: Bookmarks.

Forest, Laurie. 2017. *The Black Witch.* Toronto, Ontario: Harlequin Teen.

Foutch, Haleigh. 2017. "*The Transfiguration* Review: A Melancholy, Downright Disturbing Modern Vampire Allegory." *Collider.* Retrieved from http://collider.com/the-transfiguration-movie-review/.

Frater, Rhiannon. 2011. *Fighting to Survive.* New York, NY: Tor.

_____. 2011. *The First Days.* 1st ed. New York, NY: Tor.

_____. 2012. *Siege.* New York, NY: Tor.

Frost, Brian J. 2003. *The Essential Guide to Werewolf Literature.* Madison, WI: University of Wisconsin Press.

Fry, Carrol L. 1988. "Fictional Conventions and Sexuality in *Dracula.*" In *Dracula: The Vampire and the Critics,* edited by Margaret L. Carter, 35–38. Ann Arbor, MI: UMI Research Press.

Fusco, Katherine. 2018. "DIY Whiteness in the Age of Apocalypse." *Avidly.* Retrieved from http://avidly.lareviewofbooks.org/2018/05/24/diy-whiteness-in-the-age-of-apocalypse/.

Gallagher, Catherine, and Thomas Walter Laqueur, eds. 1987. *The Making of the Modern Body: Sexuality and Society in the Nineteenth Century.* Berkeley, CA: University of California Press.

Garber, Marjorie B. and Nancy J. Vickers, eds. 2003. *The Medusa Reader.* New York, NY: Routledge.

Gelder, Ken. 1994. *Reading the Vampire.* New York, NY: Routledge.

Gentilviso, Chris. 2015. "Todd Akin on Abortion: 'Legitimate Rape' Victims Have 'Ways to Try to Shut That Whole Thing Down.'" *Huffpost.* Retrieved from www.huffingtonpost.com/2012/08/19/todd-akin-abortion-legitimate-rape_n_1807381.html.

Gilbert, Sophie. 2018. "*Red Clocks* Imagines America Without Abortion." *The Atlantic.* Retrieved from www.theatlantic.com/entertainment/archive/2018/02/leni-zumas-red-clocks-review/552464./

Gomez, Jewelle. 1997. "Recasting the Mythology: Writing Vampire Fiction." In *Blood Read: The Vampire as Metaphor in Contemporary Culture,* edited by Joan Gordon and Veronica Hollinger, 85–92. Philadelphia, PA: University of Pennsylvania Press.

_____. 2011. "Caramelle 1864." In *From Where We Sit: Black Writers Write Black Youth,* edited by Victoria A. Brownworth. Tallahassee, FL: Tiny Satchel Press.

_____. 1991. *The Gilda Stories.* Ann Arbor, MI: Firebrand Books.

_____. 1991 "Joe Louis Was a Heck of a Fighter." In *The Gilda Stories,* 266–68. Ann Arbor, MI: Firebrand Books.

_____. 1991. Afterword. "We Take Blood, Not Life, Leave Something in Exchange." *The Gilda Stories,* 256–63. Ann Arbor, MI: Firebrand Books.

Gonzalez, Ed. 2015. "Sundance Film Review: *It Follows.*" *Slant Magazine.* Retrieved from www.slantmagazine.com/house/article/sundance-film-festival-2015-review-it-follows.

Goodwin, Megan. 2016. "When the Vampire Looks: Gender and Surveillance in *A Girl Walks Home Alone at Night.*" *Mizan Project.* April. Retrieved from http://www.mizanproject.org/pop-post/when-the-vampire-looks/

Gordon, Max. 2019. "This Is Us: Deconstructing Race, Identity and Sexual Trauma in Jordan Peele's *Us.*" *Medium.* Retrieved from https://medium.com/@maxgordon19/this-is-us-deconstructing-race-identity-and-sexual-trauma-in-jordan-peeles-us-bbaa8d6d41f

Grant, Barry Keith. 1996. "Taking Back the *Night of the Living Dead*: George Romero, Feminism, and the Horror Film." In *The Dread of Difference: Gender and the Horror Film,* edited by Barry Keith Grant, 200–212. Austin, TX: University of Texas Press.

Grant, Barry Keith, ed. 1996. *The Dread of Difference: Gender and the Horror Film.* Austin, TX: University of Texas Press.

Green, Stephanie. 2017. "Lily Frankenstein: The Gothic New Woman in *Penny Dreadful.*" *Refractory: A Journal of Entertainment Media.* Retrieved from www.refractory.unimelb.edu.au/2017/06/14/green/.

Greene, John and Michaela D.E. Meyer. Fall 2014. "The Walking (Gendered) Dead: A Feminist Rhetorical Critique of The Zombie Apocalypse Television Narrative." *Ohio Communication Journal* 52: 64 -74.

Greene, Richard, and K. Silem. Mohammad. 2010. *Zombies, Vampires, and Philosophy: New Life for the Undead.* Chicago, IL: Open Court.

Grey, Rosie. 2017. "Trump Defends White-Nationalist Protesters." *The Atlantic.* Retrieved from https://www.theatlantic.com/politics/archive/2017/08/trump-defends-white-nationalist-protesters-some-very-fine-people-on-both-sides/537012/.

Griffin, Gail B. 1988. "'Your Girls That You All Love Are Mine': *Dracula* and the Victorian Male Sexual Imagination." In *Dracula: The Vampire and the Critics,* edited by Margaret L. Carter, 137–148. Ann Arbor, MI: UMI Research Press.

Grimm Brothers. 2013. *The Grimm's Fairy Tales.* Trans. by Margaret Hunt. Mermaids Classics.

Haig, Matt. 2014. *The Radleys.* New York, NY: Free Press.

Halberstam, Jack. 2012. *Skin Shows: Gothic Horror and the Technology of Monsters.* Durham, NC: Duke University Press.

Halperin, Moze. 2016. "Feminism, Radicalization, and Injustice: The Enduring Power of the Witch Narrative." *Flavorwire.* Retrieved from http://flavorwire.com/571723/not-just-feminist-what-todays-puritan-witch-horror-stories-have-to-say-about-more-insidious-forms-of-radicalization

_____. 2014. "*A Girl Walks Home Alone at Night* Is a Protest Film ... If You Want It to Be." *Flavorwire,* November. http://flavorwire.com/490408/a-girl-walks-home-alone-at-night-is-a-feminist-protest-film-if-you-want-it-to-be.

Halpern, David. 1995. *Saint Foucault: Towards a Gay Hagiography.* New York, NY: Oxford University Press.

Haraway, Donna. 1997. *ModestWitness@Second_Millennium. FemaleMan_Meets_OncoMouse: Feminism and Technoscience.* New York: Routledge.

Harding, Kate. 2015. *Asking for It: The Alarming Rise of Rape Culture—and What We Can Do about It.* Boston, MA: Perseus Books Group.

Harper, Stephen. 2015. "'They're Us': Representations of Women in George Romero's "Living Dead" Series.'" Retrieved from http://mediawolfpack.com/wp-content/uploads/2013/11/females-in-romero.pdf.

Harrington, Erin. 2017. *Women, Monstrosity, and Horror Film: Gynaehorror.* New York, NY: Routledge.

Harvey, Day. 2018. "How *The Shape of Water* Subtly Became the Queer, Race-Aware,

#MeToo Masterpiece of 2018." *Shortlist*. Retrieved from www.shortlist.com/entertainment/films/the-shape-of-water-guillermo-del-toro-metoo-race-lgbt/346246.

Hatlen Burton. 1988. "The Return of the Repressed / Oppressed in Bram Stoker's Dracula." In *Dracula: The Vampire and the Critics*, edited by Margaret L. Carter, 117–135. Ann Arbor, MI: UMI Research Press.

Hayles, Katherine. 1999. *How We Became Posthuman: Virtual Bodies in Cybernetics, Literature, and Informatics*. Chicago, IL: University of Chicago Press.

Hayton, Heather Richardson. 2017. "The Monster Waiting Within: Unleashing Agon in the Community." In *Monsters in the Classroom: Essays on Teaching What Scares Us*, edited by Adam Golub and Heather Richardson Hayton, 211–214. Jefferson, NC: McFarland.

Heller-Nicholas, Alexandra. 2011. *Rape-Revenge Films: A Critical Study*. Jefferson, NC: McFarland, 2011.

Ho, Helen K. 2014. "Becoming Glenn: Asian American Masculinity." In *The Politics of Race, Gender and Sexuality in* The Walking Dead*: Essays on the Television Series and Comics*, edited by Elizabeth Erwin and Dawn Keetley, 31–42. Jefferson, NC: McFarland.

Hoffman, Nina Kiriki. 2008. "The Third Dead Body." In *The Living Dead*, edited by John Joseph Adams, 83–97. San Francisco, CA: Night Shade Books.

Hollinger, Veronica. 1997. "Fantasies of Absence: The Postmodern Vampire." In *Blood Read: The Vampire as Metaphor in Contemporary Culture*, edited by Joan Gordon and Veronica Hollinger, 199–212. Philadelphia, PA: University of Pennsylvania Press.

Housel, Rebecca, and Jeremy Wisnewski, eds. 2009. *Twilight and Philosophy: Vampires, Vegetarians, and the Pursuit of Immortality*. Hoboken, NJ: John Wiley & Sons.

Howell, Amanda. 2018. "The Terrible Terrace: Australian Gothic Reimagined and the (Inner) Suburban Horror of *The Babadook*." In *American-Australian Cinema*, edited by Adrian Danks et al, 183–201. Berlin: Springer.

Hubbard, Susan. 2010. *The Season of Risks: An Ethical Vampire Novel*. New York, NY: Schuster Paperbacks.

_____. 2008. *The Society of S.* New York, NY: Schuster Paperbacks.

_____. 2009. *The Year of Disappearances*. New York, NY: Schuster Paperbacks

Hughes, Bill and Sam George. 2013. "Introduction: Undead Reflections: The Sympathetic Vampire and Its Monstrous Others." *Gothic Studies* 15.1 Manchester University Press.

Hutchinson, Sean. 2016. "How Robert Eggers Made 'The Witch' a Modern Horror Classic." *Inverse*. Retrieved from www.inverse.com/article/11691-how-robert-eggers-made-the-witch-a-modern-horror-classic.

Inness, Sherrie A. 1999. *Tough Women: Women Warriors and Wonder Women in Popular Culture*. Philadelphia, PA: University of Pennsylvania Press.

Irving, Washington. 1824. "The German Student." In *Tales of a Traveller*. London, UK: John Murray.

Jackson, Dan. 2016. "Is Eleven Actually the Monster on *Stranger Things*?" *Thrillist*. Retrieved from https://www.thrillist.com/entertainment/nation/stranger-things-theory-eleven-monster.

Jackson, Kimberly. 2016. *Gender and the Nuclear Family in Twenty-First Century Horror*. New York, NY: Palgrave Macmillan.

James, Kendra. 2017. "*Get Out* Perfectly Captures the Terrifying Truth About White Women." *Cosmopolitan*. Retrieved from https://www.cosmopolitan.com/entertainment/movies/a8990932/get-out-perfectly-captures-the-terrifying-truth-about-white-women/.

Jensen, Robert. 2007. *Getting Off: Pornography and the End of Masculinity.* Brooklyn, NY: South End Press.

Jionde, Elexus. 2014. "The Curious Case of T-Dog: A Magical Negro?" In *The Politics of Race, Gender and Sexuality in* The Walking Dead: *Essays on the Television Series and Comics,* edited by Elizabeth Erwin and Dawn Keetley, 21–30. Jefferson, NC: McFarland.

Johnson, Alan. 1988. "Bent and Broken Necks: Signs of Design in Stoker's *Dracula.*" In *Dracula: The Vampire and the Critics,* edited by Margaret L. Carter, 231–243. Ann Arbor, MI: UMI Research Press.

Johnston, Elizabeth. 2016. "The Original 'Nasty Woman.'" *The Atlantic.* Retrieved from www.theatlantic.com/entertainment/archive/2016/11/the-original-nasty-woman-of-classical-myth/506591/.

Jones, Steve. Summer 2012. "Deadgirl and the Sexual Politics of Zombie-Rape." *Feminist Media Studies* 13.3: 1–15.

_____. 2011. "Porn of the Dead: Necrophilia, Feminism, and Gendering the Undead." In *Zombies Are Us: Essays on the Humanity of the Walking Dead,* edited by Christopher Moreman and Corey Rushton, 40–61. Jefferson, NC: McFarland.

Katz, Jackson. 2006. *The Macho Paradox: Why Some Men Hurt Women and How All Men Can Help.* Naperville, IL: Sourcebooks.

Kee, Chera. 2011. "'They Are Not Men … They Are Dead Bodies!': From Cannibal to Zombie and Back Again." In *Better off Dead: The Evolution of the Zombie as Post-Human,* edited by Deborah Christie and Sarah Juliet Lauro, 9–23. New York, NY: Fordham University Press.

Keesey, Pam. 2001. "The B-Movie Mystique: American Feminism at the Drive-In." *Monsterzine.* Retrieved from http://www.monsterzine.com/200107/feminism.php.

Keetley, Dawn. 2016. "*The Witch:* The Dread-Soaked Wilderness." *Horror Homeroom.* Retrieved from www.horrorhomeroom.com/category/dawn-keetley/page/24/.

Keetley, Dawn, eds. 2014. *"We're All Infected": Essays on AMC's* The Walking Dead *and the Fate of the Human.* Jefferson, NC: McFarland.

Kelly, Casey Ryan. 2016. "Camp Horror and the Gendered Politics of Screen Violence: Subverting the Monstrous-Feminine in *Teeth.*" *Women's Studies in Communication* 39.1: 86–106.

Kelly, Stuart. 2016. "*The City of Mirrors,* by Justing Cronin: Review." *The Guardian.* Retrieved from https://www.theguardian.com/books/2016/jun/16/the-

Kermode, Mark et al. 2017. "The Female Directors Bringing New Blood to Horror Films." *The Guardian.* Retrieved from https://www.theguardian.com/film/2017/mar/19/the-female-directors-bringing-new-blood-horror-films-babadook-raw-prevenge.

Kessock, Shoshana. 2014. "*Salem:* How Not to Handle History (Or Race, Gender, etc…)" *The Daily Beast.* Retrieved from https://www.thedailybeast.com/the-walking-deads-slabtown-the-real-source-of-terror-isnt-walkers-its-rape.

Kilgannonaug, Corey. 2004. "Long-Running Rivalries in Rockaways Projects Flare Into Violence." *The New York Times.* Retrieved from https://www.nytimes.com/2004/08/23/nyregion/long-running-rivalries-in-rockaways-projects-flare-into-violence.html.

Kimerling, Rachel et al. 2002. *Gender and PTSD.* New York, NY: Guilford Press.

King, Amy K. 2013. "The Spectral Queerness of White Supremacy: Helen Oyeyemi's *White Is for Witching.*" In *The Ghostly and the Ghosted in Literature and Film,* edited by Lisa Kroger and Melanie R. Anderson, 59–73. Newark, DE: University of Delaware Press.

Kiste, Gwendolyn. 2018. "W Is for Witch." *Nightmare Magazine*. Retrieved from http://www.nightmare-magazine.com/nonfiction/h-word-w-witch/.

Klein, Christopher. 2018. "The Guillotine's First Cut." *History Channel*. Retrieved from https://www.history.com/news/the-guillotines-first-cut.

Koss, Mary P. et al. Spring 1987. "The Scope of Rape: Incidence and Prevalence of Sexual Aggression and Victimization in a National Sample of Higher Education Students." *Journal of Consulting and Clinical Psychology* 55. 2: 162–71.

Kramer, Heinrich and James Sprenger. 1971. *Malleus Maleficarum*. Trans. by Montague Summers, Mineola, NY: Dover Books.

Kristeva, Julia. 1982. *Powers of Horror*. Trans. by Leon S. Roudiez, New York, NY: Columbia University Press.

Lafrance, Adrienne. 2016. "The Weird Familiarity of 100-Year-Old Feminism Memes." *The Atlantic*. Retrieved from https://www.theatlantic.com/technology/archive/2016/10/pepe-the-anti-suffrage-frog/505406/.

Lanagan, Margo. 2013. *The Brides of Rollrock Island*. Toronto, ON: Ember.

_____. 2010. *Tender Morsels*. New York, NY: Alfred A. Knopf.

Lane, Michelle R. 2013. "There Goes the Neighborhood: Racial Segregation in Richard Matheson's *I Am Legend*." Retrieved from http://michellerlane.blogspot.com/2013/08/there-goes-neighborhood-racial.html.

Latham, Rob. 1997. "Consuming Youth: The Lost Boys Cruise Mallworld." In *Blood Read: The Vampire as Metaphor in Contemporary Culture*, edited by Joan Gordon and Veronica Hollinger, 129–147. Philadelphia, PA: University of Pennsylvania Press.

Lauro, Sarah Juliet. 2017. "Introduction: Wander and Wonder in Zombieland." In *Zombie Theory: A Reader*. Minneapolis, MN: University of Minnesota Press.

Lauro, Sarah Juliet and Karen Embry. 2008. "A Zombie Manifesto: The Nonhuman Condition in the Era of Advanced Capitalism." *Boundary* 35.1: 85–108.

Ledger, Sally. 1997. *The New Woman: Fiction and Feminism at the Fin de Siècle*. Manchester: Manchester University Press.

LeFanu, J. Sheridan. 2012. *Carmilla*. New York, NY: Start Publishing.

Leon, Melissa. 2014. "*The Walking Dead's* 'Slabtown': The Real Source of Terror Isn't Walkers, It's Rape." *Daily Beast*. Retrieved from https://www.thedailybeast.com/the-walking-deads-slabtown-the-real-source-of-terror-isnt-walkers-its-rape.

Lindqvist, John Ajvide. 2010. *Let the Right One In*. New York, NY: St. Martin's Griffin.

Littlewood, Alison. 2016. "Fairy Tales: The Original Horror Stories?" *Nightmare Magazine*. Retrieved from http://www.nightmare-magazine.com/nonfiction/fairy-tales-the-original-horror-stories/.

Lorde, Audre. 1984. "The Master's Tools Will Never Dismantle the Master's House." In *Sister Outsider: Essays and Speeches*, Crossing Press Feminist Series. New York, NY: Crossing Press.

Lovecraft, H.P. 1939. "Medusa's Coil." *Weird Tales*, January. Retrieved from www.hplovecraft.com/writings/texts/fiction/mc.as.

Lowder, James, eds. 2011. *Triumph of The Walking Dead: Robert Kirkman's Zombie Epic on Page and Screen*. Dallas, TX: Smart Pop.

Luckhurst, Roger. 2015. *Zombies: A Cultural History*. Durrington, UK: Reaktion Books.

Lykke, Nina, and Rosi Braidotti, eds. 1996. *Between Monsters, Goddesses, and Cyborgs: Feminist Confrontations with Science, Medicine, and Cyberspace*. London: Zed Books.

Lynskey, Dorian. 2011. "Strange Fruit: The First Great Protest Song." *The Guardian*. Retrieved from https://www.theguardian.com/music/2011/feb/16/protest-songs-billie-holiday-strange-fruit.

Macalpine, Maggie. 2010. "Interview: Margo Lanagan on *Tender Morsels.*" *Unbound Rules.* Retrieved from http://www.unboundworlds.com/2010/03/interview-margo-lanagan-on-tender-morsels/.

Machada, Maria Carmen. 2014. "The Husband Stitch." 3–32. Minneapolis, MI: Graywolf Press.

Marinucci, Mimi. 2010. *Feminism Is Queer: The Intimate Connection Between Queer and Feminist Theory.* London: Zed Books.

Marsella, Anthony J. 2008. *Ethnocultural Perspectives on Disaster and Trauma.* New York, NY: Springer.

Marx, Karl. 1978. *Capital: A Critique of Political Economy.* Trans. by David Fernbach, London: Penguin.

Matheson, Richard. 2007. *I Am Legend.* New York, NY: Tor.

McCann, Hannah. 2016. "The Queer World of *Stranger Things.*" *Binary This.* Retrieved from https://binarythis.com/2016/12/10/the-queer-world-of-stranger-things/.

McClelland, Bruce A. 2009. *Slayers and Their Vampires: A Cultural History of Killing the Dead.* Ann Arbor, MI: University of Michigan Press.

McDermott, Kirstyn. 2011. "*Tender Morsels* not for Feminists?" *Kirstyn Mcdermott.* Retrieved from https://kirstynmcdermott.com/2011/02/02/tender-morsels-not-for-feminists/.

McFarland, Melanie. 2016. "How *Penny Dreadful's* Surprise Series Finale Betrayed Its Best Character." *Vox.* Retrieved from https://www.vox.com/2016/6/30/12053744/penny-dreadful-finale-recap-vanessa-ives-dies.

McGuire, Danielle L. 2011. *At the Dark End of the Street: Black Women, Rape, and Resistance—A New History of the Civil Rights Movement from Rosa Parks to the Rise of Black Power.* New York, NY: Vintage Books.

McIntosh, Shawn, and Marc Leverette, eds. 2008. *Zombie Culture: Autopsies of the Living Dead.* Lanham, MD: Scarecrow Press.

McNally, Cayla. 2017. "Get Out and Scientific Racism." *Horror Homeroom,* http://www.horrorhomeroom.com/get-out-scientific-racism/.

McNally, David. 2012. *Monsters of the Market: Zombies, Vampires, and Global Capitalism.* Chicago, IL: Haymarket Books.

McRobbie, Angela. 1991. *Feminism and Youth Culture: From 'Jackie' to 'Just Seventeen.'* Boston, MA: Unwin Hyman.

Meyer, Sabine. 2002. "Passing Perverts, After All?: Vampirism (In)Visibility, and the Horrors of the Normative in Jewelle Gomez' The Gilda Stories." *Femspec* 4.1.

Miller, Cynthia J., and A. Bowdoin Van Riper, eds. 2012. *Undead in the West: Vampires, Zombies, Mummies, and Ghosts on the Cinematic Frontier.* Lanham, MD: Scarecrow Press.

Miller, Madeline. 2018. "From Circe to Clinton: Why Powerful Women Are Cast as Witches." *The Guardian.* www.theguardian.com/books/2018/apr/07/cursed-from-circe-to-clinton-why-women-are-cast-as-witches?CMP=twt_books_b-gdnbooks.

Miller, Sam J. and Aviva Briefel. 2011. Introduction. *Horror After 9/11,* 1–10. Austin, TX: University of Texas Press.

Miller, Sarah Alison. 2019. "Monstrous Sexualities: Variations on the *Vagina Dentata.*" In *The Ashgate Research Companion to Monsters and the Monstrous,* edited by Asa Simon Mittman and Peter J. Dendle, 311–28. Farnham, United Kingdom: Ashgate.

Millhauser, Steven. 1998. "The Sisterhood of Night." *The Knife Thrower and Other Stories,* 45–62. New York, NY: Crown Publishers.

Mitter, Partha. 2019. "Postcolonial Monsters." In *The Ashgate Research Companion to Monsters and the Monstrous,* edited by Asa Simon Mittman and Peter J. Dendle, 329–41. Farnham, United Kingdom: Ashgate.

Mittman, Asa Simon. 2017. "Teaching Monsters from Medieval to Modern: Embracing the Abnormal." In *Monsters in the Classroom: Essays on Teaching What Scares Us,* edited by Adam Golub and Heather Richardson Hayton, 18–33. Jefferson, NC: McFarland.

Modleski, Tania. 1986. "Feminity as Mas(s)querade: A Feminist Approach to Mass Culture." In *High Theory, Low Culture, Analysing Popular Television and Film,* edited by Colin McCabe, 37–52. Manchester, United Kingdom: Manchester University Press.

Moreman, Christopher M., and Cory Rushton, eds. 2011. *Zombies Are Us: Essays on The Humanity of the Walking Dead.* Jefferson, NC: McFarland.

Moretti, Franco. 1983. *Signs Taken for Wonders: Essays in the Sociology of Literary Forms.* London: Verso.

Morgan, Felix. 2017. "Beyond *Teeth*: The Cultural History of Vagina Dentata." *OutTake.* Retrieved from http://www.outtake.tribecashortlist.com/beyond-teeth-the-cultural-history-of-vagina-dentata-60e9f020d557.

Morrow, Brendan. 2016. "'It Follows' Is Not About STDs. It's About Life As a Sexual Assault Survivor." *Bloody Disgusting.* Retrieved from http://www.bloody-disgusting.com/editorials/3387893/follows-not-stds-life-sexual-assault-survivor/.

Morton, Lisa. 2016. "Interview: Angela Slatter." *Nightmare Magazine,* Issue 44, May. Retrieved from http://www.nightmare-magazine.com/nonfiction/interview-angela-slatter/.

Mulvey, Laura. 1999. "Visual Pleasure and Narrative Cinema." In *Film Theory and Criticism: Introductory Readings,* edited by Leo Braudy and Marshall Cohen, 833–44. New York, NY: Oxford University Press.

Murphy, Bernice. 2011. "Imitations of Life: Zombies and the Suburban Gothic." In *Better Off Dead: The Evolution of the Zombie as Post-Human,* edited by Deborah Christie and Sarah Juliet Lauro, 116–138. New York, NY: Fordham University Press.

_____. 2009. *The Suburban Gothic in American Popular Culture.* Basingstoke, UK: Palgrave Macmillan.

Murphy, Patricia. 2016. *The New Woman Gothic: Reconfigurations of Distress.* Columbia, MO: University of Missouri Press.

Newitz, Annalee. 2010. "Justin Cronin Explains His Vampires in *The Passage.*" *IO9.* Retrieved from https://io9.gizmodo.com/5605835/justin-cronin-explains-his-vampires-in-the-passage-and-drops-spoilers-for-the-next-book.

O'Cuana, Emmet. 2016. "Reading Justin Cronin's *The Passage* Trilogy." *Medium.* Retrieved from https://medium.com/@EmmetOC_/reading-justin-cronins-the-passage-trilogy-2e4ab25ace68.

O'Falt, Chris. 2016. "How Robert Eggers Used Real Historical Accounts to Create His Horror Sensation *The Witch.*" *IndieWire.* Retrieved from www.indiewire.com/2016/02/how-robert-eggers-used-real-historical-accounts-to-create-his-horror-sensation-the-witch-67882/.

Olde Heuvelt, Thomas. 2016. *Hex.* New York, NY: Tor.

Opatic, Dunja. 2014. "Zombies in Revolt: The Violent Revolution of American Cinematic Monsters." *Sic: A Journal of Literature, Culture and Literary Translation* 2.4.

O'Reilly, Julie D. 2013. *Bewitched Again: Supernaturally Powerful Women on Television, 1996–2011.* Jefferson, NC: McFarland.

Orenstein, Catherine. 2002. *Little Red Riding Hood Uncloaked: Sex, Morality, and the Evolution of a Fairy Tale.* New York, NY: Basic Books.

Oyeyemi, Helen. 2014. *White Is for Witching.* New York, NY: Riverhead Books.

Paddison, Joshua. 2017. "Studying Gods and Monsters." In *Monsters in the Classroom: Essays on Teaching What Scares Us,* edited by Adam Golub and Heather Richardson Hayton, 161–74. Jefferson, NC: McFarland.

Paffenroth, Kim. 2006. *Gospel of the Living Dead: George Romero's Visions of Hell on Earth.* Waco, TX: Baylor University Press.

Palmer, Paulina. 2012. *The Queer Uncanny: New Perspectives on the Gothic.* Cardiff, Wales: University of Wales Press.

Parke, Maggie, and Natalie Wilson, eds. 2011. *Theorizing* Twilight: *Critical Essays on What's at Stake in a Post-Vampire World.* Jefferson, NC: McFarland.

Passard, Colleen. 2015. *Diary of a Witch.* Pennsuaken, NJ: Bookbaby.

Patterson, Natasha. 2008. "Cannibalizing Gender and Genre: A Feminist Re-Vision of George Romero's Zombie Films." In *Zombie Culture: Autopsies of the Living Dead,* edited by Shawn McIntosh and Marc Leverette, 103–18. Lanham, MD: Scarecrow Press.

Petherbridge, Deanna. 2014. "Witches: A History of Misogyny." *Independent.* Retrieved from https://www.independent.co.uk/arts-entertainment/art/features/witches-a-history-of-misogyny-9757605.html.

Pinedo, Isabel Cristina. 1997. *Recreational Terror: Women and the Pleasures of Horror Film Viewing.* New York, NY: State University of New York Press.

Poole, W Scott. Foreword. 2011. *Monsters in America: Our Historical Obsession with the Hideous and the Haunting.* Waco, TX: Baylor University Press.

_____. 2017. Introduction. *Monsters in the Classroom: Essays on Teaching What Scares Us,* edited by Adam Golub and Heather Richardson Hayton, 1–7. Jefferson, NC: McFarland.

Postman, Neil. 1986. *Amusing Ourselves to Death: Public Discourse in the Age of Show Business.* London, United Kingdom: Penguin.

Preston, Ted. 2010. "Deserving to Be a Vampire: The Ethical and Existential Elements of Vampirism." In *Zombies, Vampires, and Philosophy: New Life for the Undead,* edited by Richard Greene and K. Silem. Mohammad, 155–165. Chicago, IL: Open Court.

Projansky, Sarah. 2001. *Watching Rape: Film and Television in Postfeminist Culture.* New York, NY: New York University Press.

Pumfrey, Stephen. 2002. "Potts, plots and politics: James I's *Daemonologie* and *The Wonderfull Discoverie of Witches.*" In *The Lancashire Witches: Histories and Stories,* edited by Robert Poole, 22–41. Manchester: Manchester University Press.

Purkiss, Diane. 1996. *The Witch in History: Early Modern and Twentieth-Century Representations.* New York, NY: Routledge.

Randall, Kelli. 2008. "Corrupted by Skin Color: Racist and Misogynist Perceptions of Hoodoo in Maryse Condé's I, Tituba, Black Witch of Salem." *Women Writers.* Retrieved from http://www.womenwriters.net/aug08/Maryse_Conde.htm.

Read, Jacinda. 2000. *The New Avengers: Feminism, Femininity, and the Rape-Revenge Cycle.* New York, NY: St. Martin's Press.

Reynolds, Ryan. The Advocate, 26 July 2016, https://www.advocate.com/television/2016/7/26/homophobia-real-monster-stranger-things.

Rich, Adrienne. 1976. *Of Woman Born: Motherhood as Experience and Institution.* London: Virago.

Richardson, John. 2018. "The Shape of Water: An Allegorical Critique of Trump." *The Conversation.* Retrieved from https://theconversation.com/the-shape-of-water-an-allegorical-critique-of-trump-93272.

Roberston, Pamela. 1996. *Guilty Pleasures: Feminist Camp from Mae West to Madonna.* Durham, NC: Duke University Press.

Robey, Tim. 2015. "George A. Romero: Why I Don't Like *The Walking Dead.*" *Telegraph.*

Retrieved from http://www.telegraph.co.uk/culture/film/10436738/George-A-Romero-Why-I-dont-like-The-Walking-Dead.html.

Robinson, Tasha. 2019. "Does the ending of Jordan Peele's Us play fair with the audience?" *The Verge*. Retrieved from https://www.theverge.com/2019/3/25/18281033/jordan-peele-us-movie-twist-ending-reveal-questions-explained-analysis.

Rogers, Martin. 2008. "Hybridity and Post-Human Anxiety in *28 Days Later*." In Zombie *Culture: Autopsies of the Living Dead*, edited by Shawn McIntosh and Marc Leverette, 119–134. Lanham, MD: Scarecrow Press.

Romanow, Rebecca Fine. 2008. *The Postcolonial Body in Queer Space and Time*. Newcastle upon Tyne, United Kingdom: Cambridge Scholars Press.

Rosenberg, Jessica et al. 2015. "Madness, Stigma, and Religion in *American Horror Story: Asylum*. *The Monster Stares Back: How Human We Remain Through Horror's Looking Glass*, edited by Mark Chakares and Marcia Goncalves, 111–24. Oxford, United Kingdom: Inter-Disciplinary Press.

Rosenfield, Kat. 2018. "The Toxic Drama of YA Twitter." *Vulture*. Retrieved from https://www.vulture.com/2017/08/the-toxic-drama-of-ya-twitter.html.

Roth, Phyllis A. 1988. "Suddenly Sexual Women in Bram Stoker's *Dracula*." In *Dracula: The Vampire and the Critics*, edited by Margaret L. Carter, 57–67. Ann Arbor, MI: UMI Research Press.

Russell, Erica. 2017. "*The Shape of Water* and Guillermo Del Toro's Fantastical Feminist Heroines." *Nylon*. Retrieved from www.nylon.com/articles/guillermo-del-toro-shape-of-water-feminism.

Santos, Cristina. 2017. *Unbecoming Female Monsters: Witches, Vampires, and Virgins*. Lanham, MD: Lexington Books.

Sarner, Lauren. 2016. "*Penny Dreadful* Is Proving That Misandry in Feminism Can Be Fun." *Inverse Entertainment*. Retrieved from www.inverse.com/article/16975-penny-dreadful-is-proving-that-misandry-in-feminism-can-be-fun.

Scarboro, Ann Armstrong. 1992. Afterward. *I, Tituba, Black Witch of Salem*, by Maryse Condé, Trans. by Richard Philcox, 187–225. Charlottesville, VA: University of Virginia Press.

Schwartz, Alvin. 2017. "The Green Ribbon." In *In a Dark, Dark Room and Other Scary Stories*, 24–35. New York, NY: HarperCollins.

Scott, Emmy. 2019. "The Native Imagery of Jordan Peele's Us, Explained." *Vulture*. Retrieved from https://www.vulture.com/2019/03/the-native-imagery-of-jordan-peele-s-us-explained.html.

Seabrook, W.B. 1929. *The Magic Island*. New York, NY: The Literary Guild of America.

Segal, Corrine. 2017. "Stitch by Stitch: A Brief History of Knitting and Activism." *PBS*. Retrieved from https://www.pbs.org/newshour/arts/stitch-stitch-history-knitting-activism.

Seibold, Witney. 2014. "Review: *All Cheerleaders Die*." *Nerdist*. Retrieved from http://www.nerdist.com/review-all-cheerleaders-die/.

Shaviro, Steven. 2006. "The Cinematic Body." In *Theory Out of Bounds*, edited by Sandra Buckley et al. Minneapolis, MN: University of Minnesota Press.

Shelley, Percy Bysshe. 2011. *The Complete Works of Percy Bysshe Shelley: Prometheus Unbound, Ozymandias, The Masque of Anarchy, Queen Mab, Triumph of Life and More*. Charleston, SC: Nabu Press.

Shelton, Jacob. n.d. "The Best Parts of 'Chilling Adventures of Sabrina' Are Ripped Straight from Horror Properties." *Ranker*. Retrieved from https://www.ranker.com/list/sabrina-horror-movie-references/jacob-shelton.

Shildrick, Margrit. 2002. *Embodying the Monster: Encounters with the Vulnerable Self*. Thousand Oaks, CA: Sage Publications.

_____. 2001. "You Are There, Like My Skin: Reconfiguring Relation Economies." In

Thinking Through the Skin, edited by Sara Ahmed and Jackie Stacey, 160–73. Abingdon, United Kingdom: Routledge.

Short, Sue. 2006. *Misfit Sisters: Screen Horror as Female Rites of Passage.* New York, NY: Palgrave Macmillan.

Silver, Anna Krugovoy. Spring 2002. "The Cyborg Mystique: *The Stepford Wives* and Second Wave Feminism." *Women's Studies Quarterly* 30.1-2: 60–76.

Sims, David. 2016. "Female Freedom and Fury in *The Witch.*" *The Atlantic.* Retrieved from https://www.theatlantic.com/entertainment/archive/2016/02/robert-eggers-the-witch-female-empowerment/470844/.

Skal, David J. 1993. *The Monster Show: A Cultural History of Horror.* New York, NY: W.W. Norton and Company.

Slatter, Angela. 2015. *Of Sorrow and Such.* New York, NY: Tor.

Snyder, Rachel L. 2019. *No Visible Bruises: What We Don't Know About Domestic Violence Can Kill Us.* London: Bloomsbury.

Sobchack, Vivien. 1996. "Bringing It All Back Home: Family Economy and Generic Exchange." In *The Dread of Difference: Gender and the Horror Film,* edited by Barry Keith Grant, 143–163. Austin, TX: University of Texas Press.

Sorkin, Amy Davidson. 2012. "What Does Todd Akin Think 'Legitimate Rape' Is?" *The New Yorker.* Retrieved from https://www.newyorker.com/news/amy-davidson/what-does-todd-akin-think-legitimate-rape-is.

Stahler, Kelsea. 2018. "The New 'Charmed' Is a Feminist Take on the Original & Spoiler: It's Great." *Bustle.* Retrieved from https://www.bustle.com/p/the-new-charmed-is-a-feminist-take-on-the-original-spoiler-its-great-9825952.

Steiger, Kay. 2011. "Unshakable Race and Gender Politics in The Walking Dead." In *Triumph of The Walking Dead: Robert Kirkman's Zombie Epic on Page and Screen,* 100–14. Dallas, TX: Smart Pop.

Stillwell, Chloe. 2014. "Let's Talk About the Extreme Racism and Sexism of *American Horror Story: Coven.*" *Mic.* Retrieved from https://mic.com/articles/80723/let-s-talk-about-the-extreme-racism-and-sexism-of-american-horror-story-coven#.

Subissati, Andrea and Alexandra West. "Season of the Witch: Witches in Film Part 3, *The Witch* (2015) and *The Autopsy Of Jane Doe* (2016)." *Faculty of Horror: Podcasting From the Horrored Halls of Academia,* Episode 60, 25 Mar. 2018, http://www.facultyofhorror.com/2018/03/episode-60-season-of-the-witch-witches-in-film-part-3-the-witch-2015-and-the-autopsy-of-jane-doe-2016/.

_____. "Where Is My Mind: *The Stepford Wives* (1975) and *Get Out* (2017)." *Faculty of Horror: Podcasting From the Horrored Halls of Academia,* Episode 67. 27 Nov. 2018, http://www.facultyofhorror.com/2018/11/episode-67-where-is-my-mind-the-stepford-wives-1975-and-get-out-2017/.

Sumner-Smith, Karina, and John Joseph. 2010. "When the Zombies Win." In *The Living Dead 2,* edited by John Joseph Adams, 57–61. New York, NY: Night Shade Books.

Swancer, Brent. 2014. "The Mysterious Real Zombies of Haiti." *Mysterious Universe.* Retrieved from https://mysteriousuniverse.org/2014/08/the-mysterious-real-zombies-of-haiti./

Sydie, Rosalind A. 1987. *Natural Women, Cultured Men: A Feminist Perspective on Sociological Theory.* New York, NY: New York University Press.

Tallerico, Brian. 2016. "*Train to Busan* Review." *Roger Ebert.* Retrieved from http://www.rogerebert.com/reviews/train-to-busan-2016.

Todd, Molly. 2014. "Misogynist, Sexist, and Filled with Female Subjugation—*World War Z* in a Nutshell." *Write Me Away.* Retrieve from https://mollyjoycetodd.wordP.com/2014/07/02/misogynist-sexist-and-filled-with-female-subjugation-world-war-z-in-a-nutshell/.

Twitchell, James B. 1985. *Dreadful Pleasures: An Anatomy of Modern Horror.* New York, NY: Oxford University Press.

Ussher, Jane M. 1989. *The Psychology of the Female Body.* London: Routledge.

Valenti, Jessica. 2007. *Full Frontal Feminism: A Young Woman's Guide to Why Feminism Matters.* Seattle, WA: Seal.

_____. 2014. "Why do women love The Walking Dead? It might be the lack of rape scenes." *The Guardian,* June. Retrieved from https://www.theguardian.com/commentisfree/2014/jun/12/women-love-walking-dead-rape-scene.

VanDerWerff, Todd. 2017. "*The Strain* Was supposed to be FX's *Walking Dead.* What happened?" *Vox.* Retrieved from www.vox.com/culture/2017/7/30/16059374/the-strain-episode-2-recap-blood-tax-dutch.

Veeder, William. 1988. "Foreword." In *Dracula: The Vampire and the Critics,* edited by Margaret L. Carter, ix-xviii. Ann Arbor, MI: UMI Research Press.

Walker, Julia M. 1998. *Medusa's Mirrors: Spenser, Shakespeare, Milton, and The Metamorphosis of the Female Self.* Newark, DE: University of Delaware Press.

Wall, Anna. 2018. "The Shape of Ableism: Why I Will Never Watch Another Guillermo del Toro Movie." *Cripple Magazine.* Retrieved from https://cripplemagazine.com/the-shape-of-ableism-why-i-will-never-watch-another-guillermo-del-toro-movie/.

Weekes, Princess. 2018. "Was *Charmed* Ever Really a Feminist Show?" *The Mary Sue.* Retrieved from https://www.themarysue.com/charmed-feminist-show/.

Weinstock, Jeffrey Andrew. 2012. *The Vampire Film: Undead Cinema.* London: Wallflower.

Weiss, Andrea. 1993. *Vampires & Violets: Lesbians in Film.* New York, NY: Penguin Books.

Weiss, Gail. 1999. *Body Images: Embodiment as Intercorporeality.* London: Routledge.

Weissman, Judith. 1988. "Women and Vampires: *Dracula* as a Victorian Novel." In *Dracula: The Vampire and the Critics,* edited by Margaret L. Carter, 69–77. Ann Arbor, MI: UMI Research Press.

West, Alexandra. 2018. *The 1990s Teen Horror Cycle: Final Girls and a New Hollywood Formula.* Jefferson, NC: McFarland.

West, Lindy. 2017. "Yes, This Is a Witch Hunt. I'm a Witch and I'm Hunting You." *New York Times.* Retrieved from https://www.nytimes.com/2017/10/17/opinion/columnists/weinstein-harassment-witchunt.html.

Whitney, Sarah E. 2016. *Splattered Ink: Postfeminist Gothic Fiction and Gendered Violence.* Champaign, IL: University of Illinois Press.

Williams, Kevin Wayne. 2017. "*The Girl with All the Gifts*: Race Analysis." *Black Girl Nerds.* Retrieved from https://blackgirlnerds.com/girl-gifts-race-analysis/.

Williams, Linda. 1996. "When the Woman Looks." In *The Dread of Difference: Gender and the Horror Film,* edited by Barry Keith Grant, 15–34. Austin, TX: University of Texas Press.

Williams, Tony. 2011. *George A. Romero: Interviews.* Jackson, MI: University Press of Mississippi.

_____. Spring 1983. "White Zombie, Haitian Horror." *Jump Cut* 28: 18–20.

Williamson, Milly. 2005. *The Lure of the Vampire: Gender, Fiction and Fandom from Bram Stoker to Buffy.* New York, NY: Wallflower Press.

Wilson, Natalie. 2015. "Re-Composing Zombie Politics: Evolved Zombies and Female Survivors/Saviors." Paper presented at *Southwest Popular Culture Association Conference.*

_____. 2014. "Rules for Surviving Rape Culture." In *The Politics of Race, Gender and Sexuality in* The Walking Dead: *Essays on the Television Series and Comics,* edited by Elizabeth Erwin and Dawn Keetley, 129–41. Jefferson, NC: McFarland.

_____. 2011. *Seduced by* Twilight: *The Allure and Contradictory Messages of the Popular Saga.* Jefferson, NC: McFarland.

_____. 2016. "Women-Directed Horror Films Take Aim at the 'Celluloid Ceiling.'" *The Establishment.* Retrieved from https://medium.com/the-establishment/women-directed-horror-films-take-aim-at-the-celluloid-ceiling-d3001694058e.

Winnubst, Shannon. 2003. "Vampires, Anxieties, and Dreams: Race and Sex in the Contemporary United States." *Hypatia* 18.3: 1–20.

Winterson, Jeanette. 2014. *The Daylight Gate.* New York: Grove Press.

Wood, Robin. 1986. *Hollywood from Vietnam to Reagan … and Beyond.* New York, NY: Columbia University Press.

Woodend, Dorothy. 2016. "Zombie Politics: Korea's Latest Horror Flick Asks Whether People Eaters Can Digest a Hedge Fund Manager." *The Tyee.* Retrieved from https://thetyee.ca/Culture/2016/07/29/Zombie-Politics/.

Young, Elizabeth. 2018. "Black Frankenstein at the Bicentennial: Race and Political Metaphor from Nat Turner to Now." *The Common Reader: A Journal of the Essay.* Retrieved from https://commonreader.wustl.edu/c/black-frankenstein-at-the-bicentennial/.

_____. 1996. "Here Comes the Bride: Wedding Gender and Race in *Bride of Frankenstein.*" In *The Dread of Difference: Gender and the Horror Film,* edited by Barry Keith Grant, 309–37. Austin, TX: University of Texas Press.

Zumas, Leni. 2018. *Red Clocks.* Boston, MA: Little Brown and Company.

Films and Television Series

All Cheerleaders Die, 2013, film, dirs., Lucky McKee, Chris Siverston
All the Boys Love Mandy Lane, 2006, film, dir., Jonathan Levine
American Horror Story: Coven. 2013–2014, series, FX.
The Autopsy of Jane Doe, 2016, film, dir., André Øvredal
Avenged, 2012, film, dir., Michael S. Ojeda
The Babadook, 2014, film, dir., Jennifer Kent
Byzantium, 2012, film, dir., Neil Jordan
Candyman, 1992, film, dir., Bernard Rose
Charmed. 2018– , series, The CW.
Chilling Adventures of Sabrina. 2018– , series, Netflix.
Contracted I, 2013, film, dir., Eric England
Contracted: Phase II, 2015, film, dir., Josh Forbes
Crimson Peak, 2015, film, dir., Guillermo del Toro
Daybreakers. 2009, film, dirs., Michael Spierig, Peter Spierig
Deadgirl, 2008, film, dirs., Marcel Sarmiento, Gadi Harel
Doghouse, 2009, film, dir., Jake Wes
Don't Breathe, 2016, film, dir., Fede Alvarez
Fido, 2006, film, dir., Andrew Currie
Get Out, 2017, film, dir., Jordan Peele
A Girl Walks Home Alone at Night, 2014, film, dir., Ana Lily Amirpour
The Girl with All the Gifts, 2016, film, dir., Colm McCarthy
Housebound, 2014, film, dir., Gerard Johnstone
I Am Legend, 2007, film, dir., Francis Lawrence
I Am the Pretty Thing That Lives in the House, 2016, film, dir., Oz Perkins
I Walked with a Zombie, 1943, film, dir., Jacques Tourneur
Jaws, 1975, film, dir., Steven Spielberg
Jennifer's Body, 2009, film, dir., Karyn Kusama
Let Me In, 2010, film, dir., Matt Reeves
The Love Witch, 2016, film, dir., Anna Biller
The OA. 2016– , series, Netflix.
The Passage. 2019– , series, Fox.
Penny Dreadful. 2014–2016, series, Showtime.
A Quiet Place, 2018, film, dir., John Krasinski
The Shape of Water, 2017, film, dir., Guillermo del Toro
Sisterhood of Night, 2014, film, dir., Caryn Waechter
Stranger Things. 2016– , series, Netflix.
Teeth, 2007, film, dir., Mitchell Lichtenstein
Us, 2019, film, dir., Jordan Peele

Voodoo Man, 1944, film, dir., Willian Beaudine
The Walking Dead. 2010– , series, AMC.
White Zombie, 1932, film, dir., Victor Halperin
The Witch, 2016, film, dir., David Eggers
The Woods, 2006, film, dir., Lucky McKee
World War Z, 2013, film, dir., Marc Forster

Index

Numbers in **_bold italics_** indicate pages with illustrations